INTERNATIONAL DICTIONARY OF THE SECURITIES INDUSTRY

INTERNATIONAL DICTIONARY OF THE SECURITIES INDUSTRY

Stuart Valentine

M
MACMILLAN PRESS
LONDON
Macmillan Reference Books

First published 1985 by
THE MACMILLAN PRESS LTD
London and Basingstoke

Associated companies in Auckland, Delhi, Dublin, Gaborone, Hamburg, Harare, Hong Kong, Johannesburg, Kuala Lumpur, Lagos, Manzini, Melbourne, Mexico City, Nairobi, New York, Singapore, Tokyo.

British Library Cataloguing in Publication Data

Valentine, S.P.
International dictionary of securities industry.
1. Securities
I. Title
332.65 HG4528

ISBN 0-333-38240-4
ISBN 0-333-38241-2 Pbk

Printed and bound in Great Britain by
Anchor Brendon Ltd, Tiptree, Essex

INTRODUCTION

It has long been one of my hobby-horses that the essential workings of a stock market are really quite simple. Yet new investors approaching the market for the first time are apt to be thoroughly put off by the apparent complexity of the language. That is a pity, because little can be more important for someone than to use his savings for his own and his family's security. Not understanding the world of investment and blindly trusting those who use the language as a smoke-screen, rather than as the means of communication it is supposed to be, can have unfortunate consequences: at best the saver will not use his savings to their best advantage, while at worst, he could be lured into highly speculative investments by the promise of rich rewards, without appreciating the risks involved.

The language can be off-putting: indeed, the whole investment scene can sound at times like a safari park, with its inhabitants of bulls, bears, stags, cats and tigers, a veritable thundering herd of wildlife. Yet all of these have their meanings in everyday language and all of them (including the thundering herd itself) will be found in the pages of this volume.

The object of compiling this book was not, of course, to solve all financial problems and make everyone rich. Anyone looking for such a book is advised to put down this volume right now and try another. Rather, its aim is to help both those approaching investment for the first time and also those already involved to thread their way through the jargon. Those involved will already know better than I the meanings of many of the words here. But the language of investment is growing week by week, and I hope that even the experienced investor and market man will find something new here.

The world of investment is also growing more international. Phrases starting in one market gradually (or these days not so gradually) pass into other markets' terminology. As the market in securities is becoming increasingly worldwide, an attempt has been made here to explain some of the words and the institutions of overseas markets, but I am conscious that many words common in those markets may have been left out.

The other problem is the rate of growth, amounting almost to an explosion, in the language of investment. Dozens of the words and phrases in this dictionary would not have been there a year ago. Frighteningly, a year from now there will be dozens more which today are still unheard of.

So, inevitably, not everything will be here, but I hope that it will meet the needs of those who, in their own or in overseas markets, are in need of clarification and enlightenment on the meaning of particular words and phrases. Where possible I have tried to include sources of further information, by way of bibliography, in the hope that those who find the definition given here inadequate for their needs will be guided to the more detailed information in those other sources.

I should say a word or two about layout and style. A strict alphabetical order has been adopted, ignoring the fact that individual words may be separated: thus 'capitalization' comes after 'capital gain' but before 'capital redemption yield'.

Cross references to both English and foreign words contained in the body of the text are printed in SMALL CAPITALS. For foreign terminology, where the word or phrase has a close English equivalent, I have referred readers to that English translation although, occasionally, the cross-referenced English equivalent will be accompanied by background information which refers to the specific situation in the United Kingdom or the United States. Where there is no such equivalent, an explanation of the phrase has, of course, been given.

The words *bourse, Börse* and *Borsa* have been used in the appropriate national contexts, although I have sometimes used phrases such as 'the French Stock Exchanges' or 'the Frankfurt Stock Exchange' when to have used *bourse* or *Börse* would have sounded excessively pedantic.

The differences between English and American usage have sometimes caused difficulty. Though 'company' and 'corporation' may be used almost interchangeably, I have tried to be careful to distinguish between the English and American uses of the word 'stock': in the United Kingdom 'stock' is a fixed interest security; in the United States, 'stock' or 'common stock' is equity, the word for fixed interest security being 'bond'. If it is any consolation to the layman, conversations between market practitioners of the two countries often have to be clarified on this score. In any discrepancy between English and American spelling the English version has been used except where the definition in which the word appears is wholly American. The style, *-ize* and *-ization* have been used at the publisher's request, instead of *-ise* and *-isation.*

Where a word has (a) a common meaning; (b) a banking or other financial meaning; (c) a specific stock exchange meaning, I have tended to ignore the first of these, and have defined the second only when it has a relevance to a stock market, or is necessary to understand the particular use employed in a stock exchange context. Thus, for example, I have not defined the word 'average' in an insurance context, only its stock market meaning. In all cases, the specific stock exchange meaning has been defined.

Finally, I have used the word 'he' to refer to the third person singular throughout.

ACKNOWLEDGEMENTS

Anyone attempting to compile a dictionary which sets out to cover such a broad spectrum as international stock market terminology must, of necessity, rely on the active and enthusiastic assistance of others. In this case, that help has been so unstintingly given by so many people that to do them all full justice would fill far more pages than I am allotted for the purpose.

In particular, I would like to thank first and foremost Malcolm Duncan of the Milan Stock Exchange for the immense amount of help willingly given on Italian terminology. Also Bill Freund and Kenneth Fox of the New York Stock Exchange for the use of the NYSE glossary of terminology, as well as for considerable help given me in clarifying and supplementing my information on the complex American scene. In this context, my additional thanks are due to Merril Stevenson of *The Economist* for invaluable help and advice.

On other overseas markets I have been greatly assisted by the help I have received from Bertrand Jacquillat and Bruno Montier of the Chambre Syndicale des Agents de Change in Paris; by Dr. Herbert Schlicht of the Frankfurt Stock Exchange, Robert Fell, Commissioner for Securities in Hong Kong, Ada Jeung of his office and Andrew Mason of the London office of Nomura Research.

I should like to thank Dr Paul Stonham for permission to use material from his book, *Major Stock Markets of Europe,* references to which appear in various bibliographies in the text. John Wiley, the New York publishers, also gave me permission to quote from their *International Finance Handbook,* edited by Abraham M. George and Ian H. Giddy, and again the debt I owe to that volume is reflected in many of the bibliographic notes. So too is the debt to Janette Rutterford's book, *An Introduction to Stock Exchange Investment.*

On the UK domestic scene, Juliette Proudlove of the London International Financial Futures Exchange provided me with valuable information on that market's terminology, while Tony Newman and A.E. Backholer, of the Society of Investment Analysts, kindly provided help on balance sheet terminology and on the sometimes complex vocabulary of the investment analyst. Among my colleagues at The Stock Exchange I would like to thank Sheila Nicoll for providing many valuable contacts and for help with translations, together with Alan King and Tracy Alexander of the Settlement Division, who helped guide me through some of the more obscure corners of that esoteric area.

To all of those mentioned, as well as many who gave pieces of advice too numerous to mention, I extend my most sincere thanks.

Their contribution is a major one, but I must not forget those who gave me encouragement, support and help in the actual production of the volume: Jeffrey Knight, Chief Executive of The Stock Exchange, who encouraged me to undertake the task; David Clutterbuck and John Hodgson of Macmillan Press who initiated the idea and helped me to carry it to fruition; John Webster, whose technical expertise helped speed up the production process; Nigel Storer, who helped check information and fill in some of the blanks. My thanks most of all go to Ann Hanson, who not only typed and re-typed the drafts, but who was also extremely valuable in making me turn highly obscure and unintelligible definitions into something approaching both clarity and the English language. Obscurities and errors which remain are entirely, of course, my own responsibility.

A final word of gratitude to my wife Jill, whose forebearance when the evenings and weekends of what was laughingly called my spare time were devoted to 'The Dictionary'. When I emerge from the study, I only hope she remembers who I am.

To all those who have given their help, I am aware I have built up a large debit balance of favours owed. I hope I shall have the opportunity to repay them.

List of Abbreviations

The following commonly-used abbreviations and acronyms appear in the main body of the text in the alphabetical order of the full reference. Where an abbreviation or acronym has itself been used as a headword, e.g. TALISMAN, it has not been repeated here.

AASE : Association of Australian Stock Exchanges
ABS : Automated Bond System
ACT : Advance Corporation Tax
ADR : American Depository Receipt
AG : Aktiengesellschaft
AHC : Accepting Houses Committee
AIBD : Association of International Bond Dealers
AITC : Association of Investment Trust Companies
AMEX : American Stock Exchange
AMOS : AMEX Options Switching System
ARP : adjustable rate preferred stock
ASAS : American Shares Amsterdam System
ASL : Admission of Securities to Listing

BES : Business Expansion Scheme
BET : book entry transfer

CAC : Compagnie des Agents de Change
CAD : cash against documents
CAES : Computer Assisted Execution System
CAP : convertible adjustable preferred stock
CAPM : Capital Asset Pricing Model
CATS : Computer Assisted Trading System (Canada)
CATS : certificate of accrual on Treasury securities (US)
CBOE : Chicago Board Options Exchange
CD : certificate of deposit
CFTC : Commodity Futures Trading Corporation
CGT : Capital Gains Tax
CMA : cash management account
COB : Commission des Opérations de Bourse
CONSOB : Commissione Nazionale per la Società e la Borsa
CSI : Council for the Securities Industry
CTT : Capital Transfer Tax

DOTS : Designated Order Turnaround System
DTC : Depository Trust Company
DTI : Department of Trade and Industry

ECI : Equity Capital for Industry
EDSP : exchange delivery settlement price
EFP : exchange for physicals
EMH : Efficient Market Hypothesis
EOE : European Options Exchange
EPIC : Electronic Price Information Computer
EPS : earnings per share
ERISA : Employee Retirement Income Security Act
ESOP : Employee Stock Ownership Plan

FCI : Finance Corporation for Industry
FESE : Far Eastern Stock Exchange
FFI : Finance for Industry
FHLMA : Federal Home Loan Mortgage Association
FIBV : Fédération Internationale des Bourses de Valeurs
FIFO : first-in-first-out

FNMA : Federal National Mortgage Association
FOCUS : Financial and Operational Combined Uniform Single Report
FTA : Financial Times-Actuaries all share index
FTO : Financial Times Ordinary share index
FTSE : Financial Times-Stock Exchange index

GmbH : Gesellschaft mit beschränkter Haftung (see Gesellschaft)
GNMA : Government National Mortgage Association

HSI : Hang Seng Index

IBRD : International Bank for Reconstruction and Development
ICCH : International Commodities Clearing House
ICFC : Industrial and Commercial Finance Corporation
ID : International Dealer
IFC : International Finance Corporation
IHA : Issuing Houses Association
III : Investors In Industry
IMM : International Monetary Market
IRA : Individual Retirement Account
ITS : Intermarket Trading System

KAGG : Gesetz über die Kapitalanlagegesellschaften
KNI : Kam Ngan Index

LCM : Limited Corporate Member
LDMA : London Discount Market Association
LIBOR : London Inter-Bank Offered Rate
LIFFE : London International Financial Futures Exchange
LIFO : last-in-first-out
LSE : London Stock Exchange

MIB : indice Borsa Valori di Milano
MIT : market-if-touched
MLR : Minimum Lending Rate
MPDS : Market Price Display Service

NASD : National Association of Securities Dealers (US)
NASDAQ : National Association of Security Dealers Automated Quotations System
NASDIM : National Asociation of Securities Dealers and Investment Managers (UK)
NDJA : Nikkei-Dow Jones Average
NPV : no par value (shares)
NSCC : National Securities Clearing Corporation
NYFE : New York Futures Exchange
NYSE : New York Stock Exchange

OARS : Opening Automated Report Service
OFT : Office of Fair Trading
OMO : open market operations
OTC : over-the-counter (markets)

PE or PER : price-earnings ratio
PLC : Public Limited Company
PSL (1 or 2) : private sector liquidity

R4 : Registered Representative Rapid Response System
REIT : real estate investment trust
RPI : retail price index

SA : société anonyme
SAYE : Save-As-You-Earn
SEC : Securities and Exchange Commission
SEDOL : Stock Exchange Daily Official List
SEPON : Stock Exchange Pool Nominees
SESI : Stock Exchange of Singapore Index
SEOYB : Stock Exchange Official Year Book
SIA : Securities Industry Association
SIAC : Securities Industry Automation Corporation

SICAV : société d'investissement à capital variable
SICOVAM : Société Interprofessionelle pour la Compensation des Valeurs Mobilières
SIPA : Securities Investors Protection Act
SIPC : Securities Investors Protection Corporation
SLMA : Student Loan Marketing Association
S & P : Standard & Poor's Corporation
SRA : self-regulatory agency
STI : Straits Times Index
SWIFT : Society for Worldwide Interbank Financial Telecommunications
TBT : TALISMAN Bought Transfer
TOPIC : Teletext Output of Price Information by Computer
TSE : The Stock Exchange (UK) or Tokyo Stock Exchange (Japan)
TST : TALISMAN Sold Transfer
UCM : Unlimited Corporate Member
USM : Unlisted Securities Market
UTA : Unit Trust Association
VAT : Value Added Tax

World Stock Exchange Indices

Country	*Index*	*No. of Companies*	*Base date*	*Base Value*	*Frequency of Calculation*
Argentina	El Cronista Commercial-Banco Roberts	All (260 app.)	29 Dec 1977	100	daily
Australia	Australian Stock Exchange All Ordinaries Price Index (AOPI)	270 (app.)	31 Dec 1979	500	continuously
	Australian Stock Exchange All Industrial Price Index (AIPI)	80 (app.)	31 Dec 1979	500	continuously
	Australian Stock Exchange All Resources Price Index (ARPI)	190 (app.)	31 Dec 1979	500	continuously
Austria	Creditanstalt Bankverein (CA Index)	20	2 Jan 1962	100	daily
	Girozentrale und Bank der Osterreichischen Sparkassen AG (GZ-Index)	All	31 Dec 1966	100	daily
	Borsekammer (WBK Index)	43	31 Dec 1967	100	twice monthly
Belgium	Cash Market Index	All (197)	1 Jan 1980	100	daily
	Account Market Index: foreign companies	All (63)	1 Jan 1985	1000	every two minutes during trading session
	Belgian companies	All (33)	1 Jan 1980	1000	
Brazil	The Profit Index (IBV)	34	16 Aug 1965	100	daily
Canada	Montreal Composite Index	85	1956	100	half-hourly
	Industrial Index	65	1956	100	half-hourly
	Toronto "300" composite stock price index	300	1975	1000	every 15 minutes
Denmark	Copenhagen Stock Exchange Index	38	1 Jan 1973	100	daily
France	CAC Index	268	31 Dec 1981	100	at opening
	CAC Trend Indicator	50	end of previous year	100	continuously
	INSEE daily	50	end of previous year	100	at close
	INSEE weekly	220	end 1981	100	at opening
	Agefi (cash and account market)	162	2 Jan 1962	100	at close
Germany	Commerzbank	60 "blue chip" companies	1 Dec 1953	100	daily
Hong Kong	Hang Seng Index	33	31 July 1964	100	
	Far East Index	52	1 Apr 1971	1000	
Israel	Total Yields indices for stocks and bonds (TY)	all	31 Dec 1981	100	daily
Italy	Milano Indice borsa (MIB) Current Index	176	2 Jan 1983	1000	daily
	Historical Index	129	2 Jan 1975	1000	daily

Country	*Index*	*No. of Companies*	*Base date*	*Base Value*	*Frequency of Calculation*
Japan Osaka	Stock prices average (1st section)	220	4 Jan 1968	100	6 times on full business day; 3 times on half business day
	Stock prices average (2nd section)	80	4 Jan 1968	100	
Tokyo	Toyko Stock Eschange Stock prices indices (TSESPI)	all on 1st section	4 Jan 1968	100	1st and 2nd sections continuously
	Nikkei Dow Jones average	225 on 1st section	16 May 1949	100	
Korea	Korean Composite Stock price Index (KCSPI)	all	4 Jan 1980	100	half-hourly
Luxembourg	Luxembourg Shares Index	8	27 Dec 1967	100	daily at close
Malaysia	Kuala Lumpur Stock Exchange Index (KLSE)	30	1970	100	daily at close and during every recess
Netherlands	ANP-CBS Stock Market Index	53	1970	100	active 4 times daily less active twice daily
Norway	Oslo SE Composite	25	1 Jan 1972	100	daily at close
Singapore	Stock Exchange of Singapore (SES) Industrial & Commercial	32	31 Dec 1973	100	twice daily
	Straits Times industrial (ST)	30	30 Dec 1966	100	daily at close
	OCBC Indices	40	2 Jan 1970	100	daily at close
South Africa	Johannesburg Stock Exchange actuaries index (JSEA)	146	31 Dec 1959	100	continuously
	Rand Daily Mail Indices	100	1958	100	daily at close
Spain: Barcelona	The Barcelona Stock Exchange current and historical indices	89	1 Jan each year and 1 Jan 1963 for long base index	100	continuously
Madrid	Daily Index	69	31 Dec of previous year	100	daily at close
Sweden	JAPO Industrial Banks Investment	30 9 19	31 Dec 1956	100	daily at close
	Affarvarden	135	31 Dec 1979	100	daily at close
	Veckans Affarer	135	31 Dec 1972	100	weekly
Switzerland	Credit Suisse Index (CSI)	variable	31 Dec 1959	100	daily at close
	Societe Generale de Banque Suisse Index (SBSI)	variable	31 Dec 1958	100	daily at close
	Banque Nationale Suisse Index (BNSI)	variable	1966	100	weekly (Friday's prices)
United Kingdom	Financial Times-Actuaries all-share Index (FTA)	750 (app.)	10 Apr 1962	100	daily at 3.30
	Financial Times Industrial Ordinary shares Index (FTO)	30	1 Jul 1935	100	hourly

Country	*Index*	*No. of Companies*	*Base date*	*Base Value*	*Frequency of Calculation*
	Financial Times-Stock Exchange (FT-SE) 1000 Index	100	30 Dec 1983	1000	continuously
USA	Amex market value index	all (860 app.)	1 Sep 1973	100	10:15, 10:30 then every half-hour
	Dow Jones Average (see text)				
	NYSE Composite	all (1560 app.)	31 Dec 1965	50	continuously
	Standard & Poor's	500	1941/3	10	continuously
	Standard & Poor's	400	1941/3	10	continuously
	Standard & Poor's	100	2 Jan 1976	100	continuously

This table is largely based on statistics drawn up by the Brussels Stock Exchange for the F.I.B.V. in 1983. The F.I.B.V.'s permission to use it is gratefully acknowledged.

A

'AAA' or **'Triple A' rating** (US). The highest rating awarded to PREFERRED STOCK by credit rating agencies such as Standard and Poor's Corporation. Such agencies also tend to rate bonds similarly and to have an additional classification for common stocks (ordinary shares). *See also* STANDARD AND POOR'S RATINGS.

abandonner (Fr). To abandon a BOURSE transaction by the payment of an agreed premium. Such a procedure is allowed on the MARCHÉ À PRIMES where the buyer has the right to cancel a deal before settlement day on payment of a fixed forfeit called a PRIME.

Ablösbare Vorzugsaktie (Ger). *See* REDEEMABLE PREFERENCE SHARE.

above (the) market. At a price higher than the value currently ruling in the market.

above par. *See* PAR.

Abrechnungstag (Ger). *See* SETTLEMENT DAY.

a breve scadenza (It). *See* SHORT DATED.

a breve termine (It). *See* SHORT TERM.

Abschlag (Ger). A discount from a nominal or PAR rate to a lower rate, normally expressed as a percentage of the par rate. (In the United Kingdom the TREASURY BILL rate is expressed this way.)

Abschlagsdividende (Ger). *See* INTERIM DIVIDEND.

Abschluss (Ger). A deal or a bargain, carried out on the BÖRSE.

Abschnitt (Ger). *See* COUPON.

absorption. *See* TAKE-OVER BID, MERGER, AMALGAMATION.

a cavallo (It). An expression used to indicate that though no exact price was fixed for the security, it should be possible to find a buyer or seller near the stated price. For example, shares are priced 'a cavallo' at 1180. Presumably is should therefore be possible to find a buyer at 1170 and a seller at 1190.

accaparer le marché (Fr). To CORNER a market.

accaparrare il mercato (It). To CORNER a market.

acceptance (UK). (1) In the banking world, acceptance has a specific meaning with regard to a bill of exchange. In this context, acceptance is the acknowledgement by the acceptor that he will honour the bill if the drawee or other party fails to pay. Acceptance of a bill is normally signified by writing the word 'accepted' on the back of the bill and signing it. It is this specific meaning which has given the name to the ACCEPTING HOUSE.

(2) In a securities context, acceptance is the agreement by a shareholder to take up an offer made to him. Such an offer may be a RIGHTS ISSUE by a company in which he has a shareholding. It may also be some change in the conditions of this shareholding or benefit for which his agreement has to be obtained.

Alternatively, it could be the acceptance of an offer for all or part of his shareholding by another company in a MERGER or TAKE-OVER BID. *See also* ASSENT.

accepting house (UK). Specifically a member of the ACCEPTING HOUSES COMMITTEE, a group of leading MERCHANT BANKS in the City of London. All accepting houses must have a substantial involvement in the ACCEPTANCE of bills of exchange, but in a Stock Exchange context, they are important as financial advisers to companies and closely concerned with them in the raising of new money from shareholders by issues of long term loans or shares. All the accepting houses are also members of the more broadly based ISSUING HOUSES ASSOCIATION.

Accepting Houses Committee (AHC) (UK). A 16-strong group of the leading UK merchant banks. The Committee acts as the trade association for these banks and officially represents them on a number of other bodies, including the COUNCIL FOR THE SECURITIES INDUSTRY. The present members of the Accepting Houses Committee in alphabetical order are: Baring Bros; Brown, Shipley; Charterhouse J. Rothschild; Robert Fleming; Guiness Mahon; Hambros Bank; Hill, Samuel; Kleinwort, Benson; Lazard Bros; Morgan, Grenfell; Rea Brothers; N.M. Rothschild & Sons; Samuel Montagu; J. Henry Schroder Wagg; Singer & Friedlander and S.G. Warburg.

accompagnateur (Fr). A speculator, not specifically on the BOURSE, but the word is applied to someone who buys and sells shares on a short term view.

acconto dividendo (It). Account dividend. *See* INTERIM DIVIDEND.

accordarsi (It). To operate along the same lines adopted by other operators or dealers.

account, Stock Exchange (UK). A two (occasionally three) week period within which dealings in registered company shares take place. Most UK equity and company fixed interest stock is dealt in on this basis but not UK GILT EDGED STOCK. The account usually runs in a four-weekly cycle. Dealings take place in the two-week period of the account itself from the Monday of week one to the Friday of week two. (Where a public holiday occurs, which in the United Kingdom is most usually on a Monday, the account extends to the Friday of week three.) A new dealing account then begins. Settlement of all business done during the relevant account is made on the Monday of week four (*see* SETTLEMENT DAY) after all the necessary paperwork has been completed in the week following the end of the dealing account. *See also* ACCOUNT DEALING.

accountant's opinion (US). The name by which an AUDITOR'S REPORT is often known in the United States.

account day (UK). *See* SETTLEMENT DAY.

account dealing (UK). The practice of buying and selling securities within the same ACCOUNT. In this case the investor will receive from (or pay to) the broker the difference between the buying and selling price(s) (plus relevant costs such as broker's COMMISSION), on SETTLEMENT DAY. The existence of the Stock Exchange account, in which all dealings are settled on one settlement day, permits short term trading to take place (*See* ACCOUNT, STOCK EXCHANGE). Such short term dealing helps provide the market with LIQUIDITY, both in that more dealing is encouraged and also that the JOBBERS are able to deal more freely knowing that they have a period within which they can offset any LONG POSITION or SHORT POSITION they may be carrying.

account executive (US). *See* REGISTERED REPRESENTATIVE.

account settlement (UK). *See* ACCOUNT, STOCK EXCHANGE and FOR THE ACCOUNT.

accredited investor (US). An investor who is allowed, under SECURITIES AND EXCHANGE COMMISSION rules, to participate in a PLACING of shares.

accrued interest. Interest which has been earned on a fixed interest security but which has not yet been paid. Interest is normally paid half yearly, but the interest accrues on a daily basis. Any investor selling a security in between interest payment dates is therefore entitled to the interest which has been earned, or accrued, up to the date he sells it. Equally, an investor buying the stock must expect to pay the interest accrued to date. Such daily accruals of interest are normally incorporated into the price of the stock, which might be expected to fall by the amount of the interest when the half yearly payment is made. An exception to the general rule for including accrued interest in the price occurs with short dated government stocks of less than five years to maturity dealt in on the Stock Exchange in the United Kingdom. There the price quoted is a CLEAN PRICE and the amount of accrued interest is calculated separately.

acid test ratio. The current assets of a company, less its stock-in-trade, divided by its current liabilities. *See also* CURRENT ASSETS RATIO.

acquisition (UK). *See* TAKE-OVER BID.

acquisto di titoli da parte di non-residenti (It). The purchase of Italian securities by non-residents which requires the import of the necessary currency through an agent bank and its conversion into lire at the moment when the purchased securities must be paid for.

Wherever the securities are not officially listed, the Italian Exchange Bureau requires that an evaluation certificate is obtained from the stockbrokers' Executive Committee (or from the Commission for the Official List in the case of minor stock exchanges). This is in order to determine the trading price of the share.

actif (Fr). *See* ASSET.

acting in concert. *See* CONCERT PARTY.

action (Fr). A share in a company as distinct from a loan. *See also* OBLIGATION.

action à dividende prioritaire sans droit de vote (Fr). A share which may be issued by a company which has made profits in its two preceding trading years. The shares give the right to a dividend ahead of ordinary shareholders, but no right to vote in a general meeting. The dividend will be of not less than 7.5 percent of nominal value. In the event of the dividend not being fully paid for a period of three years, the shares do then confer voting rights until full payment of the dividends has been made.

action au porteur (Fr). *See* BEARER SHARE.

action avec droit de vote (Fr). *See* VOTING SHARE.

action d'attribution, action gratuite (Fr). A bonus share. *See* SCRIP ISSUE.

action de fondateur (Fr). *See* FOUNDER'S SHARE.

action de priorité, action de priviligée (Fr). *See* PREFERENCE SHARE.

action de priorité cumulatif (Fr). *See* CUMULATIVE PREFERENCE SHARE.

action différée (Fr). *See* DEFERRED SHARE.

action entièrement libérée (Fr). *See* FULLY PAID SHARES.

actionnaire (Fr). *See* SHAREHOLDER.

action nominatif (Fr). *See* REGISTERED SHARE.

action ordinaire (Fr). *See* ORDINARY SHARE.

action partiellement libérée (Fr). *See* PARTLY PAID SHARES.

action privilégiée amortissable (Fr). *See* REDEEMABLE PREFERENCE SHARE.

action sans droit de vote (Fr). *See* NON VOTING SHARE.

action sans valeur nominal (Fr). *See* SHARE OF NO PAR VALUE.

action souscrite (Fr). *See* FULLY PAID SHARE.

active bond crowd (US). The group of dealers who operate in bonds which are well and actively traded.

active market. A stock market in which trading in securities is busy. Investors in these circumstances are able to buy and to sell in large quantities at FINE PRICES.

actuals. In a FINANCIAL FUTURES market, the cash FINANCIAL INSTRUMENT as distinct from the FUTURES CONTRACT. In commodity futures markets, the term used is 'physicals' meaning the actual commodity on which the futures contract is written.

adjustable rate preferred stock (ARP) (US). A type of stock introduced in 1981 with variable rates of interest designed to keep the stock trading at close to its PAR VALUE. Several stocks however, especially those of banks, have not succeeded in maintaining their par values as their ratings have fallen.

Admission of Securities to Listing (ASL) (UK). The booklet published by the Stock Exchange in the United Kingdom which gives the details of the Stock Exchange's requirements for companies seeking a stock market listing. The booklet is often known as the YELLOW BOOK from the colour of its binding.

Adresse (Ger). A stock exchange member who is party to a securities transaction.

ad valorem. A Latin phrase, literally meaning 'to the value', used in many stock and money markets to describe the method of calculating the amount of tax and/or commission to be paid on a transaction. Where a tax or commission is *ad valorem,* the amount to be paid is usually a fixed percentage of the value of the deal to which it relates. Thus, for example an *ad valorem* tax of one percent on deals of £50,000 and £100,000 would produce £500 and £1000 of tax respectively.

Advance Corporation Tax (ACT) (UK). The CORPORATION TAX payable by a company on its dividend distributions. Under the Corporation Tax arrangements in the United Kingdom, dividends are declared and paid to shareholders on a net basis. The company however, has to gross up the net dividends by the current basic rate of income tax to arrive at a gross equivalent figure. The difference between the gross equivalent and the net figure on each dividend is shown as a TAX CREDIT to shareholders. The total of these differences on individual dividend payments is paid by the company to the tax authorities and is called Advance Corporation Tax. This payment, under present tax law, can be offset against a company's mainstream Corporation Tax on its profits, which does not become due until some time after its year end. In practical terms, the system is little different from declaring a dividend gross and deducting tax from it at source before paying the net amount to the shareholder.

BIBLIOGRAPHY *Income and Corporation Taxes Act, 1970* (HMSO, London). Glyn Saunders, *Tolley's Corporation Tax* (Tolley Publishing, London, annually).

affare (It). A DEAL or BARGAIN.

affogliamento (It). The substitution of a new stock certificate for an old one.

after hours dealings. Dealings after the official close of business on a stock exchange trading floor. For details of individual stock exchange arrangements, *see* TRADING HOURS.

aftermarket. A word occasionally applied to trading in a security following its issue. *See also* SECONDARY MARKET, which is the more common term.

agent. One who carries out dealings on behalf of a principal. In stock market terms, it applies to a broker acting on behalf of his investment client. In some stock markets of the world the role of agent (broker) is strictly separated from that of principal (market maker) but in others, where the role of both can be carried out by one and the same company, strict rules are enforced to ensure that the agent acts in that role and in his client's best interests.

agent de change (Fr). An official member of the Paris (or any other French) Stock Exchange (BOURSE). No one can deal in securities in France unless he is an accredited *agent de change* and all must be members of the COMPAGNIE DES AGENTS DE CHANGE (CAC), a public corporation responsible, along with the COMMISSION DES OPERATIONS DE BOURSE (COB), for the surveillance of French stock markets and brokers.

agente di borsa or ***agente di cambio*** (It). *See* STOCKBROKER.

Agents, Register of (UK). A register maintained by the Stock Exchange in the United Kingdom. It contains the names of those companies, investment advisers or individuals who act as agents for the public in stock market dealing and who are permitted to share commission with a Stock Exchange broking member on a prescribed scale. *See also* APPENDIX 41.

aggiotagio (It). Artificial dealing in a manner designed to create the false impression of price movement. The action is illegal.

aggiotatore (It). A dealer who seeks to provoke a price rise or fall for his personal interests and not on the basis of buying or selling orders.

aggiunta (It). A kind of option contract whereby the buyer acquires the right to buy or sell a quantity of securities two or more times the stipulated number.

aggiustamento (del) corso (It). The adjustment of the share price following a change in the company's share capital in order to be able to make an accurate comparison of the price movements of the share over a long period of time.

aggregation (UK). The term used in CAPITAL TRANSFER TAX legislation to describe the required adding together of separate gifts during a donor's lifetime to determine the rate at which CTT will be charged.

agio. This term has a number of meanings in the world of banking and finance, all to do with a 'turn' or difference : for example, the sum payable for the convenience of exchanging one kind of money for another; as silver for gold, paper for metal. Also, in somewhat archaic stock market terminology, the difference between the par value of a stock and its market price.

Aktie (Ger). A share which may be either INHABERAKTIE (bearer) or NAMENAKTIE (registered). If the latter, the holders' names are kept in the *Aktienbuch* or *Aktienregister* (share register) and ownership is evidenced by an *Aktienzertifikat* (share certificate). The shareholder may also be entitled to GRATISAKTIEN (bonus shares) or acquire ANRECHT, the right to participate in a new issue.

Aktienbuch, Aktienregister (Ger). Share register. *See* AKTIE.

Aktiengesellschaft (AG) (Ger). A company with a share capital. One of the major forms of company organization in Germany. *See also* GESELLSCHAFT MIT BESCHRÄNKTER HAFTUNG (GMBH). An *Aktiengesellschaft* has 'AG' following its name and is broadly equivalent to PUBLIC LIMITED COMPANY (PLC), in the United Kingdom.

Aktiengesetz (Ger). Company law.

Aktienhandel (Ger). Dealing in stocks and shares; the role carried out by market makers (MAKLER).

Aktienindex (Ger). A share price index.

Aktieninhaber (Ger). *See* SHAREHOLDER.

Aktienkapital (Ger). *See* SHARE CAPITAL.

Aktienkurs (Ger). *See* KURS.

Aktienmarkt (Ger). A market for shares: a stock exchange. *See* BÖRSE.

Aktien ohne Stimmrecht (Ger). *See* NON-VOTING SHARES.

Aktienzertifikat (Ger). Share certificate. *See* AKTIE.

Aktionär (Ger). *See* SHAREHOLDER.

Aktionärbrief (Ger). A report or letter to shareholders from the directors informing them of the company's results and progress.

à la criée (Fr). One of the three methods of fixing a quotation for securities traded on a French BOURSE (stock exchange), the other two being PAR CASIERS and PAR OPPOSITION. The *à la criée* system is used on the MARCHÉ À TERME, the market for forward settlement. It is a similar method to the *par casiers* system in that bids and offers are listed to find the price at which most orders can be fulfilled. The main practical difference between the two is that under the *à la criée or* AUCTION system, dealings are carried out by OPEN OUTCRY.

Securities quoted by this method are assigned to six auction groups; the CORBEILLE and five others. An auctioneer appointed by the CHAMBRE SYNDICALE DES AGENTS DE CHANGE, together with a representative of each broking firm, stands in each group which always deals in the same securities. The list of the securities traded in each group is displayed on a board and they are dealt in a fixed order each day.

The method of fixing a price proceeds along the following lines: the auctioneer opens the market in each security at its closing price at the previous TRADING SESSION. BIDS and OFFERS are called out by the brokers. The auctioneer then raises or lowers the price until he reaches a balance. This price is then chalked on the board alongside the name of the security. New orders coming to the floor during a trading session go to make further transactions for which a second price is reached, and so on. The final price reached each day is referred to as the COURS DE LA CLÔTURE or CLOSING PRICE.

BIBLIOGRAPHY *The Paris Stock Exchange, a guide for foreign investors* (Paris, January 1980).

al buio (operare) (It). To rely on hunch and intuition in securities dealing rather than on sound research.

alla pari (It). (1) An operation executed by an agent without any commission charge.

(2) With reference to securities, the term signifies that the listing or issuing price was at PAR.

alleggerire (la) posizione (It). To reduce the extent of one's POSITION in a security.

allied member (US). A senior executive of a NEW YORK STOCK EXCHANGE member firm who is not himself a full member of the Exchange.

al listino (It). At the CLOSING PRICE.

allocation. On a FINANCIAL FUTURES market the passing on of a transaction by a PIT BROKER or TRADER to a third party.

all'ordine (It). A security which must be transferred by endorsement.

all or none (US). An order from a client to his broker to execute the whole of his order at one time.

allo scoperto (It). A LONG OR SHORT position. A speculative operation.

allotment. The granting of shares to an applicant for a new issue. In the event of demand exceeding supply, the company's RECEIVING BANKERS may scale down applications so that the amount of shares alloted to an applicant may be less than the amount applied for. In some cases, an applicant may not receive an allotment at all. *See also* BALLOT.

allotment letter (UK). A successful applicant for a new share issue (*see* ALLOTMENT) will receive an allotment letter informing him of the number of shares he has been alloted. This allotment letter is in BEARER form, title to the alloted shares passing by delivery of the allotment letter, which can itself be traded on the stock market. After a period of time all holdings of the shares at that date are transferred to a share register, after which the transactions take place in registered form in the normal way and the allotment letter ceases to be of value.

al meglio (It). *See* AT BEST.

alpha. A term used in the CAPITAL ASSET PRICING MODEL (CAPM) in investment analysis. The *alpha* of a share is a statistical estimate of its superior or inferior return having adjusted for the market-related risk or BETA FACTOR. The *alpha* measures the over or under valuation of a share.

al portatore (It). A BEARER security.

altalenante (It). Fluctuations or oscillations in a share price.

alternative investments. Investments in items other than property or securities. Often such alternatives do not have a ready marketplace, sales and purchases being subject to private and direct negotiation between principals. Such alternative investments include *inter alia* coins, stamps, medals, forestry, paintings, furniture, *objets d'art,* old bank notes and share certificates of defunct companies.

a lunga scadenza (It). *See* SHORT TERM.

amalgamation. The taking over of one company by another or the merging of the interests of two companies. Sometimes called absorption. *See also* TAKE-OVER BID and MERGER.

American Depository Receipt (ADR). A document similar to an AMERICAN-FORM SHARE CERTIFICATE except that it has usually been created by a bank, not by the company which has issued the shares. The original shares remain with the bank, while the ADR, not the share certificate, circulates as a bearer document.

American-form share certificate (UK). A company share certificate which has acquired some, but not all, of the aspects of a bearer document. The certificate is issued by the company and made out in the name of the registered holder, often a bank or stockbroker, who may endorse it and pass title to another owner. Banks and stockbrokers who are the registered holders are often known as MARKING NAMES.

American Shares Amsterdam System (ASAS) (NL). The system set up in Amsterdam in 1980 to handle dealing and settlement of major American securities on a quicker and cheaper basis. American securities are dealt from 10:00 hours to 16:30 and quotation is in US dollars.

ASAS uses two specially created subsidiaries of the Amsterdam Stock Exchange for its operations: Nominee Amsterdam Stock Exchange NV and ASAS Servicing Company NV, for holding and settlement respectively. Settlement takes place on the American basis, five days after dealing.

BIBLIOGRAPHY Paul Stonham, *Major Stock Markets of Europe* (Gower Publishing, London, 1982).

American Stock Exchange, the (AMEX). The American Stock Exchange is the second largest trading floor stock exchange in the United States after the neighbouring NEW YORK STOCK EXCHANGE (NYSE). AMEX lists over 1000 securities, but generally those of smaller companies than are traded on the NYSE. Sometimes companies begin their stock exchange lives by being traded on AMEX and then later move to the NYSE Big Board; others stay with AMEX, even though they may grow large enough to qualify in terms of market capitalization, for a listing on

NYSE. Also AMEX trades in the options of some NYSE-listed stocks.

The American Stock Exchange was known as the New York Curb Exchange until 1953, taking its name from the fact that it was originally an outdoor market literally trading on the Curb, and not until 1921 did it acquire an indoor marketplace.

AMEX and the NYSE have co-operated in a number of joint ventures, notably the SECURITIES INDUSTRY AUTOMATION CORPORATION, designed to provide a more efficient data processing and settlement operation. Proposals in the past for more formal links, perhaps even amalgamation, between the two major New York exchanges have, however, come to nothing.

BIBLIOGRAPHY R. Teweles and E. Bradley, *The Stock Market* 4th edition (John Wiley, New York, 1982). Abraham M. George, 'The United States equity markets' in Abraham M. George and Ian H. Giddy (eds.), *International Finance Handbook* (John Wiley, New York, 1983), Section 6.1.

Amerikaanse Aandelen Amsterdamse Usance (NL). *See* AMERICAN SHARES AMSTERDAM SYSTEM.

Amex Options Switching System (AMOS) (US). An automatic system developed by the American Stock Exchange for sending options and contract orders to the appropriate part of the floor for execution and for transmitting details of the executed trade back to the investor.

ammissione (di) titoli a quotazione (It). The admission of securities to listing on a stock exchange.

ammortamento (It). (1) In reference to a security, the word refers to the procedure to cancel a mislaid certificate and its replacement.

(2) In relation to a loan stock issue, the redemption of the issue in conformity with the established rules.

amortissment (Fr). The repayment of a debt, either on the due redemption date or, as with some debts, by the repayment of a portion of the outstanding debt by regular drawings of bonds to be redeemed.

amortization. (1) In stock market terminology, the payment into a SINKING FUND, by a debtor, of given amounts of money which will be used to make capital repayment of a debt and any interest outstanding.

(2) Accounting for expenses or charges as they accrue rather than when paid. Such expenses include depreciation, pre-paid expenses and deferred charges.

amtlicher Markt (Ger). The official trading market of the German stock exchanges. It includes all bonds and equities admitted to official listing. Its securities all have their prices fixed by the MAKLER but there are two distinct sub-markets within the official market: the EINHEITSKURS and the VARIABLER KURS.

BIBLIOGRAPHY Hartmut Schmidt, *Advantages and Disadvantages of an Integrated Market compared with a Fragmented Market* (Collection Studies, Competition; Approximation of Legislation Series No.30, Brussels, 1977). Paul Stonham, *Major Stock Markets of Europe* (Gower Publishing, London, 1982).

analisi fondamentale (It). *See* FUNDAMENTAL ANALYSIS.

analisi tecnica (It). *See* TECHNICAL ANALYSIS.

andienen (Ger). To DELIVER the UNDERLYING SECURITY under an options contract.

Angebot (Ger). Quotation, offer, tender, bid.

an Hand lassen (Ger). To give a firm order, for a short period, to buy or sell a specified quantity of shares at a stated price.

Anlagefonds (Ger). Investment funds, such as INVESTMENT TRUSTS, UNIT TRUSTS.

Anlagekapital (Ger). Investment capital.

Anlagepapier (Ger). Investment in stocks and shares.

Anlageplan (Ger). An investment plan: a savings scheme by which shares are acquired by regular subscriptions after a planned period.

Anlagepolitik (Ger). A strategy of investment suitable to a particular investor's needs.

Anlagevermögen (Ger). Literally investment in estate. Investment in business assets, land, buildings, stock-in-trade.

Anleihewerte (Ger). *See* LOAN STOCK.

annacquare (It). To average. To carry out purchases of a security at considerably lower prices in order to reduce the average price paid for the holding. *See* AVERAGING.

Annahmeschluss (Ger). The point at which the MAKLER on a German stock exchange will receive no further orders. Used particularly in relation to trading in subscription rights.

annual accounts. *See* ANNUAL REPORT AND ACCOUNTS.

annual general meeting (AGM). The meeting of a company which must by law be held once a year, for the purposes of receiving the directors' report and statement of accounts for the year, declaring a final dividend on the shares, electing directors and auditors and fixing the remuneration of the auditors. Special resolutions may also be considered at the AGM, such as the introduction of profit sharing schemes for directors and employees. Shareholders who are unable to attend the meeting in person must be given the right to vote and are sent proxy cards to enable them to record the way in which they wish to vote.

annual report and accounts. The yearly statement which must be made to the shareholders by the directors of a company. It must contain full details of the company's activities, progress and financial position. In the United Kingdom, the amount of detail which must be given is spelled out by a series of Companies Acts from 1948 to 1981.

The annual report must contain a directors' report giving information on the overall financial results, changes in the board of directors, how much money the company has given to political and charitable causes, consolidated profit and loss and balance sheet details, turnover by activity and geographical area. A chairman's statement discussing the company's progress is also included.

Annuität (Ger). *See* ANNUITY.

Annuities (UK). Securities issued by the British Government as part of the National Debt. There are at present two such Annuities listed, one carrying a COUPON rate of 2.5 percent, the other a rate of 2.75 percent. The 2.5 percent stock was issued as long ago as 1853 to replace South Sea Stock (*see* SOUTH SEA BUBBLE) and an earlier issue of Annuities.

annuity. A fixed annual payment made to an investor, sometimes for a set period of years, sometimes in perpetuity, in return for a capital sum invested.

annuity tables. Tables of statistics designed to help an investor calculate the present value of an amount of money received each period for n periods ahead at a discount rate of x percent. Such tables are also useful in helping calculate redemption yields on fixed interest securities.

anomaly switch. The exchange of one fixed interest security for another in order to take advantage of the fact that the prices of the two are out of line and that an investor can profit from buying the one and selling the other.

Anrecht (Ger). The right, conferred by an existing shareholding, of participating in a new issue. *See also* RIGHTS ISSUE.

an Sie - von Ihnen (Ger). Literally 'to you, from you'. Called by dealers on a German Stock Exchange when they conclude a transaction, indicating who has bought and who has sold.

anstellen (Ger). To offer securities on certain conditions: not an unqualified BID OR OFFER.

Anteil (Ger). A portion or share in a general sense. Thus a share of income by way of interest or dividend, or a share in the particular sense of part ownership of a company.

Anziehen (Ger). A general rise in prices.

'A' ordinary share (UK). The designation often given to a NON-VOTING SHARE in the United Kingdom.

apertura (It). Formerly the opening price period on an Italian stock exchange. Not now used in Milan, the largest exchange.

Appendix 39 (UK). An appendix to the Stock Exchange rule book which lays down the scales of minimum COMMISSION which have to be charged by stock exchange brokers to their clients. Commissions under Appendix 39 cannot be shared with an agent. *See also* APPENDIX 41.

Appendix 41 (UK). If a broker wishes to share his commission with a bank or other agent on the Stock Exchange's REGISTER OF BANKS OR AGENT'S REGISTER he must charge commission at the rates laid down in Appendix 41, not those in APPENDIX 39. Under current Stock Exchange rules, a broker may not pass on more than 25 percent of the commission to an agent on the register of banks and not more than 20 percent to other registered agents.

The scales laid down under this Appendix and under APPENDIX 39 are to be removed no later than December 1986 when Stock Exchange brokers' commissions will become fully negotiable. *See* NEGOTIATED COMMISSIONS.

appesantimento (della) quota (It). A general fall in security prices.

application form (UK). The form which is a part of the PROSPECTUS for a new issue and on which a potential investor must apply for shares. Because potential investors must have access to all relevant information contained in the prospectus, no application forms can be issued without being accompanied by the full prospectus. A photocopy of an application form will not be accepted since an investor might have been induced to apply for an issue without having been given the chance to read the company's prospectus in full.

applicazione (It). The SPREAD of BID PRICE and OFFER PRICE. Whoever makes these prices must subsequently either buy or sell the securities at the price quoted.

Applikationskurs (Ger). The price on a German stock exchange which is used as the basis on which commission and other charges are calculated.

apport (Fr). Contribution. The proportion of a share issue bid for by an investor.

apportion. To allocate a share issue among the applicants. When a NEW ISSUE is OVERSUBSCRIBED, the MERCHANT BANK handling details of it will, in conjunction with the company, determine how the issue is to be shared out. There are no hard and fast rules about how an issue will be apportioned, but it will depend upon the size of the oversubscription, the wishes of the company for a large or small spread of shareholders and the needs of the marketplace in being able to provide a good TWO WAY MARKET when trading in the shares begins.

apportionment. The act of making an apportion. In UK Stock Exchange, settlement terminology, the word has a more specific meaning. It is the process of allocating stock from a jobbers' trading account to brokers' purchase bargains and the jobbers own withdrawals of stock. Where there is insufficient stock to satisfy a bargain completely, special rules apply in order to part-apportion it.

appreciation. A rise in the price of a share or shares.

appropriation account (UK). That part of a company's accounts which shows the distribution of total profits into retained and distributed profits.

Arbeitsgemeinschaft der deutschen Wertpapierbörsen (Ger). *See* ASSOCIATION OF GERMAN STOCK EXCHANGES.

arbitrage. (1) The buying of a security in one market with the object of selling it almost instantaneously in another at a profit.

(2) A FINANCIAL FUTURES market describes arbitrage as the purchase and sale of a FINANCIAL INSTRUMENT with a view to profiting from price anomalies.

arbitraggio (It). *See* ARBITRAGE.

arbitraggista (It). One who undertakes arbitrage buying and selling.

arrivato (It). A share price believed to have reached its peak.

Articles of Association. One of the basic documents of any company, the Articles govern the internal workings of the company, in contrast to the Memorandum of Association which covers its dealings with the outside world. The articles deal with the powers of directors, borrowing powers, the issue of shares etc. Attached as an appendix to the Companies Act 1948 in the United Kingdom was a set of draft Articles of Association called Table A which companies could adopt in full, or adapt as required. Any company not adopting its own set of Articles is deemed to be using Table A Articles.

asked price. The price asked by a market maker for a share in contrast to BID, the price offered by the market dealer to buy the security in question from potential sellers. Also called OFFER PRICE.

assaggiare (It). To take advantage of a price rise by selling part of a holding to realize some of the holders PAPER PROFIT.

Assekuranz (Ger). *See* UNDERWRITING.

assemblea generale annuale (It). *See* ANNUAL GENERAL MEETING.

assemblée d'actionnaires annuelle (Fr). *See* ANNUAL GENERAL MEETING.

assent. The agreement by a stock or share holder to a variation in his rights in respect of his holding. This variation may be a change in the terms of a loan stock or debenture, relating to interest payments or priority for repayment, for example. In the case of shares, the shareholder may agree to accept an offer for his shares from another company. While such offers remain open, stocks or shares may be dealt in on the Stock Exchange in assented or non-assented forms, depending upon whether their holders have agreed to accept the offer or not.

assented bonds. Those bonds in respect of which the holders have already given their ASSENT to the variation in rights. They can normally still be dealt in on a stock market but the price of the assented bond is likely to differ from that of its non-assented counterpart.

asset. In general terms, property of individuals, companies, partnerships and other bodies. Assets may consist of both financial and non-financial assets, short term or liquid assets, long term, illiquid assets and even intangible assets, such as goodwill.

For commercial companies, short term assets consist largely of stocks and work-in-progress, long term assets are land, buildings, plant and equipment.

In a securities market, assets are financial assets, but may be either liquid and repayable within a few weeks or months, or illiquid in that repayment may not be for several years, if at all.

It is a major function of a stock market to provide liquidity to the holders of long term or irredeemable securities by providing a market place in which an investor may convert these securities back into cash at times of his own choosing, by selling them to another investor.

asset cover. The number of times a company's outstanding debt is covered by the net assets of the company.

asset deficiency. The situation where the assets of a company fall short of its liabilities so that its debts cannot be paid in full.

asset stripping. A term applied to the taking-over of a company by another, which then proceeds to sell off the taken over company's assets piecemeal to other companies. The term came into use in the 1960s to describe such activities then being carried on by a number of entrepreneurs. Companies with relatively poor trading records and therefore low share prices but which were rich in assets, were particularly vulnerable to this type of operation. The practice fell into disrepute during the stock market crash of 1974 when the shares of companies known to be asset strippers fell very sharply and several of the companies failed. *See also* TAKE-OVER BID.

asset value. An ambiguous term which may be used to describe (1) the value of the ASSETS at cost in the company's balance sheet; (2) the current value of a company's assets or (3) the estimated realizable value on sale. Care should be taken when reading this phrase as to which value is being discussed.

Net asset value per share can be used as a yardstick in valuing shares; total assets less total liabilities divided by the number of shares in issue can produce such a figure. Figures of net current assets show cash, bank deposits, work-in-progress and debtors less current liabilities (overdrafts, creditors and other short term borrowing) and give a measure of a company's immediate financial position.

assignee. The general meaning is the person to whom any right in property passes as the result of a legal transfer or assignment of that right. For the specific meaning given to this work by the United Kingdom Stock Exchange, *see* OFFICIAL ASSIGNEE.

assignor. One who signs over his rights in a particular piece of property to another.

associate. Generally a colleague or partner. Specifically in a securities market context all persons, whether or not acting in concert (*see* CONCERT PARTY), who directly or indirectly own or deal in the shares of an offerer or offeree company in a take-over or merger transaction and who have (in addition to their normal interests as shareholders) an interest or potential interest, whether commercial, financial or personal, in the outcome of the offer. The CITY CODE ON TAKE-OVERS AND MERGERS, from which the above definition is taken, includes the following in the category of associates: the parent or a subsidiary company of one of the contesting parties; professional advisers; directors' families and trusts; pension funds of the companies; investment companies whose funds are managed by an associate; a 10 percent shareholder of either party and any company with a material trading arrangement with either offerer or offeree.

associated company. A company set up by or allied to another, but not a subsidiary. Associated companies may have interlocking directorships or shareholdings. It is usual for one company to hold between 20 and 50 percent of the shares of an associate, thus giving it effective control but not causing one to be a subsidiary of the other.

associate member (UK). A member of the UK Stock Exchange can be either a full member or an associate member. An associate member is generally not a partner in a member firm but is fully qualified for membership by having served the necessary three years' training period and passing the

Stock Exchange's examination papers. An associate member, although not a full profit sharing member of a member firm, may be a HALF-COMMISSION MAN or may be paid a salary (with or without bonus).

Association of German Stock Exchanges. A federation of the eight West German Stock Exchanges which determines common rules and standards of, for example, dealing and settlement. *See also* BÖRSE.

Association of International Bond Dealers (AIBD). An association set up in 1969 to establish uniform practices in EUROBOND and other internationally dealt fixed interest securities. Membership of the organization now totals over 650 member banks and bond dealers worldwide.

Association of Investment Trust Companies (AITC) (UK). The trade association for investment trusts in the United Kingdom. Set up in 1932 it has a membership of around 175 companies. It represents these trusts in dealings with government, the civil service and other financial institutions and bodies, including the COUNCIL FOR THE SECURITIES INDUSTRY.

associé (Fr). *See* PARTNER.

at best. The instruction given by a client to his stockbroker to execute his order immediately at the best price currently available in the market. *See also* LIMIT ORDER.

at call. Any funds which are placed by one institution with another on the basis that they are subject to immediate withdrawal. Funds are frequently placed on such terms by a UK bank with DISCOUNT HOUSE, STOCK JOBBER or MONEY BROKER. Such funds assist the borrowers with their short-term financial needs while they assist the banks in complying with the monetary control requirements laid down by the BANK OF ENGLAND. Money placed at call in this way is secured upon the assets of the institutions to which it is lent.

at par. The phrase used to indicate, in the case of a fixed interest security, that the nominal (or par) price and market price are one and the same. Sometimes also loosely applied to share prices. *See* PAR.

at-the-money option. A CALL OPTION whose EXERCISE PRICE is the same as the current market price of the underlying security. *See also* IN-THE-MONEY OPTION; OUT-OF-THE-MONEY OPTION.

Attribution (Fr). The ALLOTMENT of shares in a new issue.

auction market. A type of market for securities where the price is fixed by brokers and dealers bidding for stock around a trading post where all deals in that particular security take place. Dealings may be made by 'OPEN OUTCRY' or by the submission of written BIDS and OFFERS. The New York Stock Exchange's SPECIALIST system and the French PAR CASIERS markets are examples of different types of auction markets. *See also* À LA CRIEÉ.

audit. The examination of a company's accounts to ensure that proper records are being kept.

auditor. The independent, professionally qualified accountant who certifies to the shareholders or members, that a company's accounts have been properly kept and reflect a true and fair view of the state of the business. An auditor's report must be an integral part of the company's ANNUAL ACCOUNTS.

auditor's report. The statement attached to a company's ANNUAL REPORT AND ACCOUNTS and signed by a firm of professional accountants, signifying that the accounts have been properly kept and reflect a true and fair view of the company's financial position. *See also* QUALIFIED ACCOUNTS.

aufgelaufene Zinsen (Ger). *See* ACCRUED INTEREST.

Aufgeld (Ger). *See* PREMIUM.

Aufnahme geschlossen (Ger). The phrase called out by the MAKLER to indicate he will take no more orders before he fixes the price for a security.

Aufsichtsrat (Ger). A company's board of directors.

Auftrag (Ger). *See* ORDER.

Aufwertung (Ger). A revaluation of items in a balance sheet, such as property assets.

aumento (di) capitale (It). An increase in PAID UP CAPITAL.

au mieux (Fr). On the French BOURSES, *au mieux* means at best or at the market price. If an order is received before the start of TRADING HOURS, it will be carried out at the opening price. If the order arrives after the opening price has been fixed, it will be carried out at the first price or COURS after it has reached the floor.

Ausgabe (Ger). *See* ISSUE.

Ausgabe junger Aktien (Ger). *See* NEW ISSUE.

Ausgabepreis (Ger). *See* ISSUE PRICE.

ausgegebenes Kapital (Ger). *See* ISSUED CAPITAL.

ausgleichen (Ger). (1) To cover a position: the action of a broker when he buys or sells for his own account in order to balance the bids and offers on his book.

(2) The action of an ADRESSE to facilitate the fixing of a price for a security.

Auslands investition (Ger). *See* OVERSEAS INVESTMENT.

Auslandsinvestierungsgesetz (Ger). The German foreign investment law which regulates the trading in overseas stocks of German investors, including unit trusts.

Auslosung (Ger). The repayment of bonds, not on a fixed redemption date but by way of annual drawings by lot.

Ausreissen des Kurses (Ger). A sharp and unexpected increase in the price of a security or securities.

Ausschlussrecht (Ger). The right of an issuing house to reserve a portion of a new issue of securities for itself or its clients.

Ausschuss für Festverzinsliche Werte (Ger). The committee for fixed interest securities, one of the committees of the West German stock exchanges.

Ausschuss für Geschäfte in amtlich nicht notierten Werten (Ger). The German stock exchanges' committee for unlisted securities.

ausserbörslichen Wertpapierhandel (Ger). The unofficial or OVER THE COUNTER MARKET in West Germany, sometimes called the TELEFONVERKEHR or telephone market. The participants in this market are the West German banks and the FREIE MAKLER. Not only unlisted but also officially listed shares and bonds may be dealt in on this market. For the latter it is a method of dealing outside official German Stock Exchange TRADING HOURS and for ARBITRAGE with overseas stock markets.

aussteigen (Ger). To sell securities; to get out of the market.

aussuchen (Ger). The offer to buy or sell securities at the same price. If a broker quotes a security 'aussuchen' he indicates his intention to buy or sell the specified quantity at the stated price.

Australian Associated Stock Exchanges (AASE). Formed in 1937, the AASE is now the policy-making body for the six Australian Stock Exchanges in Sydney, Melbourne, Adelaide, Brisbane, Perth and Hobart. The AASE consists of 13 members, three each from Sydney and Melbourne, two each from

Adelaide, Brisbane and Perth and one from Hobart. The AASE determines listing requirements for companies coming to any of the exchanges, sets dealing regulations and publishes the share price indices.

Australian Associated Stock Exchanges Indices. The AASE indices were introduced in 1980 and replaced the separately compiled Sydney and Melbourne indices. The AASE indices are based on prices on both the Sydney and Melbourne trading floors, plus information from the other Australian exchanges. The base of all the AASE indices is 500 on 1 January 1980 and 24 separate industry groups are calculated, along with a number of composite groups such as metals and minerals, all resources, all industrials, all ordinaries and the 50 leading stocks.

BIBLIOGRAPHY Paul A. and Laurie J. Aron, 'The Asian Equity Markets' in Abraham M. George and Ian H. Giddy (eds), *International Finance Handbook* (Wiley, New York, 1983) Section 6.9.

authorized capital (UK). The nominal amount of capital which a limited company is authorized to raise under its ARTICLES OF ASSOCIATION. The ISSUED CAPITAL may be less than this amount at any time, but never in excess of it. Should the company wish to increase its authorized capital it has to obtain the agreement of its shareholders in general meeting.

authorized clerk (UK). A dealer with a member firm of the Stock Exchange, the authorized clerk is not a full member but may carry out clients' dealing business on behalf of his firm. He is assisted in his task by unauthorized clerks or BLUE BUTTONS.

authorized depositary (UK). An institution or firm, authorised under the UK Exchange Control Act to receive deposits of overseas securities held by UK residents. Such securities had, by law, to be placed with an authorized depositary, which also arranged the payment of interest and dividends to the shareholders in the United Kingdom. Much of the work of authorized depositaries disappeared with the ending of exchange control in October 1979 but the Act was not formally repealed and they remain in nominal existence. Authorized depositaries include banks, stockbrokers and some other financial institutions.

authorized investments (UK). Investments which may be undertaken by trustees under the TRUSTEE INVESTMENTS ACT 1961.

autofinancement (Fr). *See* INTERNAL FINANCE.

Automated Bond System (ABS) (US). A service of the NEW YORK STOCK EXCHANGE which provides current quotation and trading information for over 80 percent of NYSE-listed bonds. The system also validates, stores and matches orders for possible execution.

Automated Real-Time Investments Exchange Ltd (ARIEL) (UK). A computer-based share dealing system, established in 1972 by a group of UK MERCHANT BANKS with the object of trading shares in large blocks among themselves. Although still in existence, trading via ARIEL has not materially diverted equity business from the Stock Exchange.

autorisiertes kapital (Ger.) *See* AUTHORIZED CAPITAL.

averages. One of the methods of measuring general movements in stock market prices, popular especially in the United States, where one of the longest running measures is the DOW JONES AVERAGE of 30 industrial stocks listed on the New York Stock Exchange. The prices of the 30 securities are added together and then divided by a figure which compensates for past stock splits and stock dividends and which is changed from time to time. *See also* NYSE COMMON STOCK INDEX, STANDARD & POORS '500' INDEX.

averaging. The practice of buying additional shares in a company when the price has fallen from the original purchase price, in order to bring down the average cost per share of the investment. In this case, the investor must be confident that the share price will in fact turn and rise again and there are many in the investment world who will say that averaging is a polite term for throwing good money after bad, since a share price may continue to fall.

For CAPITAL GAINS TAX purposes in the United Kingdom, averaging in order to affect one's capital gain tax liability has been ineffective since 1982, since all acquisitions now have to be separately identified in arriving at a capital gains tax liability. *See also* INDEXATION OF CAPITAL GAINS TAX; POOLING.

avis d'attribution (Fr). *See* ALLOTMENT LETTER.

avoir fiscal (Fr). A tax credit for non-French holders of French securities introduced in the 1960s, equal to 50 percent of the amount of dividends paid to shareholders. Private shareholders in Austria, Belgium, Brazil, West Germany, Luxembourg, the Netherlands, Spain, Sweden, Switzerland, the United Kingdom and the United States are granted this tax credit, so long as their holdings in the French company do not exceed specified percentages. (5 percent for a Netherlands investor, 10 percent for a UK or US investor; 20 percent for a Swiss; 25 percent for a West German or Luxembourgeois). No *avoir fiscal* is available on French bonds.

avoirs bloques (Fr). *See* BLOCKED FUNDS.

azione (It). *See* SHARE.

azione ordinaria (It). *See* ORDINARY SHARE.

azione postergata (It). *See* DEFERRED SHARE.

azione preferenziale cumulative (It). *See* CUMULATIVE PREFERENCE SHARE.

azione preferenziale redimibile (It). *See* REDEEMABLE PREFERENCE SHARE.

azione priviligista (It). *See* PREFERENCE SHARE.

azione (di) risparmio (It). A savings share. An Italian category of non-voting cumulative preference shares which have a right to a dividend at least 2 percent (of par value) higher than that of the ordinary shares. Such shares may only be issued and listed by companies whose ordinary shares are already listed and up to a maximum of 50 percent of the capital of the company.

azione senza diritto a voto (It). *See* NON-VOTING SHARE.

azione (di) sostegno (It). Support buying of securities by banks or institutions in order to counterbalance or reduce the effect of speculative selling.

azione (di) stimolo (It). Selective purchasing of leading securities by investors or speculators in an effort to enliven stockmarket volume in order to provoke price upturns and reduce price losses.

azioni con diritto a voto (It). *See* VOTING SHARES.

azioni (di) godimento (It). Shares issued in exchange for old ones at the time of a share reduction. Such shares carry a deferred right to a dividend but no voting rights.

azioni (di) lavoro (It). Shares issued to employees as part of a PROFIT SHARING scheme.

B

baby bond (US). A bond with a nominal value lower than the conventional amount of $1000.

bacchettara (It). To sell a security.

backing away (US). A market maker's failure to deal on a price which he has quoted. The phrase might be applied primarily to the over-the-counter market in the United States, but is against the National Association of Securities Dealers' RULES OF FAIR PRACTICE.

back office. The term applied in the United States and, less commonly, in the United Kingdom to the settlement functions of stockbroking firms, dealing with benefits such as dividends etc. In US firms, sometimes referred to as 'the CAGE'.

back months. In a FINANCIAL FUTURES market, the most distant months' futures CONTRACTS currently being traded. Also referred to as deferred futures. *See also* NEARBY FUTURES.

back to back loan. An arrangement between two companies in different countries, each of which wishes to undertake an investment in the other's country. For tax or exchange control reasons they agree to finance each other's project in their own respective countries.

backwardation. A Stock Exchange term with two quite different meanings.

(1) the ability of a seller of stock on payment of an agreed premium to postpone delivery of that stock beyond the normal SETTLEMENT DAY.

(2) In the United Kingdom market a backwardation is said to occur when the selling or OFFER PRICE quoted by one jobber is lower than the buying or BID PRICE quoted by one or more of his competitors. In such circumstances it would be possible for a broker to buy shares from the first jobber and re-sell them to the second thus making a small turn for himself. Dealing 'on a back' in this way is frowned on by the Stock Exchange authorities and is proscribed by the CODE OF DEALING. A broker finding such a situation in the market is obliged to inform the jobber concerned that it exists and the jobber is then permitted to change his QUOTE.

baisse (Fr). A general fall in stock market prices; a declining price trend, taking into account the fluctuations in day-to-day prices in the market.

Baissemarkt (Ger). *See* BEAR MARKET.

Baissespekulant (Ger). *See* BEAR.

baissier (Fr). A BEAR operator in a stock market: one who expects prices to fall.

balance certificate (UK). A certificate issued by a REGISTRAR representing the balance of shares held by an investor after he has sold a part of his holding. On the sale of shares, the investor has to pass the share certificate to his broker who in turn sends it to the registrar to record the change of ownership. When only a part of a holding is sold the original certificate is cancelled and a new one issued showing the balance of the new holding.

balance sheet. The statement of assets and liabilities of a company, club, society, partnership or other business entity at its year end.

The breakdown of assets will cover separately: fixed assets, such as plant and equipment, land and buildings, investments in subsidiary and associated companies, assets leased from other companies and intangible assets such as goodwill. Next, current assets such as cash in the bank and debtors. The breakdown of liabilities includes share and loan capital, reserves, any minority interests in subsidiary companies, plus current liabilities such as trade and other creditors.

balance sheet ratios. There are a number of ratios which investment advisers and analysts derive from a company's balance sheet figures which they use in assessing the financial strength of that company. These ratios include the LIQUID ASSETS RATIO, CURRENT ASSETS RATIO and the ACID TEST RATIO.

ballot. The drawing of the names of successful applicants in a new issue of securities for which there has been an OVERSUBSCRIPTION. In such a situation it is usual for those who have applied for a large number of shares to be allotted a proportion of their total application, whereas those applying for a small number will have their applications put into the ballot for a minimum number of shares.

bank holiday (UK). Specifically a day on which the banks are closed for business, but in the United Kingdom has the more general meaning of an occasional public holiday. The meaning was acquired by the Bank Holidays Act of 1871 by which certain non-religious days in the year (generally Mondays) were declared to be bank holidays, with the object of creating more general public holidays.

Bank of England (UK). The central bank of the United Kingdom. In addition to its banking role, set out in the Bank of England Act 1946 and the Banking Act 1979, the Bank of England operates a general supervisory role over the financial institutions and markets of the City of London as a whole.

Founded in 1694 as a commercial bank, based on the plan of a Scotsman, William Paterson, the Bank of England has always had a privileged status in London banking. It was from the start a JOINT-STOCK COMPANY, whose shareholders enjoyed limited liability, whereas the other London banks were partnerships. The Bank was founded to provide a loan of £1.2 million for King William III, and so it became the government's banker and the manager of the national debt.

In the 19th century, legislation helped the Bank of England to become the only bank in England and Wales with the right of note issue and it began to acquire functions which are today regarded as central banking, rather than commercial banking, activities.

The Bank of England was nationalized in 1946 but its position as a central bank was by that time so entrenched that the transfer of its stock to public ownership was little more than a formality. It was given legislative control of the banking system with the passing of the Banking Act 1979, although some of this legislation merely put on a more formal basis the control that the Bank of England had operated for many years.

In securities markets, the Bank of England is responsible for selling debt on behalf of the government. It watches developments in the securities market generally and consults frequently with the Stock Exchange on matters of mutual interest and concern. The Bank was largely instrumental in the establishment of the PANEL ON TAKE-OVERS AND MERGERS and, later, the COUNCIL FOR THE SECURITIES INDUSTRY. It has also exercised a close interest in the changes which have taken place in the methods and operation of the Stock Exchange following the agreement between the government and the Stock Exchange which led to the ending of the RESTRICTIVE PRACTICES COURT case against the Exchange in 1983. *See also* LINK, THE; SINGLE CAPACITY.

bankrupt. An individual who has been declared unable to pay his debts. Individual members of a partnership may be made bankrupt, but a company is said to be wound up (*see* WINDING UP). For the specific Stock Exchange terminology for one of its firms being declared in default, *see* HAMMERING.

banque d'affaires (Fr). A French term roughly equivalent to, and translated as, a MERCHANT BANK. Generally speaking, a bank which lends on a medium to long term basis to corporate customers and assists them in raising such finance from other sources, most notably via an issue of stock exchange listed securities.

banque d'émission (Fr). *See* ISSUING HOUSE.

banque de virement (Fr). A clearing bank. A retail bank one of whose major functions is a money transmission service.

banque universelle (Fr). A combination of a BANQUE DE VIREMENT and a BANQUE D'AFFAIRES; in other words, one which attempts to cover the whole range of a customer's financial needs.

barca (It). To make a trading error. The term is used in expressions like 'pretendere una barca' or 'essere in barca', in order to indicate a trading mistake; for example, to have effected a sale of securities instead of a purchase and vice versa.

bargain (UK). A deal or transaction on the Stock Exchange in the United Kingdom is called a bargain. Statistics of the amount of turnover on the Exchange are published showing the number of bargains, the total value of the turnover and the number of shares traded. In order to measure the business of the UK Stock Exchange in comparison with others worldwide, the UK figures have to be halved. This is because UK Stock Exchange statistics are collected on the basis of the broker's CONTRACT NOTE which reports the deal to the client. Thus the buyer and the seller will each be informed of the deal when (in effect) one block of shares has changed hands. For details of Stock Exchange statistics *see* STOCK EXCHANGE FACT SERVICE.

barreserve (Fr). Cash holdings of an investor awaiting investment.

Barron's confidence index (US). An index of confidence published in the American financial weekly, Barron's, which traces the ratio between the intermediate and 'best grade' corporate bonds: as the ratio narrows, confidence is said to be improving and vice versa.

base date. The date on which an INDEX NUMBER commenced. All indices have a base date which may be a year, (most national income statistics are based on the average level in a particular year), a quarter or a particular point in time. Stock market indices are often based on the last of these. For example, the base date of the FINANCIAL TIMES INDUSTRIAL ORDINARY SHARE INDEX is 1 July 1935. Normally at the base date the index is given the number 100, but this is not invariable: for example, the FINANCIAL TIMES-STOCK EXCHANGE INDEX (FTSE) of 100 ordinary shares was based at 1000 on its base date of 30 December 1983, the AUSTRALIAN ASSOCIATED STOCK EXCHANGES INDICES at 500 on 1 January 1980 and the NYSE Composite Index (*see* NEW YORK STOCK EXCHANGE COMMON STOCK INDICES) at 50 on 31 December 1965.

base rate (UK). The rate quoted by British banks on which many of their lending rates are based. Base rate is adjusted by each bank according to its own position, but the individual base rates are most usually in line with one another because of the similarity of the money market conditions in which they all operate and compete. Increasingly, the banks are raising funds on the wholesale markets in London and are calculating lending rates in some instances relative to the LONDON INTER-BANK OFFERED RATE (LIBOR), rather than to their own base rates. Base rate is the British equivalent of the American PRIME RATE.

basis. In a FINANCIAL FUTURES market the difference between the CASH PRICE of a FINANCIAL INSTRUMENT and the price of a particular futures CONTRACT relating to that instrument.

basis point. *See* MINIMUM PRICE FLUCTUATION.

bear. A speculator who sells, at the current price, shares he does not already own, hoping to buy them back later at a lower price and thus make himself a profit.

bearer. The person who holds a bond or share payable to 'bearer'. He is thus its BENEFICIAL OWNER. *See also* BEARER BOND and BEARER SHARE.

bearer bond. A fixed interest security which is payable to 'bearer' and thus may be transferred by delivery. Because it may pass by delivery, it is not possible to keep a register of such bonds and their holders. To allow such owners to claim interest payments on a bearer bond, coupons are attached and the current owner claims his interest payment by clipping off the relevant coupon and sending it to the PAYING AGENT, who then forwards the payment to the holder of the bond.

bearer share. Variable income securities or shares may be issued to 'bearer' allowing him to claim dividends which have been declared. The procedure for claiming is similar to that for a BEARER BOND.

bearish. A feeling of uncertainty; an expectation that share prices will fall.

bear market. A stock market in which sellers predominate and as a result prices are generally falling. *See also* BEAR.

bear position. *See* POSITION.

bear squeeze. *See* SQUEEZE.

beat the market. To achieve greater capital gain than any rise in share prices generally would produce. Advice to investors, whether based on hunch, share tipping in newspapers and other publications, or given as a result of detailed and expensive research, is designed to help them beat the market and achieve above average capital growth. Those who have analysed the effects of investment research suggest that above average rates of return should not be taken at face value but must be related to the risk involved in the particular shares in relation to the market as a whole. Proponents of the EFFICIENT MARKET HYPOTHESIS suggest that once such risk has been accounted for, beating the market consistently and scientifically is impossible. *See also* ALPHA; BETA; CAPITAL ASSET PRICING MODEL.

bed-and-breakfast (UK). A term used to describe the short term buying and selling of shares to crystallize a tax position. If an investor held shares which he had bought at a higher than current price, he would sell them close to the end of the tax year (5th April) in order to establish a loss for CAPITAL GAINS TAX purposes. If, however, he had confidence that the shares would subsequently rise in price he would ask his broker to carry out a bed-and-breakfast transaction, buying the shares back again on the day after he had sold them.

Equally, because of the Capital Gains Tax legislation, an investor who had seen his shares rise sharply in price might wish to sell them to establish a capital gain and buy them back again on the following day to take advantage of future increases in price.

Legislative changes in 1982, which introduced INDEXATION OF CAPITAL GAINS TAX, made bed-and-breakfast deals less attractive to investors.

BIBLIOGRAPHY *Capital Gains Tax* (Tolleys Publishing, London, 1984).

begebbares Wertpapier (Ger). A negotiable instrument.

Begebungskonsortium (Ger). An issue syndicate which acts only as a selling agent for the securities, not as an underwriter. The syndicate operates on a commission basis, selling the securities to the public in its own name but on the issuer's account. Securities remaining unsold are returned to the issuer. This type of selling consortium is now less common than the underwriting syndicate, the UBERNAHMEKONSORTIUM.

being short. *See* SHORT.

below (the) market. At a price below that currently ruling in the market.

below par. *See* PAR.

ben comprato (It). Refers to a security which is systematically bought by operators who are particularly expert and normally well informed.

bénéfice (Fr). *See* PROFIT.

bénéfice par titre (Fr). *See* EARNINGS PER SHARE.

beneficial owner. The rightful, legal owner of property to whom all the benefits of that property accrue. Often the phrase is used with regard to shares where the registered holder is different from the beneficial owner. The holding of stocks and shares in the United Kingdom, for example, is often done through a NOMINEE, who holds the shares in trust for the beneficial owner. Any analysis of share ownership must take into account that an analysis of the SHARE REGISTER may not give a true reflection of the beneficial ownership of a company.

BIBLIOGRAPHY *The Ownership of Company Shares* (Central Statistical Office, London, 1979). *Survey of Share Ownership* (The Stock Exchange, London, 1983). *Stockholding, 1983* (New York Stock Exchange).

benefit. Any entitlement due to a stock or share holder as a result of purchasing or holding securities. These benefits include the right to any DIVIDEND, RIGHTS ISSUE, SCRIP ISSUE etc made by the company.

best. *See* AT BEST.

best efforts (US). One of the bases on which an investment banker will help issue securities to investors on behalf of a company. The bank does not act as an underwriter for the issue but tries to sell the securities as an agent with no financial risk and no liability for those which cannot be sold. *Contrast with* BOUGHT DEAL.

bestens (Ger). *See* AT BEST: specifically applied to a selling order. *See also* BILLINGST.

best execution rule (UK). A rule being proposed for the new dealing system in equities in the United Kingdom. The best execution rule will place an obligation on any agency dealer in the market to carry out his client's transaction at the best possible price obtaining in the market at the time of the deal.

beta factor. A measure of risk used in investment analysis. The *beta* is a statistical estimate of how closely returns to a share are expected to move in relation to returns to the whole market portfolio. When both move in unison, beta has a coefficient of one. For shares with greater-than-average risk, the beta is greater than unity. Those with less-than-average risk have a beta factor of less than unity. Investors will expect a greater return for the former and a lower return for the latter. Betas for shares listed on the Stock Exchange in the United Kingdom are calculated and published quarterly by the London Business School's RISK MANAGEMENT SERVICE.

better, to go. Of share prices, to improve or rise.

Beursplein 5 (NL). The colloquial name for the Amsterdam Stock Exchange, equivalent to Wall Street for the New York and American Stock Exchanges or Throgmorton Street in London.

Beursvoorschriften (NL). Stock Exchange regulations implemented by the BEURSWET.

Beurswet (NL). The Stock Exchange Act of 1914, the statute by which the Netherlands stock market is governed, in conjunction with the rules established by the Amsterdam Stock Exchange's governing body.

Bezugsrecht (Ger). The right of a shareholder to buy additional shares at a privileged price. *See also* RIGHTS ISSUE.

bid. In securities terminology, the offer to buy shares. (1) This may be the market maker's price at which he indicates he is willing to buy shares from existing shareholders (*see* BID PRICE).

(2) Alternatively, it may refer to a general offer by one company to buy the shares of another. *See also* AMALGAMATION; TAKE-OVER BID.

bid and asked or **bid-asked spread.** The market maker's QUOTE. *See also* ASKED PRICE; BID PRICE.

bid price. The price at which the market maker is prepared to buy shares from existing holders. This will be below his OFFER PRICE or ASKED PRICE at which he is prepared to sell shares to new holders.

'big bang'. The term coined in 1983 to describe the changes in UK Stock Exchange practices brought about following the ending of the RESTRICTIVE PRACTICES COURT case against the Stock Exchange. By an agreement reached between the Stock Exchange and the government in July 1983, the government agreed to exempt the Stock Exchange from the Restrictive Practices Act in return for certain concessions, most notably the ending of minimum COMMISSION by the end of 1986 at the latest. At first it was thought that commissions would be dismantled or de-regulated in stages, but it quickly became apparent that the ending of minimum commissions would most likely occur on one date. This 'sudden death' of minimum commissions was termed the 'big bang'.

Later the term was widened to include all the other changes likely to flow from the ending of minimum commissions, including the changes to the dealing system and the relaxation of restrictions limiting the percentage of a member firm which could be owned by a single non-member to 29.9 percent. *See also* LINK, THE; SINGLE CAPACITY.

Big Board. A name colloquially applied to the NEW YORK STOCK EXCHANGE, reflecting the fact that it lists the major American companies.

biglietto di ammissione (It). Document or ticket circulated by a company to its shareholders which authorizes them to participate at a company meeting.

big number. In quoting a security's price, the name colloquially applied to the whole number to the left of the decimal point. More loosely, any number so obvious to the parties to the deal that it does not have to be mentioned. If for example, in the United Kingdom , a share is trading at a BID PRICE of 261p and an OFFER PRICE of 264p, a dealer asked for a price would most likely say '61-64', the big number, 2, being taken as read.

bilan annuel (Fr). *See* ANNUAL ACCOUNTS.

bilanco annuale (It). *See* ANNUAL ACCOUNTS.

Bilanz (Ger). *See* BALANCE SHEET.

bill broker (UK). *See* DISCOUNT HOUSE.

billingst (Ger). *See* AT BEST: applied to an order to buy without naming a maximum price the investor is willing to pay. *See also* BESTENS.

bill of exchange. A credit instrument drawn by one party (the drawer) extending the credit and signed by the party receiving it (the drawee) acknowledging and accepting his liability for the debt at a stated future date. The drawer of the bill may obtain immediate cash by discounting the bill with a discount house or bank. A better rate can be obtained if the bill bears, as acceptor, the signature of a reputable bank or accepting house, which agrees to honour the bill in the event of the drawee's failure to do so.

blanket fidelity bond (US). *See* FIDELITY BOND.

Blankoverkauf (Ger). *See* LEERVERKAUF.

blank transfer (UK). A STOCK TRANSFER FORM in which the name of the transferee is left blank. This procedure is often used when stock exchange securities are used as security against a loan. The blank transfer will be kept by the lender who may fill in his own name and have the securities fully transferred to him as BENEFICIAL OWNER should the borrower default on the debt.

blocage des dividendes (Fr). Dividend control or limitation.

block (US). A large holding or transaction in a stock, popularly considered to be 10,000 shares or more, although there is no hard and fast rule on what constitutes a block.

blocked funds. Money which for reasons of exchange control legislation cannot be transferred outside the country concerned. It is therefore traded at a discount to the official rate of exchange for freely convertible currency.

block trading (US). The buying and selling of large blocks of shares by brokerage firms in the United States. The firms taking on a large BLOCK order will try to carry out the deal on the other side with the least possible disturbance to the market price. The broker will try to place the stock with his own clients who are interested in it or he may take a position in the stock for his own account, hoping to sell it later at a profit. If he is able to find matching buyers for a large selling order, the broker is said to CROSS the deal on the trading floor, being both the buyer and the seller, but doing the deal through the SPECIALIST.

blue button (UK). A clerk on the floor of the Stock Exchange in the United Kingdom who assists the dealers but cannot himself deal. He (or she) is officially called an unauthorized clerk. The name, blue button, derives from the blue badge which unauthorized clerks must wear to denote their status. Blue buttons are trainee dealers, they may help the AUTHORIZED CLERKS and member dealers by collecting prices for them or carrying details back to the broking firm's office.

blue chip. An equity share of a large, safe and prestigious company. Ironically, perhaps, the term is said to derive from the colour of the highest valued chip in a poker game.

blue list (US). A list of municipal bonds issued daily since 1935 by Standard & Poor's which details prices, yields etc of municipal bonds in issue.

blue sky laws (US). A name popularly applied to the laws of some states which seek to protect the public against fraudulent dealing in securities. The term is said to have derived from the words of a judge who said that a particular security had about the same value as a patch of blue sky.

bocca di barile (It). An expression used to indicate considerable purchases or sales of securities without much attention to the prices obtained.

bond. A fixed interest security. *See also* GILT EDGED STOCKS.

bon de jouissance (Fr). Sometimes called a *bon de récuperation,* it gives the holder the right to share in the net proceeds of the liquidation of a company and the preferential right to participate in a new issue if the company's fortunes revive.

bon de livraison (Fr). *See* ALLOTMENT LETTER.

bon de récuperation (Fr). *See* BON DE JOUISSANCE.

bond market. An organized market place in which fixed interest bond issues, made either by governments, companies or other issuers, may be traded.

Bon du Tresor (Fr). A Treasury bond.

bond washing (UK). The name given to the practice of selling a security *cum* dividend and buying it back *ex* dividend, thus converting income on the dividend (taxed at a higher rate) into a capital gain on which a lower rate of tax was payable.

bon marché (Fr). Cheap. *See also* MARCHÉ.

bonus Ausgabe (Ger). *See* SCRIP ISSUE.

bonus issue (UK). *See* SCRIP ISSUE.

book. A market maker's record of his buying and selling deals and, by extension, the POSITION he has in a particular security. Thus a market maker's book may be LONG of a stock if he has bought shares for which he has no immediate buyer or SHORT if he has sold stock he does not already hold. *See also* JOBBER'S BOOK.

book entry transfer (BET). A method of recording the transfer of shares by amending the records in the registrar's books and obviating the need for a share certificate. This is the system of share transfer in West Germany, principally through the KASSENVEREIN, and a similar system has recently been introduced in France. The United Kingdom Stock Exchange is currently working towards the introduction of a similar system.

book value. The value of a company's assets as shown in their 'books' or balance sheet.

boom. A generic word for rising prices, output, employment etc. In stock exchange terminology, applied specifically to a sustained rise in share prices.

borsa (It). Stock Exchange. There are ten stock exchanges in Italy: Milan, Rome, Turin, Genoa, Florence, Bologna, Naples, Venice, Trieste and Palermo. Milan, with 70-80 percent of the business, is by far the largest.

Börse (Ger). Stock Exchange. There are eight stock exchanges in the Federal Republic of Germany: the main ones are located in Frankfurt and Düsseldorf, which together account for around 80 percent of the total turnover; other smaller exchanges exist in Berlin, Bremen, Hamburg, Hanover, Munich and Stuttgart. Each *Börse* is governed under the laws of the *Land* in which it operates, but in legal terms all the exchanges are linked together.

Börsenaufsichtausschuss (Ger). The supervisory committee of the Frankfurt and Düsseldorf Stock Exchanges.

Börseneinfuhrung (Ger). A listing or quotation on a BÖRSE of company or other securities. Admission of securities to listing passes through a Listings Committee (*see* ZULASSUNGSSTELLE), a partly independent body which licenses securities prior to their listing.

Börseneinfuhrungsprovision (Ger). Listing fee.

Börsengesetz (Ger). The Stock Exchange Act of 1896 which created the German stock exchanges.

Börsenkommissar (Ger). An official appointed by the Land to sit on the Stock Exchange management committee.

Börsenkurs (Ger). *See* KURS.

Börsenmakler (Ger). A general name for an official broker on a German stock exchange. *See also* MAKLER and FREIE MAKLER.

Börsenordnung (Ger). The internal regulations of the West German stock exchanges which govern their operations under powers delegated by the BÖRSENGESETZ. THE BÖRSENVORSTAND receives its authority from the *Börsenordnung*.

Börsensachsverständigenkommission (Ger). A commission established in 1968 to investigate the improvement of practices in the West German stock exchanges.

Börsenspekulant (Ger). A share speculator.

Börsenumsatzsteuer (Ger). The turnover tax levied on transactions on a West German stock exchange and on capital raising. The rate varies from 0.10 percent on government bonds to 0.25 percent on company securities. The tax is levied at one half of the normal rates if one of the parties to the deal is an overseas resident.

Börsenvorstand (Ger). The board of governors of each of the West German stock exchanges. The *Börsenvorstand* is set up under the internal regulations governing the operation of stock exchanges (*see* BÖRSENGESETZ and BÖRSENORDNUNG) and is responsible for issuing regulations governing the operation of the exchanges and the admission of members and of companies to listing.

Börsenzulassungsstelle (Ger). The committee of the West German stock exchanges which sets and administers the regulations for the official admission of securities to listing.

borsino (It). Any room or hall in a bank where clients may follow price movements on the principal stock exchanges.

bought deal (US). An underwriting commitment by an issue syndicate to handle a new issue by buying it from the issuer and accepting the financial risk if it cannot retail the stock. *Contrast with* BEST EFFORTS.

bought stock account (UK). An account operated by the Stock Exchange settlement system. All bought bargains are posted to the bought stock account and remain in it until settlement is completed.

bourse (Fr). The French word for Stock Exchange, used primarily for the French and Belgian stock exchanges, is a widely used generic term for stock exchanges throughout Europe. In France itself there are seven *bourses* dominated by the Paris *bourse*, which accounts for over 90 percent of total capitalization. Other French *bourses* are located in Bordeaux, Lille, Lyons, Marseilles, Nancy and Nantes. They are officially created by a decree (*arrète*) of the French Ministry of Economics. Creation of a *bourse* must be approved by the CHAMBRE SYNDICALE DES AGENTS DE CHANGE.

In Belgium there are four *bourses* dominated by Brussels with smaller exchanges at Antwerp, Ghent and Liège.

boursicoteur (Fr). A speculator.

breadth (of a market). The number of securities listed on a market in which there is regular trading. *See also* DEPTH and LIQUIDITY.

break. A sharp and rapid decline in prices following an earlier rise.

breakout. A term used in technical analysis to describe the movement of a share price out of a firm pattern it had previously established.

Brief (Ger). The sale of SECURITIES.

Briefträger (Ger). Literally 'postman', a nickname for a stock exchange dealer who is a seller of securities.

British Savings Bonds (UK). A non-marketable security issued to private investors and repayable with bonus on the date shown. They return a good rate of interest and because of this holdings of the bonds by individuals are subject to a maximum figure. *See also* NATIONAL SAVINGS.

broad tape (US). Information services which, in addition to share price movements, print other news of a general financial interest to investors.

broker. An agent acting on behalf of clients in a particular field. In securities markets the stockbroker acts as agent for his client and is rewarded by way of commission. The essence of a broker is that he is an agent working on commission and not a principal or dealer acting on his own account. It is possible (although not currently in the United Kingdom) for a broking firm also to act as principal, but the two sides of the business in any transaction must be kept separate or disclosed to the client to avoid conflicts of interest.

The stockbroker not only deals for his client but may also perform a variety of other tasks for him, notably research into industries and particular companies, tax and other related financial advice etc. The broker may also operate DISCRETIONARY FUNDS on behalf of his clients, carrying out transactions and informing the client of the purchases and sales and the reasons for them. The broker may also run a valuation service for clients, keeping them informed of the progress of their own portfolio and its performance against the market as a whole. *See also* BROKER-DEALER; JOBBER.

brokerage (US). The amount charged by a BROKER for his dealing services to clients. *See also* COMMISSION.

broker-dealer. A securities firm which combines the functions of a BROKER acting as agent for clients, with that of a DEALER, acting as a PRINCIPAL for its own account. Such a combination of roles, sometimes called DUAL CAPACITY as contrasted with SINGLE CAPACITY, has for some time been a feature of securities trading in the United States and Japan, for example, but has been unknown in the United Kingdom, where single capacity has been strictly enforced by the Stock Exchange. In order to protect the investor when a firm may act in both roles, the firm must disclose to the client when it is acting as a principal and not in an agency role.

The adoption of a system of dual-capacity broker-dealers is now being considered by the Stock Exchange in the United Kingdom as the most likely basis for a new dealing system.

BIBLIOGRAPHY *The Stock Exchange: A Discussion Paper* (1984). *The Stock Exchange: The Choice of a New Dealing System for Equities* (July 1984). *The Stock Exchange: The Choice of a New Dealing System for Gilt Edged Securities* (August 1984).

brokers' contract note (UK). The notification sent by a broker to his client as soon as conveniently possible after the client's transaction has been carried out. It is normal for the contract note to be sent either on the day of dealing or the next day at the latest. The contract note shows the date of the buying or selling transaction, the stock concerned, the total CONSIDERATION, the broker's COMMISSION, TRANSFER STAMP DUTY if applicable, and any other charges, including VALUE ADDED TAX.

brokers' loans (US). Money borrowed from banks or other brokers and used in a variety of ways. It may be used by the SPECIALIST to help finance inventories of securities they hold; by broking firms to finance the underwriting of new issues of company and municipal (local authority) stock; to help finance a broking firm's own investments and to help finance the purchase of securities for customers who prefer to use the broker's credit to buy securities on MARGIN.

broker-trader. Similar to a BROKER-DEALER, a broker-trader on the LONDON INTERNATIONAL FINANCIAL FUTURES EXCHANGE is a firm, organization or individual, a member of LIFFE, acting in the dual role of BROKER and TRADER for its own account.

broking commission. *See* BROKERAGE and COMMISSION.

Bruchzins (Ger). The amount of interest calculated on a bond for a part or broken period.

brutto (Ger). Gross, before commission or other charges.

bubble. A speculation which, like a bubble, can be expected to burst. The most famous instance in the United Kingdom was the SOUTH SEA BUBBLE of 1720, when stock in the South Sea Company spiralled in value only to crash later. The wave of speculation in the South Sea stock stimulated a host of get-rich-quick schemes with shares of worthless companies being traded in the streets and coffee-houses of the City of London. Reality soon set in, however, and many speculators were ruined.

bucket shop. Originally an American expression for a gambling den, now used to describe a shady share dealing company, not associated with a recognized stock exchange or association of securities dealers.

Budget. The annual (or semi-annual) statement by the Chancellor of the Exchequer in the United Kingdom (or other Finance Minister in other countries) in which the government's revenue and expenditure for the forthcoming year are outlined and measures for the raising of the necessary revenue are announced. It is also (at least in the United Kingdom) the time at which new taxes are introduced (or abolished) and amendments are made to existing tax legislation.

Budget deficit. An actual or forecast excess of government expenditure over tax and other government revenue which therefore needs to be covered by short or long term government borrowing.

bull. In the strict sense, a speculator who buys shares hoping to sell them at a profit before SETTLEMENT DAY. More generally, an investor who expects a general rise in share prices, particularly in the short term. *See also* BEAR.

Bulldog bond (UK). A bond, denominated in sterling, issued by an overseas borrower on the United Kingdom capital market. Such issues became popular in the early 1980s, beginning with an issue by the Kingdom of Denmark in 1980.

bullish. A feeling of confidence; expectation of rising stock market prices.

bull market. A stock market in which share prices are on a rising trend. *See also* BULL.

bull position. *See* POSITION.

bunching (US). The practice of combining orders for execution as one transaction on the trading floor of a stock exchange.

Bundesaufsichtamt für das Kreditwesen (BAK) (Ger). The West German government office dealing with the control of investment funds such as UNIT TRUSTS. The BAK controls the registration of such funds and insists on annual and half yearly statements from them.

Bundesobligationen (Ger). Federal fixed interest stock. One of the methods used by the West German government to raise funds.

Bundesschatzbriefe (Ger). Federal savings bonds in West Germany.

buono del tesoro (It). Treasury bill or bond which is exempt from income tax or death duties.

buono di assegnazione (It). The coupon which gives the shareholder the right to participate in a SCRIP ISSUE in the capital of a company in proportion to the number of shares which he possesses.

buono stanza (It). A temporary document distributed by the securities clearing house while awaiting the arrival of the stock certificate.

busari (It). The official gazette of joint stock and limited liability companies. It is particularly important for the Stock Exchange as details of an issue of shares or convertible bonds must be published in the document by the companies and a minimum period of 30 days from the date of publication must be allowed to shareholders in order to exercise their rights.

Business Conduct Committee (US). A committee appointed annually by each of the thirteen districts into which the NATIONAL ASSOCIATION OF SECURITIES DEALERS

(NASD) is divided. The role of the District Business Conduct Committees, which generally consist of not more than twelve members, is to deal with any complaints from the investing public against NASD members within its district. Where appropriate, district committees may also appoint local Business Conduct Committees.

Business Expansion Scheme (BES) (UK). A scheme introduced in the United Kingdom in 1983 as an expansion of the earlier Business Start-up Scheme. Under the BES investors may put up to £40,000 a year into a company and obtain tax relief on the investment.

There are a number of limitations: no one involved or associated with the running of the company is eligible for the relief, nor are any relatives of the owners or directors. The funds must be committed for a period of at least five years, otherwise the tax authorities can 'claw back' the relief. The shares must not be listed on a recognized stock exchange nor must they be dealt in on the UNLISTED SECURITIES MARKET for a period of three years from the date of the subscription under the BES. Funds may be invested direct with one company or put into an approved fund which undertakes investment in BES-qualifying companies, while spreading risk so far as the investor is concerned.

Buttonwood Tree agreement (US). The original agreement signed on 17 May 1792 between 24 New York stockbrokers which formed the first organized stock exchange in New York. So called because the brokers met and signed the agreement under a buttonwood tree at what is now 68 Wall Street, New York. *See also* NEW YORK STOCK EXCHANGE.

buy in. To cover, offset or close out a short position in a futures market. *See also* EVENING UP; LIQUIDATION; OFFSET; SELL OUT.

buying climax. A sharp rise in price following a steady earlier increase. Often interpreted in technical analysis as the final fling of a rising share price and heralding a downward reaction.

buying-in (UK). The method of ensuring (in abnormal cases of difficulty) that a buyer of shares through a broker gets the shares he has bought. Normally there is no problem and the buyer will get his stock on SETTLEMENT DAY but in abnormal cases, he may not have been able to obtain delivery and a Stock Exchange official (called the buying-in official) can go into the market to buy in the particular security; any charges having to be met by the seller who has failed to make timely delivery. *See also* SELLING OUT.

buy on close. To buy CONTRACTS on a FINANCIAL FUTURES market at the end of a trading session at a price within the CLOSING RANGE. *See also* SELL ON CLOSE.

buy on opening. To buy CONTRACTS on a FINANCIAL FUTURES market at the beginning of a trading session at a price within the OPENING RANGE. *See also* SELL ON OPENING.

C

cabinet bid. A facility in a TRADED OPTIONS market whereby, when no tangible value applies to a deep OUT-OF-THE-MONEY OPTION, the holder may dispose of contracts to a market maker at a nominal price per contract (of 1p in the United Kingdom).

cabinet crowd (US). A group of dealers on the New York Stock Exchange who deal in relatively inactive bonds. The phrase arises from the practice of those wishing to deal filing their intentions in a pigeon hole or cabinet. *Contrast with* ACTIVE BOND CROWD.

cabinet stock (US). A relatively inactive stock. *See also* CABINET CROWD.

caduta dei corsi (It). An expression used to indicate a sudden and unexpected fall in share prices.

cage (US). That part of a broker's BACK OFFICE which handles cheques and securities in course of settlement and is screened for security purposes from the rest of the office.

call. The demand by a company or other issuer of shares or stock for payment. This may be the demand for full payment on the due date, as for example with a RIGHTS ISSUE. It may, on the other hand, be the demand for a further payment when the total amount is payable by instalments. When, in the United Kingdom, a government stock is issued, payment is frequently due by instalments to spread the flow of funds into the Exchequer. Normally a company will call for payment in full at the time of issue, although there have been in the United Kingdom a few issues, often large ones associated with the PRIVATIZATION of nationalized industries, where payment for the shares has been called by instalments.

callable (US). An issue of debt all, or part, of which may be redeemed by the issuer under specified conditions prior to its maturity. The term is also applied to PREFERRED SHARES which may be redeemed by the issuer in a similar way. Calls on such stocks are usually made by companies which believe they can replace them by issues carrying a lower COUPON, but they may have to pay a call premium to be able to do so.

call money. Money lent by banks to borrowers, which is repayable immediately on demand. *See also* AT CALL.

call option. An option to purchase shares at a known price at a specified future date. For this privilege, the buyer pays a premium, a fraction of the price of the UNDERLYING SECURITY. *See also* CLASS (OF OPTIONS); CONVENTIONAL OPTION; PUT OPTION; SERIES OF OPTIONS; TRADED OPTION.

call-over. The phrase used to describe the method of trading on some stock exchange floors. In such a market, a stock exchange official calls out the names of the listed securities in order and the dealers or brokers make a BID or OFFER for them according to the orders they have from their clients. A price is reached which reflects the balance of supply and demand for each stock. The call-over system is employed on the Belfast and Dublin floors of the Stock Exchange in the United Kingdom as well as on the French BOURSES. The system is generally successful only when there are relatively few stocks listed. There is no continuous price-making mechanism, although deals may be made during the day at the price fixed at the call-over.

call premium. Any additional amount an issuer may have to pay to redeem stocks prior to the maturity date.

calmo (It). Refers either to the calm state of the market or to a general moderate fall in prices.

campana (It). Literally meaning a bell, *campana* is a term used to define the behaviour of a dealer authorized to operate on a trading floor who, during a TRADING SESSION, declares himself to be a buyer when in fact he wishes to sell and vice versa. It is an anomalous way of dealing more typical of the minor Italian exchanges, rather than Milan, and requires great skill owing to the risks involved.

cancellation. A general banking and financial term, applied in securities markets in relation to stocks and shares which have been redeemed or exchanged for others. The old securities are called in and cancelled by destruction or defacing.

cannella (It). Normally used in expressions like *c'è una cannella aperta* or *si è chiusa la cannella,* which respectively mean that there has been a movement in share prices which is likely to be repeated and that there have been considerable sales of a security by a group or by an individual; alternatively, the end of such an action.

capacity. The role, either AGENT or PRINCIPAL, in which a firm or individual acts in the securities markets. *See also* DUAL CAPACITY; SINGLE CAPACITY.

capital. One of the most overworked words in the economic and financial vocabulary, capital has a variety of different meanings depending upon whether it is being used by an economist, an industrialist, an accountant or an investor and his financial adviser.

In economics, capital is one of the factors of production, the other two being land and labour, which combine to produce goods and services. In this meaning it is the accumulation of equipment and money from past savings and its use in current production.

An industrialist will think of capital either as his stock of plant and equipment or as the money he employs in his business, either EQUITY and long term capital or short term money loaned by banks and other financial institutions.

An accountant will probably share the industrialist's view, but regard capital as a liability (to be put on the left-hand side of a balance sheet).

An investor and his financial adviser regard capital as the savings or wealth the investor has accumulated and which they will be concerned first to conserve and secondly to increase.

W.S. Gilbert, in the operetta *Utopia Limited,* facetiously defined capital as 'to what extent they (a company's founders) mean to pay their debts'.

capital allowances (UK). Those amounts spent on items of a capital nature by an industrialist (*see* CAPITAL) which may be offset against income before arriving at the company's profit and therefore its tax liability.

Capital Asset Pricing Model (CAPM). A model of portfolio valuation which seeks to measure the risk to which an investor is exposed in holding his portfolio and to relate the rate of return to that risk. An investor using CAPM may deliberately choose a higher-than-average portfolio risk on which he would expect to receive a correspondingly higher return. The cautious investor may choose a lower degree of risk and receive a correspondingly lower reward.

The CAPM divides risk into two categories: first, the overall market risk inherent in buying and holding shares; second, the risk involved in holding particular individual securities. The former risk cannot be diversified by holding different shares, the latter risk can be diversified.

Investors following the CAPM do not seek to BEAT THE MARKET but to obtain a reasonable rate of return relative to the risk they wish to bear. The technique is thus attractive to institutional investors seeking to manage funds efficiently on behalf of beneficiaries, since it provides an objective measure of risk and return against which their performance can be measured and justified. *See also* ALPHA; BETA FACTOR.

BIBLIOGRAPHY Janette Rutterford, *Introduction to Stock Exchange Investment* (Macmillan, London, 1983). E. Eugene Carter and Rita M. Rodrigues, 'International Capital Budgeting' in Abraham M. George and Ian H. Giddy (eds.) *International Finance Handbook* (John Wiley, New York, 1983), Section 8.5.

capital autorisé (Fr). *See* AUTHORIZED CAPITAL.

capital de fondation (Fr). Founders' capital, those amounts used to start up a business.

capital d'exploitation (Fr). *See* WORKING CAPITAL.

capitale a breve termine (It). *See* SHORT-TERM capital.

capitale autorizzato (It). *See* AUTHORIZED CAPITAL.

capitale azionario (It). *See* SHARE CAPITAL.

capitale consolidato a lunga scadenza (It). *See* LONG-TERM capital.

capitale di speculazione (It). *See* RISK CAPITAL.

capitale emesso (It). *See* ISSUED SHARE CAPITAL.

capital émis (Fr). *See* ISSUED SHARE CAPITAL.

capitale nominale (It). *See* NOMINAL CAPITAL.

capitale non emesso (It). *See* UNISSUED CAPITAL.

capitale non richiamato (It). *See* UNCALLED CAPITAL.

capitale settoscritto (It). *See* SUBSCRIBED CAPITAL.

capitale versato (It). *See* PAID-UP CAPITAL.

capital gain, capital loss. The profit or loss made from the sale of a capital asset. Such gains are normally taxed at rates lower than those on income (*see* CAPITAL GAINS TAX) partly because such gains tend to arise only occasionally and partly to allow for the effects of inflation on the current value of the asset and the capital gain made. *See also* INDEXATION OF CAPITAL GAINS TAX.

Capital Gains Tax (CGT). First introduced in the United Kingdom as a tax on short term realized gains (those up to 6 months) in 1962, the tax was extended in 1965 to become a general tax on capital gains made on the sale of any form of asset. Owner occupied housing was exempt from the start, while government stocks held for at least one year were exempted from the tax in 1968. Losses can be offset against gains in arriving at a CGT liability and may be carried forward to future years. The rate of Capital Gains Tax is 30 percent and has remained so nominally since 1965. The rules, however, have changed so often in the intervening period that the relationship between the actual money gain on the disposal of an asset and the tax to be paid on it has varied enormously over the years.

At present, all gains made since March 1982 are indexed (*see* INDEXATION OF CAPITAL GAINS TAX) and no tax is payable if the real gain, after allowing for inflation, is below £5000 in 1982-83 prices. This figure is itself increased in line with changes in the retail price index in subsequent years.

In the United States, there is still a two-tier structure for Capital Gains Tax. A short term gain (defined as one made within 12 months of the purchase of the asset) is taxed at the individual's full income tax rate. A long term gain is subject to a lower rate of tax.

BIBLIOGRAPHY Capital Gains Tax Act 1979. Finance Act 1982. *Capital Gains Tax* (Tolley Publishing, London, annually).

capitalization. *See* MARKET CAPITALIZATION.

capitalization issue. *See* SCRIP ISSUE.

capitalization of reserves. The conversion of a company's RESERVES into share capital by means of a SCRIP ISSUE.

capitalized value. The value of an asset calculated according to a formula based upon the earnings of that asset at current rates of interest.

capitalism. A form of economic organization in which the supply of savings (capital) is accorded an equal role to that of land and labour. In a feudal society, land is the predominant factor of production; in a communist structure, labour is held to be the only factor. Capitalism is based on the freedom to accumulate and to use private financial savings.

capitalizzazione (It). *See* MARKET CAPITALIZATION.

capital redemption reserve fund. A fund established by a company which has issued redeemable preference shares. Each year, an amount equal to the value of the shares to be redeemed is transferred to the capital redemption reserve fund to provide funds for repayment of such capital.

capital redemption yield. The return on a stock expressed at an annual rate, representing the capital gain between the price paid and the nominal redemption value. To this must be added the FLAT YIELD to arrive at the GROSS REDEMPTION YIELD.

capital repayment. The return of capital to shareholders if a company wishes to reduce its capital in line with its trading needs. Such repayments are not treated as income and are therefore subject to capital taxation rules, not income tax legislation.

capital stock. Like CAPITAL itself, subject to a number of different meanings, including the total ISSUED CAPITAL of a company, both ordinary and preference shares.

Capital Transfer Tax (CTT) (UK). A tax introduced in the United Kingdom in 1975 to tax both assets passing to beneficiaries on the death of a donor and lifetime transfers by that donor. CTT replaced Estate Duty.

Transfers between spouses are exempt, but on all other transfers above specified minima, CTT is payable. These minima are generally raised annually in line with inflation. The rates of tax on lifetime transfers (GIFTS INTER VIVOS) at the lower end of the scale are half of those applying to transfers on death but rates of tax on higher values are taxed at the same rate. Donors transferring assets during their lifetimes must survive three years after the date of gift if the transfer is to qualify for the lower rate. The tax is cumulative and the rates are levied on the total value of gifts made over the years, except that small gifts of a few thousand pounds a year are exempt.

BIBLIOGRAPHY *Capital Transfer Tax,* (Inland Revenue). Robert Wareham and Jane Scollen, *Tolley's Capital Transfer Tax* (Tolley Publishing, annually).

capitaux errants (Fr). *See* HOT MONEY.

carry. The cost of financing a POSITION in FINANCIAL INSTRUMENTS in a futures contract.

carry over. To postpone settlement of a stock exchange BARGAIN from one account to the next. *See also* CONTANGO ACCOUNT; STOCK EXCHANGE.

carry over day (UK). The name given on the UK Stock Exchange for the first day of settlement.

carta e matita (It). Literally meaning paper and pencil, this expression is used in the stockmarket to indicate operations with speculative motives. They occur usually at the beginning of the monthly trading accounts since that allows the speculator more time to exploit the period available before settlement is required.

cash against documents (CAD) client (UK). A large investor in the United Kingdom who is given the facility in the settlement process of being paid by his broker when he delivers the relevant transfer documents and of paying cash when he knows that stock has been allocated to him on presentation of a STOCK NOTE.

cash and new (UK). A variation of a CONTANGO and a means used, in effect, to delay the settlement of a bargain to the following ACCOUNT. In practice, an investor with an outstanding deal due for settlement on the next SETTLEMENT DAY carries out a *contra* deal towards the end of the account. He then immediately restores his original position by a further purchase (or sale) for settlement on the following settlement day. As an example, an investor who has bought shares hoping for a short term profit which has not materialized before the end of the account sells, but then buys them back immediately. By this method he hopes that the shares will rise as he expects during the following account and he can then take his profit.

cash flow. The profits of a company, plus any amounts set aside for the depreciation of capital assets and to offset the effects of the increased prices of replacing stocks. Cash flow seeks to measure the amount of cash a company is receiving and its needs for current expenditure on salaries, stocks, tax payments etc.

An investor will also compare the returns on investments by measuring the cash flows they yield in terms of interest, dividends and, perhaps, capital receipts.

cash management account (CMA) (US). A type of brokerage acount introduced for private investors by Merrill Lynch in 1977. The CMA offers clients who leave deposits with the firm a cheque book and credit card facility. The client may use the account as a current (demand) account, but spare balances are automatically invested in a high interest earning MONEY MARKET FUND.

cash market. The term used on a FINANCIAL FUTURES exchange to mean the underlying currency or money market in which deals are carried out in the items to which the futures contracts relate.

cash price. The price QUOTATION obtained in the CASH MARKET.

cash sale (US). A transaction on the floor of a stock exchange which calls for settlement on the same day rather than by the normal REGULAR WAY DELIVERY. Under the latter, settlement takes place on the fifth business day after the transaction was carried out or, in the case of bonds, on the following business day.

cavallo (It). *See* A CAVALLO.

caveat emptor. A Latin phrase meaning 'let the buyer beware' and indicating the responsibility on the part of the buyer to make sure that the property or shares he is buying are free from defect. The seller is not obliged to volunteer information concerning them, and although he must answer the buyer's questions truthfully the onus is on the buyer to ask the questions.

Cedel S.A. One of the two settlement systems for EUROBOND trading (the other being EUROCLEAR), Cedel S.A. is based in Luxembourg and was established in 1970. It provides an accounting service for the transfer of eurobonds held in depositary accounts worldwide and arranges for the collection of dividends. Cedel also provides, via Citibank, finance for eurobond marketmakers, providing up to 80 percent of the value of convertible bonds and 90 percent against straight fixed interest bonds. Cedel also provides a bond lending facility between its participants.

BIBLIOGRAPHY Brian S. Quinn and Peregrine Aldred, 'The Eurobond Secondary Market' in Abraham M. George and Ian H. Giddy (eds.), *International Finance Handbook* (John Wiley, New York, 1983), Section 5.4.

cedola di dividendo (It). *See* COUPON.

central bank. The bank or other monetary authority in a country charged with assisting the government in the framing and implementation of monetary policy and with management of the country's national debt, the issue and redemption of the government's own securities, and managing the market in them.

certificat (Fr). *See* CERTIFICATE.

certificat d'actions (Fr). A bearer depositary receipt which allows the dealing on the French stock exchanges of foreign shares deposited outside France.

certificat de copropriété, certificat de trust (Fr). A unit trust certificate.

certificat d'investissement (Fr). A security introduced in France in 1982 to enable nationalized industries to attract investment funds from private investors. *Certificats d'investissement* are issued by those industries in which the government has a 100 percent shareholding but, while giving the holder the right to dividend payments they do not entitle him to vote. *See also* TITRE PARTICIPATIF.

certificate. A written or printed evidence of title. For specific reference to the stock market, *see* SHARE CERTIFICATE.

certificate of accrual on Treasury securities (CATS) (US). An investment vehicle created in 1984 as a means of selling US Treasury bonds to overseas investors in bearer form. Funds invested in the certificates were in turn invested in Treasury bonds, but the interest payments accrued and the whole paid out in one lump sum at maturity. CATS were similar to TIGER BONDS. The U.S. authorities were unhappy at the issue of Treasury bonds in full bearer form, and effectively banned further issues. Later the authorities themselves issued a partial bearer bond targeted at foreign investors.

certificate of deposit (CD). A negotiable instrument issued by a bank to a depositor, giving evidence of the deposit with the bank. The bank retains the deposit for the full term, which may vary from three months to five years, but the certificate is negotiable and may, therefore, be sold on the secondary market at any time. First introduced in the United States in 1961 they were issued, in dollar denominations, in London in 1966. Sterling certificates were first issued in 1968. Although primarily a banking instrument, CDs are subject to a FUTURES contract in both the United States and on the LONDON INTERNATIONAL FINANCIAL FUTURES EXCHANGE.

certificato azionario (It). *See* SHARE CERTIFICATE.

certified transfer (UK). A STOCK TRANSFER FORM or TALISMAN SOLD TRANSFER which is marked 'certificate lodged' to indicate that the share certificate has been sent to the company's registrar to be dealt with.

Chambre Syndicale des Agents de Change (Fr). The governing body of the stock exchanges in France. All AGENTS DE CHANGE must belong to the COMPAGNIE DES AGENTS DE CHANGE or National Brokers Association and the Association's rules, the RÈGLEMENT GÉNÉRAL DE LA COMPAGNIE DES AGENTS DE CHANGE, govern the seven French BOURSES and have the support of the Ministry of Economics.

The CHAMBRE SYNDICALE is the governing body of the Association. It is elected annually by its members and is made up of a SYNDIC (chairman) and seven Governors. The main duties of the CHAMBRE SYNDICALE are to enforce regulations on its members and the smooth running of the market.

BIBLIOGRAPHY *The Paris Stock Exchange : A Guide for Foreign Investors* (Paris, January 1980). Paul Stonham, *Major Stock Markets of Europe* (Gower Publishing, London, 1982).

charge. The pledge of security, either over fixed or non-fixed assets, in return for a loan or DEBENTURE. Loans may be secured on specific fixed assets, or against all the assets owned by a company. In the event of the borrower failing to meet his payment commitments on the loan, the charged assets may be sold for the benefit of the lenders.

chargeable assets (UK). All those assets the sale of which will give rise to a liability to CAPITAL GAINS TAX. This includes property (other than owner-occupied housing), convertible bonds and stocks, shares, land and property other than freehold land (chattels). Exempted or non-chargeable assets include straight fixed interest securities and gilt edged stocks.

chargeable document (UK). A document giving evidence of a holding in the Stock Exchange nominee company SEPON, which may be used as security for a loan being made by a bank.

charged security (UK). *See* COLLATERAL.

chartered company (UK). A trading company which carries on business under a charter granted by the Crown, rather than under the Companies Acts.

charting. The use of graphs of previous market price movements of securities. *See also* CHARTIST.

chartist. An investment analyst who subscribes to the view that share price movements follow patterns which can be identified by means of charts. The emergence of certain patterns provides buy or sell signals to investors. While chartists believe that all underlying facts about a company are reflected in the share price and that study of price movements alone will provide the key to portfolio investment decisions, the FUNDAMENTALIST believes that research into the underlying position and prospects (the fundamentals) of a company is necessary to arrive at a view on the likely future movement of its share price. Both groups have to contend with the supporters of the EFFICIENT MARKET HYPOTHESIS who believe that the stock market is efficient in adjusting quickly to all known facts about a company and reflecting those facts in its share price. They further believe that the past is no good guide to the future, and that the study of companies and their share prices will not enable investors consistently and scientifically to BEAT THE MARKET.

checking (UK). The overnight computer reconciliation between brokers' and jobbers' books prior to the bargain entering the settlement process proper.

checking the market. The action of a broker enquiring the prices of securities from the MARKET MAKERS before deciding with whom to deal.

chiamare un titolo (It). An expression used to indicate the public outcry to fix the price of a certain security at the opening or closing call.

Chicago Board Options Exchange (CBOE) (US). An exchange set up in 1973 as an offshoot of the Chicago Board of Trade for the specific purpose of trading put and call options of leading American securities. The CBOE has had spectacular success and TRADED OPTIONS have been imitated by many stock exchanges worldwide, using the techniques and terminology developed in Chicago.

Chinese wall. Deriving by analogy from the impenetrable Great Wall of China, the phrase is used to describe the substantial, if intangible, barriers which must exist between different parts of a financial organization to ensure that conflicts of interest are avoided. The allusion was made by Franklin D. Roosevelt when he referred to 'an old Chinese wall policy of isolation', (Webster's 3rd New International Dictionary).

In London, the phrase 'green baize door', representing the internal door between the master and his family on the one hand and the servants on the other, has been used to convey the same idea.

chiudere una operazione (It). An expression used to indicate an operation effected in the same number of securities in the opposite way in order to close a speculative POSITION.

chiusura (in) (It). At the closing price.

choice (UK). A word in market dealing to indicate that one jobber or market maker is quoting a price at which he will sell shares to a broker while another jobber is quoting the same price at which he will buy from the broker. The broker is said to have the choice of either buying or selling at that price.

Chubu Securities Finance Co. (Jap). One of the three securities finance companies established in Japan to lend stock and cash to securities firms to finance dealing in securities and thus to improve market liquidity. *See also* JAPAN SECURITIES FINANCE COMPANY; OSAKA SECURITIES FINANCE COMPANY.

churning. The highly dubious practice of a broker transacting large numbers of deals in DISCRETIONARY FUNDS placed with him by clients to manage on their behalf. The object of the exercise would be to generate commission. The practice is frowned upon by stock exchange and other regulatory bodies, which have introduced rules and codes of conduct to protect clients from it.

circulating capital. That money which, in a company, is invested in assets meant for resale. On receipt of payments from sales, the proceeds are re-circulated back into new stock.

City, The (UK). The financial district of London. It is called 'The City' because it is the square mile of the old City of London, bounded on the south by the River Thames, on the east by the Tower of London, on the north by Billingsgate Market and on the west by the Law Courts. The City of London, or Square Mile as it is sometimes called, has long been synonymous with finance. Tacitus in the first century AD called London 'a town of the highest repute and a busy emporium for trade and traders'. Later the Lombards, merchants and bankers from Northern Italy, carried on their business in the City and later still, the goldsmiths of the City began to provide banking facilities. The phrase 'The City' is often used as a collective noun for all the various financial and commodity markets of the United Kingdom including the Stock Exchange, the banks, discount houses, Lloyd's of London, the Baltic Exchange, the commodities markets, the gold market, the Metal Exchange and, most recently, the LONDON INTERNATIONAL FINANCIAL FUTURES EXCHANGE (LIFFE), among many others.

City Code on Take-overs and Mergers (UK). A code of practice drawn up by the PANEL ON TAKE-OVERS AND MERGERS to control the activities of all parties in a TAKE-OVER BID. The Code was first issued in 1968 and has been revised in the light of changing circumstances.

The Code does not have the force of law but all those who are engaged in dealings in the securities markets, together with the directors and advisers of commercial companies, are expected to keep to it. The Stock Exchange helps compliance by writing into its LISTING AGREEMENT a clause binding companies to abide by the terms of the Code.

The provisions of the Code fall into two categories: first, general principles of conduct to be observed when engaged in a take-over; second a series of detailed rules deriving from the general principles and which provide procedures to be followed by companies and their advisers in a take-over situation.

The Code is drawn up with listed public companies in mind, but applies also to the takeover of unlisted public companies. It does not, however, apply to private companies.

The Code is administered by the Panel on Take-overs and Mergers, a working arm of the COUNCIL FOR THE SECURITIES INDUSTRY.

BIBLIOGRAPHY *The City Code on Take-overs and Mergers* (published by The Council for the Securities Industry). The Panel on Take-overs and Mergers, *Annual Reports*.

class (of options). All options of the same type relating to the same underlying security. Options in the same security may be traded for a number of EXPIRY DATES and EXERCISE PRICES. All of these are included in the same class of options.

class (of shares). All shares or securities of a company or other issuer which have identical rights and obligations. Thus all ordinary voting shares in a company will constitute a class, but any non-voting ordinary shares of the same company will be a separate class, as will any preference or other shares.

classato (It). A security which is widely distributed among investors and which is normally considered as an excellent investment (a BLUE CHIP).

claw back (UK). A term used to describe the situation where the Inland Revenue takes back money in the hands of a taxpayer as the result of a tax concession. This clawing back of tax may be the result of a change in the taxpayer's circumstances or due to an act on his part which renders him no longer qualifying for the relevant relief. Companies too may be subject to a claw back of CORPORATION TAX relief.

clean price. The price of a fixed interest security stripped of any ACCRUED INTEREST.

clean trade (US). A deal in a BLOCK of shares by a brokerage house in which the buying and selling volumes were precisely matched and the dealer had neither to take stock on to his book nor supply any stock from it.

clearing fees. Negotiated fees in respect of transactions negotiated by a non-clearing member of the LONDON INTERNATIONAL FINANCIAL FUTURES EXCHANGE and payable by that member to the CLEARING MEMBER, in whose name the resultant contracts are registered by the CLEARING HOUSE.

clearing house. An organization set up to permit the settlement of business by providing a focal point through which accounts may be debited and credited. In the banking world, a clearing house provides for the efficient and speedy settlement of cheques drawn on one bank for payment to an account in another.

In futures and options markets, a clearing house may perform a similar function. In the United Kingdom, for example, the INTERNATIONAL COMMODITIES CLEARING HOUSE (ICCH) registers, monitors and guarantees dealings between members of the LONDON INTERNATIONAL FINANCIAL FUTURES EXCHANGE and co-ordinates financial settlement on delivery of futures transactions. London Options Clearing House (LOCH) performs similar functions for the TRADED OPTIONS market.

clearing member. A member firm of the CLEARING HOUSE for CONTRACTS in FINANCIAL FUTURES. Each clearing member firm must, in the case of the LONDON INTERNATIONAL FINANCIAL FUTURES EXCHANGE, be a member of the Exchange, but not all exchange members are members of the clearing house. All trades of non-clearing members must, however, be registered with and settled through a clearing member.

clients' accounts (UK). A term originating with solicitors who held clients' funds in bank accounts. The term now applies also to stockbrokers who hold clients' funds pending re-investment. Such funds must, under the rules of the Stock Exchange, be segregated from the broking firm's own money.

close, the. On a FINANCIAL FUTURES exchange, the 30-second period at the end of the trading session. Sometimes refers to the closing price. *See also* OPENING.

close a position. In a financial futures or traded options market, to carry out a further transaction in order to terminate liability.

close company (UK). Under UK company law a close company is one which is under the control of less than five people, whether directors or not.

closed end funds. Investment companies, such as INVESTMENT TRUSTS in the United Kingdom, whose own capital is limited in the same way as that of an ordinary trading company. Their shares may thus be traded on a stock exchange. *See also* OPEN END FUNDS.

closed end investment company (US). The American equivalent of CLOSED END FUNDS.

closely held shares. Term used to indicate that the shares of a company are held largely by a few individuals, most likely directors and those connected with them. The market in the remaining shares is likely to be a difficult one in which to deal, as even a small buying or selling order could have a disproportionate effect on the price. *See also* NARROW MARKET.

closing. The carrying out of a transaction in the securities market to offset a previous bargain. Thus an investor may sell shares he had previously bought and thus 'close his position'. He may also buy shares he had previously sold in order to take a profit (or minimize a loss). *See also* BEAR and SHORT SELLING. The term 'closing' usually has a short term connotation in that the transaction to close the investor's position follows relatively shortly after the original transaction: in the case of the United Kingdom, closing may refer specifically to closing a deal within the ACCOUNT. *See also* ACCOUNT DEALING.

closing price. The price of shares at the end of a day's stock market trading. In London, although the Stock Exchange market floor closes at 3:30pm, trading continues by telephone until about 5:00pm. Closing prices refer generally to those around this later time.

closing purchase. A TRADED OPTIONS transaction in which the writer buys an option having the same terms as the option which he has sold and thus CLOSE A POSITION and terminate his liability. *See also* CLOSING SALE.

closing range. In a FINANCIAL FUTURES market, the high and low prices recorded during the period designated as the official CLOSE.

closing sale. A transaction in which the holder of a traded option disposes of it.

closing the books. The action of a registrar in ruling off his books on a particular day in order to pay the dividend. Only those holders whose names are on the register on that day will be sent the dividend. If they have meanwhile sold the shares *cum* dividend, they will have to pass on the dividend to the buyer.

Code of Dealing, Stock Exchange (UK). A set of notes for the guidance of dealers on the trading floors of the Stock Exchange in the United Kingdom, governing their conduct towards other dealers with whom they are doing business. The provisions of the Code help to maintain an orderly market in securities on the floors of the Exchange and ensure that the etiquette of the market and its dealing practices are maintained without resort to formal rules.

collaborateurs (Fr). Correspondents of AGENTS DE CHANGE on the French stock exchanges.

collateral. Securities or other property pledged by a borrower to secure the repayment of a loan should he default.

collo, restare in (It). Expression used to indicate an error of judgement in the purchase of securities whose price has since fallen and the shares are still unsold. A PAPER LOSS.

collocare a fermo (It). The prior underwriting of part of a new issue by a bank or other institution.

Comitato Direttivo degli Agenti di Cambio (It). The Executive Committee of Stockbrokers on the Milan Stock Exchange. The Committee is an elected body and is responsible for the day-to-day running and supervision of stock market trading as well as the promotion of stock exchange business. It operates under a legally backed code and is subject to the COMMISSIONE NAZIONALE PER LA SOCIETÀ E LA BORSA (CONSOB), but has certain powers delegated by the latter, including the administration of the brokers' guarantee fund and the ability to intervene in the market to maintain continuity in the event of an insolvency.

BIBLIOGRAPHY Paul Stonham, *Major Stock Markets of Europe* (Gower Publishing, London, 1982) Chapter 4.

commercial paper. Debt issued by companies to meet their needs for short term finance.

Commerzbank index (Ger). The leading index of stocks quoted on the West German stock exchanges. The index consists of 60 securities, is based at 1953 = 100, and is calculated on a daily basis.

commissaire aux comptes (Fr). An auditor. Companies listed on a stock exchange must appoint two auditors to report to the shareholders on the accuracy of the company's accounts.

commissario di borsa (It). The local Stock Exchange Commissioner or inspector of the national body of control, the COMMISSIONE NAZIONALE PER LE SOCIETÀ E LA BORSA (CONSOB).

commission. Generally, the money paid by a client to his agent for services rendered. Stockbrokers, as agents for their clients, are usually rewarded in this way.

Different stock exchanges have different rules concerning commission which their members may charge. At one time all stock exchanges tended to have scales of commission which their members had to keep to. Gradually these minimum, or fixed commission, rules are breaking down. The commissions charged by brokers on the New York Stock Exchange were made negotiable from 1 May 1975 (*See* MAYDAY), those in Canada from April 1983 and those in Australia in April 1984. *See also* APPENDIX 39; APPENDIX 41; MINIMUM COMMISSIONS; NEGOTIATED COMMISSION.

Commissionair in effecten (NL). A type of member admitted to the trading floor of the Amsterdam Stock Exchange, who acts as an intermediary between the banks and the HOEKLIEDEN as well as trading on their own accounts.

commissionaria di borsa (It). A firm of commission dealers in securities. Though they may be authorized to enter the floor, they may not enter the trading area to effect trading operations but must, like the banks, utilize a stockbroker.

commissionario (It). A commission dealer. Unlike a broker he may also buy and sell on his own account.

Commission Baumgartner (Fr). An enquiry set up in 1971 to examine means of improving the operations of the French stock market in order to allow it to meet the needs of savers and satisfy more easily the requirements of French business.

The Commission Baumgartner identified a number of weaknesses in savers' attitudes to the stock exchanges, the operations of the participants in the market, information supplied by listed companies and the tax treatment of direct shareholding.

It also identified a lack of public awareness, interest and understanding of the stock market and, consequently, an excess of liquidity in personal saving and generally in the French economy, which was acting to the detriment of the needs of business.

To increase public awareness of the role and functions of the stock exchanges, the Commission proposed greater media coverage and the inclusion of the stock market and investment matters in university economics syllabuses.

To encourage more direct personal investment, it recommended tax relief, particularly on small portfolios, the lowering of tax on dividend income and more incentives to overseas shareholders to the holding of French shares. The Commission also suggested improved terms for SICAV (*see* SOCIETÉS D'INVESTISSEMENT À CAPITAL VARIABLE) and greater encouragement of them.

The Commission noted the inadequate information provided by companies to shareholders and said that consolidated accounts should be mandatory. Improvements in the conduct of take-overs were also recommended.

On the stockbroking side, an increase in commissions was recommended in order to improve the profitability of AGENTS DE CHANGE. They should also be allowed to adopt a corporate, rather than a partnership, structure and take in outside shareholders. Some relaxation of the rules of the BOURSE was also suggested to allow brokers to become limited market makers.

Progress was made in implementing some of the suggestions, particularly with regard to take-over offers and more market making, but the impetus thereafter faltered. *See also* COMMISSION PEROUSE; LOI MONORY.

BIBLIOGRAPHY Paul Stonham, *Major Stock Markets of Europe* (Gower Publishing, 1982), *Le Marché des Actions* (Report presented to the Minister of the Economy and Finance by the Commission charged with the study of the securities market, Paris, June 1971).

commission broker (US). An agent on a stock market or financial futures exchange who carries out orders for clients and is paid for his services by way of commission.

Commission des Opérations de Bourse (COB) (Fr). A Commission established by law in 1967 to supervise the operations of the French stock exchanges. The Chairman and members of the Commission were appointed by the Government and serve for a term of four years.

The main responsibilities of the COB are :

(1) to make sure that listed companies issue all legally required information at the specified time;

(2) to prevent insiders using information gained in the course of their work for personal gain;

(3) to register complaints against the stock exchanges;

(4) to suggest modifications to stock exchange rules;

(5) to decide, on the advice of the CHAMBRE SYNDICALE DES AGENTS DE CHANGE, on the admission of securities to the official list.

BIBLIOGRAPHY *The Paris Stock Exchange: A Guide for Foreign Investors* (Paris, January 1980).

Commissione Nazionale per la Società e la Borsa (CONSOB) (It). The national commission for the Stock Exchange, established by law in 1974, with very wide and legally backed powers, including the approval of new listings, the determination of stockbrokers' commission, the receiving of notice of transfers of company control and the scrutinizing of company accounts.

BIBLIOGRAPHY Paul Stonham, *Major Stock Markets of Europe* (Gower Publishing, London, 1982) Chapter 4.

Commissione per il listino di borsa (It). The equivalent of the COMITATO DIRETTIVO DEGLI AGENTI DI CAMBIO (the Executive Committee of the Stockbrokers) in the minor Italian stock exchanges.

Commission Perouse (Fr). An inquiry set up in 1979 to study the internal practices of the French stock exchanges, still felt to be in need of reform despite the recommendations of the COMMISSION BAUMGARTNER in 1971. The Commission Perouse divided its investigation into three main areas: legal and settlement; quotations and market dealing practices; the structure of commission.

On legal and settlement matters, the Commission suggested the introduction of a central depositary system for equities, similar to that already operating in Treasury bonds, as a simpler structure to the complexities of the current settlement system.

The Commission recommended extended trading hours for the French stock exchanges and a continuous quotation system. A further recommendation was that the practice of listing securities, both on the MARCHÉ À TERME and on the MARCHÉ AU COMPTANT, should be abolished,as should dual listings on both Paris and a provincial exchange. Furthermore, the market-making powers of the AGENTS DE CHANGE introduced in the early 1970s should be increased still further in the interests of developing depth and liquidity in the trading market.

Recognizing again the low level of remuneration to brokers on the French exchanges, the Commission Perouse recommended a further increase in the level of commissions and a lowering of government tax on share dealings.

Finally, the Commission recommended reforms of the options markets, the MARCHÉ À PRIMES and STELLAGE dealings.

Since October 1983, following the recommendation of the Commission Perouse, a security may be traded only on the cash or the forward market, but not on both. Share certificates have been replaced by a book entry process since November 1984.

BIBLIOGRAPHY Paul Stonham, *Major Stock Markets of Europe* (Gower Publishing, London, 1982).

commitment. A user of financial futures is said to have a commitment when he assumes an obligation to make DELIVERY on a futures contract. *See also* OPEN INTEREST.

Committee to Review the Functioning of Financial Institutions, (The Wilson Committee) (UK). A Committee set up in 1976 under the chairmanship of Sir Harold (now Lord) Wilson, the former British Prime Minister. Its task was to review all aspects of the operation of financial institutions and it split its work into two parts: first, the provision of funds to industry and trade; second, other aspects of the financial system. The Committee produced a final report in 1980, various research papers and 13 volumes of evidence.

BIBLIOGRAPHY *Committee to Review the Functioning of Financial Institutions (The Wilson Committee), Report and Appendices* (HMSO, London, Cmnd.7937, June 1980).

Commodity Futures Trading Commission (CFTC) (US). The body created by Congress in 1979 to regulate trading in futures contracts. In this area it performs functions similar to those of the SECURITIES AND EXCHANGE COMMISSION with regard to securities dealing.

common (US). An abbreviation sometimes used for COMMON STOCK.

common stock (US). The American term synonymous with shares in United Kingdom usage. Common stocks are securities which represent part ownership of the issuing company by the holder, with the associated risks and rewards. Both common stock and PREFERRED STOCK bear the rights and responsibilities of ownership, but common stock holders bear the greater risk and greater potential rewards in terms of dividends and capital gain if the company is successful.

BIBLIOGRAPHY *Fact Book* (New York Stock Exchange, annually). *Common stocks listed* (NYSE, annually).

Compagnie des Agents de Change (CAC) (Fr). The national association of French stockbrokers to which all AGENTS DE CHANGE must belong. Although a private association, it provides a service and regulation which is given official recognition in that its regulations, the RÈGLEMENT GÉNÉRALE DE LA COMPAGNIE DES AGENTS DE CHANGE which govern dealings on the seven French stock exchanges, are recognized by the Minister of the Economy. The Compagnie des Agents de Change works closely with the statutory body. the COMMISSION DES OPÉRATIONS DE BOURSE set up in 1967.

The governing body of the Compagnie des Agents de Change is the CHAMBRE SYNDICALE DE LA COMPAGNIE DES AGENTS DE CHANGE, which is elected annually by its members.

BIBLIOGRAPHY *The Paris Stock Exchange: A Guide for Foreign Investors* (Paris, January 1980).

Companies Act 1980 (UK). The Act which made insider dealing a criminal offence in the United Kingdom. It also established the title PUBLIC LIMITED COMPANY (PLC) instead of the old-established Limited (Ltd).

Companies Act 1981 (UK). The Act which *inter alia* allowed companies in the United Kingdom to buy back their own shares, a practice common in other countries, notably the United States, but previously illegal in the United Kingdom.

company. A separate legal entity consisting of a number of individuals associated together to carry on a business or trade. In the United States it is usually called a CORPORATION.

company doctor (UK). A term applied to a person brought on to the board of an ailing company in an attempt to save it from liquidation. The person will often have wide powers and may have to take drastic action to turn it round. Sometimes the medicine works and sometimes it does not.

company limited (UK). A company limited is the phrase used to describe the fact that the shareholder's liability in the event of a COMPULSORY LIQUIDATION of the company is limited in some way.

The concept of limited liability, although known and used earlier, did not become general in the United Kingdom until the 19th century.

The normal method of limiting liability is by the issue of shares; each subscriber or subsequent investor is committed only to the amount of cash he has put in. In some instances, when the shares are only partly paid up, the investor will be required to pay the balance in the event of a liquidation. In either case, his liability is known and limited to the extent of his commitment; he is not liable, as he would be in a partnership or one-man business, for the debts to the extent of his personal wealth.

It is possible to set up a company limited, not by shares, but by a guarantee of its members up to a specified amount. Such a company is known as a company limited by guarantee, as compared with a company limited by shares. Companies listed on stock exchanges are all companies whose owners' liability is limited by the number of shares.

company limited by guarantee. *See* COMPANY LIMITED.

company limited by shares. *See* COMPANY LIMITED.

company meetings. *See* ANNUAL GENERAL MEETING; EXTRAORDINARY GENERAL MEETING; STATUTORY MEETING.

competing market maker system or **competitive market maker system** (UK). A system of trading in securities in which the market consists of a number of dealers or dealing firms, trading as principals and competing for the business of others in the market who are acting as agents for clients. Such a market system exists in the United Kingdom with the JOBBERS and is expected to continue (with significant modifications) in the new dealing system to be introduced. In the United States, the NATIONAL ASSOCIATION OF SECURITIES DEALERS market, NASDAQ, operates on similar principles.

competitive bid (US). The issue of new securities by a company in which different underwriters, or groups of underwriters, make offers for the shares in competition with one another. The company will accept the bid it finds most attractive and the successful syndicate will then on-sell the securities to investors. The competitive bid is contrasted with the NEGOTIATED BID.

competitive trader (US). A member of the New York Stock Exchange who trades in securities on the TRADING FLOOR for an account in which he has an interest. He is also known as a registered trader.

composition agreement (UK). An agreement between the Stock Exchange and the Inland Revenue, whereby the Stock Exchange settlement centre collects TRANSFER STAMP DUTY on the transfer of TALISMAN securities and makes a composite payment to the Inland Revenue.

compound interest. The method of calculating interest on a principal amount whereby the interest is calculated, not only on the original principal, but also on any other interest which has previously been calculated and added to the balance.

The formula is usually written:

$$A = P(1 + r)^n$$

when A = the final amount
P = the original principal
r = the rate of interest credited at each period
n = the number of periods.

compra (vendita) titoli non quotati (It). A purchase (sale) of unlisted securities.

compratore a premio (It). An option buyer.

compulsory liquidation (UK). Sometimes referred to as a winding up of a company's affairs by order of the Court: the High Court Chancery Division if the liquidation is in excess of £120,000; otherwise the County Court. This will be done on a petition by an interested party, either the company itself, a creditor or, where fraud is involved, the Department of Trade and Industry. There are a number of actions which can trigger a petition for compulsory liquidation. They are: (1) the passing of a resolution by members of the company that it be wound up by the Court; (2) where the company has failed to make its statutory return to the Registrar of Companies; (3) if the company either fails to begin trading within a year of its incorporation or at some point thereafter ceases to trade for a period of one year; (4) where the number of members falls below the statutory number of two, whether for a private or public company; (5) if debts cannot be met; (6) if the Court decides it is 'just and equitable' that the company be put into compulsory liquidation.

Computer Assisted Execution System (CAES) (US). An enhancement to the National Association of Securities Dealers Automated Quotation System (NASDAQ) in February 1981. CAES is an automated order-routing and order-execution system which provides automatic execution of a transaction and creates a paper record for both buyer and seller. It began operating for selected securities in February 1981 and was linked with the INTERMARKET TRADING SYSTEM in May 1982.

Computer Assisted Trading System (CATS) (Canada). A system of trading in securities developed by the Toronto Stock Exchange. The CATS system is an on-line order entry and information retrieval system which since 1979 has been the sole facility for trading in the Toronto Stock Exchange's less active stocks. CATS handles almost two-thirds of the total number of stocks listed on Toronto. It accepts buying and selling orders and executes these orders according to AUCTION MARKET principles of price and time priority. A registered representative of a member firm sends the details of an order to the firm's CATS trader for entry into their system. It is then either executed or, if it cannot be traded at that moment, put in its place in the queue. Details of the order and whether it has been executed or put in the queue are available throughout the market on CATS terminals.

On CATS there is a pre-opening period from 09:15 to 10:00 to allow all overnight and early morning orders to be put into the system for the 10:00 opening. The opening price is calculated at a level which will allow the most trading to take place. All buying orders with a limit price above the opening price will be fulfilled, while any stock remaining is shared out among orders given at the opening price.

concert party. A colloquial term for the phrase 'acting in concert', used by the United Kingdom PANEL ON TAKE-OVERS AND

MERGERS to describe a situation where individuals agree to co-operate actively to acquire control of a company by planned purchases of shares in that company. Any two people or groups may be deemed to be acting in concert, but the following are presumed to be so unless proved to the contrary: a company with any subsidiaries or associates; a company with its directors, or with its pension fund; a person and any fund he manages on a discretionary basis or a financial adviser and his client. In a take-over, the offerer company must state in the offer document all relevant shareholdings owned by the offerer and anyone acting in concert with him while in general terms, for the purposes of the CITY CODE ON TAKE-OVERS AND MERGERS, shareholdings of the principal and anyone acting in concert with him, are treated as constituting one holding.

In the United States, any two parties acting in concert must not seek to acquire control of a company without informing the SECURITIES AND EXCHANGE COMMISSION.

con dividendo (It). *Cum* dividend. *See* CUM.

conflict of interest. The term used to describe a situation where an individual or firm may have a commercial and financial involvement in a transaction, but a legal or fiduciary duty to act in a way which would be prejudicial to their own commercial advantage. Conflicts of interest may arise in securities transactions in a number of ways, of which the following are examples. Perhaps the most obvious example concerns the position of a broker acting both as agent for his client and that of a market maker acting as a principal in the buying and selling of shares. If a stockbroking firm can act in both capacities, the legal obligation of the agent trying to get the best price for his client may well conflict with the short term commercial interest of the market maker. Rules are needed to ensure that the client has sufficient information available to enable him to verify that his transaction was carried out at the best possible terms by his agent. Other conflicts can occur when a firm manages funds on behalf of clients and is also involved in placing or underwriting new issues. Again, rules and surveillance are needed by the stock exchange or statutory authorities to ensure that where a conflict of interest is involved, the client is protected.

conflitto d'interessi (It). *See* CONFLICT OF INTEREST.

congelata (It). An expression used in reference to securities which cannot be sold without a considerable loss, owing to a notable fall in prices. The securities are, therefore, considered as 'frozen'.

conglomerate. A term originating in the United States as a popular word to describe a HOLDING COMPANY with interests in a multitude of diverse industries, for instance steel, film-making and agriculture; and diverse activities, for instance mining to retailing.

consegna titoli (It). The delivery of the certificates to the clearing house of the Bank of Italy on settlement day.

consideration. The total amount involved in a commercial transaction; the purchase or sale value. In securities trading the word refers to the value of a share, option or futures purchase or sale. Commission, taxes and other charges are often based on the total value or consideration of the deal.

consolidated balance sheet. A balance sheet showing the assets and liabilities of a company and its subsidiaries. Company law and accounting practice normally require such consolidated information to be published so that investors and financial analysts can obtain a complete picture of a group of companies controlled by a single source. The Seventh Directive of the EEC Council of Ministers extended requirements for producing consolidated accounts throughout the Community.

Consolidated stock (UK). *See* CONSOLS.

consolidated tape (US). The ticker which reports transactions in securities listed on the New York Stock Exchange whether the deal takes place on the New York Stock Exchange or on any of the regional exchanges and other markets around the United States. A separate consolidated tape operates for all stocks listed on the American Stock Exchange for all deals taking place there or on any other market. *See also* TICKER.

Consols (UK). The abbreviation for Consolidated Stock or Consolidated Loan, a type of fixed interest Government stock issued in large amounts, often as replacement for a number of maturing smaller issues which were being consolidated. The Consols are technically repayable in '1923 or after' and '1957 or after' according to their prospectuses, but they are dealt on the basis that they will never be repaid and thus enjoy only a FLAT YIELD and not a REDEMPTION YIELD.

consorzio per investimenti (It). *See* INVESTMENT TRUST.

contango (UK). The delay in settlement of a bargain on the Stock Exchange from one ACCOUNT to the next. For the agreed privilege of carrying forward settlement the instigator of the request will pay a premium.

contango day (UK). The first day of dealing for the new account when contangos are matched. It should be noted that contangos are arranged on the previous business day so that a client has time to close the bargain if a CONTANGO is not available.

contanti (It). A cash bargain.

contingent order. An order to buy (or sell) securities which will only be executed if another deal to sell (or buy) can be carried out first.

continuation (UK). A commission concession given to investors under the minimum commission rules of the Stock Exchange. Where an investor made a number of purchases of shares in the same company over a restricted period of time, the broker could charge commission, not at an individual rate on each deal, but at the rate which would have applied had the whole deal been completed at one time. There was an advantage to the investor since the minimum scales of commssion tapered: the higher the total consideration, the lower the commission rate.

continuation day (UK). *See* CONTANGO DAY.

conto profitti e perdite (It). *See* PROFIT AND LOSS ACCOUNT.

contract. (1) On a securities market, an agreement between a buyer and a seller to buy or sell securities. *See also* CONTRACT NOTE.

(2) In a FINANCIAL FUTURES market, while having the same general meaning, a contract is a binding agreement to make and take DELIVERY at a definite date of a stated amount of a specified currency or FINANCIAL INSTRUMENT.

(3) Any formal agreement between two or more parties to a business transaction.

contract grade. *See* DELIVERABLE NAME.

contract month. The month in which a futures CONTRACT matures, resulting in the delivery of the specified currency or financial instrument. *See also* DELIVERY MONTH.

contract note (UK). In a Stock Exchange context, a notification issued by a broker to his client and sent as soon as possible after the deal has been made. The contract note shows the name of the company whose shares have been bought or sold, the particular security, whether the shares or stock have been traded with or without any particular benefits attached (such as dividend, scrip or rights issue), the price paid, the total CONSIDERATION, the amount of COMMISSION and other charges such as TRANSFER STAMP DUTY, VAT, CSI levy, CONTRACT STAMP and finally the date of SETTLEMENT DAY.

contract stamp (UK). A stamp which must be affixed to a stock CONTRACT NOTE. The amount of the stamp is small: on deals of £100 to £500 it is 10p, on deals of £500-£1500 it is 30p, and above £1500, 60p.

contractual saving. Regular saving via an insurance policy, pension scheme or some other form of savings medium. The amount saved is the subject of a contract between the saver and the savings institution and cannot be terminated except usually by penalty. Most personal sector savings in the United Kingdom are now in contractual form, especially because of the growth of occupational pension schemes, membership of which is often a condition of employment. Much contractual saving is actively encouraged by the granting of tax concessions.

contrapartiste (Fr). A market maker. Originally an AGENT DE CHANGE was not allowed to be a *contrapartiste,* but the law was changed in 1972 to allow a limited form of market making, although still well short of what is done by the JOBBER in the United Kingdom or the SPECIALIST in the United States. An *agent de change* may now deal direct with clients as a principal out of normal trading hours at the last price quoted on the official market during trading hours. The deal must be unwound in the market as soon as possible.

contratto a contante (It). A cash contract normally restricted to loan securities whose settlement takes place on the third stock exchange trading session after the deal has taken place.

contratto 'contanti a giorni' (It). A contract in which settlement must take place within ten stock exchange dealing periods.

contratto (a) premi (It). An option contract.

contratto (a) pronti (It). *See* CONTRATTO A CONTANTE.

contratto (a) termine (It). A forward deal. This is the normal way of buying and selling shares and the account lasts for a maximum period of one month.

contributory pension. Occupational pension schemes are now an established fringe benefit of many employees in the United Kingdom. Over 11 million are contributors to them while a further 2 million receive pensions from them. Some schemes are contributory, with the employees themselves making contributions to the pension fund. Other schemes are non-contributory, where the employer bears the full cost of the pension contribution. Because of the tax benefits granted to money paid into occupational pension schemes, there are maximum amounts laid down to limit the amount saved through these schemes.

contro fisso (It). An operation carried out on the stock exchange for the same amount of securities for which an option has been stipulated.

controle des changes (Fr). Exchange control. Still in existence in France, despite the provisions of the Treaty of Rome relating to the free movement of capital.

controlling interest. The ability of a shareholder to influence the affairs of a company. Controlling interest, strictly speaking, means the ability to command a majority of the votes in a company, but the phrase is often used more loosely than that. It is possible, because of the fragmentation of shareholding, for one individual (or another company) to exerise a significant interest by holding 20 percent of the capital. *See* ASSOCIATED COMPANY. The PANEL ON TAKE-OVERS AND MERGERS deems that one shareholder has effective control over another's affairs if he or it owns 30 percent of the other company's shares.

conventional option (UK). The term given to an option which has been available on the UK market for a century, giving the buyer of the option the right to buy or the right to sell a given share at a fixed price at a specified future date. The difference which distinguishes a conventional option from a TRADED OPTION is that a conventional option cannot be sold to another investor. If the holder is successful in his investment and the underlying share on which he has a CALL OPTION rises in price, he will EXERCISE his option and buy the UNDERLYING SHARES. If he holds a PUT OPTION, success will come if the price of the underlying share falls and again, he would exercise his option. If on the other hand the price of the underlying share were to move against the investor, falling when he had bought a call option or rising when he held a put option, he would simply allow the option to lapse.

A conventional option may be written on a wide range of shares listed on the UK Stock Exchange and the terms are individually written for each contract. There is no standardization of EXERCISE PRICE, size of CONTRACT or EXPIRY DATE as there is with traded options.

conversion. The act of transferring from one security directly into another on the maturity of the former. Often the word is applied to government stock when the government will offer holders the right to convert into a new stock, often on favourable terms. The benefit to the government is that the average life of government debt is lengthened and the direct conversion of one stock into another minimizes disruption to the money markets caused by a large injection of cash into the banking system as the stockholders are repaid. *See also* CONVERSION RIGHTS, CONVERSION STOCKS.

(Conversion has a different meaning in law, where it refers to the wrongful diversion of funds or other property from their rightful owner.)

conversion (Fr). *See* CONVERSION. In normal circumstances, holders of stock who do not wish to convert into the new one can receive cash instead, but in the case of a CONVERSION FORCÉE the holder is given no cash option.

conversion forcée (Fr). Conversion of one stock into another where the holder of the original security is given no cash option but must take his conversion rights in the new stock, converting it into cash, if he requires, by the sale of the new stock in the market.

conversion premium. The amount by which the current price of a convertible stock exceeds its current CONVERTIBLE VALUE.

conversion price. The price of the equity at which a CONVERTIBLE LOAN STOCK can be converted.

conversion rights. The terms and conditions upon which the holder of a security may exchange it for another. The security in question may be a government stock, in which case conversion rights will be into another government stock of a later maturity date. Alternatively, the conversion rights may apply to a company's CONVERTIBLE LOAN STOCK and normally give the holder the ability to convert a fixed interest loan stock into equity shares of the company at pre-determined prices on one or a series of pre-determined future dates. The price at which conversion can be made will most likely be higher than that prevailing at the time the convertible loan stock is issued, but the company (and the stock holders) hope and expect that the market price of the equity when the conversion dates arrive will make conversion attractive to the loan stock holders.

conversion stocks (UK). Stock issued by the British Government as new issues into which holders of existing stocks can convert their holdings. Sometimes such stocks are clearly indicated by their names, such as Conversion Stock 3.5 percent, but existing holders may be offered conversion into a government stock which is not specifically called a conversion stock.

conversion value. The current market value of the shares into which a convertible loan stock can be converted.

convertibilità (It). The terms of CONVERSION of a security.

convertibility. The ability of a currency to be freely exchanged for another. Sterling returned to free convertibility for current trade and payments in 1958, when restrictions applied during and after World War II were lifted. For capital payments some restrictions remained until October 1979, when exchange control on portfolio investment was removed. Since then, British investors have been able to invest without penalty in securities worldwide. *See also* EXCHANGE CONTROL; INVESTMENT CURRENCY PREMIUM.

convertible adjustable preferred stock (CAP) (US). A PREFERRED STOCK, introduced in 1983, which gives the holder the right to convert into the equity of the company after the announcement of each quarterly dividend. Because of the conversion capability and the ability of the company to adjust the dividend on the stock, the CAPs trade close to PAR, giving holders stability of capital value.

convertible bond. *See* CONVERTIBLE LOAN STOCK.

convertible loan stock. A stock (usually paying a fixed rate of interest) which can be converted at the option of its holder into equity shares. The object of issuing such a stock is to obtain fixed interest finance at a relatively low rate of interest while making it attractive to potential holders by the offer of equity participation at a later date when the company's profitability can support an increase in share capital.

copertura (It). The MARGIN required to cover a purchase or sale of equities.

coprirsi (It). *See* HEDGE.

corbeille (Fr). The oldest trading area on the floor of the Paris *bourse* where the AGENTS DE CHANGE are to be found during trading hours. The word is often used as a symbol for the AGENTS DE CHANGE and their clerks. *See also* COULISSE.

The word is also used in Italy to refer to the circular trading ring in which the trading of securities takes place.

corner. To purchase, or otherwise gain control of, the supply of a commodity or shares in order to restrict supply and drive up the price.

corporate member (UK). A shareholder in a member firm of the Stock Exchange in the United Kingdom or a member firm itself, which is organized as a corporate entity and not as a partnership. Limited corporate members are those outside institutions which have taken a financial stake in a Stock Exchange member firm and in consequence their liability for the debts of the firm is limited to the amount of their share stake. An unlimited corporate member is a member firm of the Exchange which has elected to have a corporate structure. Its directors, who are generally members of the Stock Exchange, must still undertake unlimited liability for the debts of the company.

corporation. (1) (UK) A local authority. (2) (US) A limited company.

Corporation Tax (UK). The tax on company profits in the United Kingdom. First introduced in 1965, Corporation Tax was levied at 40 percent of profits before the distribution of dividends. Dividends themselves were then taxed at the shareholder's marginal rate. In fact, therefore, dividends were subject to double taxation. The system was revised in 1971 when an imputation tax system was introduced. Under this system, dividends are paid net and an amount equivalent to the tax due on a gross dividend is accounted for to the Inland Revenue as ADVANCE CORPORATION TAX (ACT). Any amounts of ACT paid may be offset against the company's 'mainstream' Corporation Tax (i.e. its own direct tax liability on its profits).

Corporation tax has since been set at 52 percent, with a lower rate for smaller companies. However, because of tax relief given against stock appreciation in the inflation-ridden 1970s, many companies were in fact paying little or no mainstream Corporation Tax. In his Budget speech of 1984, the Chancellor of the Exchequer set out a medium term plan for Corporation Tax, with the objective of reducing it to 35 percent by 1986/87 but phasing out the inflation reliefs.

BIBLIOGRAPHY Glyn Saunders and David Harrington, *Tolley's Corporation Tax* (Tolley Publishing, annually).

correspondent (US). A securities firm, bank or other financial institution which regularly performs services for another in a place or market to which the other does not have direct access. Securities firms may have correspondents in foreign countries or on exchanges of which they are not members. Member organizations of the NEW YORK STOCK EXCHANGE with offices in the city may also act as correspondents for out-of-town member organizations which do not possess New York City offices.

correzione errori (It). The established day on the monthly stock exchange calendar on which all bargains are checked for possible errors or discrepancies by the clearing house.

corso (It). The current price of a security on any day on the stock exchange.

corso secco (It). The net price of a loan stock excluding ACCRUED INTEREST.

cotation (Fr). *See* QUOTATION; applied to securities listed on the French and Belgian *bourses*.

côte officielle (Fr). The market for officially listed stocks on the Paris Stock Exchange. It is divided into two separate markets: the MARCHÉ AU COMPTANT, (the cash or spot market) and the MARCHÉ À TERME (the forward market). The *Bulletin de la Côte Officielle* publishes daily prices of securities traded.

coulisse (Fr). The old name for the unofficial market on the Paris *bourse*. The word is now in disuse, since the official and unofficial markets have now merged and the *coulisse* was officially dismantled in 1962.

Council for the Securities Industry (CSI) (UK). A non-statutory supervisory body for the UK securities industry, set up in 1978.

The chairman and deputy chairman of the CSI are appointed by the Governor of the Bank of England, while all the major UK bodies concerned with the securities markets are represented on the Council. These bodies are the COUNCIL OF THE STOCK EXCHANGE, ACCEPTING HOUSES COMMITTEE, ASSOCIATION OF INVESTMENT TRUST COMPANIES, British Insurance Association, Committee of London Clearing Bankers, ISSUING HOUSES ASSOCIATION, UNIT TRUST ASSOCIATION, National Association of Pension Funds, Confederation of British Industry and the Consultative Committee of Accountancy Bodies.

The objectives of the CSI are to maintain the highest ethical standards in securities dealing; to keep under constant review the evolution of the securities markets and the practices and codes of conduct of its participants; to scrutinize the effectiveness of regulation; to be in a position to investigate cases of alleged misconduct and breaches of codes of conduct or best practice; to initiate new policies and codes as necessary other than those wholly within the scope of an individual association; to resolve differences of principle between constituent parties; to consider the need for changes in legislation relating to securities trading and to liaise with the European Commission on securities industry matters and on the implementation of the EEC Capital Markets Code of Conduct.

The CSI is a voluntary body, relying for its effectiveness on the support of its constituent bodies. Although the Council's recommendations on matters are not legally binding, they are nonetheless effective because of the close-knit nature of the UK securities markets.

To finance the activities of the CSI, a levy of 60p is made on all contract notes in respect of transactions in sterling securities over a level of £5000.

BIBLIOGRAPHY Supervision of the Securities Markets : non-statutory aspects, *Bank of England Quarterly Bulletin*, September 1978, pp 390-397. Council for the Securities Industry, *Annual reports. Code of Conduct for Dealers in Securities* (CSI booklet series, No. 1). *Rules governing substantial acquisitions of shares* (CSI, No.2). *Guidelines for personal dealings by fund managers* (CSI, No. 4). *Statement on Insider Dealing* (CSI, No. 5).

Council of the Stock Exchange (UK). The governing body of the Stock Exchange in the United Kingdom. The Council frames and publishes rules and regulations relating to securities trading in the United Kingdom and the Republic of Ireland. Since 1973, the Stock Exchange has incorporated not only London, but also the out-of-London exchanges and is not only the Stock Exchange of the United Kingdom, but also of the Republic of Ireland.

The Council consists of 51 members: of these, 35 are elected by the London membership, eleven by the various units around the country; since January 1984 there have been five lay members appointed who sit as representatives of the public interest. In addition, the Government Broker is a member of the Council *ex officio*.

The Council divides its work into a number of standing committees: quotations, membership, technical services, settlement services, member firms accounts, disciplinary and appeals, and property and finance. The lay members of the Council make up the majority of members of the appeals committee and the entire membership appeals committee.

coupon. The word has two distinct, but related, meanings. (1) In the case of a BEARER BOND the coupon is the warrant attached to the certificate which has to be detached and sent to the PAYING AGENT in order to receive the interest payment. This coupon states the amount of interest due at each payment date. Hence the word coupon has acquired its second meaning: (2) the nominal rate of interest attached to a fixed interest security: thus a 5 percent fixed interest stock pays five pounds a year per £100 nominal stock. The coupon rate is not to be confused with the YIELD, which is the actual rate of return achieved, depending upon how much money is invested at current prices.

coupon bond. *See* BEARER BOND and COUPON.

coupon sheet. The sheet of coupons accompanying a BEARER BOND or BEARER SHARE. *See also* COUPON.

coupures (Fr). The total number of individual shares in a class comprising a total issue or class of issue.

cours (Fr). The market price of a share at any given time on the French or Belgian *bourses.*

cours d'application (Fr). The buying and selling prices on the BOURSE which are applied by the broker to certain transactions carried out on behalf of his clients. The equivalent of a PUT-THROUGH, the *cours d'application* must be at one of the prices quoted on the trading floor at the previous trading session.

cours de la clôture (Fr). The prices of shares at the closing of the market.

cours de la demande (Fr). The BID price of a security on the *bourse.*

cours de l'offre (Fr). The OFFER price of a security.

cours d'émission (Fr). *See* PRIX D'ÉMISSION.

cours d'introduction (Fr). The offered price of a newly issued security on the morning of its introduction. The *cours d'introduction* is set by a committee under the auspices of the COMPAGNIE DES AGENTS DE CHANGE based on the bids received from potential investors in the company. *See also* PRIX D'OFFRE.

cours d'ouverture (Fr). The price of a share at the opening of the trading session. Also called the *premier cours.* The degree of change of opening prices from their previous close is regulated by the CHAMBRE SYNDICALE DES

AGENTS DE CHANGE. On the cash market, French bonds must not differ by more than 2-3 percent from the previous close and shares by not more than 4-5 percent. If supply and demand are so out of balance that these limits would be exceeded, the Chambre Syndicale will fix a price and reduce supply or demand by the amount needed to give balance at the maximum price change. If supply and demand are so out of balance that less than 20-25 percent of orders can be executed, trading in that security is suspended for the day. On the forward market if the opening price differs by more than 8 percent from its previous close, trading is halted to give buyers and sellers the opportunity to confirm or cancel their orders and trading is later resumed.

cours limité (Fr). A limit price. *See* LIMIT ORDER.

cours moyen (Fr). *See* MIDDLE PRICE.

cours touché (Fr). Limit orders which coincide with the current market quote.

courtage (Fr). Commission. The brokerage commissions on French securities on the French *bourses* are set according to the following schedule:

	Bonds	*Convertibles and Shares*	
		on Paris	*on a regional exchange*
Consideration (Francs)	%	%	%
up to 600,000	0.5	0.65	0.75
600,001 to 1.1m	0.33	0.43	0.50
1.1m to 2.2m	0.25	0.325	0.375
over 2.2m	0.165	0.215	0.25

The phrase is also used to describe commission on the German exchanges. *See also* MAKLERGEBÜHR.

BIBLIOGRAPHY *The Paris Stock Exchange: A Guide for Foreign Investors* (Paris, 1980). Paul Stonham, *Major Stock Markets of Europe* (Gower Publishing, 1982).

courte échéance, à (Fr). *See* SHORT TERM.

courtier (en valeurs mobilieres) (Fr). Formerly a dealer on the COULISSE but since they were officially suppressed in 1962, most have become official *agents de change.*

cover. In financial markets, cover has a number of different meanings:

(1) The first relates to some form of collateral security. In a financial futures market, cover has two meanings in this context: *(i)* the purchase of futures contracts to offset a previously established short position and *(ii)* the security provided (in cash or other acceptable form) by a clearing member to the clearing house, by a non-member to a member or by the client to a member to cover variations in the value of existing contracts resulting from market price changes. *See also* INITIAL MARGIN, VARIATION MARGIN. In a TRADED OPTIONS market, cover is the UNDERLYING STOCK, securities pledged as collateral for a written option. *See* OPTIONS WRITER.

(2) Cover has the second meaning of the number of times a company's dividend could be paid out of current earnings. This is usually referred to as 'times covered'. The figure gives an indication of the company's ability to pay dividends even should it suffer a bad year so far as earnings are concerned. A well covered dividend is less likely to be reduced if a company has a bad year than one which is accounting for all, or almost all, a company's annual earnings.

BIBLIOGRAPHY *A Guide to Financial Statistics* (Financial Times, London, 3rd edition, 1984).

cover, dividend. *See* DIVIDEND COVER.

cravatta, fare una (It). Expression used to explain the undoing of a position at a lower price than the speculator might have been able to obtain if he had been able to operate in his own time; a FORCED SALE.

Crédit Lombard. (Fr). *See* LOMBARD CREDIT.

criée, à la (Fr). *See* À LA CRIÉE.

cross, crossing. (1) The simultaneous buying and selling of the same BLOCK of securities. Brokers are not permitted to cross a deal within their own offices except in very special situations: exchanges in a number of countries have a 'crossing rule' to the effect that all such deals must be crossed on the floor of an exchange to test the price and allow other investors or market makers to participate in the deal should they so wish.

(2) On a financial futures market, a cross has a similar meaning, with other brokers in the pit having the right to intervene in the deal.

crowd. The dealers wishing to deal in a particular stock who gather around a SPECIALIST trading post or around a pitch or pit in a traded options or financial futures market.

cum. Latin, meaning 'with'. It has many uses in the securities markets to describe the rights attaching to a security: thus a share bought or sold *cum* a benefit confers the right to that benefit on the buyer. Among phrases in common usage are *cum* rights, meaning that the buyer acquires the right to participate in an announced RIGHTS ISSUE; *cum* DIVIDEND; *cum* SCRIP or *cum* CAPITALIZATION and, less common, *cum* DRAWING.

cumulative preference shares. Shares which not only have a preferential right to receive a fixed dividend ahead of any ordinary shareholder, but in addition have the right to any arrears of the preference dividends which may have built up. *See also* PREFERENCE SHARES.

cumulative preferred (US). The American equivalent of CUMULATIVE PREFERENCE SHARES.

cumulative voting (US). A method of voting for company directors which enables the shareholder to multiply the number of his shares by the number of directorships being voted on and cast the total for one director or a group of directors. A holder of ten shares would normally cast his ten votes for each of twelve nominees to the board of directors. In total he therefore has 120 votes and under the principle of cumulative voting, he may cast his 120 votes for one nominee or 60 for each of two, etc. Cumulative voting is required under the corporate laws of some States and is permitted by most others.

curb market (US). *See* KERB MARKET.

curb trading (US). *See* KERB TRADING.

currency funds. Funds which collect the savings of a group of relatively small savers and invest them in a number of currencies to diversify risk. The vehicles chosen for the currency investment may be interest bearing bank accounts or other essentially short term assets.

current assets. Short term assets which could reasonably be expected to be in cash or convertible into cash within one year. Current assets consist of cash itself, bank balances, stock and work-in-progress, debtors (excluding bad and doubtful debts) and listed investments held as current assets rather than trade investments.

current assets ratio. The relationship of the current assets of an organization divided by its current liabilities as shown in the balance sheet.

current liabilities. Short term claims on a company such as bank overdrafts, other short term borrowing, creditors, dividends and tax payable.

current return (US). An American term for YIELD.

cushion (US). The period between the issue date of a stock and the first date on which the issuer can call it in for repayment. A bond may be issued with a final date of maturity of 25 years, but may be called in for repayment by drawing (*see* DRAWN BOND) at any time after (say) ten years. The first ten years' life of the bond is therefore the investor's cushion to protect him from the loss of his anticipated income for the life of the bond.

CUSIP number (US). A computerized number allotted to every security in the United States since 1970 and which allows every security to be uniquely identified. CUSIP stands for Committee on Uniform Securities Identification Procedures.

D

Dachgesellschaft (Ger). *See* HOLDING COMPANY.

daily settlement price. The daily closing price used by the CLEARING HOUSE in a FINANCIAL FUTURES market to MARK TO MARKET all OPEN CONTRACTS for the purpose of calculating VARIATION MARGIN. *See also* EXCHANGE DELIVERY SETTLEMENT PRICE.

data di rimborso or ***data di scadenza*** (It). *See* REDEMPTION DATE, MATURITY DATE.

date d'échéance (Fr). *See* REDEMPTION DATE.

dated stock. An interest bearing security with a fixed date of repayment or MATURITY. The term is usually applied only to government stocks to differentiate them from undated government issues. Since no company interest bearing issues are undated, there is no point in drawing the distinction. Sometimes the dated government stock is repayable on a specific REDEMPTION DATE; more frequently, such a stock carries two dates, indicating that the stock will be redeemed after the first and at or before the second.

Dauerschuldverschreibung (Ger). *See* PERPETUAL DEBENTURE.

dawn raid (UK). A phrase used to describe a practice which had a brief active life on the UK Stock Exchange in the early 1980s. A potential bidder for a company would instruct his broker to go into the market at the start of business and bid for stock in the TARGET COMPANY at a price usually well in excess of the prevailing level. The object was to buy a holding of stock up to 29.9 percent of the capital of the target company (*see* TAKE-OVER BID) as a base on which to launch a possible offer for the remaining share capital later.

The practice received a good deal of hostile comment, principally because the board of the target company had no time to assess the merits of the bid or to advise their shareholders; also the method tended to favour those large investors who were in minute-by-minute touch with the market, compared with small investors who could not be so well informed.

In response, the Stock Exchange and the Council for the Securities Industry (CSI) investigated the practice, and following a moratorium on such dealings the CSI issued a set of rules in December 1980 governing substantial acquisitions of shares, defined as holdings in excess of 15 percent but less than 30 percent. In essence, these rules delayed the speed with which such acquisitions could be made and ensured that all shareholders had seven days in which to react.

Following further difficulties in 1982, these rules were amended to delay acquisition leading to full blown bids (which in effect had been exempted from the earlier rules) thus giving time for the offeree company's directors to respond to an unwelcome approach.

BIBLIOGRAPHY Council for the Securities Industry, *Rules Governing Substantial Acquisitions of Shares* (CSI, No.2, revised April 1982). Council for the Securities Industry, *Annual Reports*, years to March 1981 and March 1982.

day order (US). An order which is placed with a price limit for execution, if possible, during only one trading session. If execution of that order within the specified time proves impossible, the order is automatically cancelled. A similar expression is used in financial futures trading. *See also* LIMIT ORDER.

day trading. The establishment and liquidation of a POSITION in stock or

FINANCIAL FUTURES markets within one trading day so as to eliminate an open position by the end of the day.

deal. A TRADE OR BARGAIN made on a market.

dealer. A general term for a professional trader in a financial marketplace, be it foreign exchange, commodities or other financial contracts. The dealers may be MARKET MAKERS or agents for the investing public. Thus, in UK stock exchange terminology, dealers may be either BROKERS OF JOBBERS, the former acting as agents, the latter as market makers. *See also* MAKLER.

dealer bank (US). A banking organization which acts as a regular MARKET MAKER or primary dealer in US government bonds.

debenture. Loans which are secured on the fixed or floating assets of a company.

debenture holder. The holder of a part or the whole of a DEBENTURE STOCK. In the event of the borrower defaulting on the interest or capital repayment, the debenture holder has the right to appoint a RECEIVER FOR DEBENTURE HOLDERS to sell the assets and thus secure repayment of the loan.

debenture stock. The original DEBENTURE may be split into units which can be traded on a stock exchange. Such a stock and its units are referred to as debenture stock, which may be traded in any amount on the market.

debit balance (US). On a customer's margin account that position of the purchase price of the stock, bonds or commodities which is covered by credit extended to the customer by the broker. *See also* MARGIN.

debole (It). A weak market; falling market prices.

debordant (It). A method of placing an order to buy or sell securities at a fixed price, which allows the deal to be executed partially during a stock exchange trading session, provided that the set or limit price is obtained.

debordare (It). This expression is used when the price of the security on the stock market surpasses the exercise price of the option. By selling all the underlying securities at that price, the buyer of the option recuperates all that he paid and makes a profit.

debt. (1) The amounts owing by individuals, partnerships, companies or indeed countries.

(2) The term in stock market parlance is often used to describe the whole of a company's borrowing, which may consist of a number of DEBENTURE STOCKS and LOAN STOCKS as distinct from its SHAREHOLDERS' FUNDS.

debt/equity ratio. The relationship between a company's borrowing and its shareholders' capital funds. *See also* GEARING and LEVERAGE.

Deckungsgeschäft (Ger). A stock exchange transaction to provide COVER or to offset a commitment already made.

découvert (Fr). An uncovered position on the stock market. A BEAR who is in the position of finding that the stock which has been the subject of the bear sale has risen in price.

Deed of Settlement (UK). Generally a trust established by one or more settlers for the benefit of others. In UK Stock Exchange terminology, the document of 1802 which governs the fundamental rules of the Exchange.

deep discount bond, deep discount stock. Stock issued at a low price compared with the par value and redemption price. The rate of interest and the running yield are low, indeed may be zero, with most or all of the benefit to the investor coming from the capital gain between the issue and redemption prices. The benefit of deep discount bonds to the issuing company is the low interest commitment; to the high rate taxpayer they provide (relatively low tax) capital gain instead of (more highly taxed) income. *See also* ZERO COUPON BOND.

default. The failure of a legal or commercial entity to honour debts when due. *See also* HAMMERING.

deferred futures. The most distant months of a futures contract, also referred to as back months or back positions. *See also* NEARBY FUTURES.

deferred shares. A part of the ordinary share capital of a company, deferred shares give full voting rights to their holders and, in a liquidation, similar rights as to the holders of ordinary shares. However, deferred shares do not rank for dividend until after a certain date or until the company's profitability reaches a certain level.

deficit financing. The methods by which a government raises the money to cover the annual difference between its spending and the amount it raises by taxation. There are a number of ways in which such a deficit may be financed. These are borrowing from overseas, printing more banknotes or creating more bank deposits. Other methods include borrowing on short term from the banking system or raising long term funds by the issue of marketable and non-marketable securities. Raising long term money is the method preferred by the monetary authorities as it takes money out of circulation and is less inflationary than any of the other methods.

definitive certificate. A certificate signifying ownership of shares which are paid for by instalments. Once the amount to be subscribed has been fully paid, the definitive certificate is issued to replace the temporary evidence of title.

defunct company. A company which has gone out of business and has been wound up. The Stock Exchange in the United Kingdom used to issue a REGISTER OF DEFUNCT AND OTHER COMPANIES containing details of those companies whose shares used to be listed. This book is no longer separately published, but details are incorporated into THE STOCK EXCHANGE OFFICIAL YEAR BOOK.

BIBLIOGRAPHY *The Stock Exchange Official Year Book* (Macmillan, London, annually).

dégrèvement de charges fiscales doubles (Fr). *See* DOUBLE TAXATION RELIEF.

delayed opening (US). The postponement of the opening of trading on a US stock exchange beyond the normal time because of market conditions that have been judged by a market official to warrant such a delay. Reasons for the delay might be an influx of either buying or selling orders, an imbalance of buyers and sellers or imminent company news which demands time for the market to assimilate it.

***del credere* agent.** An agent who, for an additional commission, undertakes to guarantee payment to his principal for any deals he undertakes with a third party.

deliverable names. Those FINANCIAL INSTRUMENTS which are specified in the rules of a FINANCIAL FUTURES exchange which may be offered when making delivery of an actual instrument in satisfaction of a futures CONTRACT.

delivery. (1) The transfer of securities to their new owner.

(2) The tender and receipt of an actual FINANCIAL INSTRUMENT or cash in settlement of a financial futures CONTRACT.

(3) In TALISMAN, the United Kingdom settlement system for equities, the process of transferring effective control of stock from the selling BROKERS to the buying JOBBERS on SETTLEMENT DAY.

delivery month. The month in which a FINANCIAL FUTURES contract matures, resulting in DELIVERY of cash, the specified currency or other financial instrument.

delivery notice. The written notice given by a seller of his intention to make delivery against his open, short futures position on a particular day. *See also* NOTICE DAY.

delivery points. Those physical points designated by financial futures exchanges at which the financial instrument covered by a futures contract may be delivered in fulfilment of such a contract.

delivery settlement price. *See* EXCHANGE DELIVERY SETTLEMENT PRICE.

de minimis non curat lex. A Latin phrase translated as 'the law does not concern itself with small things'. The phrase is often abbreviated to *de minimis,* and in a financial context means small amounts which are exempted from certain pieces of tax legislation because of their trivial size.

denaro (It). The BID price for a particular security.

denaro caldo (It). The availability of short term or sight money for investment on condition that it may be returned at 48 hours notice.

denaro e lettera (It). *See* BID AND ASKED.

Department of Trade and Industry (DTI) (UK). The Department of State in the United Kingdom which has overall responsibility for the securities markets. The Department is responsible, *inter alia,* for issuing licenses to firms to allow them to deal in securities, but exempts those dealers who are members of a recognized stock exchange or dealers' association. In practice, therefore, such organizations have day-to-day control of their members delegated to them by the Department.

depletion accounting (US). A term used in accountancy practice in the United States to describe the method of accounting for the depletion of natural resources. Basically, a charge is made against earnings based on the amount of the resource extracted or used up during the accountancy period.

déport (Fr). *See* BACKWARDATION.

deporto (It). *See* BACKWARDATION.

deposit/deposit set (UK). A term used in the TALISMAN settlement system to cover the lodging of stock by selling BROKERS in preparation for delivery to JOBBERS. The deposit set is the documentation making up the deposit and normally consists of transfer form, certificate and sale docket.

Depository Trust Company (DTC) (US). A central securities certificate depository through which members effect security deliveries between each other by means of computerized book-keeping entries, thereby reducing the physical movement of certificates. The New York Stock Exchange is the major shareholder.

deposit withdrawal (UK). In the TALISMAN settlement system, the withdrawal of a DEPOSIT prior to its being delivered to the purchaser.

dépôt facultatif des titres (Fr). The deposit of securities with brokers as part of the settlement process in the French securities markets. The COMMISSION PEROUSE recommended the replacement of this system by a more general INSCRIPTION EN COMPTE or credit accounting or book entry method.

depreciation. Charges against a company's profits to allow for the loss in value during the accounting period of fixed assets. The amount does not involve a cash transfer, the object of the exercise being to write off the value of the asset in question over its useful life. There are several methods accepted for accounting for depreciation including the straight line method, where a fixed amount a year is written off, and the declining balance method, where a given percentage of the balance remaining is written off each year.

depth (of a market). The extent to which a market can absorb sales or purchases of blocks of stock without moving the price significantly. One of the indicators of market quality used by the New York Stock Exchange to measure performance. NYSE defines market depth as the amount of buying and selling pressure a stock can withstand before its price moves significantly. On this criterion, on a 1000 share trade, prices show no movement or the minimum movement of one-eighth for about 85 percent of deals. *See also* BREADTH; LIQUIDITY.

dernier cours (Fr). Closing price of a security on the BOURSE. Instructions given by an investor to buy or sell at *dernier cours* may only be given on the MARCHÉ À TERME or forward market and not on the MARCHÉ AU COMPTANT or spot market. *See also* PREMIER COURS.

Designated Order Turnaround System (DOTS) (US). An electronic system for small orders introduced on the New York Stock Exchange (NYSE) in 1975. The system deals with orders of up to 599 shares and handles over five million market orders a year. Member firms wishing to deal on DOT transmit the order from their offices to the relevant TRADING POST on the floor of the NYSE. After the order has been executed, the deal is reported back, generally within two minutes.

Deutsche Auslandskassenverein Aktiengesellschaft (AKV) (Ger). A depository set up in 1970 in Frankfurt by the German domestic securities depositories to act as trustee for foreign securities held by foreign banks, to encourage foreign registered equities to seek official trading on the German stock exchanges and to participate in the international clearing of securities.

Devisen-Ausschuss (Ger). The foreign exchange committee of the Frankfurt and Düsseldorf Stock Exchanges.

Devisenkontrolle (Ger). *See* EXCHANGE CONTROL.

dictum meum pactum. The motto of The Stock Exchange in the United Kingdom, meaning 'my word is my bond'.

difference. On the United Kingdom Stock Exchange, the ACCOUNT system enables a short term investor to buy and sell the same securities within the account. The difference is the amount of the cheque which the broker pays to him on SETTLEMENT DAY. Conversely, if the investor is unsuccessful in his dealings, the difference is the amount he has to pay his broker.

difference account. In a FINANCIAL FUTURES transaction, the account rendered to a client by his broker upon the closure of the client's POSITION. *See also* DIFFERENCE.

differential (US). *See* ODD-LOT.

dilution of equity. The 'watering down' of an individual's stake in a company by an issue of new shares from which he is excluded or in which he chooses not to participate. Such dilution can occur as the result, for example, of a PROFIT SHARING issue to employees or the conversion of a CONVERTIBLE STOCK into equity shares. In a RIGHTS ISSUE, existing shareholders, by being offered the chance to subscribe additional cash for more shares pro rata to their existing holding, are given what is called PRE-EMPTIVE RIGHTS which enable them to maintain their percentage stake in the company. To the extent they choose not to take up their rights, however, they will suffer dilution of their equity stake.

direct deposit/withdrawal (UK). A facility in the TALISMAN settlement system available to JOBBERS, MONEY BROKERS and banks whereby they can deposit or withdraw funds direct from their accounts with the settlement centre.

director. One appointed by shareholders to run the affairs of a company. The directors may be either working directors of the company or non-executive directors. The board of directors issues an annual report to its shareholders and recommends to shareholders the rate of dividend a company shall pay.

Director-General of Fair Trading (UK). The head of the OFFICE OF FAIR TRADING. The post was created under the Fair Trading Act of 1973 which, *inter alia,* brought together much of the existing legislation on the monopolies and mergers policy. The Director-General is responsible under the Act for making recommendations to the Secretary of State for Trade and Industry on matters relating to competition in the supply of goods (and services, since 1976). His office is under a duty to collect information on the subject, to establish a register of restrictive trading agreements which are presumed to be against the public interest, unless those party to the agreement prove otherwise, if necessary after the matter has been heard by the Restrictive Practices Court.

The Director-General will recommend action to the Secretary of State in relation to mergers and take-overs, but his recommendations are not binding.

He also has duties relating to the Consumer Credit Act, 1974, including the granting and revocation of licenses under the Act.

director's interest (UK). The extent to which the director of a limited company owns shares in that company. The financial involvement of a director in his company is encouraged as an earnest of his commitment to the company and is closely watched by other shareholders. Directors, by the nature of their position, have much greater knowledge about a company's affairs than the outside shareholders. The directors, therefore, have to be careful about the acquisition and disposal of their shares in case such purchases and sales render them liable to prosecution for INSIDER DEALING under the COMPANIES ACT 1980. The Stock Exchange issued a MODEL CODE FOR DIRECTORS DEALINGS in 1977, which set down guidelines for directors in their share transactions, in order to help protect them from misguided criticism under what was then a non-statutory method of supervision and investigation.

discount. To make allowance for. Applied to share markets when a particular piece of news has already been allowed for in the current share price. Thus good results may be expected from a company, so that when they duly appear the share price might actually fall.

discount, at a. The phrase used to indicate that a share price is standing below its issue price or, in some cases, its nominal value.

discount broker (US). A type of stock broker who appeared in the United States following MAYDAY, 1 May 1975, and the ending of fixed commissions by the New York Stock Exchange. The discount broker offers his clients a basic dealing and execution service but without advice or management of portfolios. For the basic service, the discount broker charges a lower or discounted commission than the FULL SERVICE BROKER. Discount brokers are often used by individual investors and have secured a significant proportion of business in this sector.

discounted cash flow. A method of assessing the return on a capital investment by calculating the present value of cash flows to be received over the life of the investment.

discount house (UK). One of the members of the LONDON DISCOUNT MARKET ASSOCIATION, a group of financial companies in the City of London which specializes in the buying and selling of short term government and commercial paper, providing funds to the borrowers and using funds borrowed from the banks and other members of the monetary sector. The discount houses are a unique feature of the financial system in London and play a central role in the monetary control arrangements operated by the Bank of England. The discount houses have, since the late 19th century, been intermediaries between the commercial banks on the one hand and the central bank, the Bank of England, on the other. It has been through the medium of the discount houses that the Bank has alleviated cash and liquidity shortages in the banking system. Such a shortage would first show itself by the action of the banks demanding the return of their money at call and short notice, which they had placed with the discount houses on a secured basis. In order to raise the funds needed to cover their holdings of short term financial assets, the houses are able to turn to the Bank of England.

The Bank always makes the funds available, but at rates of its own choosing, rates which reflect the way the Bank wishes to see interest rates move generally. In the past, the rate at which the Bank lent might have been the penal Bank Rate (Minimum Lending Rate between October 1972 and August 1981 and now in abeyance) or at market rates.

During the Competition and Credit Control regime of 1971-81, money placed by the banking institutions with the discount houses was an eligible reserve asset without limit. In return, the discount houses undertook to keep certain ratios of their funds in public sector assets.

Since August 1981, under the amended system of monetary control then introduced, the banking institutions are obliged to keep a specified amount of their funds with the discount houses, while the Bank of England continues to operate through the discount houses when it wishes to influence interest rates in the money markets. The Bank now does this primarily by buying commercial bills from the discount houses, at rates specified by the Bank, when it wishes to relieve a shortage of funds rather than lending through the discount window.

In the securities markets, the discount houses are major holders of SHORT GILTS, which they hold as income earning assets. Their gilt edged assets are generally of less than five years to maturity, although in periods of volatile interst rates even such short gilts have, on occasions, caused heavy capital losses to the houses if rates have suddenly and unexpectedly risen sharply.

BIBLIOGRAPHY E.R. Shaw, *The London Money Markets* (Heinemann, London, 3rd edition, 1981). 'Monetary control - provisions' *Bank of England Quarterly Bulletin*, September 1981, pp 347-350.

discount market (UK). *See* LONDON MONEY MARKETS; DISCOUNT HOUSE.

discretionary account. *See* DISCRETIONARY FUNDS.

discretionary funds. Amounts of money placed with stockbrokers by investors, leaving the broker to decide on the distribution of the investments. Normally the broker will carry out the deals for discretionary clients and inform them afterwards of the nature of the deal and the reasons for it. The Stock Exchange lays down guidelines for its member firms dealing with discretionary funds. The COUNCIL FOR THE SECURITIES INDUSTRY lays down in a Code of Conduct for Dealers in Securities that a dealer managing clients' funds (whether or not on a discretionary basis) should set out in writing his terms and conditions for managing such funds, which include the fees to be charged, the arrangements for the custody of cash and securities, for the payment of interest on uninvested balances and for the reporting to the client of transactions and valuations.

dissolution. The winding up of a company or a partnership. In the case of a company, the winding up will be by due process of law as described in COMPULSORY LIQUIDATION or VOLUNTARY LIQUIDATION.

A partnership may be wound up by the retirement or death of one of the partners, by his giving notice of intention to withdraw, his bankruptcy or simply at the end of an agreed period.

distributed profits. Profits paid out by way of dividend to shareholders. *See also* DIVIDEND; ADVANCE CORPORATION TAX.

distribution. Used in the United Kingdom in two contexts (1) dividend payments, where such payments may be referred to as a distribution or dividend distribution.

(2) A SCRIP ISSUE or RIGHTS ISSUE may also be called a distribution or share distribution.

(3) (US) *See* PRIMARY DISTRIBUTION; SECONDARY DISTRIBUTION.

diversification. (1) The spreading of a portfolio among a number of different investments to offset some of the risk of direct shareholding.

(2) The buying by a company of another with activities in an area different from that of

the acquiring company. Alternatively, the establishment by a company of a new activity. In all cases, the objective is to offset the risks and/or a cyclical nature of profits in the area of activity in which the company is currently engaged.

dividend. The amount paid out by a company to the holders of its preference, ordinary and deferred shares. Being the risk capital of the business these equity shares rank for dividend only after the interest on loan capital has been paid. Dividends are declared by the directors of a company and voted on by shareholders in general meeting. In the United Kingdom, the shareholders can vote to accept a recommended dividend or reduce it, they cannot vote to increase the recommendation of the directors.

Dividends in the United Kingdom are declared and paid on a net basis, with an appropriate TAX CREDIT. If a shareholder is not a taxpayer, he may reclaim the tax credit. If he pays tax at higher than basic rate he must account to the tax authorities for the difference in due course. *See also* ADVANCE CORPORTION TAX; DISTRIBUTED PROFITS; INTERIM DIVIDEND.

dividend cheque. The cheque payable to the shareholder in respect of the dividend declared by the company. *See also* DIVIDEND WARRANT.

dividend control (UK). An order by the government to freeze or restrain the growth of dividends paid by a company. The measure was used as part of a general restraint on prices and incomes at various times during the 1960s and 1970s in the United Kingdom but was abandoned in 1979.

dividend cover. *See* COVER.

dividende (Fr and Ger). *See* DIVIDEND.

dividende intérimaire (Fr). *See* INTERIM DIVIDEND.

Dividendenstop (Ger). *See* DIVIDEND CONTROL.

dividend exclusion (US). The small amount (currently $100) of annual dividend on which investors do not have to pay Federal (national) taxes. Also the extent to which a company receiving dividends does not have to pay further tax on them. *See also* FRANKED INCOME.

dividend mandate (UK). The authority signed by a shareholder instructing the company's registrar to pay the due dividends direct to a bank account.

dividendo (It). *See* DIVIDEND.

dividendo semestrale (It). Half-yearly dividend.

dividend warrant (UK). The document by means of which a dividend is passed to shareholders. It consists of two parts, a cheque payable to the shareholder and a counterfoil giving details of the amount of the dividend per share, the total number of shares held, the amount of TAX CREDIT allowed and the amount of the net payment due to the shareholder.

dividend yield. The amount of the annual dividend expressed as a percentage of the current price of the share. *See also* EARNINGS YIELD.

division d'action (Fr). *See* SPLIT.

document. Written evidence of entitlement to property or a benefit from it. A generic term which, in stock market terminology, would include CERTIFICATES, DIVIDEND WARRANTS, LETTERS OF ALLOTMENT etc.

dollar bond (US). An issue of bonds on the US capital markets by an overseas borrower. Also referred to as a YANKEE BOND.

dollar certificate of deposit. *See* CERTIFICATE OF DEPOSIT.

dollar cost averaging (US). The American term for AVERAGING.

dollar premium (UK). *See* INVESTMENT CURRENCY PREMIUM.

dont (It). *See* CALL OPTION.

dopo borso (It). The period following the close of the stock exchange trading session, during which deals may continue to be made.

Doppelbesteuerungsnachlass / Doppelbesteuerungserleichterung (Ger). Double taxation relief.

double bottom. An expression used in the TECHNICAL ANALYSIS of stock market trends to indicate that the price of a stock has, for a second time in a short period, reached the same low point and has then turned upwards again. Sometimes also referred to as a W formation, because of the shape of its pattern, the significance of which could therefore lead to an overall improvement in the price trend.

double option. The right either to buy or to sell shares at a future date at a specified price. *See also* PUT OPTION; CALL OPTION; TRADED OPTION.

double prime (Fr). *See* STELLAGE.

double taxation relief. The relief given to holders of securities whereby the tax authorities in the country of the recipient give relief on income to the extent that it has already borne tax in the country of origin. Double taxation relief is given only in respect of income arising in countries with which a double taxation treaty has been negotiated.

double top. An expression used in technical analysis to describe the pattern of a share price which has reached a second peak at a level similar to an earlier one, but has not exceeded it. The significance of a double top is that the price may then begin to show a downward trend. It is also sometimes referred to as an inverted W formation.

Dow Jones Industrial Average (US). One of the widely quoted share indices in the United States; it consists, like the FINANCIAL TIMES INDUSTRIAL ORDINARY INDEX in the United Kingdom, of 30 shares. In addition to the industrial average, there are also averages for transportation stocks, utilities and a composite index which, as its name implies, is an amalgam of the others. The transportation index covers 20 railway, airline and trucking (road haulage) stocks, the utilities index consists of 15 stocks, while the composite includes all 65. The averages are not weighted according to market capitalizations, but are calculated simply on price changes. *See also* NEW YORK STOCK EXCHANGE COMMON STOCK INDICES; STANDARD AND POORS 500 INDEX.

down tick (US). A term used to describe a transaction made at a price lower than the previous transaction. To signify such a move, a minus sign would be displayed alongside the price of the security at the TRADING POST on the NYSE floor. *See also* UP TICK.

Dow Theory (US). A theory of stock market analysis based upon the performance of the DOW JONES INDUSTRIAL AVERAGE and the transportation average. The theory says that the market is on an upward trend if one of these averages advances above a previous important high, accompanied or followed by a similar advance in the other. When the averages dip below important lows, this is regarded as confirmation of a downward trend. This approach to analysis may also be applied to other market indices and averages.

Dow Theory divides price movements into three parts: a primary trend, the long term cyclical movement of prices which may last several years; a secondary movement of shorter duration around this trend and, finally, the day-to-day fluctuations. This latter is unimportant in Dow Theory. What is important is the movement of the secondary trend. If a downward secondary movement halts and then reverses at a level higher than an earlier reversal, the primary trend is judged to be continuing upwards. A similar conclusion is reached if the secondary trend peaks at a higher level than previously.

A further important factor is the interrelationship between the industrial and transportation averages. One must confirm the other: one moving on its own is insufficient and may give incorrect signals to investors. Dow Theory, like all technical analysis, has its firm adherents as well as attracting scepticism from other analysts.

drawing. The act of selecting which bonds will be repaid in an issue where it is laid down that repayment will be made on such a basis.

drawn bond. A fixed interest security which has been drawn by lot for repayment.

droit attaché (Fr). *See* CUM DIVIDEND.

droit de souscription (Fr). *See* RIGHTS ISSUE.

droit de timbre (Fr). Stamp duty. *See also* IMPÔT DE BOURSE.

drop lock loans (UK). A type of loan stock issued by companies which is used to convert short term borrowing into long term loans when interest rates reach a pre-determined level.

dual capacity. The ability of stockbrokers to act both as agents for investors and as principals, buying and selling on their own books. In order to protect the investor in any conflict of interest which the broker/dealer may face in such a structure, rules for full disclosure of the capacity in which the broker is acting are necessary. In addition, information on the prices in the market at the time the trade was made should be available in order to verify that the deal was done at the best possible price for the client.

In the United Kingdom, a system of SINGLE CAPACITY has been rigorously enforced in the past, keeping the roles of the BROKER as agent and the JOBBER as principal quite separate. This situation is likely to change over the next few years.

BIBLIOGRAPHY *The Stock Exchange, A Discussion Paper* (April 1984). *The Choice of a New Dealing System for Equities* (The Stock Exchange, London, July 1984).

durante (It). Additional price fixings and bargains made during the trading session other than the official opening and closing dealings in the main trading rings.

durée (Fr). *See* MATURITY.

E

early deposit (UK). The deposit with the TALISMAN settlement centre of stock by selling brokers in advance of settlement day. The stock is held in trust until delivery on the settlement day.

earnings per share (EPS). The amount of annual profit or earnings attributable to each ordinary share, after tax, interest on loan stock and other borrowings and dividends on preference shares have been paid. Earnings may be either distributed as dividends or retained for future use in the business.

earnings report (US). A statement, sometimes also referred to as an income statement, showing a company's earnings or its losses over a given period. The United Kingdom equivalent is the PROFIT AND LOSS ACCOUNT. *See also* BALANCE SHEET.

earnings yield. The ratio of EARNINGS PER SHARE after allowing for tax and interest payments on fixed interest debt, to the current share price. The inverse of the PRICE EARNINGS RATIO. *See also* YIELD, DIVIDEND YIELD.

easier. Used to describe a market in which prices are tending to fall.

écart (Fr). The SPREAD; the difference between the buying and selling prices quoted by a dealer in a stock.

échéance (Fr). The date on which a coupon attached to a bond falls due for payment. Also the maturity date of the loan itself.

Effectenclearing BV (NL). The Dutch securities clearing organization maintained by the Amsterdam Stock Exchange. Delivery and receipt of stock can take place without physical delivery through this system.

effective date (US). The date, normally 20 days after the filing of a REGISTRATION statement with the SEC, when distribution of a security can be made.

Efficient Market Hypothesis (EMH). The Efficient Market Hypothesis says that given full access to all information, the market's current price of a share is the best estimate of future returns. Markets are said to be efficient if share prices adjust quickly to information. There are said to be three levels, or degrees, of efficiency against which it is possible to test securities markets statistically to assess their degree of efficiency. These three are weak form, semi-strong form and strong form. A market is said to show weak form efficiency when prices in the market fully reflect all past price changes. To achieve semi-strong form efficiency, prices must reflect all publicly available information about the shares, while strong form efficiency is not achieved until prices reflect all information about a company whether publicly available or not.

The Efficient Market Hypothesis has its origins in the RANDOM WALK theory of share price movements, which argues that future price movements are independent of past changes and that the most likely estimate of tomorrow's prices are the levels they are today.

The EMH, because it suggests that investors cannot systematically and scientifically beat the market, has caused much controversy since it might be extended to show that investment research cannot help investors achieve above average rates of return, after allowing for risk. Thus, if the market is only weak form efficient, meaning that future price movements are independent of past changes, there would appear to be little scope for CHARTIST or DOW THEORY methods of research, which are based on share prices establishing particular patterns which can be used to predict future price changes to investors' advantage.

In its semi-strong form, the EMH, suggesting that current share prices reflect all publicly available information, calls into question the benefits of fundamental research, based on the interpretation and analysis of known data about a company.

There has been much research carried out on various markets to test the EMH. Much of this research has been based on US stock market prices, although some work on UK prices and, to a lesser extent, European markets, has also been undertaken. The proponents of the EMH are convinced that their research shows US and UK markets in particular to be semi-strong form efficient. Many securities markets analysts disagree.

BIBLIOGRAPHY Simon Keane, *Efficient Market Hypothesis* (Philip Allan, Oxford, 1983). Janette Rutterford, *Introduction to Stock Exchange Investment* (Macmillan, London, 1983), Chapter 9.

Effekten (Ger). Marketable securities, including both bonds and shares.

effeti (It). *See* SECURITIES.

Einführung an der Börse (Ger). The granting of a new listing on a German Stock Exchange. In order to obtain such a listing, which must be for a minimum of Dm500,000, the company will, through a syndicate of issuing houses, submit an application to the listings committee or ZULASSUNGSSTELLE of the exchange on which the listing is being sought. The listings committee requires a prospectus, *Einführungsprospekt*, which has to include information on the history of the company, its directors, its finances and trading record on an up-to-date basis.

Einführungsprospekt (Ger). *See* EINFÜHRUNG AN DER BÖRSE.

Einheitskurs (Ger). The single price quotation system of dealing on a German exchange. This is just one of the systems employed and may be compared with the continuous quotation market, VARIABLER KURS. The Einheitskurs is established by the MAKLER who fixes the price of each security for each trading session, in relation to supply and demand. The *Makler* attempt, in fixing the price, to maximize the turnover in the stock. Trading on the basis of this price takes place once a day at approximately 11:45 am.

Einschuss (Ger). *See* PAID UP CAPITAL.

Electronic Audit Trail (US). A system being introduced by the New York Stock Exchange to capture and record all details of all transactions as a data base for the automatic surveillance of dealings.

Electronic Price Information Computer (EPIC) (UK). A system designed by the Stock Exchange, London, for the electronic distribution of prices in computer readable form and via the Stock Exchange's closed circuit television system, TOPIC.

émission (Fr). The issue of new shares.

emissione (It). The issue of new shares.

émission sous droit de souscription (Fr). *See* RIGHTS ISSUE.

Emissionspreis (Ger). The offer of a new issue.

Emissionsprospekt (Ger). The prospectus for a new issue.

Emissionssyndikat (Ger). A syndicate of banks acting together for the purpose of handling a new issue of securities.

émittent (Fr). A bank handling a new share issue.

Employee Retirement Income Security Act (ERISA) (US). An Act passed by Congress in 1974 to help those employees not covered by profit sharing schemes or tax allowable pension schemes, to save for retirement. The law allowed such employees to set up

INDIVIDUAL RETIREMENT ACCOUNTS (IRA). The Act was amended in 1982 to allow all employees to take advantage of IRA, and such accounts, offered by banks, stockbrokers and other financial institutions, became very popular.

A further provision of the 1974 legislation laid a duty on pension fund trustees to monitor the performance of their fund managers. This has led to the development of analyses of investment performance to help trustees satisfy the requirements of the Act.

Employee Stock Ownership Plan (ESOP) (US) The major vehicle in the United States for profit sharing by employees in the companies for which they work. Employee Stock Ownership Plans spring from legislation passed by Congress in 1974. A company introducing an ESOP subscribes cash for common stock (shares) of the company which are deposited with a trust for the benefit of all participating employees. The stock does not immediately become the property of the employees but is vested with them gradually over ten or fifteen years. All full time employees of a company introducing an ESOP must be able to participate and schemes must be drawn up in a way which does not give greater proportionate benefit to the higher paid employees, although it is permissable to allot stock in proportion to levels of salary.

Stock put into the trust is a tax allowable expense for the company and is not taxable in the trust.

When the stock is vested with the employees it is either taxed as a capital gain, not income, or it can be placed, without tax penalty, into an INVESTMENT RETIREMENT ACCOUNT (IRA) where it will be taxed only as it is drawn out. *See also* EMPLOYEE RETIREMENT INCOME SECURITY ACT (ERISA).

BIBLIOGRAPHY *ESOPS : An Employer Handbook* (US Senate Committee on Finance (Washington, 1979). *Employee Ownership: A Handbook.* (National Center for Employee Ownership, Arlington, Va., 1982). Thomas Marsh and Dale McAllister, ESOPS Tables; A Survey of Companies with Employee Stock Ownership Plans, *Journal of Corporation Law* (Spring 1981). Corey Rosen, 'Employee Stock Ownership Plans: a new way to work', *Business Horizons* (September-October 1983).

emprunt (Fr). *See* LOAN STOCK.

emprunt indexé (Fr). *See* INDEX LINKED STOCK.

enfranchisement. The granting to shareholders of NON-VOTING SHARES the right to vote in future. Issues of non-voting shares were made to allow outside investors to buy and thereby share in the profits, but the control of the company remained in the hands of the founders or original shareholders who held the voting shares. In recent years, investors, particularly the large institutional investors, have brought pressure to bear on companies with such issues outstanding to grant the right to vote. Many have done so, although a few non-voting issues remain.

En Nom-Beteiligung (Ger). Participation by a bank in a new issue of securities.

en soignant (Fr). An order placed by a client through an agent to buy or sell securities at discretion. A type of flexible LIMIT ORDER in which the agent will adjust the number of shares in the order according to the availability of shares on the market at that price.

en souffrance (Fr). In arrears. A term applied to loans or interest payments which are unpaid on the due date.

equazione or ***equivalenza borsa*** (It). The expression used to describe a situation when an investor resorts to more than one transaction in order to achieve a desired result. For example, instead of a STELLAGE (put) option for 50 shares, one buys a call option for 100 shares and also executes a forward sale for 50 shares.

equipment trust certificate (US). A type of security, usually issued by a rail company, to pay for equipment. Title to this specific equipment, such as a locomotive, is held by a trustee until the notes are paid off. An equipment trust certificate is usually secured by a first claim on the equipment itself.

equity. (1) The ordinary share capital of a company as distinct from its LOAN CAPITAL. The equity is the risk capital of the company; its owners, the shareholders, are the owners of the company, having the right to elect the directors and share in the profits by way of dividend. *See also* ORDINARY SHARES, DEFERRED SHARES, NON-VOTING SHARES.

(2) In the United States, in addition to having a meaning similar to that above, equity also refers to the value of securities or COMMON STOCK over the debit balance in a MARGIN account.

(3) On the FINANCIAL FUTURES markets, equity is the residual value of the total INITIAL MARGIN and VARIATION MARGIN assuming the LIQUIDATION of the contract at the current market price. It is possible for the equity to be either positive or negative at any one time, depending upon the success of the contract.

Equity Capital for Industry (ECI) (UK). A body formed in 1976 to subscribe additional risk funds for British industry. ECI's funds were subscribed by a variety of large financial institutions such as pension funds and insurance companies, investment and unit trusts. The initial capital of ECI was £41m and was intended to help small and medium sized companies unable to raise equity capital elsewhere. After a life of seven years, it was merged along with FINANCE FOR INDUSTRY into a new grouping, INVESTORS IN INDUSTRY, in 1983.

Eröffnungskurs (Ger). The opening price of a stock at a trading session.

esclusione dalla borsa (It). To exclude an operator from the trading floor of an Italian stock exchange for reasons of insolvency.

escompter (Fr). To discount. In stock market terms to mark down a price in anticipation of an event.

escrow account (US). The term used to designate an account which is held by a third party until both of the principals have carried out their sides of the bargain. An escrow account, for example, was opened with the Bank of England to deal with Iranian assets frozen by the US government during the negotiations for the release of the American hostages held in Teheran in 1980.

esecuzione coattiva di borsa (It). A special settlement procedure adopted by a stock exchange in the case of the insolvency of an operator.

eseguito (It). The communication to the client confirming that his transaction has been carried out.

essere una barca (It). *See* BARCA.

Estate Duty (UK). For many years the tax on the estate of a deceased individual, estate duty was replaced in 1975 by CAPITAL TRANSFER TAX.

estratto (It). Refers to a DRAWN BOND which must be reimbursed at or above the nominal value, according to the rules established for the issue.

estrazione (It). The act of drawing the numbers of an issue for reimbursement. *See* DRAWN BOND.

eurobond. A medium and long term interest bearing issue made on the international capital markets and denominated in a currency other than that of the centre in which it is being issued. Eurobonds are issued by governments, other public bodies and companies of international standing.

Euroclear. One of the two major clearing systems for the EUROBOND market, Euroclear was set up in Brussels in 1968 by Morgan Guaranty Trust Company. In addition to providing clearing, accounting and coupon collecting services, Euroclear also helps provide liquidity in the eurobond market through finance made available by Morgan Guaranty. Finance is made available to dealers in the market on the basis of the security provided by the securities held by the dealers or on the basis of bank guarantee.

eurocurrency. The term used to describe a currency which is held by a depositor in a bank outside the country of origin of that currency. Thus eurocurrencies may be dollars held in an account with a bank in London, Deutsche Mark held via Switzerland, or yen held in New York. Eurocurrencies, more particularly eurodollars, have their origins in the 1950s when communist governments of eastern Europe feared that their dollar balances held in the United States might be blocked by the American authorities. They therefore transferred their balances to banks in London. The countries still had the use of the dollars, the bank in London now held the balance of dollars, so payments could not be blocked and the banks discovered two other things. First, there were borrowers who wished to borrow those dollars and second, they could afford to give depositors a more favourable rate of interest than could American banks in the United States. This was because of the Federal Reserve System's REGULATION Q which fixed a maximum rate of interest which could be paid on deposits. Because individual deposits and advances were large, finer rates could be quoted and the market developed rapidly, attracting many US and other banks to London, which was the main centre for the eurocurrency markets. Other centres, such as Zurich, Paris and the Far East, have now also developed.

In recent years, the eurocurrency market grew rapidly following the oil price increases of 1973 and 1979. Those oil exporting countries frequently chose to invest their surplus funds at short term in the eurocurrency markets, where they acquired the name 'petrodollars'. These balances, deposited with banks throughout the world, were on-lent, often to the less developed countries whose balance of payments had been severely hit by the oil price rise itself. The extra funds they had had to use to pay for the oil were thus re-cycled back to them. However, these loans were often at short notice and at fluctuating rates of interest. Such was the ease with which many countries were able to borrow that many eventually found themselves unable to meet the interest payments, let alone pay back any of the capital.

Since many of the loans were placed on a short term basis, any demand from lenders for repayment could place the borrowing countries under severe difficulty. In the early 1980s, arrangements had to be made, first with the commercial banks themselves, then with the International Monetary Fund, to roll over these loans to prevent any country defaulting on its debts. Such default would have been disastrous for the world's banking systems and for the economic welfare of developed, as well as developing, countries.

The International Monetary Fund has become concerned about the growth of eurodollars because of their short term, volatile nature and also because of the lack of effective control by the national monetary authorities.

European Options Exchange (EOE). A market for TRADED OPTIONS in a number of European securities established in Amsterdam in 1978. Modelled on the CHICAGO BOARD OPTIONS EXCHANGE it is recognized as a stock exchange under Dutch law and is a TRADING POST on the floor of the Amsterdam Stock Exchange. The European Options Exchange trades gold and silver options as well as options in specified currencies and securities. *See also* TRADED OPTIONS.

evening up. The buying or selling of a futures contract to cancel or offset an existing market position. *See also* BUY IN.

ex. A Latin term literally meaning 'from' or 'out of'. Widely used in the securities markets to denote that a security is being sold without a benefit which has been announced, such as a dividend, a rights or a capitalization issue.

ex acconto (It). Without right to the interim dividend.

***ex* all.** A share sold without rights to any or all declared benefit(s).

***ex* capitalization (*ex* cap).** Indicates that a share has been sold without the right to the capitalization, or SCRIP ISSUE, which has been announced.

ex cedola (It). *See* EX COUPON.

excess shares (UK). In a RIGHTS ISSUE, those shares not taken up by the original allottees and which may be bid for by other holders who would like more shares than they have been allocated under the rights issue.

exchange. An abbreviated version of stock exchange or other market for financial securities. The plural, exchanges, however, often refers to the currency exchange markets but can also be used to refer collectively to stock markets throughout the world.

exchange control. The set of rules introduced by governments to prevent, hinder or just make more expensive, the ability of their residents to invest in other countries and, occasionally, to restrict the inward flow of investment. Most countries now allow free movement of funds for ordinary trade and commerce, so-called current account items, since that is where such trade would appear in the country's balance of payments statistics. Many still place restrictions on the free movement of capital, whether to set up plant and machinery or to buy shares in overseas companies. One exception to this is the United Kingdom where, since October 1979, residents have been free to invest anywhere in the world without penalty. The Exchange Control Act 1947, which previously limited such investment, has not been repealed, its provisions merely put into abeyance. *See also* INVESTMENT CURRENCY PREMIUM.

Exchange Delivery Settlement Price (EDSP). In a FINANCIAL FUTURES market, the price determined by PIT TRADING and, in the case of LONDON INTERNATIONAL FINANCIAL FUTURES EXCHANGE, short term interest rate contracts selected average quotations by banks against which OPEN CONTRACTS posted for delivery through the CLEARING HOUSE, are settled.

Exchange Equalization Account (UK). A fund set up in 1932 as a department of the Treasury, but operated by the Bank of England, to smooth out fluctuations in the sterling exchange rate against other currencies. When sterling was on a fixed rate system the Account was used to keep it within the internationally agreed limits by buying sterling to support the rate when commercial and speculative pressures were driving it down. When other pressures were causing it to rise, a rather less common occurrence, the Account was used to sell sterling to moderate the increase. Since sterling was floated in June 1972, the Account has been the vehicle through which the authorities act when wanting to initiate or resist a particular market movement but changes are not now required to meet international agreements.

exchange fee. *See* TRANSACTION CHARGES.

exchange for physicals (EFP). The offer by a financial futures broker to execute simultaneously a cash and a futures transaction, in opposite directions, at a fixed price differential.

exchange rate futures. A FINANCIAL FUTURES contract in which the FINANCIAL INSTRUMENT on which the contract is written is a given amount of a specified foreign currency. The objective of an exchange rate futures contract is to help protect the buyer against an adverse movement in that currency. For example, a trader knows that he will have a certain amount of a foreign currency coming to him in, say, three months' time. He fears that because of exchange rate fluctuations he might receive less in terms of his domestic currency in three months than he would if he had the foreign currency to convert now. In that case he would sell exchange rate futures contracts now in that currency. If his fears are justified, the hedger will, when he actually receives the foreign currency, convert it into his domestic currency at the then going rate, but he will also be able to sell his futures contract at a profit, thus helping to offset the poorer rate of exchange he has received.

On the other hand, if his fears proved ill founded, and the exchange rate had moved in his favour by the time he received the foreign currency, he would receive an unexpected bonus from the exchange but would have suffered an offsetting loss on his futures contract.

The object of an exchange rate futures contract, as with an INTEREST RATE FUTURES contract, is to offset the uncertainty of market movements.

***ex* coupon.** A stock sold without right to the next interest payment due.

***ex* dividend (*ex* div).** A share sold without the right to the recently declared dividend payable to holders on the share register at a particular date some short time in the future. To avoid confusion, stock exchanges declare a particular day on and after which the shares are traded without rights to the dividend. For example, in New York a stock is dealt *ex* dividend from the day five days before that declared by the company as the cut-off date. If a company declared that a dividend will be payable to shareholders registered on a particular Friday, for example, the stock will be dealt *ex* dividend as from the preceding Monday. This is to take account of the fact that the New York settlement rules specify that settlement takes place five days after the deal has been made.

ex dividendo (It). *See* EX DIVIDEND.

ex divitto (It). *See* EX RIGHTS.

***ex* drawing.** A bond sold on the basis that it will not participate in the next drawing for repayment. *See* DRAWN BOND.

execution. The completion of a deal; a TRADE or BARGAIN.

exempt dealers (UK). A term used in the PREVENTION OF FRAUD (INVESTMENTS) ACT 1958 to designate those bodies whose dealers are exempt from the provisions of the Act. They include banks and recognized associations of dealers, as well as stockbrokers who are members of the Stock Exchange in the United Kingdom. They are exempt because they are subject to other rules and disciplines which give adequate protection to the investors using their services.

exercise an option. To convert an option into the UNDERLYING SECURITY at the agreed price in the case of a CALL OPTION. Conversely, to demand that the WRITER of a PUT OPTION takes the underlying security at the agreed price

exercise date. The fixed date upon which an OPTIONS CONTRACT may be converted into the UNDERLYING SECURITY. Traded options are usually available for expiry dates three, six and nine months ahead.

exercise notice. A formal notification that the holder of a CALL OPTION wishes to buy the UNDERLYING SECURITY at the EXERCISE PRICE. Alternatively, the notification that the holder of a PUT OPTION wishes to sell.

exercise price. The price per share at which the buyer of a CALL OPTION may buy the UNDERLYING SECURITY. Conversely, the price per share which the buyer of a PUT OPTION may obtain for the underlying security.

***ex* new.** *See* EX RIGHTS and EX SCRIP.

ex optione (It). *See* EX RIGHTS and EX SCRIP.

expiry date. The last date upon which an option may be exercised or traded. Also known as the exercise date. *See also* EXERCISE AN OPTION.

exportation de capital (Fr). The outflow of capital by way of real or PORTFOLIO INVESTMENT in other countries.

***ex* rights.** Shares not having the benefit of an impending RIGHTS ISSUE.

ex saldo (It). Without right to the final dividend.

***ex* scrip.** Shares not having the right to participate in an impending SCRIP ISSUE.

external debt. The amount owed collectively by a country to outsiders.

extra (US). An abbreviation for extra dividend. A term used in the United States to describe a dividend which may be paid in cash or by way of extra stock in addition to the normal dividend.

extraordinary general meeting (EGM). A meeting called to discuss special business of a company. Such a meeting may be summoned by the directors or by shareholders owning ten percent of the shares with voting rights.

extraordinary resolution. A resolution of which prior notice has been given may be discussed at a company meeting but, to succeed, must have the support of 75 percent of those voting, either in person or by proxy.

F

face value. Sometimes referred to as nominal or PAR value, face value is the term used to describe the value of a bond in terms of what the company will repay when the loan matures.

faible (Fr). A general downward movement in, or weakening of, stock market prices.

fail position (US). A failure to deliver or receive stock. The phrase is used to describe the situation where stock market transactions cannot be settled because the seller has not delivered the stock to his broker who is unable therefore to pass it to the buyer.

failure. *See* INSOLVENCY.

Fälligkeit (Ger). *See* MATURITY.

Fannie Mae (US). The colloquial name for the FEDERAL NATIONAL MORTGAGE ASSOCIATION (FNMA) and in the plural (Fannie Maes) for securities issued by it.

Far Eastern Stock Exchange (HK). One of the four Stock Exchanges currently operating in Hong Kong, the Far Eastern Stock Exchange (FESE) was established as recently as 1969 and stimulated the establishment in the early 1970s of two further exchanges in the territory. The FESE is now the largest of the four exchanges in terms of turnover.

Many companies have their stock listed on more than one exchange and although individuals cannot be members of more than one exchange, company brokerage firms may trade on all four.

Moves are now afoot which should lead to the amalgamation of the four exchanges into a single exchange in the relatively near future. *See also* HONG KONG STOCK EXCHANGE, KAM NGAN STOCK EXCHANGE, KOWLOON STOCK EXCHANGE.

Far East Index (FEI) (HK). One of the three stock market indices relating to shares in the Hong Kong markets, the other two being the HONG KONG INDEX and the KAM NGAN INDEX. The Far East Index covers 52 stocks traded on the Far Eastern Stock Exchange, about 25 percent of the total. Each stock is weighted in relation to the number of shares traded over the preceding five years. There are nine sub-indices of the Far East Index, covering land and construction, commercial and industrial, textiles, utilities, banks, shipping, hotels, docks and investment services. In addition to the price index, the Far East Index also shows average YIELD and PRICE-EARNINGS RATIO for the stocks it covers.

The Far East Index was based on a figure of 1000 at 1st April 1971.

BIBLIOGRAPHY Paul H. and Laurie J. Aron, 'The Asian Equities Markets' in Abraham M. George and Ian H. Giddy (eds.), *International Finance Handbook* (Wiley, New York, 1983), section 6.9.

fare (la) coda 'accordarsi' (It). Literal meaning: to get into line. *See* ACCORDARSI.

fare (una) cravatta (It). *See* CRAVATTA.

fare denaro (It). *See* DENARO.

fare lettera (It). *See* LETTERA.

fare media (It). *See* AVERAGING.

fattore di rettifica (It). The necessary adjustment to the price of a security following a capital increase etc, made in order to be able to compare current and previous prices.

features. Those securities or sectors of the market which, in the course of a day's trading, have been particularly active and subject to large rises or falls in their prices.

Federal Cartel Office (Ger). The German Government department which is officially responsible for supervising changes in the control of companies. The German legislation against restraint of trade lays down that the Federal Cartel Office must be notified of any major take-over or merger plans and the Office may object to them.

federal funds (US). The excess funds of banks in the United States which are available for overnight lending to others who are short of funds. The federal funds rate, at which these amounts are placed, is one of the most closely watched indicators of money market and financial conditions.

Federal Home Loan Mortgage Corporation (FHLMC) (US). Performs a function for normal residential mortgages similar to that provided for Federal Housing Administration mortgages by the FEDERAL NATIONAL MORTGAGE ASSOCIATION. The FHLMS provides support for the market by buying mortgages from its members, providing the support of its guarantee and selling them on to other investors. Colloquially known as Freddie Mae.

Federal National Mortgage Association (FNMA) (US). A federal agency established in the United States in 1938 to create a SECONDARY MARKET in mortgages issued by the Federal Housing Administration. Originally wholly government-owned, the Association was split into three parts in 1954 and FNMA became part privately owned. In 1968 the FNMA became wholly privately owned and retained its function of providing liquidity, with special assistance loans going to the GOVERNMENT NATIONAL MORTGAGE ASSOCIATION (GNMA).

The main function of FNMA is to buy government-insured and guaranteed mortgages when the supply of mortgage funds is low and to sell them when the demand for new mortgages falls and supply is relatively plentiful in relation to demand.

FNMA raises its funds by the issue of short term notes, the interest rate on which is related to the U.S. Treasury bill rate. It also issues longer term debentures which are bearer instruments of $10,000 and $25,000, in which there is a good secondary market. Colloquially known as Fannie Mae.

Federal Reserve System (US). The central banking system of the United States, set up in 1913. The System consists of the Board of Governors, the Federal Reserve Board, situated in Washington D.C., which acts, along with its various committees, including the Federal Open Market Committee, as the central decision-making authority. In addition, there are twelve Federal Reserve districts, each of which has its own Federal Reserve Bank, to carry out day-to-day central banking operations for the member banks in their areas.

From the securities markets' viewpoint, the Federal Reserve System is important in that it fixes the minimum MARGIN requirements which must be met for the purchase of securities on credit under REGULATION T.

Fédération Internationale des Bourses de Valeurs (FIBV) (Fr). An informal group of the world's stock exchanges which was formed in 1961 to provide a forum within which common problems could be discussed and ideas formulated for the promotion of securities markets worldwide. The FIBV has its headquarters in Paris. It initiates and co-ordinates much research work on stock markets, bringing together the facts and experience of exchanges in different parts of the world.

fee. A fixed charge made for a service; often used in contrast to COMMISSION, which varies with the value of the deal.

fermé (Fr). A tendency of stock market prices to rise.

fermo (It). (1) Used in reference to a market tendency, the word means 'bullish'.

(2) Referring to a transaction, it means a forward deal for the stockmarket account which, in Italy, is of one month's duration.

fest (Ger). The German equivalent of FERMÉ.

festverzinslich (Ger). Fixed interest.

feuille de coupons (Fr). *See* COUPON SHEET.

fidelity bond (US). An amount of insurance which all brokers must take out to protect against loss, forgery and fraudulent trading by members and staff.

fiduciary. Held, kept or issued in trust.

filiale (It). *See* SUBSIDIARY COMPANY.

fill or kill. (1) (US) A term used on stock markets to indicate that if an order cannot be transacted at once it is to be withdrawn and not to be left with the market.

(2) On FINANCIAL FUTURES markets, an order which has been offered or bid in the PIT three times and is then cancelled if not executed at once.

final accounts. The annual accounts, notably the profit and loss account and balance sheet, drawn up at the end of a company's FINANCIAL YEAR. The final accounts are audited by a firm of independent auditors who present a report on them to the company's shareholders. *See also* ANNUAL REPORT AND ACCOUNTS, QUALIFIED ACCOUNTS.

final dividend. The dividend paid by a company to its shareholders out of its profits for the year. A motion to pay a final dividend must be approved by shareholders in general meeting. Shareholders at that meeting can vote to approve the level recommended by the directors or they can vote to reduce it; they cannot, however, vote to increase the directors' recommendation. A company's board of directors may in the course of a year declare and pay an INTERIM DIVIDEND. *See also* DIVIDEND.

Finance Act (UK). The Act of Parliament which implements the changes introduced by the government in the spring Budget each year. Normally an annual event, it is sometimes necessary for a government to introduce Budget legislation at different times during the year, in which case another Finance Act, usually designated Finance (No.2) Act, will have to be passed.

Finance Bill (UK). The changes to the financial regulations are contained in the Finance Bill which has to pass the necessary parliamentary stages before it receives the Royal Assent and becomes law as the FINANCE ACT. Like other legislation, the stages in the passage of a Finance Bill through Parliament are: First and Second Readings, Committee Stage, Report and Third Reading, House of Lords and Royal Assent. However, a Finance Bill differs from other legislation in that the House of Lords stages are purely formal. The House of Lords may not amend the Finance Bill: control of finance, therefore, is unambiguously with the elected House of Commons.

Finance Corporation for Industry (FCI) (UK). A company formed in 1945 along with INDUSTRIAL AND COMMERCIAL FINANCE CORPORATION to provide capital for the expansion of British industry. FCI, set up with capital provided by the long-term savings institutions, concentrated on larger amounts of lending from £250,000 to £1million. FCI and ICFC were merged in 1973 to form FINANCE FOR INDUSTRY which itself became INVESTORS IN INDUSTRY in 1983.

Finance For Industry (FFI) (UK). Formed in 1973 by the merger of FINANCE CORPORATION FOR INDUSTRY and INDUSTRIAL AND COMMERCIAL FINANCE CORPORATION. Finance For Industry was to lend money on medium term, up to fifteen years, for the expansion of British industry. Finance For Industry had equity capital supplied by the banks and the financial institutions but raised large amounts of loan capital by way of stock exchange issu Finance For Industry itself be INVESTORS IN INDUSTRY (III) in 198

Financial and Operational Combined Uniform Single (FOCUS) report (US). The report, invariably known by its acronym, which all securities broking firms must file with their exchange or association and which details the firm's financial position. Reports on some aspects of their business must be filed monthly, others are required on a quarterly basis.

financial futures. The generic name given to financial contracts which allow investors and those exposed to a financial risk, to hedge or offset that risk by selling it to someone else willing to take it on. These may be foreign exchange and interest rate risks as well as general movements in stock market prices. The idea originated with contracts to buy or sell forward such things as wheat, cocoa, tea, copper etc.

Financial futures are contracts specifying a future date of delivery or receipt of a specified amount of a FINANCIAL INSTRUMENT. Financial futures began in the United States on the Chicago Mercantile Exchange in 1972 as a means of helping those exposed to financial risk to offset it.

The volatility of interest and exchange rates in the early 1970s had made the need for such instruments much more pressing. The object is to allow a trader or company to lock into a current level of interest or exchange rates and thus be able to ignore such fluctuations in making future plans. This is done by buying or selling contracts on a financial futures exchange. Such transactions will later be reversed to make a profit to offset any adverse movements of interest or exchange rates or stock market prices in the meantime. Anyone using a financial futures contract may, in the eventual outcome, gain or lose by using it compared with not doing so. The benefit he gains is that of [illegible]ity of cost at the time he [illegible]. Financial futures ex[illegible]everal financial centres [illegible] throughout the world, [illegible]w York, Sydney and [illegible] the United Kingdom [illegible]N INTERNATIONAL [illegible]XCHANGE (LIFFE).

financial futures exchange. An organized market on which trading in financial futures contracts takes place.

financial instrument. In a FINANCIAL FUTURES contract, the underlying currency, fixed interest security or deposit which is specified in the contract.

financial intermediary. Any financial institution which stands between the ultimate borrower of funds and the saver who provides them. Thus banks, insurance companies and pension funds are examples. Financial intermediaries act not as agents but as principals. They take deposits or other contributions and use them in their own names, but they have a fiduciary duty to their depositors or beneficiaries who provided the funds.

The role of a financial intermediary is to act as a channel to improve the flow of savings into productive investment. They take savings in relatively small amounts and lend to companies and other borrowers in large amounts. They help provide certainty to the borrower, while the financial intermediaries give security, spread of risk and, especially in the case of the banks, liquidity to the savers who know they can withdraw cash at times of their own choosing.

Financial Times-Actuaries all share index (FTA) (UK). The most comprehensive of the stock market indices published in the United Kingdom. The FTA consists of 750 shares of companies listed on the Stock Exchange: these 750 account for over 90 percent of the total market capitalization of all listed companies. In addition, the index is divided into eight major equity groups: capital goods, consumer goods, other industrial goods, oils, financials, investment trusts, mining and overseas traders. Within some of these groups, notably capital, consumer and other industrial goods and finance, there are some 32 sub-groups.

The daily publication of the FTA indices began in 1962 as a collaboration between the *Financial Times*, the Institute of Actuaries and its Scottish counterpart, the Faculty of Actuaries, drawing on the original indices produced by the actuarial bodies on a monthly basis since 1929. Changes in the constituents of the index are frequent as companies fail or merge and are replaced by new ones.

The indices making up the FTA are calculated on an arithmetic basis and each share is weighted according to its issued share capital. A rise in the share price of the largest company in the market has, therefore, a much greater effect on the index than number 750.

The indices are calculated just once a day and, in addition to all the price calculations, DIVIDEND YIELD and EARNINGS YIELD, together with PRICE EARNINGS RATIO, are calculated for all the equity groups and their sub-groups as well as for the overall index.

BIBLIOGRAPHY *A Guide to Financial Times Statistics, 3rd edition* (Financial Times Business Information, London, 1984).

Financial Times Industrial Ordinary share index (FTO) (UK). The oldest of the current stock market indices published in the United Kingdom. The Financial Times Industrial Ordinary share index, also more briefly known as the FT Index or the FT 30 share index, consists, as its colloquial name implies, of 30 leading industrial and commercial shares, excluding financial and mining issues.

The shares were originally chosen at 1 July 1935, when the index was based at 100, as being representative of British industrial and commercial stocks. Some of its original constituents have had to be replaced from time to time, but a little over a third of those originally chosen remain as constituents of the index.

The FT Index is calculated every hour from 10:00 to 3:00 and a final calculation is made at around 5:00 to represent the closing level for the day.

In addition to the price index, DIVIDEND YIELD, EARNINGS YIELD and PRICE EARNINGS RATIO are also calculated on the closing value.

The index is unweighted and geometric based. Each share price thus counts equally, irrespective of the number of shares of that company in issue. The value of the index is calculated by multiplying together the share prices of the 30 constituents, each divided by their original prices and taking the thirtieth root of the total. *See also* FINANCIAL TIMES-ACTUARIES ALL SHARE INDEX, FINANCIAL TIMES-STOCK EXCHANGE INDEX.

BIBLIOGRAPHY *A Guide to Financial Times Statistics, 3rd edition* (Financial Times Business Information, London, 1984).

Financial Times-Stock Exchange Index (FT-SE) (UK). The newest of the stock market indices published in the United Kingdom. The FT-SE index, popularly known as 'Footsie' consists of 100 of the leading stock market securities ranked in terms of market capitalization. These 100 shares account for some 70 percent of the total market capitalization of domestic securities listed on the UK Stock Exchange.

The FT-SE index was based on prices at the close of business on 30 December 1983 and given the index number of 1000 at that date.

The major purpose of the index is to provide a vehicle on which TRADED OPTIONS and FINANCIAL FUTURES contracts can be written, and such contracts have been traded since early May 1984.

The index is an arithmetic, weighted index, and adjusted as necessary to take account of changes of constituents, capital changes, rights issues and scrip issues, by a chain linking procedure which keeps the index at the same level before and after the capital or other change. In addition to any changes caused by the take-over of a company in the index, the constituents are reviewed on a regular quarterly basis and changed as appropriate. Generally a 90-110 rule applies: if a share in the index falls below position 110 in the ranking order by market capitalization it will be removed from the index automatically on the quarterly review date and be replaced by another. If a share not previously included rises above position 90 it will join the index constituents and another will drop out.

The index is calculated on a minute by minute basis by the Stock Exchange's EPIC computer system and published on the TOPIC viewdata system as well as being displayed on the market floor and distributed to the press and broadcasting media.

BIBLIOGRAPHY *The 100 Share Index : a supplement to the Stock Exchange Fact Service* (The Stock Exchange, London, 1984).

financial year. The period, normally of twelve months, which is the annual accounting period for companies or, indeed, the government. Different countries have different conventions but in the United Kingdom the financial year runs from 1 April to 31 March. *See also* FISCAL YEAR.

finding both sides. The action of a broker who on receiving an order, instead of executing it by the recognised stock exchange dealing procedure, identifies a client who wishes to deal the other WAY and thus undertakes both sides of the bargain. Stock exchanges around the world have rules which seek to make sure that where such a deal is done, the price is fair to both parties and does not undermine the market making process. *See also* CROSS; PUT THROUGH.

fine corrente (It). A stock market order which must be executed within the same trading account, which in Italy is one month.

fine mese (It). Synonym of *a termine.* That is a forward transaction for the stockmarket account of one month.

fine prices. Prices of securities in a marketplace where the difference between the buying and selling prices are close. Such a situation arises in a market with many buyers and sellers and with good and efficient methods of dealing.

fine prossimo (It). A stockmarket order to execute either in the current or next stockmarket account.

firm. In English law, a firm is strictly the name for a partnership but is often used loosely to mean any business entity. Most stockbroking units on the Stock Exchange in the United Kingdom are partnerships and often collectively and correctly referred to as 'member firms'.

firm commitment (US). The undertaking given by an underwriter to buy the shares which are the subject of a public offering. The underwriter then on-sells the securities to the investing public at a slightly higher price and thus makes his profit on the transaction. If, however, investors do not take up the shares, the underwriter bears the loss. The UK equivalent is the OFFER FOR SALE. *Contrast with* BEST EFFORTS.

firm hands, in. Used to indicate that shares are held by those who regard them as a long term, not a speculative, investment.

firm order (US). (1) An order placed by a member firm of a stock exchange on its OWN ACCOUNT.

(2) An order given by a client which remains GOOD 'TIL CANCELLED or until the expiry of a given time limit.

firm quote. A quote given by a MARKET MAKER or BROKER-DEALER which is given without conditions.

first closing date (UK). The initial date up to which an offer to the shareholders of a target company by a bidder must remain open. Under the CITY CODE ON TAKE-OVERS AND MERGERS, an offer must remain open initially for a period of 21 days after its posting. If revised, it must be kept open for at least 14 days from the posting of the revision.

first-in-first-out (FIFO). A term used in accounting and in other contexts to determine which assets acquired at different times are being identified in a given disposal. To illustrate, let us assume assets were acquired as follows: 500 units in January, 300 in February, 1000 in March. In April, 700 units were disposed of. This 700 would be identified first with the 500 acquired in January and the balance of 200 would be applied to the February purchase. A subsequent disposal of 600 would first be identified with the balance of 100 left from the February purchase and 500 would then be deemed to have come from the March purchase of 1000.

first notice day. On the FINANCIAL FUTURES markets the first date, varying with different contracts, on which notice of intention to deliver actual FINANCIAL INSTRUMENTS against futures CONTRACTS can validly be made. *See also* DELIVERY.

First Section (Jap). The major section of the Tokyo, Nagoya and Osaka Stock Exchanges, which have more stringent listing requirements than the SECOND SECTION on each of these markets.

The main criteria for a listing on the First Section of the Tokyo Stock Exchange are that the company must : (1) have been trading for at least five years; (2) have earned stipulated levels of profit for at least three years; (3) have paid specific levels of dividends for three years; (4) have at least 2,000 shareholders; (5) have at least 10 million shares in issue; (6) possess a market capital stock of at least 500 million yen; (7) have tangible assets per share of at least 100 yen.

Shares can be delisted if these stipulations are not maintained.

BIBLIOGRAPHY Paul H. and Laurie J. Aron 'The Asian Equity Markets' in Abraham M. George and Ian H. Giddy (eds.) *International Finance Handbook* (John Wiley, New York, 1983), Section 6.7. *Securities Markets in Japan* (Japan Securities Research Institute, Tokyo, annually).

fiscal. Relating to the raising of public revenue and the methods of doing so.

fiscal year. The twelve month period which is used as the basis for assessing an individual's, a firm's or a company's tax liability. In the United Kingdom it runs from 6 April in one year to 5 April of the following year.

In the United States, the fiscal year for tax purposes begins on 1 October and ends 30 September of the following year. However, the term is often used in the United States to refer to a company's FINANCIAL YEAR.

fissato bollato (It). The CONTRACT NOTE for a stock market transaction.

five percent policy (US). The name given to the guideline issued by the NATIONAL ASSOCIATION OF SECURITIES DEALERS to its members on the question of the mark up on share prices which they on-sell to customers. First issued in 1943 following a survey of members, the five percent policy is only a guide and there may be occasions when a higher rate is justified by the relevant factors involved in a deal, or indeed when even a lower rate is not justified by the effort needed to complete the deal. The relevant factors justifying the amount of mark up include the type of security involved, its availability in the market, the price of the security, the size of the deal, the pattern of mark ups generally in a particular security and the nature of the member's business.

BIBLIOGRAPHY *NASD Manual - Rules of Fair Practice* (NASD, Washington D.C.).

fixed assets. The semi-permanent assets of a business which are not used up in the day-to-day process of manufacturing, distributing or supplying services, although they may need to be replaced over time. They include land, buildings, plant and equipment.

fixed charges (US). The fixed expenses of a company such as loan interest, which must be met before any return to equity holders is made. In the United Kingdom they are often called PRIOR CHARGES.

fixed commissions. *See* COMMISSION.

fixed costs. The expenditure of a business which must be incurred irrespective of output and not varying with it.

fixed debenture. A fixed loan provided by a lender or lenders with a charge on a specific item or items of a company's fixed assets as security.

fixed interest debt. Liabilities of a company which bear a fixed annual nominal rate of interest.

fixed price offer for sale (UK). An OFFER FOR SALE of securities for which the offer price to potential shareholders is fixed in advance. Anyone wishing to buy an allotment of the shares will send an application form, plus his cheque, for the number of shares he wishes to buy. However great the demand for the issue, the investor will only have to pay the fixed price. On the other hand if demand is excessive, the allocation may be made by ballot for small applications and many bidders will not receive any allotment of the shares. Larger applications in such a situation may be scaled down. A fixed price offer for sale is contrasted with an offer by TENDER.

fixen (Ger). A BEAR operation; the selling of securities a speculator does not possess in the hope of buying them back later at a lower price, thus closing the deal at a profit.

Fixer (Ger). A BEAR.

fixings. *See* GOLD FIXING.

flag. An expression used in TECHNICAL ANALYSIS to describe a particular share price pattern. After a prolonged rise or fall in price, a flag is established when, for a period, the price moves consistently between similar highs and lows, thus establishing a rectangular pattern on a time scale.

flat income bond (US). This term means that the price at which a bond is traded includes consideration for all unpaid accruals of interest. Bonds which are in default of interest or principal are traded flat. Income bonds which pay interest only to the extent earned, are usually traded flat. All other bonds are usually dealt in 'with interest', which means that the buyer pays the market price plus interest accrued since the last payment date.

flat market. A stock market on which there is little business and no significant movement up or down in share prices.

flat yield. The annual income yield from a security calculated by the annual monetary return divided by the price and expressed as a percentage. Also known as the interest yield or running yield.

flexible trust. A type of unit trust (mutual fund) where the type of investment, for example fixed interest securities, equity, property etc, is left to the discretion of the managers within limits set down by the trust deed.

float a company. To set up a new company and sell shares in it to outside holders. Used especially of a company whose shares are being traded on a stock exchange for the first time. Also used loosely, meaning to establish a company.

floating assets. The assets in a company which are regularly turned over, as opposed to the FIXED ASSETS. Floating assets include stock in trade, cash and other liquid assets.

floating capital. Money and other short term assets available for the day-to-day running of a business.

floating charge. Any security raised on the variable or floating assets of a company. Only when and if a receiver is appointed by the debenture holder, does the charge crystallize on the floating assets then in the company's ownership. *See also* FLOATING DEBENTURE.

floating debenture. A loan raised against the security of the floating assets of the company. *See also* FLOATING CHARGE.

floating debt. Government debt of a short term nature such as the TREASURY BILL.

floating rate bond. A domestic loan issue, the interest on which varies with short term money market conditions. Also referred to as a floating rate loan.

floating rate loan. *See* FLOATING RATE BOND.

floating rate note. A variable rate security issued by borrowers on the EUROBOND market. The rate of interest is not fixed at the outset but varies during the life of the note according to comparable rates in the short term money markets. At times, when conditions are uncertain, floating rate notes have accounted for a substantial proportion of new issues on the eurobond market.

floor. *See* TRADING FLOOR.

floor broker. A term originating in the United States where it is used both on the NEW YORK STOCK EXCHANGE (NYSE) and on the futures and options markets. On the NYSE a floor broker is one who executes orders to buy or sell securities on the floor of the Exchange for other members. *See also* COMMISSION BROKER and INDEPENDENT BROKER. A similar definition applies to the financial futures markets where orders may be transacted for members who themselves may or may not have a presence on the floor of the exchange.

floor official (US). An employee of a stock exchange who settles trading disputes between members.

floor trader. *See* TRADER.

floor transaction. A trade or deal between buyer and seller carried out in the PIT by members of a FINANCIAL FUTURES exchange.

flotante (It). The issued share capital: the amount of securities effectively in circulation with the general investing public.

flotation. The issue of shares in a company coming to a stock market for the first time.

flower bonds (US). A name given to Treasury bonds which are specially designated as being acceptable at par by the tax authorities in settlement of estate taxes payable on death.

fluctuation. The rise and fall of securities or other prices on a trading market.

fondi comuni di investimento (It). Investment funds.

fondo debole (It). An expression used to indicate a market where prices are generally lower than previously.

fondo sostenuto (It). An expression used to indicate a market where prices are slightly better than previously.

fonds (Fr). Stock.

fonds communs (Fr). *See* UNIT TRUSTS.

fonds consolidés (Fr). Consolidated stock. *See* CONSOLS.

fonds de placement (Fr). *See* UNIT TRUSTS.

fonds d'état (Fr). Government stocks.

fonds publics (Fr). *See* FONDS D'ÉTAT.

Footsie (UK). The colloquial name for the FINANCIAL TIMES-STOCK EXCHANGE INDEX.

for cash. The sale of shares which are to be paid for at once and not at the end of the ACCOUNT. By convention, in the United Kingdom cash settlement means within 48 hours. Government stocks in the United Kingdom are usually dealt for cash because of the very large sums involved.

forced conversion. The enforced switch of one security into another at the instigation of the issuer.

forced sale. A sale of securities at a time not of the seller's choosing, but as a result of pressure from a creditor.

foreign bonds. Fixed interest securities issued by overseas governments and companies which are traded on a domestic stock exchange. They may be denominated in the currency of the issuer or that of the country in which they are being traded.

foreign currency securities. Any stock or share denominated in a currency other than that of the country in which it is being traded. Interest or dividends are payable in the same currency as is repayment. Where exchange control is in operation, purchase of such securities by nationals will be subject to regulations laid down by the government and may involve the payment of a premium to obtain the necessary currency. *See* INVESTMENT CURRENCY PREMIUM.

foreign exchange options. Options contracts developed by and traded on the Philadelphia Stock Exchange. The option gives the buyer the right to buy or sell currency at a fixed price on or before a specified date. The Philadelphia Exchange began trading in foreign currency options in December 1982 and currently trades them in six currencies: sterling, Deutsche Marks, Swiss francs, Canadian dollars, yen and French francs.

forfeit of shares. The forced surrender of shares by a holder who fails to pay an additional CALL on partly paid shares.

form of charge. A legal instrument by which a borrower mortgages his assets to a lender.

form of renunciation (UK). *See* LETTER OF RENUNCIATION.

formula investing (US). A term used to describe a method of investing by reference to a given set of data or a formula. As the market moves in a particular way or breaks predetermined points, the formula will determine that the investor moves out of common stock (shares) and into preferred stock or bonds and vice versa.

for the account (UK). The term used to denote that a stock exchange bargain in equity and other company securities in the United Kingdom is to be settled according to the normal settlement practice. Settlement of bargains done in a particular account is made on the sixth business day after the end of that account, irrespective of the actual day within the account when the bargain was made. *See also* ACCOUNT, SETTLEMENT DAY.

forward market. A market in which deals are made not for cash but for future settlement.

Fosiegedragsregelscade (NL). The Dutch code on public bids and mergers introduced in 1975. The code set up a Mergers Commission and required copies of all documents relating to take-overs to be filed with the Amsterdam Stock Exchange's Board of Governors.

Fotra stocks (UK). An acronym for 'free of all taxes to residents abroad'. They are stocks issued by the British government to encourage overseas investors to buy GILT EDGED STOCK. Interest on such stocks is paid on a gross basis to overseas holders, but on a net basis to United Kingdom residents. Not all British government issues qualify for this treatment.

founders' shares (UK). Shares subscribed by the original owners of a business, sometimes with special voting rights which allow them to exercise control of specific and fundamental matters afffecting the company. They may sometimes also receive a special dividend after the holders of the ordinary shares have been allocated theirs.

frais de cotation (Fr). The annual fee for LISTING on a French *bourse*.

franco valuta (It). Clause by which securities are delivered without payment.

franked income. Income received by an investor which has already borne tax and is therefore not taxable again in the investor's hands. The phrase applies particular to the financial institutions as investors.

Fraud (Prevention of) Act. *See* PREVENTION OF FRAUD (INVESTMENTS) ACT.

Freddie Mae (US). The colloquial name for the FEDERAL HOME LOAN MORTGAGE CORPORATION.

free and open market (US). A market in which the laws of supply and demand are given unrestricted expression in determining prices. It is contrasted with a controlled market subject to regulation of supply and demand and hence price.

free issue. *See* SCRIP ISSUE.

free market. A market in which securities may be traded easily, quickly and cheaply without moving the price by an appreciable amount. The phrase has overtones similar to FREE AND OPEN MARKET.

freeriding (US). The retention of shares in a successful new issue by the underwriters or dealers in the hope of making a substantial profit. Such an action, also referred to as withholding, which will be at the expense of the investing public, is banned by the rules of the National Association of Securities Dealers which insist that it is 'inconsistent with high standards of commercial honor and just and equitable principles of trade'.

freie Makler (Ger). Independent dealers, also sometimes generically called BÖRSENMAKLER, on the German Stock Exchanges who deal for their own account. They are not official dealers or KURSMAKLER but are admitted to the exchanges by the governing bodies, the BÖRSENVORSTAND, to deal in securities on the unofficial market of the BÖRSE. They may also carry out some dealings in the official market. Two *freie Makler* sit on the Börsenvorstand itself, along with representatives of credit institutions, the Kursmakler, deputies and representatives of issuers and investors.

Freiverkehr (Ger). The free market or regulated unofficial market on the German Stock Exchanges. Trading on this market takes place in securities which are not suitable for listing on the official market because they are traded elsewhere or only tradable in small amounts. Supervision of this market is in the hands of a committee for unlisted securities (AUSSCHUSS FÜR GESCHÄFTE IN AMTLICH NICHT NOTIERTEN WERTEN) and the dealers are the FREIE MAKLER. Although trading in this market is permitted under German law, the investor in the market cannot demand the right to have his order executed at a posted bid or offer price and orders are mainly done at individual prices, referred to usually as PREIS rather than KURS.

friendly society (UK). Originally local mutual help societies in case of illness or other need, friendly societies have become a tax efficient way of saving. Because of their significant tax advantages, the amounts saved in such societies are closely controlled. Building societies in the United Kingdom are a form of friendly society and still presently controlled by the Registrar of Friendly Societies.

front end loading. The practice with certain savings schemes of taking expenses for running it, including the salesman's commission, out of the investor's initial payments. Such schemes grew rapidly in the United States in the 1960s. They were restrained by an Act of Congress in 1970, which allows an investor to get back all or most of his premium if he withdraws from the contract early in its life.

full service broker (US). A name given to the type of U.S. stockbroker who continues to offer a full range of services for his clients including fund management, research and financial advice. This type of broker is contrasted with the DISCOUNT BROKER.

fully paid shares. Shares on which no further CALL can be made. Shareholders buying such shares have no further liability to contribute to the deficiency of a company in the event of a winding up. Most securities are normally traded nowadays in fully paid form. The exceptions normally occur with new issues, particularly large issues which could cause cash and liquidity problems for the investors (and for the banking system) if the subscription was taken at one time. Government stock issues in the United Kingdom are sometimes issued on a partly paid basis, with one or two further calls within six months or so. A number of PRIVATIZATION issues have also been issued first in partly paid form with subsequent calls.

fully subscribed (issue). An issue of securities for which there are sufficient subscriptions to take up the full amount on offer.

fund. The sum total of money subscribed for a savings scheme or project and by extension, the scheme itself. *See also* MANAGED FUND, MUTUAL FUND.

fundamental analysis. The method of investment analysis which concentrates on the fundamentals of a company such as its products, markets and management. Investment analysis of this sort seeks to establish prospects for a company's profits, earnings and, indirectly, its share price. It is contrasted with TECHNICAL ANALYSIS which seeks to predict changes in share prices based on patterns of past behaviour of the share price itself.

fundamentalist. An investment analyst who believes in FUNDAMENTAL ANALYSIS rather than TECHNICAL ANALYSIS or CHARTING.

fundamental research. *See* FUNDAMENTAL ANALYSIS.

funded debenture. A loan stock, provision for the repayment of which is met by annual transfers to a sinking fund.

funded debt. Government debt which has no fixed date of repayment, such as Consolidated Stock or CONSOLS. Used more loosely to mean long dated stock issued by a government to replace a shorter dated stock, thus lengthening the life of the debt.

fundierte Schuld (Ger). *See* FUNDED DEBT.

funding. Lengthening the life or maturity of debt. Normally associated with government debt, where the authorities issue a long dated stock to replace a shorter dated one, it may also be applied to the action of a company which repays short term bank borrowing by the proceeds of a long term stock issue.

Funds, the (UK). A Victorian name for government stocks collectively. Lady Bracknell in Oscar Wilde's *The Importance of Being Earnest* notes with approval the financial standing of one of the other characters : 'A hundred and thirty thousand pounds! And in the Funds! Miss Cardew seems to me a most attractive young lady…'

fungible. A word deriving from the legal term 'fungibles' meaning movable effects which perish by being used; fungible is used in a stock exchange context to refer to securities in course of settlement. In the United Kingdom, sold securities of a particular share issue are put into a pooled account from which purchases are allocated. *See also* TALISMAN, SEPON.

fuori borsa (It). Transactions effected outside the official market and/or outside market hours.

fuori prezzo (It). An order to buy or sell securities which was not effected as the prices fixed on the stock exchange were either too high or too low.

fusion (Fr). *See* AMALGAMATION, MERGER. Mergers via the *bourses* are controlled by the CHAMBRE SYNDICALE through its RÈGLEMENT GÉNÉRAL DE LA COMPAGNIE DES AGENTS DE CHANGE.

BIBLIOGRAPHY *Règlement Général de la Compagnie des Agents de Change* (Paris, October 1983). Paul Stonham, *Major Stock Markets of Europe* (Gower Publishing, London, 1982).

futures. Contracts for the delivery or receipt of a given quantity of a deliverable asset at a specified future date. Originating in commodities markets, futures contracts have now been established in FINANCIAL INSTRUMENTS such as interest rates, exchange rates and movements in stock market indices. This development, a feature of the uncertainty and volatility in financial markets in the 1970s, began as an offshoot of commodity futures markets in Chicago and has now spread worldwide. *See also* FINANCIAL FUTURES.

futures contract. *See* CONTRACT.

futures exchange or **futures market.** An organized market place where FUTURES contracts in commodities or FINANCIAL INSTRUMENTS may be traded.

G

gap (US). The word used to describe a situation where the range of prices at one TRADING SESSION does not overlap the TRADING RANGE at the previous session.

garantie de cours (Fr). *See* HEDGING.

garanzia (It). Generally used in the stockmarket in reference to a deposit of securities as collateral.

garanzia a mantenersi (It). The right of a stockbroker to ask for MARGIN from clients greater than that established by the COMMISSIONE NAZIONALE PER LA SOCIETÀ E LA BORSA (CONSOB).

gearing (UK). Called leverage in the United States, gearing is the term used to describe the proportion between a company's fixed interest loan and preference capital and its equity. A company is said to be highly geared if the ratio of borrowing to equity is high. The earnings per share available to equity capital will rise or fall more sharply the more highly geared a company is. For example, if the earnings of a company with one million shares in issue rise from £1m to £1.5m the earnings per share rise from £1 to £1.50 or 50 percent. If that same company were to have to meet interest payments or prior charges on its outstanding debt of £500,000 a year, the earnings available to ordinary shareholders would rise on the above example from £500,000 to £1million, an increase of 100 not 50 percent. In good times, a relatively high gearing is good for a company's ordinary shareholders since increases in profits flow directly through into equity earnings which rise more than proportionately. In bad times the reverse is true, with shareholders' equity earnings falling sharply if high prior charges have to be met.

geben (Ger). Selling or offering of securities.

Gebildete Prüfungskommission für Insider-Fragen (Ger). The German Committee for Insider Trading. The Prüfungskommission exists for each German *börse* and is a supervisory body set up to identify and act against insider trading.

gedeckt (Ger). Secured or guaranteed, as in *Gedeckterkredit,* meaning secured borrowing.

Geld (Ger). Demand for securities, buying.

Genehmigteskapital (Ger). The AUTHORIZED CAPITAL of a company.

general mortgage bond (US). A bond which is secured by a blanket coverage on the company's property but which may rank behind the claims of one or more other outstanding mortgages.

Genussschein (Ger). A participating certificate giving its holders the right to dividends or to participate in specified profits of a company without conferring full rights of ownership. For example, Audi-NSU issued such certificates in the late 1960s giving the holder the right to participate in the licence income from the development of the Wankel engine. Such issues are not common.

geregelter Freiverkehr (Ger). The regulated free market or the semi-official market on the German Stock Exchanges. A market half way between the official and the unofficial markets, shares traded are dealt in by the FREIE MAKLER.

Gesellschaft (Ger). A company under German law which may be either in the form of AKTIENGESELLSCHAFT (AG) or Gesellschaft mit beschränkter Haftung (GmbH).

Gesetz über die Kapitalanlagegesellschaften (KAGG) (Ger). The German law governing the activities of investment companies. *See also* BUNDESAUFSICHTAMT FÜR DAS KREDITWESEN.

geschlossener Fonds (Ger). *See* CLOSED-END FUNDS.

gesprochene Kurs (Ger). The estimated price of a security when there have been no actual deals in it at a trading session.

Gessler Report (Ger). A report on the German banking system published in 1979 which *inter alia* contained information on the shareholdings of German banks in industry.

Gewinnanteilschein (Ger). *See* DIVIDEND WARRANT.

Gewinnmitnahme (Ger). *See* PROFIT TAKING.

ghiacciare (It). Term used to indicate the immediate acceptance of an offer on the stockmarket.

giardinetto (It). The DIVERSIFICATION of a PORTFOLIO of shares and bonds issued by various companies operating in different sectors in order to split and limit investment risks.

gifts *inter vivos*. Gifts made to others by a donor who is still alive. A phrase used, for example, in the UK CAPITAL TRANSFER TAX legislation under which such gifts are less harshly taxed than if they pass on death.

gifts tax (US). The American equivalent of CAPITAL TRANSFER TAX.

gilt edged stock. (1) (UK). The phrase used to describe government and government guaranteed securities on which there is no risk of default. The market in such stocks exists within the Stock Exchange in the United Kingdom and accounts for between 75 and 80 percent of the total daily turnover in the market. Gilt edged stocks are available in a variety of forms: straight fixed interest stock, paying a fixed annual dividend throughout its life, a rate or COUPON which was set at the market rate at the time of issue; a low coupon stock, also offering a fixed rate of interest but issued at a large discount and attractive to those paying high rates of tax on income. *See also* INDEX LINKED STOCK; VARIABLE RATE STOCK.

(2) (US) Gilt edged has a different meaning in the United States. There it is a high grade bond issued by a company which has a good profit record and has demonstrated its ability to meet the payments of interest on its bonds without difficulty or interruption.

Ginnie Mae (US). Popular name for the GOVERNMENT NATIONAL MORTGAGE ASSOCIATION (GNMA) and in the plural, for securities issued by the Association.

giocare in borsa (It). To speculate, to play the market.

gioco di borsa (It). Playing the market.

girata (It). Endorsement of a stock certificate to the new holder.

giro d'affari (It). *See* TURNOVER.

giver. One who has purchased shares but wishes to carry out a CONTANGO to delay payment until the following SETTLEMENT DAY.

give up. On a FINANCIAL FUTURES market, the assignment by a FLOOR BROKER of a floor transaction to another member.

In the United States, the phrase has many different meanings, including the 'giving up' by one dealer to another of a third member's name if the first dealer is acting on behalf of that third member in a transaction on the New York Stock Exchange.

The phrase may also be used if an investor places an order through one broker but requests that it be settled through another. A further meaning refers to an order in which the participating underwriter will not guarantee the sale of the securities.

Give up was also used to refer to the instruction by a client to a broker receiving commission for a deal to give up part of that commission to another broker. This procedure is now outlawed by the New York Stock Exchange.

Glass-Steagall Act (US). An Act of Congress passed in 1933 with the prime objective of separating the commercial side of banking in the United States from investment banking. (The Act also imposed interest rate ceilings on bank deposit accounts and established the Federal Deposit Insurance Corporation to provide deposit protection for bank customers.) The Act has had significant implications for the degree to which brokers and banks have been able to compete with one another.

Glattstellung (Ger). To sell a position in a security.

godimento (It). Date from which the securities rank for dividends or interest etc.

godimento regolare (It). Ranking for normal rights.

go-go fund. A phrase believed to have been borrowed from enthusiastic controllers of the NASA space programme, to describe an investment fund which was being actively traded in order to achieve maximum capital gain and a price somewhere in the financial stratosphere. Temporarily successful in the early 1970s, some of the go-go funds fell to earth later.

going naked. *See* NAKED WRITER.

going short. *See* SHORT.

going out price. The price of a security as quoted in the STOCK EXCHANGE DAILY OFFICIAL LIST.

golden handshake. The payment made by a company to a director or senior employee as compensation if the company terminates his contract before expiry.

golden parachute. A term used to describe the payment made to directors of a company who, having lost a take-over battle, are leaving the merged organization.

golden share (UK). A term applied to a share which has particular voting rights and which can be used to exercise a veto in certain circumstances. The term is most frequently applied in PRIVATIZATION issues to the share in a company retained by the British government which can be used to prevent the privatized company being acquired by another company contrary to the government's wishes.

gold fixing. The meetings which take place twice a day between the five gold bullion dealers in London. At these meetings the price of gold is determined according to supply and demand and the price is used as the determining price of gold bullion trading and contracts worldwide.

gold options. Options traded on the EUROPEAN OPTIONS EXCHANGE in Amsterdam since 1981, by means of which investors can trade gold for future delivery. The trading contract is ten troy ounces of fine gold.

gonfiato (It). A security whose price is considered exaggeratedly high.

good delivery. The delivery of stock with no impediment in settlement of a stock exchange bargain.

good marking names. *See* MARKING NAMES.

good 'til cancelled. A phrase used in US stock markets and on futures exchanges worldwide to indicate instructions given to a broker that the order is to remain effective until either executed or cancelled. The term 'open order' has the same meaning. In a FINANCIAL FUTURES market, the instruction normally contains provision for the automatic expiry of the order at the end of the LAST TRADING DAY for the FINANCIAL INSTRUMENT to which the order relates.

government bond. A security issued by a government and therefore regarded as of the highest standing. In the United Kingdom, the phrase 'government stocks' is more commonly used; *see* GOVERNMENT SECURITIES.

Government Broker (UK). A member of the Stock Exchange used by the government to transact its buying and selling operations in GILT EDGED STOCK on the market. By tradition, the Government Broker is the senior partner of Mullens & Co. and is responsible for advising the Treasury via the Bank of England on its dealings in the market as well as for executing the business. *See also* OPEN MARKET OPERATIONS.

government guaranteed stock (UK). An issue of stock, usually by a PUBLIC CORPORATION, on which the government has guaranteed the payments of interest and principal.

Government National Mortgage Association (GNMA). A government agency whose function is to channel money into government-backed funds. The issuing of securities (Ginnie Maes) by the Association enables private funds to be mobilised in the mortgage market. GNMA is the sister organization of the FEDERAL NATIONAL MORTGAGE ASSOCIATION (FNMA).

government securities. *See* GILT EDGED STOCK; INDEX LINKED STOCK; VARIABLE RATE STOCK.

Gower Report (UK). A report on investor protection commissioned from Professor L.C.B.Gower by the Department of Trade in 1981. Its terms of reference were:

(a) to consider the statutory protection now required by (i) private and (ii) business investors in securities and other property, including investors through unit trusts and open-ended investment companies operating in the United Kingdom;

(b) to consider the need for statutory control of dealers in securities, investment consultants and investment managers; and

(c) to advise on the need for legislation.

Professor Gower issued a discussion document in 1982 and invited comments. On the basis of these and further detailed work, the Gower Report was published in January 1984.

Professor Gower's basic recommendations may be summarized in the report as follows: (1) The Prevention of Fraud (Investments) Act should be replaced by an Investor Protection Act. Its administration should be the responsibility either of the Department of Trade and Industry (DTI) or a self-standing Commission answerable to the Secretary of State. (2) The Act would make it a criminal offence to carry on investment business unless registered to do so. (3) Registration would be either direct with the DTI (or the Commission) or through membership of a self-regulatory agency (SRA) recognized by it. (4) Basic requirements and prohibitions would be laid upon those engaged in investment business. (5) Rules of conduct would be laid down by the DTI for those businesses registered directly with it and provision would be made for revoking licences. (6) An SRA would not be recognized unless it satisfied conditions regarding its membership and protection of investors which were at least equal to those laid down by the DTI and the ability to monitor observance of them. (7) Recognized SRAs would be responsible for their members and for ensuring observance of their rules. (8) The Act would lay down provisions for a harmonised system of regulation of public offers for sale and would contain an up-dated version of the prospectus requirements of the Companies Act 1948.

BIBLIOGRAPHY L.C.B. Gower, *Review of Investor Protection, Cmnd 9125*, (HMSO, London, 1984).

Granny bonds (UK). The nickname given to index-linked securities issued by the British government in the 1970s which at first could only be purchased by those men and women over retirement age. The object of the bonds, which were non-marketable national savings securities, was to protect retirement pensioners' savings from the erosion caused by the high rates of inflation. Subsequently, the bonds were made available to savers as a whole.

Graphiques de la Bourse de Paris (Fr). A booklet issued fortnightly by the Paris Stock Exchange showing the price and volume traded of all securities listed on the forward market and the leading 50 shares quoted on the cash market.

Gratisaktie (Ger). *See* SCRIP ISSUE.

green baize door. *See* CHINESE WALL.

greenmailing (US). A colloquial term coined in the United States in the early 1980s to describe the practice of purchasing a block of shares by another company or group of individuals in a company, which was known or expected to be hostile to a take-over bid. The target company, afraid that such a block could be useful if sold to a potential bidder as a spring board from which to launch a full take-over bid, might be persuaded to buy back the block of its own shares at a substantial profit to the original purchaser(s).

green shoe clause (US). A clause in an underwriting contract allowing the issuing syndicate to purchase additional shares at the original offer price.

grida (It). The trading ring on the floors of the Italian Stock Exchanges.

grossed-up redemption yield. The net redemption yield on a security to which the income and capital tax liabilities of a recipient have been added to calculate the equivalent gross yield.

grossing up. Some dividends and other income from securities is received net of tax. To calculate a tax liability on such income, an amount equivalent to a notional tax figure is added to the net amount. Tax is then calculated on this notional gross figure.

gross interest. The amount of interest paid on a security before deducting tax.

gross redemption yield. The total yield of a security, including both anticipated income and capital growth for the whole period up to the date of maturity and repayment. The gross redemption yield is calculated before any allowance has been made for the holder's tax liability.

gross yield. The return from a share or other security before account is taken of tax. The term may be applied both to the flat yield and the redemption yield.

group accounts. The consolidated profit and loss accounts of a group of companies.

groupement d'actions (Fr). A reorganization of a company's share capital.

growth share (UK). A share which is expected to achieve above-average increases in its capital value, earnings and dividends as the result of the company's prospects.

growth stock (US). The US equivalent of GROWTH SHARE.

Gründeranteilschein (Ger). A FOUNDERS' SHARE.

Gründkapital (Ger). Share capital.

guaranteed stock. A security for which income and repayment is guaranteed by a third party, either a company's parent company or, in the case of a public body, the government.

Guichetkommission (Ger). *See* UNDERWRITING COMMISSION.

H

half-commission man (UK). The employee of a stockbroking firm who is remunerated not by a salary (although he may be paid a small annual retainer) but by being paid a half of the commission on business which he has brought to the firm. The half-commission man is less prevalent now than he used to be on the Stock Exchange, although ASSOCIATED MEMBERS may still share in the profits of their firms by way of an annual bonus.

hammering (UK). The term used to describe the announcement of the failure of the partners in a Stock Exchange firm. The term comes from the traditional method of announcing such a failure when a WAITER on the Stock Exchange floor would strike his desk three times with a hammer to call for the attention of members before declaring that the named partners had notified the Stock Exchange Council that they were unable to comply with their bargains and had been declared defaulters.

handeln per Erscheinen (Ger). To deal in securities before deliverable documents are available.

Hang Seng Index (HSI) (HK). One of the three stock market indices used for the various Hong Kong Stock Exchanges, the other two being the FAR EAST INDEX and the KAM NGAN INDEX. The Hang Seng Index is the oldest of the three, having been established in 1969, although on a base of 100 on 31 July 1964. The index is an arithmetic and weighted index of 33 stocks, which together represent 70 percent of the total turnover.

hard dollars (US). Actual commissions paid to brokers. *Contrast with* SOFT DOLLARS.

Haussemarkt (Ger). *See* BULL MARKET.

Hausse (Ger). A rising trend of stock exchange prices.

Haussespekulant (Ger). A bull, one who expects stock market prices to rise.

haussier (Fr). *See* BULL.

head and shoulders. A term used in TECHNICAL ANALYSIS to describe a particular pattern of price movement. The pattern resembles the outline of a person's head and shoulders, that is a level period, followed by a sharp rise which is maintained for a while before falling back, perhaps to another price plateau. A head and shoulders formation is said to herald a fall in the price of stock.

heavy (priced) share. A share with a high quoted price in relation to the generality of prices in a particular market. The phrase does not necessarily imply that a share is expensive in terms of its price-earnings ratio or other criteria; it may simply mean that there are few shares in issue to which the company's earnings are attributable. Doubling the number of shares in issue would halve the price at which they are quoted, but the price-earnings ratio would be unchanged.

There are differences in philosophy between investors in different markets regarding share prices. For example, in the United Kingdom, investors seem to prefer to buy a lot of shares at relatively low prices. In the United States, however, investors appear to prefer heavily priced shares and, consequently, whereas the average share price in the London market is around £2 and it is unusual for a share price to exceed £10, in the United States the average share price is around $20.

hedge. (1) To offset any possible adverse changes in the value of assets held by the purchase or sale of a FINANCIAL FUTURES or OPTIONS contract.

(2) The instrument used to offset the risk.

hedger. One who buys or sells a FINANCIAL FUTURES or OPTIONS CONTRACT in order to offset his financial risk.

hedging. The act of offsetting financial risk by the use of a FINANCIAL FUTURES or OPTIONS CONTRACT.

heutegültig (Ger). Valid for today. An expression used to denote that a sale or purchase order is valid only for the day on which the order is given.

higgledy-piggledy growth. A term used by Rayner and Little in a series of articles in the 1960s, to describe the relative unpredictability of stock market earnings, dividends and security prices, a forerunner of the EFFICIENT MARKET HYPOTHESIS.

high coupon. A high nominal rate of interest being paid on a fixed interest stock. *See also* COUPON.

hoeklieden (NL). Members of the Amsterdam Stock Exchange, the *hoeklieden* specialize in particular securities or types of security and act both as intermediaries and as principals for their own account. They are a combination of BROKER and JOBBER.

hoekman (NL). *See* HOEKLIEDEN.

holding. An investment in a particular company or other security.

holding company. A company established with the objective of holding the whole, or a substantial part, of the share capital of another company or a group of subsidiaries.

Holdinggesellschaft (Ger). *See* HOLDING COMPANY.

holding over. The deferment of settlement of a stock exchange deal until the next settlement day.

Hong Kong Federation of Stock Exchanges. A body set up by the authorities in 1973 to prepare the way for a merger of the four separate Hong Kong Stock Exchanges and to establish common methods of regulation.

Hong Kong Stock Exchange. One of the four stock markets in Hong Kong, now moving towards amalgamation. The Hong Kong Stock Exchange is the oldest, but not now the largest, of the four, although it still has the largest number of foreign member firms and the greatest number of overseas securities listed.

The trading system is an auction market at trading boards. Dealing is done in ROUND LOTS by those who wish to buy or sell, writing the price on the trading board and the stock being bid for by the dealers on the floor of the Exchange. Settlement is on the following trading day.

To be listed on the Hong Kong Stock Exchange, a company must have a paid up capital of HK$20 million, of which at least 25 percent must be available to the market. *See also* FAR EAST STOCK EXCHANGE; KOWLOON STOCK EXCHANGE; KAM NGAN STOCK EXCHANGE.

BIBLIOGRAPHY The Hong Kong Stock Exchange *Year Book.* The Hong Kong Stock Exchange *Monthly Gazette.* Paul H. and Laurie J. Aron, 'The Asian Equities Markets' in Abraham M. George and Ian H. Giddy (eds.) *International Finance Handbook* (John Wiley, New York, 1983).

honorary market officials (UK). Officials appointed by the Council of the Stock Exchange who act as arbitrators in trading disputes between dealers and who are responsible for administering certain rules of dealing.

horizontal integration. The merger of two or more companies whose activities are concerned with the same level of economic production, for example retailing. *Contrast with* VERTICAL INTEGRATION.

hot issue. A term used by the NATIONAL ASSOCIATION OF SECURITIES DEALERS (NASD) to describe a security for which there is expected to be wide investor enthusiasm and a sharp price rise following the issue. NASD makes specific reference in its RULES OF FAIR PRACTICE to hot issues and the ways in which dealers must act when handling them. *See also* FREERIDING.

hot money. Short term capital which can be moved quickly by its owners from one money market to another in search of the highest rate of interest. Generally invested in bank deposits or risk-free government securities, the flow of hot money across the exchanges can cause difficulties for countries on their trading accounts by the effects on the relative exchange rates.

House, the (UK). The colloquial name for the Stock Exchange and its trading floor in the United Kingdom. (In other contexts, the House may also mean the House of Commons, the House of Lords or Christ Church, Oxford, so be careful.)

hypothecation (US). The pledging of securities as collateral for a loan on MARGIN account.

I

identification rules (UK). Rules laid down in the Finance Act 1982, in connection with the INDEXATION OF CAPITAL GAINS TAX. Prior to 1982, whenever an investor bought or otherwise acquired more of the same CLASS OF SHARES, they were pooled with all others of that class and a single pool price calculated. When part of the pool was disposed of, the pool price was that used for calculating any liability to Capital Gains Tax.

The rules of indexation meant that pooling had to be ended and early acquisitions of shares made at different times had to be separately identified. The basic rules now are that when an asset is partly disposed of, the shares making up the disposal shall first be identified with any acquired within the preceding twelve months. If more than one acquisition has been made in that time, each acquisition shall be dealt with on a FIRST-IN-FIRST-OUT (FIFO) basis.

For acquisitions made more than twelve months prior to disposal, each acquisition is identified on a LAST-IN-FIRST-OUT (LIFO) basis.

BIBLIOGRAPHY Capital Gains Tax Act 1979. Finance Act 1982. *Capital Gains Tax* (Tolley Publishing, London, annually).

immobilazione (It). *See* FIXED ASSETS.

impact day (UK). The day on which a company publishes details of a new issue. Under United Kingdom new issue requirements, the bank to any new issue is required to apply to the Bank of England for a place in the queue of new issuers. The Bank maintains an orderly queue to avoid too many companies and other borrowers all wanting to raise money at the same time thus ruining all chances of success, as well as causing liquidity problems in the short term money markets.

The Bank will allot each potential borrower an impact day and the merchant bank, along with the company's other advisers, will work towards this date to get all the details finalized. If, by the time the date is reached, conditions in the market have become less favourable to the success of an issue, the issue may be postponed, in which case a new impact day has to be sought.

impiombato (It). A dealer who finds himself with a portfolio of securities whose book values are higher than those on the current market. As a result he is unable to operate on the market without incurring a loss on his transactions.

imposta sul plusvalore di capitale (It). *See* CAPITAL GAINS TAX.

impôt de bourse (Fr). Stamp duty payable in France on all securities except those traded on regional exchanges. On bonds and debentures payable within seven years, the rate is 0.3 percent of transactions up to Ff 1 million and 0.15 percent on the balance.

imputation system (UK). The system of corporation tax which has been in existence in the United Kingdom since 1973. The essence of the imputation system is that tax on both distributed and undistributed profits shall be identical. Any tax credit given to shareholders with their dividend and paid over to the tax authorities as Advance Corporation Tax is a deduction against the company's mainstream Corporation Tax. Prior to 1973, dividends bore tax in the hands of shareholders but were not allowable as an offset against a company's own tax on its profits. In effect, therefore, tax was levied more heavily on distributed than on undistributed profits, in order to encourage companies to retain and plough back profits.

inactive bond crowd (US). *See* CABINET CROWD.

in-and-out trading (US). *See* DAY TRADING.

in apertura (It). *See* APERTURA.

in battuta (It). Refers to a security which is the object of considerable trading in one or more stock exchange TRADING SESSIONS.

incentive shares. Shares alloted by a company under a SHARE OPTION SCHEME or a PROFIT SHARING plan to its employees.

income bond. (1) (UK) A savings investment scheme, the principal object of which is to concentrate on providing income for its participants rather than capital growth.

(2) (US) A bond issued by a company which pays income to its holders when profits are earned. In some instances, accruals of unpaid income on such bonds may be accumulated as a claim against the company.

income debenture. A loan which pays interest out of profits earned by the company.

income statement. *See* EARNINGS REPORT.

income tax. The principal tax on the earnings of individuals in the United Kingdom. Income tax at the current basic rate is deducted at source on all interest payments made by a company on its loan capital. For shares, dividends are paid net to shareholders but a tax credit, equal to the basic rate of tax on an equivalent gross dividend, is also given to the shareholder. A basic rate taxpayer has no further liability to tax; a shareholder liable to tax at rates higher than the basic rate will later have to pay the balance to the tax authorities. The company pays the sum total of the tax credits to the tax authorities as ADVANCE CORPORATION TAX (ACT).

BIBLIOGRAPHY Income and Corporation Taxes Act 1970 (HMSO, London). *Tolley's Income Tax* (Tolley Publishing, London, annually).

income yield. (1) The total return in terms of income to an investor over the life of the asset or for as long as he holds it.

(2) For an alternative usage *see* FLAT YIELD.

inconvertible stocks/bonds. Stock or bonds which cannot be converted into others at maturity.

incrociare (It). To match one or more purchase-bargains by sales bargains for the same securities and in the same stock exchange TRADING SESSION.

indenture (US). A written agreement under which BONDS and DEBENTURES are issued and which sets out such details as rate of interest, maturity date and other terms and conditions.

independent broker (US). A member on the floor of the New York Stock Exchange who executes orders for other brokers having more business at that time than they are able to carry out themselves, or for firms who do not have their Exchange member on the floor. Formerly known as two-dollar brokers from the time when these independent brokers received two dollars per one hundred shares for executing such orders. The fees of independent brokers are paid by the COMMISSION BROKERS. *See also* FLOOR BROKER.

indexation. *See* INDEX LINKING.

indexation of Capital Gains Tax (UK). CAPITAL GAINS TAX was introduced in the United Kingdom in 1962 on short term gains and extended in 1965 to all gains. Subject to certain exceptions and small gains, Capital Gains Tax was levied on the disposal of assets on nominal increases in their value. Between 1965 and 1982, the RETAIL PRICE INDEX in the United Kingdom rose from the equivalent of 100 to over 500. Sellers of assets were paying Capital Gains Tax on gains brought about by inflation when the real value of the asset may actually have fallen in value.

To remedy this situation, the Finance Act of 1982 introduced an indexation allowance so that only real gains made after March 1982 would be liable to Capital Gains Tax, subject to specified restrictions. These restrictions were : (1) the asset must have been held for at least twelve months; (2) a nominal gain must exist (losses could not be indexed); (3) indexation was available only to inflation after March 1982.

Subject to these rules, an indexation allowance could be added to the acquisition costs (total buying price, plus expenses) in arriving at a figure of capital gain. The indexation allowance was calculated according to the formula :

$$\frac{RD - RI}{RI}$$

where *RD* is the retail price index in the month of disposal of the asset, *RI* is the retail price index in the month twelve months after the month of acquisition of the asset, or in March 1982, whichever is the later.

The total cost, plus this indexation allowance, is then subtracted from the total sale proceeds to arrive at the amount of capital gain to be taxed. If the allowance is more than the nominal gain, the amount of indexation allowance is limited to the amount of the nominal gain.

Special rules apply to the buying and selling of shares to establish which acquisitions qualify for indexation. These are referred to as the IDENTIFICATION RULES.

Indexation also applies to a figure of realized gains which is free from Capital Gains Tax. This figure was fixed at £5000 for 1982/83 and is raised annually in line with changes in the retail price index.

BIBLIOGRAPHY Finance Act 1982. *Capital Gains Tax* (Tolley Publishing, London, annually).

index, stock exchange. *See* INDICES, STOCK EXCHANGE.

index fund. An investment fund whose shareholdings mirror a particular share index.

index linked stock (UK). A series of British Government securities first issued in 1981 which carry a COUPON rate of 2 or 2.5 percent but with both interest and principal linked to the general RETAIL PRICE INDEX. The first issues of these stocks were available only to pension funds and life assurance companies, but were later extended to all in 1982. Index linked stocks traded on the Stock Exchange were just one of a variety of index linked instruments issued by the British Government in the late 1970s as protection to savers against inflation. Others were issued via the NATIONAL SAVINGS movement and included non-tradable bonds issued to pensioners, so-called GRANNY BONDS, later also extended to all savers.

index linking. The concept of making a monetary payment dependent upon a measure of the change in retail prices to shield people against the effects of inflation. Many variables can be index linked, including wages and salaries, loans, capital gains, interest payments etc. Index linking achieved widespread use in Brazil in the 1960s and was partially introduced in other countries in the 1970s. Index linking is, nonetheless, unpopular with governments who say that it reduces people's awareness of the dangers of inflation. *See also* INDEXATION OF CAPITAL GAINS TAX.

index number. A statistical technique designed to measure the change in a particular variable over a period of time, starting from a given base date. The two basic types of index number are Laspeyres and Paasche. Index numbers of stock exchange prices are often of the Laspeyres type and constructed on base period quantities and prices. Thus the formula is :

$$\frac{\sum p_1 q_o}{\sum p_o q_o}$$

when: $\sum$ *is the sum of the constituents' prices and shares issued*
p_o is the price of a constituent at the base date
p_1 is the current price
q_o is the number of shares on issue at the base date

See also INDICES, STOCK EXCHANGE.

index of retail prices. *See* RETAIL PRICE INDEX.

indice Borsa Valori di Milano (M.I.B.) (It). The official stock market index calculated by the Milan Stock Exchange on securities traded there. There are two general indices, one current and one historic. Each index is sub-divided into fifteen industry sectors.

The current index consists of all securities listed on the Milan Stock Exchange. The base date of the current index is 3 January 1983 when it was given the figure of 1000. It is calculated daily based on the closing prices of the securities.

The historic index comprises 129 stocks and its base date is 2 January 1975. Like the current index, its base is 1000 and it, too, is calculated daily at the close of business.

indice della azione (It). See INDICES, STOCK EXCHANGE.

indice des actions (Fr). *See* INDICES, STOCK EXCHANGE.

indice Mediobanca (It). The stockmarket index of the leading medium term banking institute, Mediobanca.

indices, stock exchange. Calculations made on an INDEX NUMBER basis to indicate the movements in the general level of prices of securities listed on stock exchanges. All securities markets have at least one index, calculated either by the Exchange itself or by an outside body such as a bank, newspaper or association of actuaries. Many exchanges have a number of different indices, designed to meet different needs.

There is no single set pattern for stock market indices: some are based on a selection of shares listed, others on the whole market; some are weighted by market capitalization or turnover, some are unweighted; most are based on an arithmetic calculation, a few on a geometric basis; most are based on a figure of 100, but this too varies.

Abbreviated details of the main indices in the major world stock markets are given in the appendix to this dictionary: each of them is more fully described in individual entries.

Individual Retirement Account (IRA) (US). A pension plan with tax advantages originally introduced in the United States in 1974, but widened in its scope in 1982. Any worker can now set up an individual retirement account and obtain a tax deduction for his contributions up to $2000 a year. The legislation allows this tax relief providing that the investment is made through an intermediary such as a mutual fund (unit trust), insurance company, bank or through a stockbroker. Investment in the employee's own company shares via an approved pension, share ownership or thrift plan is also permitted.

Any employee can set aside these funds, but they cannot be realized until he is within a few months of the retirement age of 60. Tax is not levied on the funds in an Investment Retirement Account and withdrawals from it after the permitted date are taxed at the saver's marginal rate of income tax.

Funds in IRAs can be used to purchase a wide range of assets, including high-yielding fixed interest securities, company stocks and shares and bank certificates. Gold, jewellery and works of art are, however, specifically exempt.

The purpose of the legislation was to give employees an incentive to save for retirement and to reduce burdens on federal budgets in the future. It was also hoped that the incentives would help to improve the rate of savings in the United States, which is low in comparison with other economically developed countries, to stimulate industry and help bring down inflation and interest rates. *See also* EMPLOYEE RETIREMENT INCOME SECURITY ACT; EMPLOYEE SHARE OWNERSHIP PLAN; KEOGH PLAN.

Industrial and Commercial Finance Corporation (ICFC) (UK). A body set up by the clearing banks and the Bank of England in 1945, to supply medium and long term lending in amounts of up to £1 million to small and medium sized British companies. Merged with its sister organization, FINANCE FOR INDUSTRY, the latter itself became INVESTORS IN INDUSTRY in 1983.

ingolfato (It). An excessively speculative market where dealers have overbought or oversold.

ingresso in borsa (It). Permission to operators to enter a stock exchange trading floor.

Inhaberaktie (Ger). *See* BEARER SHARE.

Inhabereffekten (Ger). Bearer securities generally, both shares and bonds.

Inhaberobligation (Ger). *See* BEARER BOND.

Inhaberpapier (Ger). A security in bearer form.

inherent worth. The value of a share calculated in relation to the fundamental position of a company and its profits. *See also* FUNDAMENTAL ANALYSIS.

in-house funds. Funds which are under the management of a financial institution which may also be a market participant in its own name. *See also* DISCRETIONARY FUNDS.

initial margin. The deposit which a user of U.S. stock markets or of FUTURES markets must make on purchasing or selling a CONTRACT. The amount of the deposit represents only a fraction of the total value of the contract. *See also* FINANCIAL FUTURES; MARGIN; MAINTENANCE MARGIN; VARIATION MARGIN.

innerer Wert (Ger). *See* INHERENT WORTH.

in prezzo (It). Where the current price on the stock market is within the established price limits and the transaction may therefore be concluded.

inscribed stock (UK). An old method of registering stock, which existed side by side with registered stock. A piece of paper was issued showing that the holder's name was written in the register, but the paper did not have the value of a CERTIFICATE. The practice of inscribed stock has been discontinued and REGISTERED STOCK is now the norm.

inscription en compte (Fr). A system for the settlement of transactions on the French Stock Exchanges involving the establishment of credit accounts or depositories. The system is already used for Treasury bonds and was recommended for equities as well by the COMMISSION PEROUSE.

insider. One who trades in a security with beneficial or inside knowledge not available to the world at large and who, by so doing, makes a profit for himself. Long considered reprehensible by all stock market regulators and outlawed in the United States, insider dealing has now also been made illegal in the United Kingdom and France. In the United Kingdom, for example, insider dealing was made illegal under the COMPANIES ACT 1980. The European Commission published a code of conduct in 1977 relating to securities trading which *inter alia* deals with insider trading. This code, however, is a recommendation to member states and is not legally binding on them. In countries where insider dealing is not illegal, it is controlled by the stock exchange authorities who will themselves take action to punish those who have acted on inside information or aided them.

insider dealings. *See* INSIDER.

insolvency. The inability to meet one's debts as they fall due; applies to individuals, partnerships and companies but different rules apply to the way in which affairs are resolved. *See* BANKRUPT; WINDING UP.

insolvenza di borsa (It). Stockmarket insolvency. In such cases the COMITATO DIRETTIVO DEGLI AGENTI DI CAMBIO intervenes to settle the insolvency.

Inspector, Stock Exchange (UK). *See* STOCK EXCHANGE INSPECTOR.

Instinet (US). Short for Institutional Networks Corporation, Instinet is registered with the SECURITIES AND EXCHANGE COMMISSION as a stock exchange. The system collects price quotes from market makers, both on stock exchange trading floors and on NASDAQ, and allows institutional investors nationwide not only to find the best bid and offer in the markets, but also to deal electronically at the best price found. *See also* NATIONAL ASSOCIATION OF SECURITIES DEALERS AUTOMATED QUOTATION SYSTEM (NASDAQ).

institutional investors. Institutions whose prime function is to gather the savings of individuals and give them financial protection through insurance, pensions or the spreading of risk. The resources they obtain from individuals are used to invest in earning assets such as government securities, equities and other company security issues, property etc. Institutional investors include pension funds, insurance companies, unit trusts (mutual funds) and investment trusts. The growth of such institutional investors has greatly increased over the past quarter of a century. Many reasons can be put forward for this: the growth of pensions as a benefit of employment; legislation to encourage long term saving for retirement; tax benefits to encourage people to undertake other long term contractual saving; increased fluctuations of interest rates and stock market prices, which has encouraged people to entrust their savings to institutions; and rising inflation, which has swollen the institutions' resources, are just a few. In many countries throughout the world institutional investors are taking an increasing proportion of company securities at the expense of the individual investor.

BIBLIOGRAPHY *Stock Exchange Survey of Share Ownership (1981),* (Stock Exchange, London, 1983). *Shareholding, 1983* (New York Stock Exchange).

institutionelle Anleger (Ger). *See* INSTITUTIONAL INVESTORS.

instrument. Originally the meaning was simply a formal written document which evidenced a financial transaction. The word has widened its meaning and now, used in an investment context, is the means by which an investment is carried out. Financial instruments, in the widest sense, can include bank accounts, other savings plans, investment and unit trusts, shares, financial futures and options contracts.

interamente sottoscritto (It). *See* FULLY SUBSCRIBED (ISSUE).

inter-broker dealers (US). Firms which are involved in the U.S Treasury bond market providing liquidity to the PRIMARY DEALERS. The function of the inter-broker dealers is to buy and sell Treasury bonds with the dealers, allowing the latter to structure their portfolios according to the maturity spread they require and to offset undue risk by being too heavily committed in a particular maturity range. In the dealing system for gilt edged securities now being discussed in the United Kingdom, inter-broker dealers may also emerge in that market.

inter-company loans market (UK). One of the short term money markets in London, the inter-company loans market developed in the late 1960s when bank lending was restricted; it enabled companies with short term borrowing needs to raise money from other companies with a surplus of short term funds. Usually such transfers were arranged via brokers and the amounts were unsecured. Although figures are difficult to come by, it is thought that this market faded from the financial scene in the mid-1970s and the passing of the Banking Act 1979, requiring deposit-takers to obtain a licence from the Bank of England, makes the re-emergence of such a market unlikely.

interesse (It). *See* INTEREST.

interesse della parte maggioritaria (It). *See* CONTROLLING INTEREST.

interessenza di minoranza (It). A minority interest in a company. *See* MINORITY SHAREHOLDER.

interessewahrend (Ger). Buying or selling orders which are left with the dealer to execute in the best interests of the client. An instruction to deal AT BEST rather than a LIMIT ORDER.

interest. (1) The payment for borrowed money. *See also* RATE OF INTEREST.

(2) A holding or investment in a security. *See also* SHAREHOLDING.

Interest Equalization Tax (US). A tax introduced by Congress in 1963 to discourage American investors from buying overseas issues of securities made on the US financial markets. Overseas borrowers had found the United States a congenial place to raise long term funds because interest rates generally were lower there than in other developed capital markets, notably those of western Europe. The object of the tax which was levied on purchases of such securities was to make it just as expensive to borrow in the United States as elsewhere and to encourage overseas borrowers to use other markets. Both they and US borrowers began to do so in great numbers and the Interest Equalization Tax is often cited as one of the factors which led to the rapid growth of the EUROBOND market. The tax was repealed in 1974.

interest rate. *See* RATE OF INTEREST.

interest rate futures. Contracts on a FINANCIAL FUTURES exchange denominated in a particular deliverable short or long term financial instrument such as a three month certificate of deposit. The object of an interest rate futures contract is to offset the risk that rates of interest will move against a HEDGER before he is in a position to carry out his underlying transaction. If the outcome is indeed adverse, the profit from his futures contract will help offset the higher interest he has to pay or the lower interest he receives at the later date.

interest warrant. The instruction sent by a company's registrar authorizing the payment of interest due. The warrant consists of a cheque payable to the beneficiary and a counterfoil showing the amount of interest payable and the tax deducted.

interest yield. *See* FLAT YIELD.

intérêt (Fr). *See* INTEREST.

intérêts accumulés or ***intérêts courus*** (Fr). *See* ACCRUED INTEREST.

interim dividend. A dividend payment made on account during the course of a company's financial year. Usually announced at the time of the interim results, the interim dividend, unlike the final dividend, does not have to be agreed in general meeting.

Interimsschein (Ger). Interim certificates issued pending the preparation of the final certificate.

interim statement (UK). A statement made by a company on its trading results and prospects in the first half of its financial year. It usually consists of half yearly accounts, which may be unaudited, together with a statement by the chairman.

interinale (It). The slip of paper which acts as a temporary document of bargains concluded.

Intermarket Trading System (ITS) (US). An electronic communications network, begun on a pilot basis in 1980 and now linking seven trading floors of stock exchanges in the United States. ITS was designed to stimulate competition among them in stocks listed either on the NEW YORK STOCK EXCHANGE (NYSE) or the AMERICAN STOCK EXCHANGE (AMEX) and one or more regional exchanges. Through ITS any broker or market maker on the floor of any participating stock exchange can locate participants elsewhere in the country, to carry out a deal whenever he sees via ITS a better price than is being quoted on his own trading floor.

intermediary, financial. *See* FINANCIAL INTERMEDIARY.

internal debt. That part of a country's national debt which is owed to its own nationals. *See also* EXTERNAL DEBT.

internal finance. Company finance which is raised from the profits made by the company, as opposed to that raised from outside by a bank loan or stock exchange issue. Most internal finance comes from retained profits and in the United Kingdom such finance accounts for around two-thirds of the financing needs of industrial and commercial companies.

International Bank for Reconstruction and Development (IBRD) (The World Bank). Founded along with its sister organization, the International Monetary Fund, as a result of the Bretton Woods conference of 1944, the IBRD provides financial guarantees and lends long term finance to countries to help them develop their economies. Capital is subscribed by the sovereign states which are members of the Bank, but the Bank also raises substantial amounts of long term loans on the capital markets of the world to allow it to carry out its work. It also operates through two affiliates, the INTERNATIONAL FINANCE CORPORATION and the International Development Association.

International Commodities Clearing House (ICCH) (UK). The organization which clears all transactions carried out between members of the LONDON INTERNATIONAL FINANCIAL FUTURES EXCHANGE (LIFFE). In addition to providing clearing facilities, it also guarantees all transactions, thus facilitating both dealing and settlement.

ICCH was originally established in 1888 as the London Produce Clearing House and changed its name in 1973. In addition to the facilities it offers to financial futures trading, ICCH also provides its services to the various commodities markets, including cocoa, coffee, rubber, sugar, vegetable oil and wool. ICCH also operates in overseas centres such as Hong Kong, Sydney and Kuala Lumpur.

International Dealers (IDs) (UK). A special category of Stock Exchange dealing company set up in April 1984 to deal, as principals, in overseas securities in competition with overseas dealers. International Dealers must have capital of at least £500,000 and must be members of the UK Stock Exchange. Outsiders, however, may own up to 49 percent of an International Dealer organization.

International Finance Corporation (IFC). Founded in 1956 as an affiliate of the INTERNATIONAL BANK FOR RECONSTRUCTION AND DEVELOPMENT to help mobilize lending to developing countries.

International Monetary Market (IMM) (US). A division of the Chicago Mercantile Exchange, one of the major commodities exchanges in the United States. The IMM was formed in May 1972 to trade in FINANCIAL FUTURES contracts, particularly in CURRENCY FUTURES.

BIBLIOGRAPHY Marilyn P. Skony, 'The Foreign Exchange Futures Market' in Abraham M. George and Ian H. Giddy (eds.), *International Finance Handbook* (John Wiley, New York, 1983), Section 2.5.

international securities. Securities which are dealt in on a number of stock exchanges throughout the world and which are widely held by residents of different countries.

interrogation device (US). A computer terminal which provides market information, such as the price of the last trade, quotes and volumes of business done, either on a tape or video display unit.

interstanza (It). The settlement of intermarket transactions through the respective clearing houses of the Bank of Italy.

intervento (It). Intervention. A term to indicate repeated purchases of a security in order to counteract a fall in prices caused by consistent sales.

in-the-money option. A CALL OPTION whose EXERCISE PRICE is below the price at which the UNDERLYING SECURITY is being traded in the market. Conversely, a PUT OPTION the exercise price of which is above the current market price. *See also* AT-THE-MONEY OPTION; OUT-OF-THE-MONEY OPTION.

intrinsic value. (1) *See* INHERENT WORTH.

(2) In an OPTIONS CONTRACT, the intrinsic value is the difference between the EXERCISE PRICE and the price of the UNDERLYING SECURITY. A CALL OPTION has intrinsic value if the exercise price of the option is lower than the current market price. Equally a PUT OPTION has intrinsic value if the exercise price is above the current market level. *See also* IN-THE-MONEY OPTION.

introduction. A particular method of listing shares on a stock exchange for the first time. An introduction may be contrasted with a PLACING or an OFFER FOR SALE in that the shares which are the subject of an introduction will already be quite widely held by shareholders other than directors and no new money is being raised either by the company itself or by the directors from sales of their shareholdings. The purpose of an introduction is to provide a wider market for the shares of the company and perhaps an enhanced value by virtue of being listed. The company may also be in a more favourable position to raise new money later as a result of its stock exchange listing.

introduction à la bourse (Fr). A listing of shares on a French or Belgian stock exchange.

inverted market. A futures market in which the contracts for the months nearer to maturity are selling at a PREMIUM over those of the more distant months, thus reversing the normal pattern.

investissements miracles (Fr). *See* ALTERNATIVE INVESTMENT.

Investitionsportefeuille (Ger). *See* PORTFOLIO.

investitore instituzionale (It). *See* INSTITUTIONAL INVESTOR.

investment. The outlay of money to purchase an interest earning or dividend paying asset. Investment may be either 'real', by which is meant buying of goods, plant, equipment, land etc or 'portfolio', the buying of securities or other type of financial instrument.

investment bank (UK). A non-clearing bank which exists to invest money on a medium to long term basis in small and medium sized companies. Such investment may be by way of equity participation or by means of loan finance.

investment banker (US). Also known as an UNDERWRITER, the investment banker is the middleman between a corporation (company) issuing new securities and the public. The usual practice is for one or more investment bankers to buy a new issue outright from the directors of a corporation and form a syndicate to sell the stocks to investors. In the United Kingdom a similar function is performed by a MERCHANT BANK acting as an ISSUING HOUSE.

investment company (US). A company which uses its capital to invest in the securities of others. It may be a CLOSED END FUND or an OPEN END FUND. In the United Kingdom, such investment companies are known as either INVESTMENT TRUSTS or UNIT TRUSTS, respectively.

investment counsel (US). *See* INVESTMENT ADVISER.

investment currency (UK). Foreign exchange for overseas investment purposes which could only be purchased from a special fund of currency, generally at a premium, under the exchange control rules operating in the United Kingdom until 1979. *See also* EXCHANGE CONTROL; INVESTMENT CURRENCY PREMIUM.

investment currency premium (UK). The premium quoted as a percentage which had to be paid by UK residents wanting to buy currency for overseas investment purposes prior to the ending of exchange control in 1979. The pool of investment currency was replenished by sales of overseas investments and the level of the premium was determined by supply and demand. At one period, although all the currency for an investment overseas had to be taken from the pool at the premium rate, 25 percent of proceeds from the sale of overseas assets had to be surrendered at the official rate with only 75 percent eligible to take advantage of the investment currency premium.

investment income. The annual return from an investment, either real or portfolio.

investment income surcharge (UK). An additional tax, levied in the United Kingdom on investment income, latterly at 15 per cent on amounts of investment income in excess of £7100. The investment income surcharge was abolished by the Finance Act 1984.

investment portfolio. *See* PORTFOLIO.

Investment Protection Committees (UK). Committees set up in the United Kingdom by the major groups of investing institutions, the pension funds and insurance companies, to act as the channel of liaison with the companies whose shares they hold. They may make recommendations to companies on matters involving the issue of shares (for example, they are against the issue of non-voting shares) and generally discuss with companies matters which affect them as major shareholders.

Investmentsparen (Ger). An investment plan for regular savings.

investment trust (UK). A CLOSED END FUND used by small investors to spread their investment risk. The investment trust, which may be either a general fund or may specialize in a particular type of security, sector of the economy or area of the world, is a corporate entity registered under the Companies Acts and a listed Stock Exchange security bought and sold by investors in the normal way. Its value is determined by supply and demand in the market, rather than by the value of its underlying securities.

Investment Trust Companies, Association of (UK). *See* ASSOCIATION OF INVESTMENT TRUST COMPANIES.

investor. One who places funds in an asset on which he expects a return, either via income, capital gain or both. The investor may put his funds into real or PORTFOLIO INVESTMENT.

Investor Protection, Review of (UK). *See* GOWER REPORT.

Investors In Industry (III) (UK). A company, formerly known as FINANCE FOR INDUSTRY, which was created in 1983 as a means of assisting small and medium sized British companies to raise equity and loan finance.

Investors In Industry is owned by the London and Scottish clearing banks, which own 85 percent of its capital, with the other 15 percent held by the Bank of England. In addition, money is raised via the domestic and international capital markets on long term loans.

Besides its financing activities, the group is also involved in management consultancy, corporate financial advice and pension fund management.

In addition to its base in London, Investors In Industry has overseas subsidiaries in the United States, France and the Republic of Ireland.

invisible exports. The export of services, as opposed to goods, from a country. Anything intangible which earns foreign currency can be considered an invisible export. Included are interest, profits and dividends on overseas investments, tourist expenditure in the country, earnings from insurance, banking, stock market transactions, shipping and aviation services, consultancy services provided overseas, even the earnings overseas of pop music groups. The United States, the United Kingdom and West Germany are the world's major earners on the invisibles account, which forms part of a country's balance of payments' current account.

irredeemable debenture. A secured loan stock with no final date of repayment.

irredeemable stock. A government stock with no fixed date of repayment. *See also* CONSOLS; FUNDED DEBT.

issue. (1) The total amount of a company's stock listed on a stock exchange. *See also* ISSUED SHARE CAPITAL.

(2) The act of distributing that stock. *See also* NEW ISSUE; SCRIP ISSUE; RIGHTS ISSUE.

issue price. The price at which shares are sold to investors for the first time. *See also* OFFER FOR SALE; OFFER PRICE; TENDER.

issued share capital. The total number of shares made available to the public and the total nominal value of that issue. Should be contrasted with MARKET CAPITALIZATION, which is the total value of the securities based on current stock market prices.

issuing house (UK). Strictly speaking, one of the members of the ISSUING HOUSES ASSOCIATION but more loosely any merchant bank or dealer in securities which sponsors the issue of a new security on the Stock Exchange or an over-the-counter market. The issuing house will have been closely involved in the work leading up to the issue and will have advised the company on its timing, the price and all other formalities relating to it.

Issuing Houses Association (IHA) (UK). A group of 60 or so leading MERCHANT BANKS in the United Kingdom which are specifically concerned with corporate finance and the sponsoring of NEW ISSUES. The IHA was formed in 1945 and acts as the trade association for the issuing houses. *See also* ACCEPTING HOUSES ASSOCIATION; COUNCIL FOR THE SECURITIES INDUSTRY.

J

Jahresabschluss (Ger). Annual accounts.

Jahresbericht (Ger). Annual report.

Jahreshauptversammlung (Ger). *See* ANNUAL GENERAL MEETING.

Japan Securities Finance Company (Jap). One of the three securities finance companies whose role is to lend stock or cash to securities houses and thus help liquidity in the Japanese markets. Formed originally in 1927, the Japan Securities Finance Company dealt with the needs of the members of the Tokyo Stock Exchange. Following a reorganization in 1956, it now covers the Sapporo, Nagoya and Fukuoka exchanges as well. *See also* OSAKA SECURITIES FINANCE COMPANY, CHUBU SECURITIES FINANCE COMPANY.

BIBLIOGRAPHY *Securities Markets in Japan* (Japan Securities Research Institute, Tokyo, annually).

jobber (UK). A MARKET MAKER on the UK Stock Exchange, a jobber is in competition with his fellow jobbers on the market for the brokers' business. There are at least two jobbers in all actively traded stocks so that the BROKER, when acting as agent for his client, always has a choice of the best possible price. There are, in total, 17 firms of jobbers on the UK Stock Exchange; some of these are very large and cover most major stocks in the market, while others are quite small and only cover specific areas of the market, notably the GILT EDGED market.

Under proposals now being made by the Stock Exchange, the competitive jobbing system, with the market makers unable to act as agents and deal with clients, may soon be replaced by a competitive market making system where the dealers may act in the capacity of both agent and principal. Such changes are likely to be introduced after the ending of minimum commissions, scheduled for the end of 1986 at the latest. *See also* COMPETING MARKET MAKER.

BIBLIOGRAPHY For a description of the jobbing system, there are many descriptive books on the present operation of the Stock Exchange, including: Janette Rutterford, *Introduction to Stock Exchange Investment* (Macmillan, London, 1983), Chapter 1. H.D. Berman, *The Stock Exchange* (Pitman, London, 1973). J. Dundas Hamilton, *Stockbroking Today* (Macmillan, London, 1979). For a description of the proposed new system, see *The Stock Exchange: A Discussion Document* (The Stock Exchange, London, April 1984). *The Choice of a New Dealing System for Equities* (July 1984). *The Choice of a New Dealing System for Gilt-Edged Securities* (August 1984).

jobber's book (UK). The record of a jobber's POSITION in the securities in which he trades. A jobber's book may be described as LONG to show when he has stock on his book for which he has not yet found a buyer, SHORT when he has sold stock he does not possess, and level when neither of these situations is true.

Jobbers' Index (UK). A Stock Exchange publication detailing which jobbers make markets in particular stocks. Popularly known as 'Squirts' Guide', a squirt being a trainee who was inexperienced in checking the market and needed his guide to tell him which jobbers to approach.

jobber's pitch (UK). One of the hexagons or other trading positions on the floor of the London Stock Exchange at which the competing jobbers stand to receive orders from the brokers.

jobbers' price spread agreement (UK). *See* OPENING PRICE CONVENTION.

jobber's quote (UK). The SPREAD between the buying and the selling price of securities quoted by a jobber when asked the price by a broker wishing to deal in the stock concerned.

jobber's spread (UK). *See* SPREAD, JOBBER'S QUOTE.

jobbers' touch (UK). Jobbers are in competition with one another for the brokers' business. When he goes into the market, a broker may be faced with three different BID and OFFER PRICES. One jobber may quote 101-104, a second 102-105, and a third, 103-106. In this case, the jobbers' touch in the market is 103-104, the difference between the third jobber's price for buying from the broker and the first jobber's price for selling to him. *See also* CHOICE and BACKWARDATION.

jobber's turn (UK). The profit made by a jobber on a deal. Sometimes mistakenly used to refer to the difference between the BID and OFFER prices of one jobber. The jobber's spread, however, is not his profit. His role is to make a market and he will frequently move his prices to try to attract business. He has no guarantee that if he buys a share at, say, 103, he will be able to sell it at 106. He may in the event be able to sell for 104 or, if the market suddenly turns against his expectations, for below the 103 he paid.

jobber trade. An expression used on the LONDON INTERNATIONAL FINANCIAL FUTURES EXCHANGE (LIFFE) to describe the purchase or sale and subsequent liquidation of the same number of contracts in a FINANCIAL INSTRUMENT for the same DELIVERY MONTH executed on the same trading day. *See also* DAY TRADING.

jobbing firm (UK). *See* JOBBER.

joint stock company (UK). A rather archaic term for a company registered under the Companies Acts. Originally used to describe a company with shares as compared with a private company. All companies are now 'joint stock' and thus the term has all but fallen into disuse except for banks, where the phrase joint stock banks is still occasionally used.

jouer à la bourse (Fr). To play the market; to gamble on the stock exchange.

jouissance (Fr). The date from which a newly issued stock is expected to pay interest.

jour de règlement (Fr). Settlement day.

jour seulement (Fr). Valid for the day. An order given by a client to his broker on the understanding that it will lapse if it cannot be carried out within the next trading session.

K

Kaffirs. The name given to South African gold mining stocks. At one time the main market in such shares was in London, and although Johannesburg and even New York now trade extensively in them, a major market still exists in London, where a considerable number of these stocks are listed.

Kam Ngan Index (KNI). One of the three stock market indices of Hong Kong, the other two being the HANG SENG INDEX and the FAR EAST INDEX.

Kam Ngan Stock Exchange. One of the four Stock Exchanges of Hong Kong, the Kam Ngan Stock Exchange was founded in March 1971 by a group of members from the Chinese Gold and Silver Exchange. In terms of members and market capitalisation, Kam Ngan is second in size to the Far East Exchange.

Kapital (Ger). *See* CAPITAL.

Kapitalanlage (Ger). *See* INVESTMENT.

Kapitalanlagegesellschaften (Ger). Investment companies which are controlled by the GESETZ ÜBER DIE KAPITALANLAGEGESELLSCHAFTEN.

Kapitalertragssteuer (Ger). *See* WITHHOLDING TAX. The rate of withholding tax in Germany is 25 percent on convertible bonds and equities for foreign holders.

Kapitalexport (Ger). The outflow of capital overseas for investment purposes.

Kapitalgewinn (Ger). Capital gain.

Kapitalisierung (Ger). *See* MARKET CAPITALIZATION.

Kapitalmarkt (Ger). The capital market.

Kapitalverlust (Ger). Capital loss.

Kapitalzuwachssteuer (Ger). Capital gains tax. There is no separate capital gains tax in Germany, although speculative gains on assets held for less than six months are charged at income tax rates. Gains on the sale of shares in privately owned companies may also be subject to tax, again at income tax rates, but with a tax free amount allowed.

Kassa, per (Ger). A cash transaction.

Kassenobligationen (Ger). Medium term notes issued by the public authorities in West Germany as security for loans.

Kassenverein (Ger). Central depositories for securities in West Germany. Almost all transfers of securities are done through the *Kassenverein* and a special foreign depository exists for international business.

Keogh Plan (US). A personal retirement plan with tax advantages which can be undertaken by the self employed. Tax is not levied on contributions but only on withdrawals as they are made (usually after retirement). *See also* INDIVIDUAL RETIREMENT ACCOUNT.

kerb market. An unofficial name for trading in securities outside a recognized stock exchange. The name derives from the fact that such trading often took place on the street.

kerb trading. On a FINANCIAL FUTURES EXCHANGE, the execution of a deal after the close of the official market.

Kommunalobligationen (Ger). Local government bonds.

Konsolidierte Bilanz (Ger). *See* CONSOLIDATED BALANCE SHEET.

Kontrahent (Ger). A contracting party to a stock market transaction.

Körperschaftssteuer (Ger). Corporation tax.

Kowloon Stock Exchange. The newest and by far the smallest of the four HONG KONG STOCK EXCHANGES, the Kowloon market was founded in January 1972 and enjoyed considerable turnover in its early years. Today, however, its turnover constitutes less than one percent of total trading on all four exchanges.

Krugerrand. A coin minted by South Africa and containing an ounce of gold. Popular as a means of buying gold among small investors.

Krumm sein (Ger). An expression used to indicate that a transaction cannot be carried out. To wish, for example, to carry out an ODD LOT transaction on the VARIABLER KURS where the rules permit trading only in a ROUND LOT.

kulanter Kurs (Ger). An advantageous price.

Kulisse (Ger). A word derived from COULISSE on the French market and used collectively to describe the institutions and brokers dealing on the market on their own account.

Kupon (Ger). *See* COUPON.

Kurs (Ger). The price or quotation of a listed stock on the German Stock Exchanges. There is an implication in the term *Kurs* as opposed to *Preis* of a flow of business, rather than an individual transaction at a one-off price. *See* FREIVERKEHR. Within the German official market there are both single quotations (EINHEITSKURS) and continuous quotation (VARIABLER KURS) sectors

Kursblatt (Ger). The daily official record of stock market quotations and prices.

Kurskommission (Ger). The quotations committees of the two large Stock Exchanges in Germany, namely Frankfurt and Düsseldorf. They include representatives of the banks and of securities market participants and are responsible for ensuring that new issues conform to the necessary listing requirements.

Kursmakler (Ger). An official broker on a German Stock Exchange. The *Kursmakler* is responsible for determining the prices of individual securities at the EINHEITSKURS by assessing the amount of supply and demand and determining a price which maximises turnover. On the VARIABLER KURS the *Kursmakler* is responsible for determining the price of a security at the beginning of a trading session in the same way and is responsible for maintaining continuous prices throughout the session of trading. The term *Kursmakler* is often translated into English variously as broker, jobber and specialist. This translation is, however, somewhat misleading since the *Kursmakler* is unique to the German system and his functions differ substantially from those of the participants in the Anglo-Saxon markets. The *Kursmakler* is engaged in the official market only and has a two-fold function: he acts as an intermediary for those banks and other participants admitted to deal on a stock exchange, in addition to fixing the prices according to the balance of supply and demand for those securities for which he has been alloted responsibility, as outlined above. The *Kursmakler* acts only as an intermediary between other market participants and is not allowed to deal with members of the investing public. *See also* FREIE MAKLER.

BIBLIOGRAPHY Rolf E. Breuer, 'Frankfurt Equity Markets', in Abraham M. George and Ian H. Giddy (eds.) *International Finance Handbook* (John Wiley, New York, 1983), Section 6.4. Paul Stonham, *Major Stock Markets of Europe* (Gower Publishing, London, 1982).

Kursmaklerkammer (Ger). The association of official brokers. It is a public body representing the KURSMAKLER, supervising them and allocating securities among them, and is responsible for controlling settlement of prices and for editing the KURSBLATTE.

Kurspflege (Ger). Changes made to prices in line with changed market conditions. Used in particular in the fixed interest market when securities are taken up by an issuing house, there being a shortage of firm buyers in the market.

Kurzfristig (Ger). Short term.

Kux (Ger). A mining company share.

L

lame duck. A term applied in the 19th century to a jobber who was unable to comply with his bargains; now a general term for an industrial company unable to stand on its own financial feet and in need of state support.

lanciare una società (It). *See* FLOAT A COMPANY.

langfristig (Ger). *See* LONG.

lapsed option. An OPTIONS CONTRACT which has expired and has not been exercised. *See also* EXERCISE AN OPTION.

last-in-first-out (LIFO). The phrase used to describe one method of identifying which stocks or securities are being disposed of. For the converse *see* FIRST-IN-FIRST-OUT. For the purposes of the INDEXATION OF CAPITAL GAINS TAX introduced in the United Kingdom in the Finance Act of 1982, shares which were acquired at different times more than 12 months prior to a disposal, are identified on a last-in-first-out basis.

BIBLIOGRAPHY Finance Act 1982. *Capital Gains Tax* (Tolley Publishing, London, annually).

last trade (US). The latest deal which took place in a particular security. Details of the last trade are printed on the TICKER including the size of the bargain and the price at which the deal took place.

last trading day. On a FINANCIAL FUTURES exchange, the final day during which trading may take place in a DELIVERY MONTH. Futures contracts outstanding at the end of the last trading day must be settled by the delivery of the specified FINANCIAL INSTRUMENT to which they relate or, in some markets, by a cash settlement.

late tape (US). The phrase used to indicate that because trading is so heavy, information on the CONSOLIDATED TAPE is falling behind the market.

Laufzeit (Ger). The unexpired period to maturity of a loan.

launch a company. Identical in meaning to FLOAT A COMPANY.

lavorare in parita (It). To deal net, that is at a price which includes an element of commission.

lavorare in tendenza (It). To buy or sell securities in line with the market trend for speculative rather than investment purposes.

lead manager. The ISSUING HOUSE or bank which is the principal one concerned in a syndicated loan or securities issue.

Leerverkauf (Ger). *See* BEAR.

legal list (US). A list of investments selected by various states in which certain institutions and financial trustees, such as insurance companies and banks, may invest. Legal lists are often restricted to high quality securities meeting certain specifications. *See also* PRUDENT MAN RULE. In the United Kingdom the equivalent is TRUSTEE SECURITIES governed by the Trustee Investments Act.

legato (ordine) (It). An order which ranks behind another transaction in order of execution.

leichter (Ger). A general drifting downwards in stock market prices.

le second marché (Fr). *See* SECOND MARCHÉ, LE.

lessee (US). In a securities market context, someone who rents a seat on a stock exchange from an existing owner for an annual fee.

lettera (It). Term used on the trading floor to indicate that a dealer wishes to sell the securities.

lettera da ripartizione (It). *See* ALLOTMENT LETTER.

letter of allotment (UK). *See* ALLOTMENT LETTER; PROVISIONAL ALLOTMENT LETTER.

letter of application (UK). The form attached to a PROSPECTUS for a new issue which an applicant must complete in order to apply for an ALLOTMENT of the shares.

letter of renunciation (UK). A form, in the style of a letter, signed by the holder named on an ALLOTMENT LETTER or a PROVISIONAL ALLOTMENT LETTER who wishes to renounce his right to the shares specified in the allotment. The letter of renunciation is addressed to the directors of the company and informs them of the named holder's wish to renounce the allotment in favour of the person(s) named on the REGISTRATION APPLICATION FORM.

lettre d'attribution (Fr). *See* ALLOTMENT LETTER.

leverage (US). The effect on a company's EARNINGS PER SHARE when it has bonds (fixed interest stock), preferred (preference) shares or both, outstanding. The earnings per equity share will be more volatile the higher the borrowing element. The term is synonymous with the UK term GEARING.

leveraged buy-out. A term originating in the United States but now spreading to the United Kingdom. It refers to the practice of someone (often a director or a senior employee) buying control of one company (usually part of a group) on borrowed funds. *See also* MANAGEMENT BUY-OUT.

liabilities. All the claims outstanding against a company including the capital subscribed by shareholders, SHAREHOLDERS' FUNDS which have been put into reserves, loan capital outstanding as well as short term items such as creditors, bank loans, declared dividends, tax payments due etc.

libération (Fr). The payment for a new issue of shares. *See* SUBSCRIPTION.

Liberierung (Ger). *See* LIBÉRATION.

life (of a bond or stock). A fixed interest security's unexpired period to maturity; sometimes used to indicate the full period of the loan from issue to maturity.

limit. *See* LIMIT ORDER.

limitato (ordine) (It). A stockmarket order with a maximum or minimum price limit. *See* LIMIT ORDER.

limite (Fr). *See* LIMIT ORDER.

limited. *See* PUBLIC LIMITED COMPANY.

limited corporate member (LCM) (UK). A corporate shareholder in a Stock Exchange member firm. Although normally a member firm's directors and shareholders must agree to accept unlimited liability, limited corporate members were first allowed in the late 1960s to help member firms raise outside capital. At first the maximum outside shareholding was fixed at 10 percent but was raised in 1982 to 29.9 percent. It is likely that over the next few years this limit will again be raised, perhaps to allow full ownership. In the particular type of Stock Exchange member firms called INTERNATIONAL DEALERS, a limited corporate member may already own up to 49 percent.

limited liability. The extent to which a shareholder is responsible for the debts of a company. This responsibility is limited to the amount he has subscribed (or may be called upon to subscribe in the case of PARTLY PAID

SHARES). Liability may also be limited by guarantee rather than shares, but this is less usual. *See also* COMPANY LIMITED.

limited market. A market in which it is difficult to deal in a reasonable quantity of a stock.

limit order. The price beyond which an investor is not prepared to go. In giving instructions to his broker, the investor will specify the highest price he is prepared to pay to buy a security or the lowest price he is prepared to accept for selling a security. The word is also used on FINANCIAL FUTURES markets in a similar context. *See also* DAY ORDER for a specific financial futures market usage. In the United States, the limit order may also be referred to as a limited order or a limited price order.

limit order system (US). The limit order system automatically files orders which are to be executed when a specific price is reached. The system now includes any DAY ORDER and GOOD 'TIL CANCELLED order.

limit up or limit down. *See* PRICE LIMITS.

line (of shares) (UK). A BLOCK of shares.

link, the (UK). The relationship between minimum commissions and the maintenance of single capacity in the United Kingdom stock market. The argument runs that the fixing of scales of minimum commissions by the Stock Exchange assures brokers of a given reward for each transaction undertaken. As a result the BROKERS are prepared to bring all their deals to the market (the JOBBERS). If minimum commissions were to go, brokers would seek to replace lost revenues by finding the counterparty to a deal for themselves, thus cutting out the market place or taking stock on to their books as principals. The jobbers, the link argument continues, would not sit idly by. They would also seek direct access to clients and the whole concept of SINGLE CAPACITY would break down.

With the agreement of the Stock Exchange to end the fixing of minimum commissions by the end of 1986 at the latest, the question of the maintenance of single capacity was put to the test. As a result, the Stock Exchange has made proposals for a future dealing system which, if implemented, will allow dealers to act as both principals and agents, subject to reporting of information and other safeguards for the investor.

liquid. Of assets, the ease with which they may be converted into cash immediately and without loss. The word is used in a variety of contexts in the financial markets, but always with a similar meaning.

liquidare (un) contratto di borsa (It). To settle a stockmarket contract by payment and delivery of the certificate.

liquidare la posizione (It). To sell all securities previously bought for forward delivery. LIQUIDATION of a POSITION.

liquid assets ratio. Generally, the ratio to total assets of those assets which can be converted with ease and without loss into cash. In banking, however, the liquid assets ratio is usually expressed as a proportion of deposit liabilities.

liquidation. (1) The repayment of a debt.

(2) The WINDING UP of the affairs of a company.

(3) The process of converting securities into cash.

(4) The act of buying or selling to offset an existing position.

See also BUY IN, SELL OUT, EVEN OUT for specific meanings in a FINANCIAL FUTURES context.

Liquidationskasse (Ger). The corporation for options trading in West Germany. The traders in this market are stock exchange members approved by the *Liquidationskasse* or LOMBARDKASSE. Trading takes place in Frankfurt and Düsseldorf and both puts and calls are traded in a few shares. Approval for trading is given by the Federal Finance Minister and the BÖRSENVORSTAND and supervision is exercised by the Committee for Options Dealing of the relevant stock exchange.

liquidator. Someone appointed to carry out the WINDING UP of a company. *See also* RECEIVER.

liquidity. (1) The degree of cash or short term assets held by an investor or investing institution.

(2) The ease with which a security can be converted into cash immediately and without loss.

(3) By extension, the ease with which securities as a whole in a market can be converted into cash (and vice versa) without causing a movement in prices.

liquid market. *See* LIQUIDITY.

listed company. Sometimes referred to as a quoted company, a listed company is one whose shares have obtained a listing or quotation on a recognized stock exchange. The phrase is confined to full listing and not generally extended to, for example, a company whose shares are traded on the UNLISTED SECURITIES MARKET or OVER-THE-COUNTER MARKETS.

listed securities. The securities of issuers, whether company, government, local authorities etc, which have been given a listing on a recognized stock exchange.

listing. The act of allowing the securities of an issuer to be traded on a stock market. *See also* QUOTATION.

Listing Agreement (UK). The undertaking which has to be adopted by a resolution of a company's board of directors before its shares can be listed on the UK Stock Exchange. One of the principal objects of the Listing Agreement is to secure the immediate release of information which might reasonably be expected to have a material effect on market activity in and prices of listed securities. Such information includes both regularly recurring matters such as dividends, interim results etc and also exceptional matters, such as a take-over approach.

BIBLIOGRAPHY *Admission of Securities to Listing (Yellow Book)* (The Stock Exchange, London).

listing requirements. The conditions which an issuer must fulfil before securities can be admitted to listing on a stock exchange. Different exchanges around the world have different requirements, some more stringent than others. The basic requirements for a listing on the UK Stock Exchange, for example, are that a company must have a minimum MARKET CAPITALIZATION of £500,000 and make available sufficient shares to enable LIQUIDITY to develop in the market; normally 25 percent of a company's share capital must be made available to satisfy this last criterion.

On the New York Stock Exchange some of the considerations used to determine whether or not a company's shares should be listed include nationwide interest in the company and a minimum of one million shares held among not less than 2000 ROUND-LOT holders. The publicly held shares should have a minimum market capitalization of $16 million and the company should have net income in its latest financial year of at least $2.5 million before tax and $2 million in each of the preceding two years.

The basic criteria for a listing on the Paris BOURSE are that a company must have paid a cash dividend in each of the preceding three years and must have a minimum of 300,000 shares outstanding with a total par value of Ff40 million. In addition, at least 25 percent of the issued share capital must be in public hands. (On a regional exchange, only 80,000 shares need be outstanding). These requirements are minima laid down by the COMPAGNIE DES AGENTS DE CHANGE (CAC) and in practice, companies applying for listing will have share capital well in excess of the minimum figure. This also tends to be true of listings in the United Kingdom and on the New York Stock Exchange.

listino ufficiale di borsa (It). The official Milan Stock Exchange list of prices.

lists closed (UK). The phrase used to indicate that the subscriptions for a NEW ISSUE of shares have been at least sufficient to cover the amount of stock on offer. In an offer for sale, subscription lists usually open at 10:00 on a particular day. If the issue is a popular one and it is clear that the issue is FULLY SUBSCRIBED, the announcement will be made that lists opened at 10:00 and closed at 10:01 and applications will be dealt with as described in the entry OFFER FOR SALE.

load (US). The amount of the OFFER PRICE for an open end mutual fund (unit trust), over and above the market value of the securities. The excess is used for administrative expenses. The load is usually charged only on purchase. *See also* FRONT END LOADING.

loan, back-to-back. *See* BACK-TO-BACK LOAN.

loan capital. That part of the capital of a company which consists of loans rather than shares, the holders being creditors of the company rather than shareholders. Loan capital consists of both DEBENTURE and LOAN STOCK.

loan docket (UK). A document issued by the Stock Exchange settlement centre to MONEY BROKERS for their use when depositing stock. It identifies details of the stock loan for which the deposit is being made.

loan stock. A security issued by a company in respect of a loan made by investors. Loan stocks are often unsecured, unlike a DEBENTURE, which is secured by a fixed or floating charge on the assets of the company. Loan stock holders rank alongside all other unsecured creditors in the event of a winding up of the company. The holders bear rather more risk therefore than DEBENTURE HOLDERS and unsecured loan stocks are unlikely to find willing investors unless issued by companies of the highest standing. In the United Kingdom in recent years there have been few issues of loan stocks or debentures because the high rates of interest ruling in the market have deterred company treasurers from undertaking long term commitments at such rates.

local. A dealer on a FINANCIAL FUTURES or TRADED OPTIONS market who deals for his own account and is independent of a large financial organization. Locals are found particularly in the Chicago markets and give additional LIQUIDITY to those markets.

local authority bonds (UK). Securities issued by local government borrowers, usually at fixed rates of interest. They are often nonmarketable securities issued direct to the general investing public by way of advertisement. *See also* LOCAL AUTHORITY STOCKS; LOCAL AUTHORITY YEARLING BONDS.

local authority stocks (UK). Long term securities issued by local government borrowers and listed on the Stock Exchange. These stocks may range for up to 25 years and although mostly issued at fixed rates of interest, in recent years VARIABLE RATE STOCK and INDEX LINKED STOCK have also been issued.

local authority yearling bonds (UK). Short term local government bonds often of one year maturity, hence the name, but sometimes issued for periods of up to three and even five years. Introduced in the mid-1960s, the bonds are issued in blocks, often with several authorities participating in an issue on identical terms of interest and repayment. On the maturity of the bond the amount of the loan is frequently rolled-over into another yearling bond at a rate of interest then ruling in the market. *See also* ROLL-OVER.

locked in. An expression used to describe the position of an investor who cannot (or is unwilling to) sell his security. This might be because trading in the security has been suspended by the stock exchange authorities. Alternatively he may not want to sell the security, perhaps because the proceeds will be subject to CAPITAL GAINS TAX whereas, by waiting for a short time, he can sell without being liable to tax. The phrase has a specific meaning in the United Kingdom with regard to PROFIT SHARING schemes under the Finance Acts 1978 and 1980. An employee alloted shares under these schemes is locked in for a period of two years during which he cannot sell the shares. After that period he may sell, but he will be liable to pay income tax on his benefit unless he keeps the shares for a total of seven years.

Loi Monory (Fr). A scheme introduced in 1978 by M. Réné Monory, the then French Minister of Finance, to encourage investment by individuals in stocks and shares issued by French companies. Briefly, a tax-paying family unit, basically husband and wife, could receive full tax relief on new investment of up to Ff5000 a year; additionally, in respect of the first two children a further Ff500 was allowable for each, while for every subsequent child a further annual investment of Ff1000 was allowed. The scheme was originally introduced in 1978 for four years but was later extended to the end of 1982.

Subsequently, the original *Loi Monory* was amended by M. Jacques Delors, successor to M. Monory as Minister of Finance: investors may now place Ff10,000 a year into stocks and shares while benefitting from a 20 percent tax credit on such investment. Households may have two such savings accounts, so that the maximum for a family unit is Ff20,000 a year.

BIBLIOGRAPHY Bruno de Maulde, *The Monory Act and the French Stock Market* (Speech delivered at the Stock Exchange, London, 13 September 1979, in the Chairman's Lecture series).

Lombard credit. A loan secured on readily realizable security, such as stocks and shares.

Lombardkasse (Ger). *See* LIQUIDATIONSKASSE.

Lombard Street (UK). In mundane geographical terms, a street in the City of London but in practice a synonym for banking and short term money markets in the United Kingdom. Named after the Lombards, the merchants of northern Italy from the city states of Genoa, Florence, Venice and Lucca, who set up as financiers in the City of London (among many other places throughout Europe) following the expulsion of the Jews from England by Edward I in 1290. The Lombards were the forerunners of modern day bankers in the United Kingdom and the name Lombard Street is a permanent reminder of the fact.

London Discount Market Association (LDMA) (UK). The association of discount houses in London, the LDMA consists of eleven discount houses, namely Alexanders Discount; Cater Allen; Clive Discount; Gerald Quin, Cope; Gerrard and National; Jessel, Toynbee and Gillett; King and Shaxson; Page and Gwyther; Seccombe, Marshall and Campion; Smith St Aubyn and Union Discount.

The members of the LDMA enjoy a unique place in the money markets of London and in the monetary control arrangements administered by the Bank of England. *See* DISCOUNT HOUSE.

London Inter-Bank Offered Rate (LIBOR) (UK). The rate offered by first class commercial banks for funds on the inter-bank market in London. LIBOR has achieved an importance far beyond this arcane use, the three month rate having become the major reference point for calculating the interest rate on much bank lending, rates being quoted at a percentage above LIBOR. The reason for LIBOR replacing in some measure the banks' own base rates as a reference point for interest rates, has been the growth in the percentage of commercial bank funds taken on the inter-bank market, rather than through the branch networks.

London International Financial Futures Exchange (LIFFE) (UK). The financial futures market established in the Royal Exchange, London, in September 1982. The market deals in currency futures in sterling against the dollar, Deutsche Mark, yen and Swiss franc and in interest rate futures based on 3-month sterling and dollar certificates of deposit and a 20-year government stock rate. In addition, it now also trades contracts in US Treasury bonds and in the movement of share prices via the FINANCIAL TIMES-STOCK EXCHANGE INDEX (FT-SE).

London money markets (UK). The markets for short term funds in London, through which the banks adjust their cash and liquidity positions. Principal among the markets is the traditional discount market (*see* DISCOUNT HOUSE). The discount houses borrow funds AT CALL and at short notice from the banks and other financial institutions. These funds are invested in a wide variety of short term assets including Treasury bills, certificates of deposit, commercial bills, local authority securities and short dated government stocks. The discount houses, by borrowing from one bank and repaying their loans to another, are effectively ironing out the flow of liquid assets between the banks. All lending in this market is secured and if the houses are short of funds overall they have borrowing rights from the Bank of England, either by the Bank buying bills from them or by lender of last resort (discount window) facilities.

Over recent years, the traditional London discount market has been supplemented by a number of other short term money markets, often called parallel markets, including the sterling and eurodollar interbank markets, the sterling and dollar certificate of deposit markets and the local authority and instalment finance company markets. The differences between these and the traditional discount market are that these markets are essentially direct borrowing and lending markets through brokers and the transactions are generally unsecured.

BIBLIOGRAPHY E.R. Shaw, *The London Money Markets* (Heinemann, London, 3rd edition, 1981).

London Stock Exchange (LSE) (UK). The major stock market in the United Kingdom. Strictly speaking, the London Stock Exchange has, since the unification of the UK Stock Exchanges in 1973, been the London unit of The Stock Exchange of the United Kingdom and the Republic of Ireland. It is still, however, often referred to as the London Stock Exchange, particularly in an international context.

The origins of the London Stock Exchange can be traced to the coffee houses of 17th century London. Here dealers would congregate to buy and sell the shares of joint stock companies. Eventually, the dealers felt the need for a private meeting place of their own, which they called the Stock Exchange. This enabled them to restrict membership and to enforce rules of conduct on the participants. The London Stock Exchange, established on its present site in the late 18th century, laid down its first rules in the early 19th century and they have a continuing history of evolution since then.

During the 19th century, many smaller stock exchanges were established around the country to meet the vast demands for capital to expand local industry, trade and communications. An amalgamation movement began shortly after the second world war and the exchanges were all eventually amalgamated into one organization in 1973. *See also* STOCK EXCHANGE, THE.

long. (1) In economic terminology, a stock with more than 15 years to run to maturity.

(2) On the UK Stock Exchange, a security with ten years or more to maturity; the difference in terminology is caused by the definition of LONG in the scales of minimum commission, due to be phased out by the end of 1986.

(3) The position of a market maker who has unsold supplies of a particular stock on his BOOK; in that case, he is said to be long of the stock. *See also* SHORT.

(4) In a FINANCIAL FUTURES context, the word used to describe the position of someone who has bought one or more futures

CONTRACTS and has not yet closed out his POSITION by a closing sale.

long hedge. The purchase of futures CONTRACTS with a view to protecting or HEDGING the holder's position. *See also* HEDGER.

long stock. *See* LONG.

long tap (UK). The TAP stock which the GOVERNMENT BROKER is currently using to supply demand for stock with over ten years to run to maturity.

long term. Over fifteen years in usual economic terminology.

Losanleihe (Ger). A bond on which no interest is paid, but payment of a premium occurs when repayment of the bond is made by a drawing. *See* DRAWN BOND.

lot (Fr). The minimum MARKET CAPITALIZATION of a share issue on the BOURSE. *See also* LISTING REQUIREMENTS.

lotto (It). Minimum trading lot which is a number of shares or a par value for bonds.

low coupon stock. A gilt edged stock with a low nominal rate of interest. Usually issued at a low price to attract those investors more concerned with capital gain than with income.

lump sum investment. A scheme of investment under which the investor makes a single payment rather than a series of regular monthly or quarterly contributions.

luogo (di) esecuzione degli ordini di borsa (It). The Stock Exchange in which the transaction was executed. As many securities are multi-listed, it is often important to know where the deal was executed.

M

mainstream Corporation Tax (UK). *See* CORPORATION TAX.

maintenance margin. In a FINANCIAL FUTURES contract, the minimum margin which a customer must keep in his account with a member of the futures exchange in respect of all OPEN CONTRACTS after deducting all amounts due for the INITIAL MARGIN and the VARIATION MARGIN.

majoration (Fr). Multiple application for shares in a new issue. *See* STAG.

Makler (Ger). A dealer on the German Stock Exchanges. *Makler* may be official dealers (BÖRSENMAKLER or KURSMAKLER) or independent dealers (FREIE MAKLER). The *Makler* are the market makers, with the banks and credit institutions effectively acting as the brokers. For a more detailed description of the roles of the different types of *Makler, see* KURSMAKLER and FREIE MAKLER.

Maklergebühr (Ger). The brokerage paid to a MAKLER for his market-making services; for share dealing it is one percent of consideration on equities and a sliding scale on bonds ranging from 0.075 percent of nominal or par value for a deal of up to DM50,000 down to 0.0075 percent on a deal in excess of DM5million.

Maklergeschäft (Ger). A bargain made by a MAKLER for his own account, although normally he is only allowed to CROSS orders.

Maloney Act (US). *See* NATIONAL ASSOCIATION OF SECURITIES DEALERS (NASD).

managed bonds. Savings schemes in which the investment is switched regularly between different types of investment: gilt-edged, equities, property, overseas securities, according to how the manager sees prospects for the moment.

managed fund. A fund established by a financial intermediary for the latter to employ on behalf of the investor. *See also* DISCRETIONARY FUNDS.

management buy-out. The purchase of a specialist part of a large conglomerate by its managers and the establishment of such an entity as an independent company. Management buy-outs became popular both in the United Kingdom and the United States in the late 1970s and early 1980s as disillusion set in with the concept of large conglomerates popular in the 1960s. Managements were often assisted in the buy-out by tax reliefs and large bank borrowings.

management shares. *See* SHARE OPTION SCHEMES.

manager. *See* LEAD MANAGER.

mancata risposta (It). When the counterparty of an option deal does not declare his intention on the expiry of the option. This will require the intervention of the COMITATO DIRETTIVO DEGLI AGENTI DI CAMBIO.

mani (It). A word used in reference to unknown operators or speculators who are behind a massive movement in the prices of securities.

manipulation (US). The buying and selling of shares in order to create the illusion of market activity or to raise or lower the price, thus inducing others to buy and sell. An illegal operation.

marchand de titres (Fr). A MARKET MAKER in securities.

marché (Fr). A market. Widely used in combination with other words or phrases to produce a variety of different meanings; for example, *bon marché* (a good market) also means 'cheap'; some other common usages follow.

marché à options (Fr). One of the MARCHÉS CONDITIONNELS on the French Stock Exchanges. The *marché à options* is equivalent to the market in CONVENTIONAL OPTIONS in the United Kingdom rather than the traded options market. On the *marché à options* buyers may purchase a put option (OPTION DE VENTE) or a call option (OPTION D'ACHAT) which give the right to exercise the option at a fixed price on any one of nine monthly expiry dates. *See also* MARCHÉ À PRIMES.

marché à primes (Fr). Like the MARCHÉ À OPTIONS, the *marché à primes* is one of the MARCHÉS CONDITIONNELS. On it, a buyer may purchase the right to buy, but not to sell, a specified number of securities at a pre-determined price for up to three months ahead on one of three monthly expiry dates. On the *marché à primes,* the buyer may abandon his bargain before settlement day on payment of a fixed forfeit (*prime).*

marché à terme (Fr). The market for forward delivery, as opposed to the MARCHÉ AU COMPTANT or spot market. On the *marché à terme* around 250 of the most active stocks are traded. The bargains are firm ones but settlement and delivery are delayed until the next settlement period. Since October 1983, securities can be quoted on either the spot or forward market, but not both as used to be the case. Clients dealing on this market must provide a cover or margin which is a percentage of the amount of their dealings and which must be adjusted in line with changes in price. The amount depends upon the nature of the cover provided: cash or Treasury bonds to the value of 10 percent of the deal; French fixed interest securities or gold, 25 percent and cover provided by other securities, 40 percent. The *marché à terme* is itself divided into the MARCHÉ DES REPORTS and the MARCHÉS CONDITIONNELS.

marché au comptant (Fr). The cash or spot market as opposed to the MARCHÉ À TERME. All officially listed securities are negotiable on this market where they may be bought and sold in any quantities for immediate payment and delivery.

marché de l'argent (Fr). The money market for short term funds, as compared with the longer term capital market.

marché des capitaux (Fr). The generic term for the markets in long term funds - the capital market.

marché des reports (Fr). The CONTANGO market. This market operates once a month on the day after settlement day and allows buyers to sell their shares at a fixed price and to buy them back again at the same price on the settlement day of the following month. Sellers buy their shares and re-sell them on the settlement day of the following month.

As the buying position usually exceeds the selling position, the market fixes a contango rate which is paid by the buyers. For those securities for which the selling position exceeds the buying position, the market fixes a rate to be paid by the sellers, called *déport* or BACKWARDATION.

marché des valeurs (Fr). A general term for a securities market.

marché hors côte (Fr). An unofficial OVER-THE-COUNTER MARKET within the French *bourses.* Trading on this market is carried out by the AGENTS DE CHANGE. Securities are divided into two sectors: the special section, on which are traded the securities of those companies which have given an undertaking to the COMMISSION DES OPERATIONS DE BOURSE that they will publish information normally required of listed companies and that they will apply for a listing of their shares within three years; the other, or ordinary, section deals in the securities of other companies.

Transactions in these markets are for cash and the AGENTS DE CHANGE are responsible for the prices at which dealings take place, but take no responsibility for the underlying quality of the shares. *See also* SECOND MARCHÉ.

marché monetaire (Fr). *See* MARCHÉ DE L'ARGENT.

marchés conditionnels (Fr). The general name for the MARCHÉ À PRIMES, the MARCHÉ À OPTIONS, STELLAGE and OPERATIONS DU DOUBLE.

Marge (Ger). The difference between a dealer's BID PRICE and OFFER PRICE: the spread.

margin (US). The proportion of the full price of the shares paid by a client to his broker when he buys securities on credit. The amount of margin is fixed by the Federal Reserve Board and is varied from time to time: over the post-war period it has fluctuated between 50 and 100 percent.

There is much less use of margin trading in the United Kingdom, partly because of the ACCOUNT dealing system and partly, it is said, because the prices of individual shares are much lower than in the United States.

In the FINANCIAL FUTURES markets, margin is required against OPEN CONTRACTS in particular financial instruments. Margin consists of INITIAL MARGIN, VARIATION MARGIN and MAINTENANCE MARGIN.

margin call (US). The demand upon a customer by the broker to place the required MARGIN, whether in cash or securities. The call is made at the same time as a purchase and thereafter additional calls are made if the margin falls below a predetermined level set by the New York Stock Exchange or the member firm, which may be above the minimum levels set by the Federal Reserve Board.

margine (It). The positive or negative difference between the current price of a security and the price at which it was bought or sold.

mark (UK). *See* MARKING.

mark down. To lower the price of securities. Market makers may lower their prices to attract buyers and deter sellers. Usually this is done following bad news, either generally or about a particular company. Marking down of prices is a reaction to find a level which may equate new amounts of supply and demand and stimulate turnover.

market. (1) A meeting place in which willing buyers find willing sellers and agree on prices for exchange. The original concept was of a physical location where buyers and sellers would meet, but today a market can be nothing more than information and order flows by telephone or electronic means. It is now no exaggeration in financial terms to talk of a world market in money and financial instruments.

(2) The generality of prices in a market place used, for example, in the phrases: 'the market was stronger' or 'the market moved higher', meaning a general rise in prices of the commodities traded in that marketplace.

(3) The collective noun for the jobbers or other market makers on an exchange.

(4) Sometimes used as an abbreviation for market price, as in the phrase 'the market is 102-103', meaning that the best available buying price in the market is 103 and the best selling price 102.

marketable securities. Stocks and shares which have been admitted to trading on a stock exchange.

market capitalization. (1) The total value of a company's securities at current prices. The total number of shares in ISSUE multiplied by the price gives the figure of market capitalization.

(2) Market capitalization may also refer to the total valuation of all securities listed on a stock exchange or the total value of particular types of securities (e.g. equities, government stocks).

market depth. *See* DEPTH (OF A MARKET).

market if touched (MIT). A price order which automatically becomes a MARKET ORDER if the price is reached.

market maker. One who trades in the market as a PRINCIPAL and actively seeks to encourage trading by changing his prices to tempt buyers or sellers to trade. It is possible for a market maker to be a monopolist, as in the New York Stock Exchange's SPECIALIST system, or in competition with his fellow market makers for brokers' or other agents' business; such a situation occurs, for example, in the London market via the jobbing system and in the United States through the NATIONAL ASSOCIATION OF SECURITIES DEALERS (NASDAQ) market.

In the changes to the market dealing system now being planned for securities trading in the United Kingdom, the system most likely to be adopted is that of competing market makers. Firms which become market makers will be able to act in DUAL CAPACITY should they wish to do so. It is also envisaged that there will be a role for those firms who wish to confine their activities either to the role of principal or that of agent. *See also* JOBBER; LINK, THE; SINGLE CAPACITY.

BIBLIOGRAPHY *An Introduction to the NASD* (NASD, 1983). *The Choice of a New Dealing System for Equities* (The Stock Exchange, London, July 1984).

market order (US). An order to buy or sell a stated amount of securities at the best price obtainable in the market after the order is presented to the TRADING CROWD. *See also* GOOD 'TIL CANCELLED; LIMIT ORDER; STOP ORDER. A similar meaning is attached to a market order on a FINANCIAL FUTURES exchange.

market partnership. A situation in which two MARKET MAKERS normally in competition with one another agree to form a temporary dealing partnership in a particular security, sharing the profits or losses between them. Not a common occurrence, such market partnerships are normally the result of a special and difficult situation.

market price. (1) The current price of a security in the market; sometimes referred to just as 'the market'.

(2) (US) Additionally, the last reported price at which a security has been sold.

Market Price Display Service (MPDS). A closed circuit TV system run by the Stock Exchange in London which distributes, on a nationwide basis, the prices of some 750 securities traded on the market, along with company news information. *See also* TOPIC.

market report. The news and information on the day's trading events on a stock exchange. The market report will highlight strong and weak sectors of the market and shares which showed a notable rise or fall, commenting on the reasons for the movement. *See also* FEATURES.

market size. The amount of shares in a transaction which the market can comfortably handle. The market size of any particular security depends upon the number of shares in issue and available for trading in the market. It thus varies considerably from one issue to another. *See also* FREE MARKET; NARROW MARKET.

market value. The price of a company's securities in the market. The market value will be dependent upon the relative supply and demand for that security in the market and will be based on prospects for the company's products, the strength of its finances, its prospects for a take-over bid, market sentiment and many other factors. The market value of a security bears little relation to its nominal value, although special rules limit a company's ability to make new issues of shares if the market value is below its nominal value.

marking (UK). The noting, for permanent record, of a price at which a share transaction took place. Marking on the UK Stock

Exchange states simply the price, not the quantity of shares traded nor the WAY (i.e. buying or selling). If a broker goes to mark a price and a deal has already been marked at the same price, he does not mark it again. The marks are published in the STOCK EXCHANGE DAILY OFFICIAL LIST the following day.

marking names (UK). Banks, stockbrokers and others are recognized as good marking names for the collection and payment of dividends paid out on AMERICAN-FORM SHARE CERTIFICATES. Those agents who are not regarded as good marking names are referred to as other names. A list of good marking names appears annually in THE STOCK EXCHANGE OFFICIAL YEAR BOOK.

Markt (Ger). *See* MARKET.

Markt beherrschen, der (Ger). *See* CORNER.

Marktbericht (Ger). *See* MARKET REPORT.

Marktbewertung (Ger). *See* MARKET CAPITALIZATION.

mark to market. An expression used on the FINANCIAL FUTURES market to describe the daily adjustment of a customer's account to reflect profits and losses on OPEN CONTRACTS based on the closing market prices at the end of the day.

Marktpreis (Ger). *See* MARKET PRICE.

Marktumständen (Ger). The state of the market.

mark up. (1) An increase in the market makers' prices for shares. The opposite of MARK DOWN and done with the same end in view; to arrive at a new price which will equate the flow of demand and supply and produce an active level of turnover.

(2) The amount added to a share price by a dealer, over and above the amount he paid for it when he on-sells it to an investor.

matching. The checking of each day's purchases and sales of futures contracts so that buyers and sellers agree the number and price of the contracts covered by each floor transaction.

maturity. (1) The date on which a security will be repaid on the stated terms. Sometimes this is not one specified date but a range during which the stock will be repaid. Thus British Government stocks are often quoted with two maturity dates, for example 2010-2013, meaning that the stock will be repaid not before the year 2010 and not after 2013.

(2) In a FINANCIAL FUTURES contract, the period within which the contract may be satisfied by delivery; that is, the period from the FIRST NOTICE DAY to the LAST TRADING DAY of the contract.

maturity date. *See* MATURITY.

maximum price fluctuation. The maximum amount by which the contract price can change, either up or down, during one trading session, as fixed by a FINANCIAL FUTURES exchange. Once the upper and lower PRICE LIMITS are reached on a particular contract, further trading in the contract will not be permitted for a specified period, following which trading can continue without limit for the remainder of the day. If the maximum price fluctuation is reached during the last hour of trading, trading in that contract is halted for the remainder of the day.

Mayday (US). 1 May 1975. The day on which minimum commissions came to an end on the New York Stock Exchange. Whether or not the choice of date was designed to make the international distress signal an apposite comparison, brokers and the media seized on the pun and the name has stuck. During the months following Mayday, the number of broking firms on the New York Stock Exchange declined sharply as commissions were reduced.

medium gilts (UK). Generally, government securities with between five and fifteen years to MATURITY. For Stock Exchange commission purposes, however, a stock between five and ten years to maturity.

mediums. *See* MEDIUM GILTS.

medium term. Generally regarded in economic terms as five to fifteen years; less than five is short term; over fifteen is long term.

meglio (al) (It). *See* AT BEST.

Mehrheitsbeteiligung (Ger). A controlling interest in a company.

member. In a general stock exchange or FINANCIAL FUTURES context, anyone who has a seat or otherwise is in full membership of the exchange. *See also* ASSOCIATE MEMBER; CORPORATE MEMBER; HALF COMMISSION MAN; MEMBER CORPORATION; MEMBER FIRM.

member corporation (US). A brokerage firm on the New York Stock Exchange which is organized as a corporation (company) with at least one officer or employee who is a member of the Exchange. For the UK equivalent *see* CORPORATE MEMBER.

member firm. In both the United States and the United Kingdom, a securities organization which belongs to a stock exchange and is structured as a partnership. In the United Kingdom, all the PRINCIPALS of the firm must be members of the Stock Exchange; in the United States, at least one general partner or employee must be a member of the Exchange.

member organization (US). Either a MEMBER CORPORATION or a MEMBER FIRM of the New York Stock Exchange.

members voluntary winding-up (UK). *See* VOLUNTARY LIQUIDATION.

Memorandum of Association (UK). The document drawn up by the founders of a company showing its name, registered office, its objects, details of its share capital and the liability of its members in the event of WINDING UP.

mercato (It). *See* MARKET.

mercato azionario (It). *See* STOCK MARKET.

mercato calmo (It). A market characterized by a dominance of orders to sell and therefore with falling prices.

mercato contrastato (It). A market in which it is difficult to pick out a precise trend owing to imbalances between selling and buying orders.

mercato debole or ***mercato pesante*** (It). A BEARISH market.

mercato (in) denaro (It). A BULLISH market.

mercato fermo (It). A positive or firm market trend in which purchases prevail over sales.

mercato inattivo (It). A weak market with little volume.

mercato (in) lettera (It). A negative market trend in which sales prevail over purchases.

mercato nervoso (It). A market characterized by continual price variations in both senses.

mercato parallelo (It). In the stockmarket it refers to a third market where unlisted securities are traded without any controls or regulations.

mercato (dei) premi (It). The options market.

mercato primario (It). The primary market in new issues.

mercato pulito (It). A market uninfluenced by speculative positions.

mercato resistente (It). A steady market.

mercato riflessivo (It). A slightly falling market.

mercato ristretto (It). The regulated market, created in 1977, for trading in unlisted securities.

mercato secondario (It). The secondary market in securities.

mercato selettivo (It). A market in which only a few leading securities manage to remain immune from a general negative trend.

mercato (di) sportello (It). Stockmarket transactions in listed and unlisted securities executed outside the official market.

mercato stabile (It). A stable market where prices fluctuate very little.

mercato tendente al rialzo (It). *See* BULL MARKET.

mercato tendente al ribasso (It). *See* BEAR MARKET.

mercato (a) termine (It). The forward market in shares.

merchant bank (UK). A bank in the United Kingdom which is more involved with such matters as corporate finance and financial advice, mergers, amalgamations and take-overs and the management of investments, than in the retail deposit-taking business. The major merchant banks are usually members of the ACCEPTING HOUSES COMMITTEE or the ISSUING HOUSES ASSOCIATION or both, but there are banks outside these two groupings which might be referred to as merchant banks. The name arose in the 19th century when traders or merchants engaged in international trade began to add to their normal business the practice of the ACCEPTANCE of other, less well known, merchants' bills of exchange, thus enabling them to obtain credit at better rates of interest or discount. This business became so profitable that some merchants began to specialize in this banking function to the exclusion of their trading activities, but the name merchant bank still remains.

merger. The amalgamation of two businesses into a new trading or corporate entity. The term has the overtone of an amalgamation of equals rather than the take-over of one company by another, but is often used more loosely. *See also* TAKE-OVER BID.

meta da savio or ***meta da matto*** (It). An expression used in the Italian Stock Exchanges to signify that prices have risen sufficiently to allow a speculator to reduce his position and make a considerable profit.

Metageschäfte (Ger). Arbitrage transactions where the two parties share the profit or loss.

middle price. The price half way between the buying and selling prices of securities. This may be at the close of business or at a time during the day. It is also sometimes referred to as the middle market price.

migliorando. (It). Splitting an order to buy or sell in order to obtain a better price.

Minderheitsbeteiligung (Ger). A minority interest (less than 50 percent) in a company. *Contrast with* MEHRHEITSBETEILIGUNG.

minimum commission (UK). *See* COMMISSION.

Minimum Lending Rate (MLR) (UK). A term used in British banking from 1972 to 1981, MLR was the penal rate at which the Bank of England would lend money to a DISCOUNT HOUSE if the Bank wished to engineer a rise in short term interest rates. From 1972 to 1978, MLR was calculated by a formula based on the weekly TREASURY BILL tender; but from 1978 until it was put into abeyance in 1981 as part of revised monetary control arrangements, MLR was fixed by the monetary authorities. It was briefly revived in January 1985 as a means of bringing about a rise in interest rates to defend the exchange rate for sterling.

minimum price fluctuation. On a FINANCIAL FUTURES exchange, the smallest change possible in the price of a given contract. Otherwise known as basis point, point or tick.

Minoritätsbeteiligung (Ger). A minority holding. *See also* MINORITY SHAREHOLDER.

minority shareholder. (1) Any shareholder in a company who has voted against a resolution supported by a majority of other shareholders. The minority shareholder has certain rights in the event of a winding up of the company, designed to protect his interests.

(2) Any holder of shares in a company which is taken over by another company, who does not accept the take-over offer and who remains a minority shareholder in what has become a subsidiary of the larger company.

Mitarbeiteraktien (Ger). Shares issued by way of bonus, for example, to employees under a profit sharing scheme.

mit Dividende (Ger). *Cum* dividend.

Mitläufer (Ger). *See* TRITTBRETTFAHRER.

Mittelfristig (Ger). *See* MEDIUM TERM.

Mittelpreis, Mittelkurs (Ger). *See* MIDDLE PRICE.

Model Code (for directors' dealings) (UK). A code of conduct drawn up and published by the Stock Exchange, which lays down guidelines for company directors to follow when dealing in the shares of their companies. The object of the Code is to encourage directors to own shares in their companies and to help protect them from misinformed criticism in dealing in those shares.

The latest version of the Code was issued in April 1981 following revisions undertaken in the light of the provisions of the Companies Act 1980.

The Code goes beyond the requirements of the law in a number of respects and lays down that:

(a) directors should not deal in the shares of their companies on short term considerations;

(b) directors should not deal in their companies' shares for a period of two months preceding the announcement of such recurring information as profits, statements and dividends, whether or not the information is price sensitive;

(c) directors should not deal prior to an exceptional announcement of a price sensitive nature, even where they do not fall within the narrowly defined prohibitions contained in the Companies Act.

The Code also includes dealings by directors in another capacity, for example as trustees and with funds managed on behalf of directors by professional fund managers. The Code is expected to be enforced, too, by companies in respect of dealings by executives and other employees who are not directors, but who are in possession of information by virtue of their employment.

monetarism. The body of economic thought which places great reliance on the control of the money supply as a means of achieving economic growth without inflation. Excessive growth of the MONEY SUPPLY is seen primarily as the fault of governments, which are encouraged by monetarism not to run a large scale BUDGET DEFICIT. The concept of monetarism, if not the name, is an historic one, first put forward by the 16th century economist Jean Bodin, who sought to explain the sharp rise in prices then taking place in Europe by relating it to the inflow of silver (then the basis for various currencies) from the discoveries in the New World. Refined in the early 20th century by the American economist Irving Fisher, into the 'Quantity Theory of Money', the concept went into decline until revived by the studies of Milton Friedman at the University of Chicago in the 1950s. Not until the late 1960s, however, did his views become more widely accepted, and they have enjoyed considerable vogue since the early 1970s.

monetarist. One who is a supporter of MONETARISM.

monetizzare (It). To REALIZE an investment at a profit.

money at call. *See* CALL MONEY and AT CALL.

money broker (UK). (1) In the United Kingdom Stock Exchange, one of six firms of stockbrokers who act as channels, borrowing stock from institutional holders and supplying it to the JOBBERS. The money brokers' role is especially important in the GILT-EDGED market, where settlement of deals normally takes place within 48 hours of dealing; in order to be able to deliver stock they have sold, the jobbers may borrow it from financial institutions through the intermediary of a money broker. By providing this stock borrowing facility, the money brokers assist the liquidity of both the gilt edged and equity markets in London.

(2) More generally, financial intermediaries who act as channels for short term funds flowing between borrowers and lenders.

money market fund (US). A mutual fund (unit trust) whose funds are invested in high yielding money market instruments such as federal (government) securities, CERTIFICATES OF DEPOSIT (CD) and COMMERCIAL PAPER. Its object is to make such high yield instruments available to individuals as well as to the large institutional investors.

money market preferred stock (MMP) (US). An instrument introduced to the American investment scene in late 1984. It carries a rate of dividend that may be varied at frequent (less than two-monthly) intervals. This keeps the return in line with short term money market rates, and gives the investor security of capital as well as a good rate of interest.

money supply. The amount of money, however defined, available in a country at any time. An economic concept given added importance by the re-emergence of MONETARISM in the late 1960s and 1970s, money supply can be measured in a number of ways, all of which may be valid, but which sometimes show quite different trends one from another. All measures of the money supply, whether defined narrowly or widely, include cash in circulation; most include bank deposits repayable on demand and capable of being transferred by cheque, while some of the wider definitions also include bank deposits subject to a period of notice and deposits held in institutions other than banks. The measures of money supply currently in use in the United Kingdom alone are:

- M_0 — The narrowest definition of the money supply; introduced in 1983 and sometimes referred to as the wide monetary base. M_0 is defined as notes and coin in circulation with the public, plus banks' till money and banks' operational balances with the Bank of England.
- M_1 — notes and coin in circulation plus sterling sight deposits of the private sector with the banks.
- M_2 — notes and coin in circulation plus private sector non-interest-bearing sterling sight deposits, retail interest bearing bank deposits and private sector holdings of retail building society deposits and national savings bank ordinary accounts.
- £M_3 — The constituents of M_1 (above) plus private sector sterling time bank deposits.
- M_3 — The constituents of £M_3 (above) plus private sector foreign currency bank deposits.

In addition to these money supply definitions, the United Kingdom authorities also calculate and publish two measures of a wider concept, private sector liquidity. These two measures are defined as follows:

- PSL 1 — The constituents of M_1 (above) plus private sector sterling time bank deposits with an original maturity of up to two years, plus private sector holdings of sterling bank certificates of deposit, plus private sector holdings, money market instruments such as bank bills, Treasury bills and local authority deposits, as well as certificates of tax deposits.

PSL 2 Includes all the above items in PSL1 plus private sector holdings of building society deposits, except term shares and SAYE accounts and National Savings instruments (excluding SAYE and longer-term deposits).

The United Kingdom monetary authorities now set targets for monetary growth for the year in terms of M_0 and sterling M_3. (£M_3).

monitoring (UK). The tripartite procedure for supervising changes taking place in Stock Exchange arrangements in the United Kingdom. The monitoring procedure involves the Department of Trade and Industry, the Bank of England and the Stock Exchange. It was set up following the agreement between the government and the Stock Exchange in 1983, which removed the Stock Exchange from the Restrictive Trade Practices Act. The monitoring body's role is to supervise and examine the effects of the ending of minimum commissions, scheduled for the end of 1986 at the latest. It is also responsible for monitoring the other consequential changes resulting from that abolition, including the changes in market structure and membership arrangements, in order to ensure, in the words of the Secretary of State for Trade and Industry, 'the evolution and development of the Stock Exchange as an efficient, competitive and suitably regulated central market which affords proper protection to investors'. (*House of Commons Hansard,* Cols. 1194-5, 27 July 1983; quoted in *Review of Investor Protection (the Gower Report)* para 5.06).

Monopolies and Mergers Commission (UK). A body set up in the United Kingdom to examine the extent to which monopoly exists in the supply of goods and services and to make reports to the Secretary of State for Trade and Industry.

Originally set up under the Monopolies Act of 1948, it now operates under the 1973 Fair Trading Act. The Secretary of State for Trade and Industry and the Director-General of Fair Trading can refer cases to the Commission for investigation.

A monopoly under the legislation is defined as one supplier accounting for 25 percent of the supply of the particular goods or services to the market (or more than one supplier acting in concert to restrict competition). If the Commission finds that such a monopoly is acting against the public interest, the Secretary of State may take action to remedy or prevent the harm which the Commission has identified. Alternatively, the Director General can negotiate agreements with the monopolist to remedy the harm caused.

Mergers may also be referred to the Commission on the advice of the Director General if such a merger would intensify a monopoly or if assets of more than £15 million are involved. The Secretary of State can, if the Commission advises against a merger, ban it or, if it has already taken place, reverse it. In normal circumstances, once a take-over has been referred to the Commission, it cannot be proceeded with until the Commission has carried out its investigation.

monopoly. In strict economic theory terms, the supply of goods or services by a single supplier. Regarded as undesirable and now regulated by law in most countries, monopolies are controlled in the United Kingdom under a series of legislation dating from 1948, but currently under the Fair Trading Act of 1973. *See also* MONOPOLIES AND MERGERS COMMISSION.

montante (It). The sum of the capital invested plus accumulated interest.

mortgage bond, mortgage debenture. A BOND or DEBENTURE secured by a mortgage on a property.

moscone, fare un (It). The short term purchase or sale of a security in the hope of making a profit; a speculative transaction.

mouvere (la) posizione (It). To substitute some securities in a PORTFOLIO with others in order to take advantage of a market trend or corporate news or performance.

movimento (di) simpatia (It). Where a positive or negative market trend in a certain security also spreads to other securities in the same sector. *See also* SWITCHING.

multinational company. A company with operations and administrative offices in a number of different countries.

mündelsicher Wertpapiere (Ger). A security in which funds may be invested by trustees.

municipal bond (US). A bond issued in the United States by a state or a political subdivision, such as a county, city, town or village. The term also designates bonds issued by state agencies and authorities. In general, interest received on municipal bonds is exempt from federal (government) income tax as well as state and local taxes within the state of issue. For the UK equivalent, *see* LOCAL AUTHORITY STOCKS.

Muttergesellschaft (Ger). *See* PARENT COMPANY.

mutual fund (US). The American name for a UNIT TRUST, an OPEN-END FUND, which allows small investors the opportunity to spread their risk over a variety of securities.

N

Naamloze Vennootschap (NV) (Neth). The most common type of organization for a company whose shares are traded on the Amsterdam Stock Exchange. Similar in concept to the British PUBLIC LIMITED COMPANY.

Nachbörse (Ger). AFTER-HOURS DEALINGS on a stock exchange.

Nachdeckungspflicht (Ger). A shortfall in security against a loan and the need to bridge the gap by the giving of additional security.

Nachzugsaktie (Ger). *See* DEFERRED SHARE.

naked bond (US). An unsecured DEBENTURE or LOAN STOCK.

naked writer. An OPTION WRITER who undertakes to supply shares he does not own at a specified price to the buyer of an option. He will hope to buy the option back at a lower price, thus making himself a profit, without having to supply the shares. If the transaction turns out to be unsuccessful, the naked option writer may have to buy back the option at a higher price, thus causing himself a loss instead of his anticipated profit.

name day (UK). The second day of the settlement process for transferring shares dealt in FOR THE ACCOUNT on the UK Stock Exchange. Also called ticket day. Tickets for bargains dealt in the preceding account must be issued on this day.

Namenaktie, Namenpapier (Ger). *See* REGISTERED SHARE.

narrow a spread. To reduce the gap between a market maker's BID PRICE and OFFER PRICE.

narrow market. A market for a particular security in which only a small amount of the stock may be traded before the price is affected. Generally, the term is applied to the market in a share with only a small MARKET CAPITALIZATION and/or where the shares are substantially held by the directors and associated persons. *See also* CLOSELY HELD SHARES.

National Association of Securities Dealers,The (NASD) (US). An association of brokers and dealers in the United States dealing in the OVER-THE-COUNTER MARKETS.

NASD operates under the provisions of the Maloney Act of 1938, a piece of legislation which amended the SECURITIES EXCHANGE ACT of 1934 to permit the formation of self-regulatory associations of dealers and brokers which would register with the SECURITIES AND EXCHANGE COMMISSION (SEC). NASD was registered in 1939 and is in fact the only such association organized in accordance with the provisions of the Maloney Act. NASD sets rules and guidelines for its members.

Members of the NASD are entitled to participate in investment banking and over-the-counter securities business on a preferential basis, to distribute new issues of securities which have been underwritten by NASD members and to join in distributing shares which have been sponsored by NASD members. Applicants for membership have to pass stringent examinations and once successful, have to subscribe to standards of ethical conduct set by the Association. The Association's rules and regulations are, in turn, subject to the approval of the Securities and Exchange Commission. The NASD is controlled by a board of 27 governors while, for administrative purposes, the members are divided into 13 districts, each of which has its own committee.

The dealers belonging to the Association trade in competition for clients' business in nearly 3700 securities on a nationwide basis by means of the NATIONAL ASSOCIATION OF SECURITIES DEALERS AUTOMATED QUOTATIONS SYSTEM (NASDAQ).

BIBLIOGRAPHY *Manual of the National Association of Securities Dealers Inc.* (Washington, June 1983).

National Association of Securities Dealers Automated Quotations System (NASDAQ) (US). An automated information network established in 1971 which provides brokers and dealers in the United States with price quotations of securities traded on the OVER-THE-COUNTER MARKETS.

NASDAQ is a highly computerized communications system which stores and transmits up-to-the-minute price quotations for nearly 3700 domestic and foreign securities. Through the system, a national network of some 3300 broker-dealer firms, as well as professional traders and investors, have immediate access to the quotations of all dealers who make markets and whose quotations are entered and up-dated throughout the day. The system automatically identifies the market makers with the best prices in particular securities.

The NASDAQ system operates on three levels: level 1 provides the subscriber with the highest bid and offer quotations for each security; level 2 provides the subscriber with access to all BID AND ASKED quotations and quotation sizes of each REGISTERED MARKET MAKER who is entering quotes to the system; finally, the level 3 service, which is available only to the registered market makers, also provides the ability to enter quotations to the system.

Companies whose securities are quoted on NASDAQ must have at least two BROKER-DEALERS registered as market makers undertaking to maintain a regular market in the stock. NASDAQ itself monitors the quality of the market and may take disciplinary action against dealers who, while entering quotations to the system, are guilty of BACKING AWAY when a counter-party wishes to deal at the quoted price. The NASDAQ market surveillance department has the ability to reconstruct dealing patterns for up to sixty days in order to investigate complaints.

The COMPUTER ASSISTED EXECUTION SYSTEM, introduced in February 1981, has added a dealing facility to the information system to which NASDAQ had previously been confined.

National Association of Security Dealers and Investment Managers (NASDIM). A body of dealers in stocks and shares outside the Stock Exchange in the United Kingdom. Formerly the Association of Licensed Dealers in Securities, it changed its name to include investment managers in November 1981. It is now recognized by the Department of Trade and Industry and its members are exempted from individual licensing under the Prevention of Fraud (Investments) Act.

National Companies and Securities Commission (Australia). The federal supervisory body of securities dealing in Australia since 1981. Prior to that date, securities market regulation was primarily the responsibility of the individual states.

national debt. The amount of money owed by the state. Such debt may be held by residents of the state itself, in which case it is internal debt, money owed by one economic sector to another, or it may be held by residents of overseas countries, in which case it is termed external debt. It is sometimes argued that only the external debt is a burden on the nation since only on this debt do interest payments go overseas, thus constituting a drain on the country's reserves of foreign exchange. Internal debt, however, remains a debt owed by one generation to the next and the interest payments on it may call for additional taxation to be necessary to SERVICE it.

National Girobank (UK). Founded in 1968 as the National Giro, the National Girobank was renamed in 1978. It was originally set up to modernise the money transmission services of the Post Office and its objective was to provide a cheap and efficient money transmission service to rival that of the commercial banks. At first, the National Giro only accepted deposits and made transfers between accounts. Since 1978 it has provided not only money transfer services but also standing orders, personal loans, cheque cards, deposit accounts, budget accounts and travel facilities, in other words, many of the services provided by a commercial bank to its personal customers. To all intents and purposes, National Girobank is now a public sector commercial bank.

nationalization, nationalized industries. *See* PUBLIC ENTERPRISE.

National Market Advisory Board (US). A board established in 1975 by the Securities and Exchange Commission to advise that body on the implementation of a NATIONAL MARKET SYSTEM for securities embracing all exchanges and dealers.

national market system (US). The concept of a nationwide market place for securities trading, linking dealings in the same securities, no matter which stock exchange member received the original order. *See also* INTERMARKET TRADING SYSTEM.

National Savings (UK). NON-MARKETABLE SECURITIES issued by the British Government and aimed primarily at personal savers. Most of the securities issued as part of National Savings have various tax advantages, some being free of all tax. For this reason, limitations are placed on the amount of any one security which an individual may hold. National Savings securities include National Savings Certificates, BRITISH SAVINGS BONDS, accounts in the NATIONAL GIROBANK and PREMIUM BONDS.

National Savings Register (UK) (formerly the Post Office Register). A method by which savers can invest in British Government stocks listed on the Stock Exchange. Stocks may be purchased, up to £10,000 worth per day, by means of direct application at post offices rather than using a stockbroker. For relatively small purchases, buying via the National Savings Register is cheaper than using a stockbroker and interest on stock held on the National Savings Register may receive interest on a gross basis. The drawback is that orders are amalgamated for purchase, so an investor cannot deal immediately at a price he has been quoted; the second disadvantage is that not every GILT EDGED stock may be bought through the register.

National Securities Clearing Corporation (NSCC) (US). A clearing corporation established in 1977 which working through the SECURITIES INDUSTRY AUTOMATION CORPORATION helps speed up the clearing process and cut down on the physical movement of stock. The NSCC helps match transfers of stock and makes the necessary net adjustments to member firms balances held in the DEPOSITORY TRUST CO, itself a subsidiary of NSCC.

nearby futures. In a FINANCIAL FUTURES exchange, those financial or commodities futures contracts which are closest to maturity. *See also* DEFERRED FUTURES.

near money. Sometimes called quasi money, near money consists of assets which perform some of the four functions of money but not all of them. The four functions of money are that it is a medium of exchange, a store of value, a unit of account and a standard of deferred payments. Near money, for example, can be a building society deposit or some other highly liquid asset, which may perform the store of value function effectively in that it can be stored for later use and (with interest added) lose little, if any, value. It does not, however, perform the function of acting as a medium of exchange; it has to be converted into something else (cash or bank deposit) before it can be so used.

negative real rate of interest. A real rate of interest is the return on an investment after allowing for the annual rate of inflation. Thus with a NOMINAL INTEREST RATE of, say, 10 percent and an inflation rate of, say, 8 percent, the real rate of interest is 2 percent. A negative real rate of interest occurs when the rate of inflation is greater than the nominal rate of interest, for example if the nominal rate were 10 percent and the rate of inflation 12 percent.

negotiable. The ability of a financial instrument to be transferred by delivery, the buyer or transferor thereby acquiring good title to it. Few British securities are negotiable in this way, the majority being REGISTERED STOCKS and REGISTERED SHARES. Overseas stocks may frequently be BEARER SHARES which are negotiable.

negotiated bid (US). A term used in the new issue market. It is the offer to a company by a single underwriter or group of underwriters to take up an issue of the company's stock to sell it on to the investing public. The use of this method, rather than organizing a competitive tender from a number of underwriters, leads to a close and often continuing relationship between an underwriter and the company, similar to that which exists in the United Kingdom between a company and its merchant bank and stockbroker. *See also* COMPETITIVE BID.

negotiated commission. The term applied to a stock (or other) market where the agent's or broker's commission is a matter between the client and the broker and not subject to a scale laid down by the stock exchange authorities. Commissions on the New York Stock Exchange have been negotiable since 1975, in Canada since 1983 and in Australia since 1984. Negotiated commissions are expected to be introduced in the United Kingdom no later than the end of 1986 under an agreement reached between the Stock Exchange and the British Government in July 1983.

negotiation. A method of dealing in securities which are not widely traded. The transaction is subject to individual negotiation rather than being made through an established dealing mechanism.

Nennwert (Ger). *See* NOMINAL VALUE.

net asset value. *See* ASSET VALUE.

net change. The movement in the price of a security between the end of one day's trading and the next. The figure is usually shown in the newspaper columns of prices immediately to the right of the CLOSING PRICE figure thus:

	Closing price	*Net change* + or −
ABC plc	432	−5
XYZ plc	143	+7
XZZ plc	117	...

The last blank space indicates no net change on the day.

On the UK market, the net price change is the change in the MIDDLE PRICE of the quotes which the individual newspaper takes; this may be from the Stock Exchange's EPIC computer service or it may be directly from jobbers. The important thing to note is that both this net change figure and the actual price are based on prices indicated by the market, not prices at which deals took place.

net distribution basis. *See* PRICE EARNINGS RATIO.

net position. The number of FINANCIAL FUTURES contracts bought or sold which have not been OFFSET by opposite transactions.

net price. A price for shares in a transaction quoted by a broker to his client, which includes an allowance for the broker's commission and other charges or fees. Normally, when a broker acts as agent for his client he will quote the price in the market for the shares and add his commission as a separate item when he renders the contract note to his client. On occasion, however, the broker may quote his client a net price, particularly, but not exclusively, when the broker is acting not as an agent but as a principal, in which case this fact must be disclosed to the client.

Nettohandel (Ger). Trading on a net basis. *See* NET PRICE.

net yield. The return to an investor on a security after allowing for the normal rate of tax on the income. Because net yields are different for different categories of investor they are not published as such. So investors should always be conscious that the gross yield on different securities may not be an adequate guide to the net yield to the individual investor, depending upon the tax status of the investment. *See also* DIVIDEND YIELD; GROSS REDEMPTION YIELD; GROSS YIELD; REDEMPTION YIELD.

Neuausgabe, Neuemission (Ger). *See* NEW ISSUE.

new issue. (1) The raising of additional capital for a company by the issuing of new securities. The issue may be one of loan or new equity capital issued either to new or existing shareholders. When the issue is of equity and the shares are already widely held, the existing shareholders may be offered PRE-EMPTIVE RIGHTS to buy additional shares in proportion to their existing holdings in order to maintain their stake in the company. Occasionally investors may be offered such a RIGHTS ISSUE in the form of a LOAN STOCK or CONVERTIBLE LOAN STOCK. The issue, as a loan rather than equity, thus causes no DILUTION OF EQUITY for the existing shareholders. A loan stock may also be issued by a company as a separate exercise.

(2) The issuing of securities of a particular company on a stock exchange for the first time. Such an issue is referred to as a new issue irrespective of whether or not any new money is being raised by the company or its existing shareholders. Such a new issue may be made by way of INTRODUCTION, PLACING or OFFER FOR SALE.

new time (UK). Dealing in the last two days of one ACCOUNT on the UK Stock Exchange for settlement on the account day of the following account. In effect, the investor buys for settlement 16 or 17 working days forward. New time dealings begin on the Thursday prior to the end of the old account.

New York Futures Exchange (NYFE) (US). The New York Futures Exchange is a subsidiary of the New York Stock Exchange and was founded in 1979 to deal in FINANCIAL FUTURES contracts under the regulatory authority of the COMMODITY FUTURES TRADING COMMISSION (CFTC).

NYFE began trading in August 1980 in futures contracts based on 90-day U.S. Treasury bills, 20-year Treasury bonds and five foreign currencies - sterling, Canadian dollar, yen, Deutsche Mark and the Swiss Franc. However, the market was unsuccessful and trading in these contracts ceased.

In 1982 a new futures contract based on the NYSE Composite Index (*see* NEW YORK STOCK EXCHANGE COMMON STOCK INDICES) was approved by the CFTC and trading in this contract began in May of that year. In 1983, as part of the CFTC pilot scheme, NYFE began trading an option on its NYSE Composite Index futures contract. Both the futures and the options contract have proved highly successful.

BIBLIOGRAPHY *Fact Book* (New York Stock Exchange, annually).

New York Stock Exchange (NYSE) (US). The largest Stock Exchange in the world in terms of both market capitalization and annual turnover. Founded in 1792 when 24 brokers met under a buttonwood tree on Wall Street. The name 'New York Stock & Exchange Board' was adopted in 1817 and changed to the New York Stock Exchange in 1863. The NYSE operates a seat system with 1366 individual members holding seats and the price of these seats varies according to supply and demand.

The Board of Directors of the NYSE consists of ten public representatives, ten Exchange members and a full-time chairman and president.

BIBLIOGRAPHY *Marketplace : A brief history of the New York Stock Exchange* (NYSE). *Fact Book* (New York Stock Exchange, annually).

New York Stock Exchange (NYSE) Common Stock Indices (US). A group of stock indices measuring movements in market prices on the New York Stock Exchange. The NYSE Composite Index covers all the stocks listed on the Exchange. Its base is 31 December 1965 and at that date was given the value of 50. The index is weighted according to the number of shares in issue of each stock. The index is computed continuously throughout the trading day and published on the ticker tape. Point changes in the index are converted to dollars and cents to provide an easily understood measure of the changes in the average price of stocks. In addition to the NYSE Composite Index, these are sub-indices for the four groups: industrial, transportation, utilities and finance. *See also* AVERAGES.

BIBLIOGRAPHY *Common Stock Indexes* (NYSE). *Index wall chart* (NYSE, annually).

nicht ausgegebenes Kapital (Ger). *See* UNISSUED CAPITAL.

nicht eingerufenes Kapital (Ger). *See* UNCALLED CAPITAL

nicht notierte Werte (Ger). *See* UNLISTED SECURITIES.

nicht rückzahlbare Schuldverschreibung (Ger). An undated or IRREDEEMABLE DEBENTURE.

Nichtveranlagungsbescheinigung (Ger). A voucher giving exemption from withholding tax on the income from shares held by non-residents of Germany.

Niessbrauchnutzer (Ger). *See* BENEFICIAL OWNER.

Nikkei-Dow Jones Average (NDJA) (Jap). One of the major measures of stock price changes on the Tokyo Stock Exchange. The NDJA consists of 225 stocks on the FIRST SECTION of the Tokyo Stock Exchange. It is an unweighted arithmetic AVERAGE and takes no account of the weight, or market capitalization, of its constituents; thus a price change in the securities of one of its smallest constituents will have the same effect on the index as a similar change in the price of one of the largest companies. *See also* TOKYO STOCK EXCHANGE (TSE) INDEX.

nil distribution basis. *See* PRICE EARNINGS RATIO.

nil paid. Shares on which no payment has yet been made, but which are being dealt in on a stock market. These shares usually arise from a NEW ISSUE, often a RIGHTS ISSUE of securities. In the United Kingdom, shares may be traded in PROVISIONAL ALLOTMENT LETTER form for a period of 21 days up to the day on which the CALL on the issue must be made. Because the price at which a rights issue is made is at a discount on the market price, the rights issue shares have value in their own right. Those existing holders who do not wish to take up the rights may, therefore, be able to realize that value by selling the shares in the market.

Nochgeschäft (Ger). The purchase of a right to exercise an option to buy shares at a stated future date.

nominale (It). (1) Par value. (2) A price fixed on a stock exchange floor for a security in which no actual deals were struck.

nominal interest rate. The COUPON rate of interest paid on a security or other financial instrument. *See also* REAL RATE OF INTEREST.

nominal price. (1) The nominal, face or par value of a share. All shares in the United Kingdom must possess a nominal value, shares of NO PAR VALUE not being allowed by law. The most common nominal price is 25p, but this can vary from 1p to £5 (both rare). At one time company dividends were often declared as a percentage of nominal value but with decimalization of sterling and the change to the IMPUTATION SYSTEM of Corporation Tax, it is now most common to declare the dividend as so many pence per share, ignoring any reference to the nominal value.

(2) A price quotation for a futures contract or security where no actual dealing took place.

nominal share capital. *See* AUTHORIZED CAPITAL.

nominal value. *See* NOMINAL PRICE and PAR.

Nominalwert (Ger). *See* NOMINAL PRICE.

nominativo (It). *See* REGISTERED BOND; REGISTERED SHARE.

nominee company. A company formed by a bank or other organization for the purpose of holding shares on behalf of the BENEFICIAL OWNER. The nominee company carries out all the paperwork and other chores associated with the documentation of share holding and arranges for the necessary transfers when a share is sold. Nominee companies must consult the beneficial owners in the event of a RIGHTS ISSUE, TAKE-OVER BID or other matter affecting the rights of the shares.

Pension funds often find it convenient to hold their shares in nominee names, and with the growth of such funds as holders of UK company equity, the percentage of shares held on a company register in nominee names has now risen to over one-third of the total number of shares of UK companies in issue.

Since 1976 companies whose shares are held in nominee names have had the right to obtain details of the beneficial owners of those shares but few, except in exceptional circumstances, have taken advantage of this power.

non-assented bonds. Bonds being traded in the market whose holders have not given their assent to a change in the rights attached to the bonds. *See also* ASSENTED BONDS.

non-business day. A day, either normally or by special decree, designated a day on which financial business will not take place, Saturdays, Sundays and Bank or Public Holidays being the most obvious examples. In the event of a financial instrument falling due for payment or repayment on a non-business day, the following business day is substituted.

non-callable bonds (US). Securities which do not give the issuer the right to call them in for repayment before the date of maturity or for a specific period between the issue date and the first date on which the stock may be called.

non-clearing member (US). A stock exchange member firm which does not clear or settle its own dealings on behalf of clients, but sub-contracts the task to another firm.

non-competitive bid (US). Offers from small investors for United States government bonds which may be submitted not stating a bid price, but stating that the investor is willing to pay the eventual STRIKING PRICE for the bonds based on the tenders submitted by the large competitive tenderers.

non-contributory pensions. Company pension schemes under which the employee who will ultimately benefit from the scheme does not pay any contribution towards it, the cost being wholly borne by the employer. Generally regarded as being a very favourable benefit of employment, the drawback for the employee is that should he leave his employment before he becomes entitled to his pension he will not receive back any contributions (having not himself made any). He may, however, be entitled to a preserved pension right from the date on which he would have become eligible for a pension had he stayed.

non-cumulative preference shares. Shares which are entitled to a dividend (normally a fixed percentage) after the interest payments have been met but ahead of the claims to dividend by ordinary shareholders. Sometimes, if a preference dividend is not paid, the arrears will accumulate and must be paid before any ordinary dividend is payable in future. These are called CUMULATIVE PREFERENCE SHARES. Preference shares which are not entitled to such accumulation of dividend arrears are called non-cumulative preference shares.

non-executive director. An independent director of a company who takes no part in the day-to-day running of the business. The role of the non-executive director is to provide, on behalf of shareholders, outside experience and expertise, both to encourage and perhaps on occasions to restrain, the executive directors. Non-executive directors with effective powers are now actively encouraged in the United Kingdom through PRONED.

non-marketable securities. (1) Securities which are not listed on a stock exchange.

(2) Securities which, although listed, are not easily bought and sold and in which there is, therefore, a NARROW MARKET.

non-resident. One whose normal place of residence is outside the country concerned. In securities transactions, non-resident status has a number of important effects; where exchange control is in place there will be restrictions on the buying and selling of securities between residents and non-residents. There may be restrictions on the remittance of interest, profits and dividends to non-residents. Non-residents will, in any event, normally be subject to WITHHOLDING TAX on dividends sent to them.

non valeur (Fr). A share or other financial instrument of little value.

non versé (Fr). The uncalled portion of PARTLY-PAID SHARES.

non-voting share. A share which does not entitle the holder to a vote in the affairs of the company. Usually on the UK Stock Exchange called an 'A' share. Although not banned in the United Kingdom, either by law or by Stock Exchange regulation, non-voting shares have become unpopular with investors, particularly institutional investors, in recent years and many companies with non-voting shares have enfranchised the holders. Some non-voting shares remain, however, for reasons associated with legal requirements (in the case of commercial television companies whose voting shareholders are answerable to the Independent Broadcasting Authority) or because of the wishes of the small number of voting shareholders. *See also* ENFRANCHISEMENT.

no par value (NPV). Shares which do not possess a nominal or PAR VALUE. Such a method of not expressing a par value is not allowed in the United Kingdom where securities must be given a nominal value. In the United States, however, the issue of shares of no par value is quite common and from time to time the matter is debated in this country. One problem with par value is that special rules apply to the raising of new money when existing securities stand at a discount on par value, which makes the raising of new money difficult in such circumstances.

normal market size. *See* MARKET SIZE.

note (US). A short term security issued by public authorities and companies.

note d'information (Fr). A preliminary prospectus, issued by a company, which must be sent to the listing authorities, the COMMISSION DES OPÉRATIONS DE BOURSE and the COMPAGNIE DES AGENTS DE CHANGE. The prospectus must contain information on the number of shares to be issued and their price, together with details of the company, its financial state, history, directors etc.

notice day. A day on which notices of intent to DELIVER pertaining to a specified DELIVERY MONTH are issued in the FINANCIAL FUTURES market.

Notierung (Ger). A price quoted on the stock market.

notleidend (Ger). In arrears.

not-to-press. In a poorly traded stock a buyer may agree not to press the jobber to deliver the stock on normal settlement day, in order to give the jobber a chance to acquire the necessary stock for delivery.

nouvelle émission (Fr). *See* NEW ISSUE.

nuovo emissione (It). *See* NEW ISSUE.

nursery finance. The provision of funds either by way of loan or equity to companies in the early stages of development. Also called venture capital.

O

obbligazione (It). *See* DEBT.

obbligazione a portatore (It). *See* BEARER BOND.

obbligazione dello Stato (It). *See* GOVERNMENT BOND.

obbligazione garantita (It). *See* SECURED DEBENTURE.

obbligazione irredimibile (It). *See* IRREDEEMABLE DEBENTURE.

obbligazione non garantita (It). *See* UNSECURED LOAN STOCK.

obbligazione redimibile (It). *See* REDEEMABLE DEBENTURE.

obbligazione senza data (It). *See* UNDATED STOCK.

obbligazionista (It). *See* DEBENTURE HOLDER.

objects clause (UK). The clause in a limited company's MEMORANDUM OF ASSOCIATION which defines the objects for which a company was formed. At one time any contract entered into for a purpose which was outside the scope of the objects clause could not be enforced, but under the Directive of the EEC on company law any transaction entered into in good faith can now be enforced even if it is outside the scope of the objects clause.

obligataire (Fr). A bond holder.

obligation (Fr). A debt security, as opposed to an EQUITY or ACTION. Usually a fixed interest security, although not invariably so.

Obligationär (Ger). A bond holder.

obligation au porteur (Fr). *See* BEARER BOND.

obligation convertible en action (Fr). *See* CONVERTIBLE STOCK.

obligation de caisse (Fr). A medium term bond issued by banks and not traded on the BOURSE.

obligation de société privée (Fr). A bond giving a preferential entitlement: a preference bond.

obligation d'Etat (Fr). A government bond.

obligation émise par des collectivités publiques ou semipubliques (Fr). A bond issued by public or semi-public bodies. One of the types of debt instrument which may be listed and traded on the Paris BOURSE.

obligation garantie (Fr). *See* SECURED DEBENTURE.

obligation irremboursable (Fr). *See* IRREDEEMABLE DEBENTURE.

obligation sans date d'échéance (Fr). *See* UNDATED STOCK.

obligation sans guarantie (Fr). An unsecured debenture.

obligationsinhaber (Ger). A debenture holder.

odd lot (US). A block of shares which is less than the normal amount or ROUND LOT which is traded on a US stock exchange. For odd lot trading, the price per share is normally slightly higher than the price for a round lot and brokerage commission, too, may be slightly higher. This is known as the odd lot differential.

off board (US). A term used to refer to transactions in an OVER-THE-COUNTER market in unlisted securities or to a transaction in listed shares which is not transacted on a stock exchange in the United States.

offene Position (Ger). Open position. *See* POSITION.

offer. To open negotiations by offering terms in a general commercial sense in the hope that the terms will be accepted. (1) In securities terminology, the word can be used as an abbreviated form of a number of phrases including a TAKE-OVER BID (an offer for one company's shares by another), an OFFER FOR SALE (an offer of shares to the public) or the OFFER PRICE for shares in the market (the price at which the market makers will sell to the investor). Care has to be taken, therefore, in interpreting the precise way in which the word is being used, although the context will normally make this clear.

(2) The indication of the willingness on the part of a FINANCIAL FUTURES dealer to sell a futures CONTRACT at a given price.

(3) A similar meaning to the financial futures' use of the word is also applied in the United States securities markets. *See also* BID; OFFER PRICE.

offer for sale (UK). The most common way in which a new issue of shares is made to the public for the first time, although other methods such as INTRODUCTION, PLACING and PROSPECTUS ISSUE are also possible.

Where the sale of shares to be issued is in excess of £3 million, an offer for sale is the method encouraged by the Stock Exchange. This is because an offer for sale gives as large a number of investors as possible the chance to invest in the security being offered. The offer for sale, therefore, helps ensure a wide distribution of shareholdings and a good trading market in the shares once they have been issued.

The offer for sale method involves the ISSUING HOUSE buying the shares from the company or from its directors (if the original owners are willing to sell some of their shares as part of the offer for sale) and on-selling them to the investing public.

This process of selling the shares to the public involves the issue of a long and detailed PROSPECTUS which gives, among other things, details of the company's share capital and any indebtedness it may have, details of the directors, senior employees and the company's professional advisers including their bankers, auditors, solicitors (attorneys), stockbrokers and registrars. There follows a description of the history of the company and its main business activities, its major customers (particularly if it is highly dependent upon one customer), its major suppliers (again important if the company is highly dependent upon a single or limited source of supply.

The offer for sale prospectus goes on to detail what the proceeds of the issue will be used for and a statement that the company's working capital is adequate for its present requirements.

Details of the company's past trading record are given and a profits forecast may follow, although this is not obligatory.

The next major part of the prospectus document contains an accountants' report showing the past five years' trading record of the company, together with the latest consolidated balance sheets and voluminous notes on the company's fixed assets, investments, share capital, reserves, borrowings and a source and application of funds' statement.

A history of the company's share capital structure is also required and details from the ARTICLES OF ASSOCIATION outlining voting rights, the powers of the directors, the company's borrowing powers, details of subsidiary and other companies, the directors' share interests in the company, plus details of relevant contracts not entered into in the ordinary course of business and including the agreement with the issuing house regarding details of the offer for sale. There will also be a statement from the company's financial advisers stating that they have given, and not withdrawn, their consent to the issue of the prospectus document; in other words, that their good names stand behind it.

Finally, the prospectus will contain an APPLICATION FORM which an investor will fill in if he wishes to apply for an ALLOTMENT of the shares. This will be sent to the RECEIVING BANKER who will deal with the applications and despatch of allotments.

An offer for sale may either be a FIXED PRICE OFFER FOR SALE or a TENDER offer. In the former, the issuing house fixes the price at which the shares will be offered to the investing public and will call for applications at that price. In a tender issue, the issuing house will usually fix a minimum price and ask investors to bid for the shares at or above that minimum.

In addition to the prospectus which is published in booklet form, the offer for sale has also, under Stock Exchange rules, to be advertised, the advertisement to include the full prospectus, in two leading newspapers. Such an advertisement may run to several pages of closely-typed broadsheet newsprint.

offer period (UK). The period for which an offer of shares in a take-over situation must remain open for acceptance. Under the rules of the CITY CODE ON TAKE-OVERS AND MERGERS, this period must be at least 21 days from the announcement of the offer. If there is a revised offer, an extension of a further 14 days is allowed.

No offer shall remain open for more than 60 days after the initial announcement, except with the permission of the Panel on Take-overs and Mergers and such permission is not normally granted unless a competing offer has been made. During the offer period, trading in the shares may continue and all interested parties may deal in them. All such dealings must, however, be reported, both to the Stock Exchange authorities and the press, no later than 12 noon on the following business day.

offer price. (1) The price (sometimes called the asked price) at which a MARKET MAKER indicates he is willing to supply securities to a buyer. A market maker will usually quote two prices, one at which he is prepared to buy from a seller (the BID PRICE) and the other at which he is prepared to sell to a buyer (the offer price).

(2) The phrase has a similar meaning specifically with regard to UNIT TRUSTS (mutual funds). The offer price is that at which the unit trust managers are prepared to sell units to the investing public, the bid price that which they will give for units which investors wish to sell back to them.

offerta (It). *See* OFFER.

offerta di acquisto (It). *See* TAKE-OVER BID.

Offerte (Ger). *See* OFFER.

off floor. A transaction or transactions in listed securities which take place by telephone or means other than by the normal trading procedure on a market floor.

Office of Fair Trading (OFT) (UK). The body established by the Fair Trading Act 1973, to supervise the working of the Act, to draw up registers of restrictive trading agreements and to attempt to remove such agreements which act against the public interest. Where a company or association does not voluntarily abandon the agreement, the OFT is empowered, through its Director-General, to refer the agreement to the Restrictive Practices Court for trial. This was the mechanism by which the Stock Exchange was expected to face the Court in 1984. By an agreement reached between the Stock Exchange and the British Government in July 1983, the Stock Exchange agreements were removed from investigation by the Court, in return for which the Exchange agreed to make certain changes to its rules, including the appointment of lay members to its ruling Council and the abandonment of its MINIMUM COMMISSION rules by the end of 1986 at the latest. *See also* 'BIG BANG'; DUAL CAPACITY; NEGOTIATED COMMISSION; SINGLE CAPACITY.

Official Assignee (UK). An official appointed by the Stock Exchange to supervise and wind up the affairs of a member firm whose partners have been declared defaulters and have been subject to HAMMERING. It is the duty of the Official Assignee to deal with outstanding administrative matters, to collect the debts owing to the firm and to pay out clients who have outstanding claims against the firm from the STOCK EXCHANGE COMPENSATION FUND.

Official List (UK). *See* STOCK EXCHANGE DAILY OFFICIAL LIST.

official quotation (UK). The CLOSING range of prices quoted in the STOCK EXCHANGE DAILY OFFICIAL LIST. The closing range is compiled from the quotations given by the jobbers in a security at the close of business. This quotation has legal recognition in that in any question of valuation of securities, the middle price of those quoted in the List would be used.

offire in vendita (It). *See* OFFER FOR SALE.

offre publique d'achat, offre publique d'échange (Fr.) A TAKE-OVER BID; if the bid is made on cash terms it is called an *offre publique d'achat*; if it is made in terms of the exchange of shares in the TARGET company for those of the offerer, it is called an *offre publique d'échange.*

Offers in France are now governed by a decree of 1978 which defines more clearly than before the conditions under which the take-over shall be made. As a result, all take-overs have to be submitted to the take-over committee of the CHAMBRE SYNDICALE DE LA COMPAGNIE DES AGENTS DE CHANGE for approval in principle, while a bid can also be vetoed within three days by the Ministry of the Economy.

If an offer is approved, a notice is posted in the *Bulletin de la Côte Officielle* giving details of the offer which must remain open for at least one month. The offerer's application for approval must contain the minimum and (if any) the maximum number of shares the offerer undertakes to buy, the offer price and whether the bid is in cash or in shares. Usually a bid involving a purchase of less than ten percent of the shares of a company is not admissable.

An offer is conditional upon acceptances being received in respect of a minimum number of shares, while if a maximum number has been fixed by the offerer, acceptances are dealt with on a *pro rata* basis according to the number of acceptances received. Shareholders in the offeree company may withdraw their acceptances at any time up to ten days before the expiry of the offer. Thereafter acceptances cannot be withdrawn. On the other hand, the offerer may not cancel his offer unless there is a competing bid for the offeree company.

In dealings in the shares of a company subject to a take-over bid, a 100 percent MARGIN must be provided with any order for shares in the offeree company on the forward market: dealings on the MARCHÉS CONDITIONNELS are suspended.

offset. To carry out a transaction in order to cancel out a previous obligation. *See also* LIQUIDATION.

offshore funds. Investment schemes in which the company running the scheme is legally based outside the tax regime of the country whose residents are investing in it. Frequently the host country for the company deliberately offers legal or tax privileges; at other times, the tax regime is simply more beneficial to such schemes than that of the investors' country of residence. Such host countries are often referred to as TAX HAVENS and include the Bahamas, Bermuda, the Cayman Islands, the Channel Islands, Lichtenstein, the Netherlands Antilles, among many others.

ohne Bezugsrecht (Ger). *See* EX-RIGHTS.

ohne Kupon (Ger). Ex coupon. *See* COUPON.

ohne Dividende (Ger). *See* EX-DIVIDEND.

omnibus account. On the LONDON INTERNATIONAL FINANCIAL FUTURES EXCHANGE (LIFFE) an account with a COMMISSION BROKER who is a member of LIFFE, used by either another member or a non-member and which combines the transactions of two or more clients of the latter.

onderhandse market (Neth). A subdivision of the Netherlands capital market, the *onderhandse* market is one on which private loans are raised. Long term savings institutions such as insurance companies and pension funds supply long term loans to industry and government with the commercial banks acting as brokers.

on floor. Transactions in securities concluded in the normal manner on the trading floor of a stock exchange.

open contracts. CONTRACTS on a FINANCIAL FUTURES market which have been either bought or sold and have not been OFFSET either by a subsequent contrary transaction or by taking delivery of the FINANCIAL INSTRUMENT or physical commodity. *See also* POSITION.

open end fund. An investment fund which operates by selling units to investors on a continuing basis and stands ready to buy back its units from investors who wish to sell. The amount of money it has at its disposal is not therefore fixed, but increases or decreases depending upon its success, or otherwise, in attracting net additions to its funds from its investors. The funds so subscribed are then invested in a range of assets, giving either or both income and capital gain and spreading the risks of small individual investors. An open end fund is contrasted with a CLOSED END FUND. Open end funds are generally called UNIT TRUSTS in the United Kingdom and MUTUAL FUNDS in the United States.

open end investment company. *See* OPEN END FUND.

opening, the. (1) The beginning of trading on a financial or securities market.

(2) On a FINANCIAL FUTURES market, the period at the beginning of a trading session, officially designated by the exchange authorities, during which all transactions are considered to have been made at the opening.

(3) Loosely, the OPENING PRICE.

Opening Automated Report Service (OARS) (US). A scheme introduced by the New York Stock Exchange in 1980 to help the SPECIALISTS marshal orders prior to the opening of the market and reduce the number of delayed starts. The scheme began as a pilot study dealing with orders of up to 299 shares in some stocks received before the opening, but has now been increased to orders of up to 5099 shares in any listed stock.

opening price or **opening range.** (1) The upper and lower prices at which the first BID and OFFER are made at a trading session on a FINANCIAL FUTURES market.

(2) A further meaning in a financial futures market context is the price at which the first transactions of the trading session are made, usually a period of about two minutes following the first trade of the session.

(3) The price made by the market makers at the beginning of a trading session on a stock exchange.

opening price convention (UK). An agreement among the jobbers on the UK Stock Exchange that they will quote the same SPREAD between their bid and offer prices when first approached by a broker seeking the quote. The agreement is about the spread between the prices, not the prices themselves; thus one jobber may quote 120-123 as his buying and selling prices, another may quote 119-122 but there is a spread of 3p in both instances. Once a broker has indicated that he wishes to do business with a particular jobber, the jobber might then be prepared to negotiate within his spread, depending upon the WAY of a broker's order, its size and other considerations.

opening purchase. An initial transaction in an OPTIONS CONTRACT by which the buyer becomes the holder of an option.

opening sale. A transaction whereby the seller assumes liability for the performance of an OPTIONS CONTRACT and thereby becomes the WRITER of an option.

open interest. In a FINANCIAL FUTURES context, the sum total of CONTRACTS which have been bought and sold and remain outstanding, not having been OFFSET.

open market. A market in which buying and selling takes place between willing buyers and sellers and is freely available to all actual and potential users. The prices in such a market are determined by the supply and demand for the commodity or security in question and are freely arrived at on that basis.

open market operations (OMO). The buying and selling by the government or its agency of government securities, either on a stock exchange or through recognized dealers in such stocks who provide the market for them. Open market operations are undertaken by the monetary authorities of a country to restrict or to expand the supply of cash and liquidity to the banking system. By selling securities on the open market, the authorities restrict credit by receiving cheques drawn by the investors on their commercial bank accounts (which are counted as part of the money supply) to pay for the securities. Conversely, they can expand credit by buying their own securities on the open market and supplying cheques which the sellers pay into their commercial bank accounts.

The movement in bank deposits and consequently in the banks' cash and liquid assets, may force them to restrict or encourage them to expand their lending to customers, thus having important secondary effects on the market for credit, interest rates etc.

Open market operations only work well if the banking system has ratios which are imposed upon it, either by law or by the central bank, if the central bank has control of the supply of assets which go to make up that ratio and there is a sufficiently large market in the government stocks to allow such transactions to take place without disrupting the market and its price-making mechanism. Thus the countries which make most use of open market operations in the conduct of their monetary policies are the ones which most fulfil those conditions, notably the United Kingdom and the United States.

open offer. A general offer to buy a holder's shares in a company. Usually such an offer results from a TAKE-OVER BID, or when a company or its directors wish to buy in outside holdings of its shares.

open order. An order to a broker to buy or sell shares or CONTRACTS on the FINANCIAL FUTURES markets which remains uncancelled or unexecuted.

open outcry. The method of trading used on some stock exchanges and all FINANCIAL FUTURES markets, where all BIDS and OFFERS are audible to all members on the floor who are trading in the stock or other financial instrument. This method of trading is implemented by all participants with an interest in the security congregating in one area around a PIT or TRADING POST so that all can hear the flow of orders and participate if they can to carry out the deals they wish to transact.

open position. *See* POSITION.

opérateur à prime (Fr). *See* OPTION DEALER.

opération à prime (Fr). *See* MARCHÉ À PRIMES.

opération à terme (Fr). *See* MARCHÉ À TERME.

opération de couverture (Fr). The act of covering a transaction for future delivery. *See* MARCHÉ DES REPORTS.

opérations du double (Fr). A transaction whereby an investor buys OPTIONS both to buy and sell the securities in question. *See also* MARCHÉ À OPTIONS; MARCHÉ À PRIMES; STELLAGE.

operatore (di) borsa (It). A stockmarket operator.

operatore differenziale (It). A speculative operator who buys or sells with the intention of cancelling the contract before the end of the same stockmarket account which lasts for one month.

operatore in contratti a premio (It). *See* OPTION DEALER.

operazione (di) borsa (It). A stock exchange transaction.

operazione (a) contanti (It). A cash transaction which must be concluded and settled on the third stockmarket session after it has been made. Bonds are normally traded cash, whereas shares are normally traded forward for settlement at the end of a month.

opposition d'intérêts (Fr). *See* CONFLICT OF INTEREST.

option. The right given to an investor either to buy or to sell a given quantity of a stock at a set price at or before a specified future date in return for the payment of a PREMIUM. *See also* CALL OPTION; CONVENTIONAL OPTION; PUT OPTION; TRADED OPTION.

option, conventional. *See* CONVENTIONAL OPTION.

option, traded. *See* TRADED OPTION.

option d'achat (Fr). *See* CALL OPTION. A TRADED OPTIONS market does not exist in Paris, but it is possible to buy a call option or a put option (OPTION DE VENTE) for a period up to nine months ahead.

option dealer. A buyer or seller of options.

option de vente (Fr). *See* PUT OPTION. *Also contrast* OPTION D'ACHAT.

option money. *See* PREMIUM.

options contract. An agreement between the buyer and the seller of an option, whereby the latter grants to the former the right to buy (call) or to sell (put) a specified number of shares at a pre-determined price at or before an agreed future date.

Optionsschein (Ger). In a new issue, the right given to shareholders to buy more shares at a pre-determined price. The right can itself be traded on the stock exchange. A similar situation exists in the United Kingdom where anyone alloted shares in a RIGHTS ISSUE may sell them on the market in NIL PAID form.

option writer. An investor who, in an OPTIONS CONTRACT, agrees either to supply shares at a pre-determined price at a future date (on a call option contract) or one who agrees to buy shares from another investor at a pre-determined price in a put option contract.

opzione (It). The right to participate in an increase in the share capital of a company. *See* RIGHTS ISSUE, PRE-EMPTIVE RIGHTS.

opzione doppia (It). *See* STRADDLE.

orario (di) borsa (It). *See* TRADING HOURS.

order. An instruction given by a client to his broker to buy or to sell securities.

order driven. The phrase used to describe a stock market trading system in which dealings and prices largely react to the flow of orders. An order driven system is contrasted with a QUOTE DRIVEN system, in which market makers adjust their prices or quotes in order to attract business. The SPECIALIST system operated by the NEW YORK STOCK EXCHANGE is regarded as the prime example of an order driven system.

order imbalance (US). Such a preponderance of buying or selling orders that a trading price cannot be established. In these circumstances trading may be suspended in that stock until balance is restored.

ordinary share. The risk capital of a company, often called the equity capital and hence the ordinary shares of a company being called equity shares. In the United States, such shares are usually referred to as common stocks, which makes it important to note whether one is consulting an American or a British source of information, the word STOCK having a different meaning in a UK context.

Ordinary shares give holders the rights of ownership of the company, such as the right to share in the profits by way of dividend and capital gain, usually the right to vote in general meeting and to elect and dismiss directors. (*But see also* NON-VOTING SHARES). Ordinary shares also confer the obligations of ownership and may result in the loss of an investor's money if the company is unsuccessful. In addition to the ordinary shares, some companies may also issue DEFERRED SHARES.

ordine (di) borsa (It). A stockmarket order to buy or sell securities.

ordine (di) chiamata (It). The order in which the securities are called, one by one, at the trading rings on the floor of the Italian Stock Exchanges.

ordine scalare (It). A SCALE ORDER; an order to buy or sell a certain security in which the maximum number is indicated, as well as partial amounts to buy or sell at various prices.

organi locali di borsa (It). Local stock exchange bodies. These include the local Chamber of Commerce, the Stock Exchange Deputation and the stockbrokers' executive committee (Comitato Direttivo degli Agenti di Cambio in Milan or Commissione per il Listino in the minor exchanges.)

Osaka Securities Finance Company (Jap). One of the three securities finance companies in Japan, the others being the TOKYO SECURITIES FINANCE COMPANY and the CHUBU SECURITIES FINANCE COMPANY. The Osaka company operates for the Osaka and two other Japanese exchanges and its object is to help provide liquidity for the members of those markets by supplying cash or securities as required.

oscillazione (It). Price fluctuations of a security.

osservatore alle 'grida' (It). A bank official with a permit to enter the trading rings on the floor of a stock exchange to allow him to follow more closely the performance of the market.

other names (UK). A MARKING NAME which is not regarded as a good marking name.

out-of-the-money option. An option, the EXERCISE PRICE of which is above the current market price of the UNDERLYING SECURITY, if the option is a CALL OPTION, or below the current price in the case of a PUT OPTION. *See also* TRADED OPTIONS. The price of an out-of-the-money option is lower than that of an IN-THE-MONEY OPTION since the former has no INTRINSIC VALUE, only TIME VALUE.

outside broker. A dealer or intermediary in stock and share dealing who is not a member of a recognized stock exchange.

outside shareholder. A shareholder who is unconnected with the company in any other way. An individual or institutional investor. Contrasted with the INSIDER.

overbought. Stock whose price is believed to be too high as a result of excessive buying pressure in relation to its underlying position and prospects. The word is often used in a TECHNICAL ANALYSIS sense to indicate that the trend in the price of the share in relation to the market as a whole is out of line.

overhang. The known existence of a large potential seller of shares. Such knowledge will act as a restraint on any increase in the price of the share, since the seller will take advantage of strong buying interest and meet that demand from his holding.

oversold. The opposite of OVERBOUGHT; the situation where selling pressure on a security has temporarily driven the price lower than is justified on FUNDAMENTAL ANALYSIS grounds, or whose price pattern suggests that it is too low and may soon rise.

oversubscription. The excess demand for a NEW ISSUE of shares. When an ISSUING HOUSE makes an OFFER FOR SALE of shares to investors and calls for applications, investors as a whole may believe that the price is too low in a FIXED PRICE OFFER FOR SALE and so collectively bid for more shares than are available in total. In the case of such an oversubscription, the issuing house will scale down the applications to a level which will just cover the amount of shares available. The prospect of an oversubscription, which can occur even in a new issue by TENDER, will tempt investors to STAG the issue, hoping for an allotment which they can sell immediately at a profit.

over-the-counter (OTC) markets. Markets, other than recognized stock exchanges, on which securities are dealt. In the United States, the over-the-counter market is primarily a telephone market and at one time used to deal mainly in the securities of companies without sufficient track records, shareholdings or other factors to allow them to seek a listing on a stock exchange. Bonds of all types are principally dealt in on over-the-counter markets. Dealers in these markets may act both as principals and as agents for clients.

The phrase contains overtones of being less regulated than the markets provided by stock exchanges and in several countries the principle of CAVEAT EMPTOR applies.

In recent years there has been a growth of over-the-counter markets in a number of countries; the principal OTC market in the United States is that provided by the NATIONAL ASSOCIATION OF SECURITIES DEALERS, while in France, the MARCHÉ HORS-CÔTE and the SECOND MARCHÉ, although within the Paris *bourse*, are over-the-counter markets. In Japan, the over-the-counter market is said to be small, organized trading in second-line stocks having been absorbed into the stock exchanges with the establishment of the second section of the Tokyo, Osaka and Nagoya Stock Exchanges in the early 1960s. Trading in OTC stocks in Japan is carried on within the offices of the securities companies and regulated by the SECURITIES DEALERS ASSOCIATION of Japan.

In the United Kingdom, there are several small OTC markets trading in securities not listed on the Stock Exchange; details of the quotations of prices in the securities of companies traded on these markets are published daily by paid advertisements in financial newspapers but no details of the amounts of trading are available.

On the Stock Exchange itself, securities not admitted to full listing may be officially traded on the UNLISTED SECURITIES MARKET (USM) while others which do not qualify or have not sought quotation on this market may be dealt in by Stock Exchange brokers for their clients on an occasional *caveat emptor* basis.

The origin of the phrase appears to have been in the United States around the 1870s. Investors could buy securities through recognised private banks as well as via a stockbroker. These private banks had counters rather like the commercial banks of today. The phrase over-the-counter therefore passed into the language to differentiate securities bought from a private bank or dealer rather than those bought through the auction market of a STOCK AND EXCHANGE BOARD.

own account. A dealer or member firm in the market buying and selling securities as principal in his, or its, own name.

ownership. *See* BENEFICIAL OWNER.

P

pacchetto (It). A BLOCK of shares.

paid up capital. The amount of AUTHORIZED CAPITAL which has been subscribed by shareholders. Normally, issued capital is fully paid on issue but there may be occasions on which payment is made by instalments. This has occurred several times in the United Kingdom, most frequently with large PRIVATIZATION issues where the amounts involved have been so large that subscription in full at one time would have caused the issue to be unpopular with investors and led to disruption in the flow of funds in the money markets. Occasionally, but rarely, the amount of issued capital may remain partly paid for a long period, the balance, UNCALLED CAPITAL, being a potential liability of the shareholder in the event of the company being wound up. *See also* FULLY PAID SHARES and PARTLY PAID SHARES.

paid up shares. PAID UP CAPITAL in share, not debt, form.

painting the tape (US). The (illegal) action of carrying out fictitious transactions in the hope of creating artificial interest in the stock by giving the impression of active trading interest. *See also* TICKER.

pair (Fr). *See* PAR.

Panel on Take-overs and Mergers (UK). A body set up in 1968 to supervise and make rulings on TAKE-OVER BIDS. The Panel was set up by nine representative bodies involved in the securities markets in London, namely the ACCEPTING HOUSES COMMITTEE, ASSOCIATION OF INVESTMENT TRUST COMPANIES, British Insurance Association, Committee of London Clearing Bankers, Confederation of British Industry, ISSUING HOUSES ASSOCIATION, National Association of Pension Funds, COUNCIL OF THE STOCK EXCHANGE, and the UNIT TRUST ASSOCIATION.

Concern over the conduct of certain take-over bids in the 1950s caused the Governor of the Bank of England to set up a working party in 1959 of those bodies most connected with take-over bids, to devise improved standards of conduct in this area. This working party produced notes of guidance but not until 1967 was the working party, supplemented now by other bodies, re-convened in the light of further disquiet about take-over activity and the tactics of some of those involved. The result was the first CITY CODE ON TAKE-OVERS AND MERGERS (the Take-over Code). At the same time, the Panel was also established to oversee the operation of the Code.

The chairman and his deputy are appointed by the Governor of the Bank of England and the members are drawn from its supporting institutions, including now the chartered accountancy profession. In addition to the Panel itself, an Appeal committee, presided over by a distinguished former judge, is appointed to re- assess disciplinary cases.

The role of the Panel has been to develop and publish a set of rules and practice notes, which should be followed by a public company engaged in a take-over. The Panel is also available to give verbal guidance in particular cases and the speed of its response is one of its great strengths.

The sanctions available to the Panel are public or private censure and reference to the machinery of the relevant association for disciplining the offender. Additionally, the offender can be deprived of access to the securities markets for a temporary period or, indeed, permanently.

The Panel on Take-overs and Mergers has been since 1978 a working arm of the COUNCIL FOR THE SECURITIES INDUSTRY and is staffed by a director general and a permanent staff.

BIBLIOGRAPHY The Panel on Take-overs and Mergers, *Annual Reports. The City Code on Take-overs and Mergers* (Council for the Securities Industry, London).

paper. A company's securities either in DEBT or EQUITY form.

paper bid. A TAKE-OVER BID for a company to be paid for by the issue of securities of the offerer.

paper profit (loss). A profit (or loss) on securities which is not yet a REALIZED PROFIT or loss, but one which exists only on paper.

papier (Fr). *See* PAPER.

par or **par value.** The nominal price of a SHARE, DEBENTURE or LOAN STOCK. The par value bears no relation to the market value of that security, which depends upon supply and demand in the market and what investors are willing to pay for it. Consequently, a security may stand in the market either at par (equal to its nominal price) above or below par.

parallel markets. *See* LONDON MONEY MARKETS.

parallel pooling. *See* POOLING.

par casiers (Fr). One of the three types of quotation for securities on the French *bourses,* the others being À LA CRIÉE and PAR OPPOSITION. On the cash market, a system of *casiers* (pigeonholes) is used, one *casier* for each security. Fixed blocks of *casiers* are assigned to different broking firms and each firm is responsible for collecting all orders which belong to its block. At the beginning of each trading session, a representative of the broking firm, standing at his appointed place on the trading floor, receives all the orders from the other firms and, together with his own firm's orders, he lists the buying and selling orders. His duty then is to fix a price which maximizes the amount of stock which can be traded.

parcel. A BLOCK of shares which changes hands on a stock market.

parco buoi (It). The area on an Italian Stock Exchange floor where the public may follow the trading session.

pareggiare (la) posizione (It). To buy or sell the same number of securities to close a speculative POSITION.

parent company. A company owning 51 percent or more of one or a number of operating subsidiaries.

pari (Fr) and (It). *See* PAR.

parificazione (dei) corsi (It). To add the value of accumulated interest on a bond to its market price.

pari passu. Equal in all respects. The documents for a new issue of shares will state that the newly issued shares will rank *pari passu* with all existing issues, meaning that, with any exceptions stated, the new shares rank equally with all the others of the same CLASS previously issued.

parità (It). (1) In the case of a capital increase, *parità* indicates that the stockmarket value of the right is equal to its theoretical value.

(2) If an intermediary deals *in parità* it means he deals net of any commission. *See also* NET PRICE.

Parkett (Ger). *See* PARQUET.

par opposition (Fr). In conjunction with the PAR CASIERS and À LA CRIÉE methods of trading, *par opposition* is one of the methods of quotation used on the French *bourses. Par opposition* is the method used to determine quotations on the cash market for securities which are also traded on the forward market and to limit the difference between the two to a maximum of two percent. *See also* MARCHÉ À TERME.

parquet (Fr). Originally the official market on the Paris BOURSE, now a general word for the whole market. Until 1962, the AGENTS DE CHANGE had a monopoly on dealings in stocks in the official list and their market was popularly known as *parquet* (floor). This was in contrast to the dealings in other securities carried out on what was known as the COULISSE (the wings of a stage, behind the scenes) by the COURTIERS. The *coulisse* was suppressed in 1962 and the distinction between *parquet* and *coulisse* disappeared. The same word is also used in Italian, meaning a stock exchange trading floor.

participant. (1) A bank or issuing house which is a member of a syndicate responsible for providing a loan to a borrower. (2) In the UK settlement system, a participant is a user of the system.

participating preference shares. Shares which, in addition to being entitled to a fixed dividend before any payment is made on the ordinary shares, are also entitled to a share in the profits by way of an additional, fluctuating dividend, if the company is successful. *See also* PREFERENCE SHARES.

participating preferred (US). The American equivalent of PARTICIPATING PREFERENCE SHARES.

participation aux bénéfices (Fr). *See* PROFIT SHARING.

participation en nom (Fr). The participation by a bank or other financial organization in a new issue of shares or bonds and the announcement of that participation by the publication of the bank's name on the prospectus. *See also* TOMBSTONE.

partito (It). A security which has reached a level which makes it no longer a good buy.

partly paid shares. Shares on which the owner is liable to a further CALL. *See also* PAID UP CAPITAL.

partnership. A commercial arrangement between two or more individuals in which they share in an enterprise in common with a view to profit. Partnerships in the United Kingdom are governed by the Partnership Act of 1890. In such a partnership arrangement, all partners are jointly and severally liable for the debts of the enterprise, without limit. Professional practices, such as those of solicitors, accountants and stockbrokers, are often carried on in partnership. For example, in the United Kingdom the great majority of Stock Exchange member firms are partnerships, although this is not now necessarily true of the organization of member firms of other exchanges.

parts (Fr). Management shares in French companies which may be traded on the stock exchanges.

par value. *See* PAR.

passaggi (It). The various prices bid and offered at the trading ring before the effective price is fixed. Such preliminary prices only serve as an indication of a trend and have no other value.

passare (di) mano (It). Indicates that a company no longer belongs to the traditional group of control but has passed into other hands.

passare (la) mano (It). When the initiative in a series of operations in a security passes from one operator to another.

passed dividend. The omission of a dividend payment by a company.

passifs (Fr). *See* LIABILITIES.

passing a dividend. *See* PASSED DIVIDEND.

Passiven (Ger). *See* LIABILITIES.

pay-as-you-go. The concept of paying for pensions out of current income rather than out of an accumulated pension fund. Pensions to former employees in Britain are only on a pay-as-you-go basis for public service employees whose pensions are met by current government revenue. Almost all other pensions are paid out of funds accumulated during the pensioner's working life. In France, however, pay-as-you-go is much more widely used although, because of the dangers to employees if a company fails, government guarantees are provided. *See also* PENSION FUND.

pay day. *See* SETTLEMENT DAY.

paying agent. A bank or other financial institution via whom the dividends or interest on bearer shares and bonds are paid. *See also* BEARER BOND and BEARER SHARE.

payment date (UK). The date on which registrars despatch dividends to shareholders in the company or interest payments to debenture and loan stock holders.

PaySOP (US). A variation on the EMPLOYEE STOCK OWNERSHIP PLAN (ESOP) whereby employers can receive additional tax relief on their payrolls of 0.75 percent, in order to contribute money towards a separate and additional ESOP. Many major U.S. companies have adopted such a scheme as an addition to employee benefits.

pennant. A term used in TECHNICAL ANALYSIS of stock market prices to indicate a type of FLAG. In a pennant, however, the movement between the high and low is not consistent and a triangular shape emerges instead of a rectangle, with the pattern showing a narrowing of the spread between the high and low as time passes.

penny stocks. Low priced, often speculative, shares. In the United Kingdom, a penny stock is, strictly speaking, one whose market price is in single figures, that is less than 10 pence. However, it is more loosely applied to any low priced stock. In the United States, where investors prefer HEAVY PRICED SHARES, a penny stock is regarded as one with a market price of less than one dollar.

pension fund. A fund to which employers (and sometimes employees as well) contribute in order to build up a capital sum to provide employees with a pension in retirement. For many reasons, including the growth of the occupational pension as an attractive employment benefit and the rise of inflation, the flow of money into pension funds has resulted in the United States and, most particularly, in the United Kingdom, in the pension funds becoming a dominant force in the securities markets. In addition to stock market investments via government stocks and equities, pension funds are also heavy investors in property and overseas securities. In addition to the self-administered pension funds run by some large companies, many long term insurance companies manage pension funds on behalf of client companies. They, too, have shown a marked growth in importance in recent years and now account for a further substantial amount of equity holdings, again particularly in the United Kingdom. *See also* PAY-AS-YOU-GO.

performance fund. An investment or unit trust or other savings scheme, the object of which is higher-than-average capital gains and income growth. In order to achieve such gains, the securities in the portfolio may be very actively bought and sold in order to make quick short term profits which, it is hoped, will add up to a good rate of growth in the longer term. The problem with the theory is that shares can fall as well as rise in the short term and the TRANSACTION COSTS can offset the benefits of short term gains.

per Kassa (Ger). A cash transaction.

perpetual debenture. A loan secured on the assets of a company but which, unlike most such stocks, will never be repaid.

personal sector. One of the four divisions into which the economy is divided and between which flows of funds are measured. The other three sectors are the public sector, corporate sector and overseas. The personal sector includes, in the United Kingdom, not only individuals but also unincorporated businesses and charities. The personal sector is an important supplier of funds to the capital markets, either directly or via a FINANCIAL INTERMEDIARY. Normally the personal sector has a substantial surplus of savings over investment which it makes available to the two major borrowing sectors, namely the public sector and the corporate sector.

pesante (It). (1) A speculative position not adequately covered by sufficient margin deposits.

(2) If used in reference to the market, it signifies a predominance of sales and falling prices.

petite bourse (Fr). A phrase sometimes used for the late afternoon trading session on the Paris *bourse* which co-incides with the opening of the New York market. *See also* SÉANCE COMPLÉMENTAIRE.

petition. An official plea made to a Court for the COMPULSORY LIQUIDATION or WINDING UP of a company or the BANKRUPTCY of an individual or partnership.

petrodollars. The name coined to describe short term funds in the hands of the oil exporting countries which were not used to buy imports or undertake long term capital investment at home, but were used to invest in short term EUROCURRENCIES.

Philadelphia options (US). *See* FOREIGN EXCHANGE OPTIONS.

physicals. *See* ACTUALS.

picking winners. Choosing those shares which are expected to be more successful than average and thus achieve above average rises in value compared with, for example, one of the stock market indices. Picking winners is an attractive aim for those investors looking for capital gain, but the EFFICIENT MARKET HYPOTHESIS suggests that it may be as fruitless as the medieval alchemists' search for the substance to turn base metal into gold.

The phrase has also been used to describe the aim of the British Government in its industrial assistance policies of the 1960s and 1970s. The object was to identify those companies with outstanding prospects but a lack of immediate management and financial resources, and to invest government funds in them to help realize their potential.

pieno (It). A share which still has attached to it the coupon for the last dividend or right to a capital increase.

pigiare (It). To persist in selling a security, notwithstanding a market of little volume and, therefore, incapable of absorbing such sales without a sharp adverse price movement.

pink sheets (US). A list of securities dealt in on over-the-counter markets, together with their prices. A similar service in the United Kingdom has also been dubbed with the same name.

piove (It). *See* BEAR MARKET.

pit. The area or areas set aside in a futures market for the trading in a particular type of CONTRACT. Those dealers interested in the particular contract gather round the pit and buy and sell on an OPEN OUTCRY basis.

pit broker. A member of a futures exchange who executes orders in the pit for other members who have a presence on the floor of the exchange, but who choose not to carry out their own FLOOR TRANSACTIONS.

più interessi (It). Without interest; means that one must add the accumulated interest to the market price quoted.

placement (Fr). *See* INVESTMENT.

placement (US). *See* PLACING.

placing. One of the methods used to make a new issue of shares to investors, the others being an OFFER FOR SALE, INTRODUCTION or PROSPECTUS ISSUE. In a placing, the shares are not offered generally to the public but are placed in the hands of a group of large investing institutions. A placing is much cheaper than an offer for sale, for example, because it does not have to be so extensively advertised, but it has the drawback that not all investors have the opportunity to buy at the same price. For this reason, stock exchanges tend to restrict them to small issues (of less than £3 million of equity in the United Kingdom) where there is not expected to be wide public interest in the issue to be placed. In all other circumstances, the sale must be by prospectus or offer for sale, to allow the widest possible distribution of shares to all those investors who wish to participate. In the United States, a placing is called a placement or private placement.

placing broker. A stockbroker acting for a company making a new issue of shares by means of a PLACING. The broker arranges to place the shares in the firm hands of long term investing clients.

plan d'investissement (Fr). A method of building up holdings in a unit trust by means of regular monthly subscriptions.

plus tick. *See* UP TICK.

plus valore di capitale (It). *See* CAPITAL GAIN.

point. (1) A unit of measurement or change in an index. For example, an index number rising from 703 to 717 is said to have risen by 14 points.

(2) On a FINANCIAL FUTURES market, the MINIMUM PRICE FLUCTUATION of a contract on the market.

(3) In the United States, a point, when applied to shares (common stocks), means one dollar, thus a share price changing from \$20 to \$21 is said to have moved by one point. On a fixed interest bond, a point is reckoned as \$10, since a bond is quoted as a percentage of \$1,000. In the case of a bond, therefore, a point is equal to one percent.

pompato (It). A share whose price is considered excessively high following considerable and steady, planned buying.

pooling (UK). (1) The term used to describe the former method of amalgamating packages of securities acquired at different times for CAPITAL GAINS TAX purposes. Thus 1000 shares might have been bought at £2 per share, followed by a later purchase of another 1000 in the same company at £2.50 per share. In computing the base price on which any future Capital Gains Tax liability would be worked out, the two holdings would be amalgamated, or pooled, so that the holding in the above example would consist of 2000 shares at an average, or pooled, price of £2.25 each. The practice of pooling was ended by the Finance Act 1982. As a result of the provisions of that Act for the INDEXATION OF CAPITAL GAINS TAX, pools of shares which had been acquired prior to April 1981 were frozen and the pooled price continued to apply. Any future acquisitions, however, had to be separately identified for making calculations of liability to Capital Gains Tax. As the result of representations made by the life assurance companies, a form of pooling, called parallel pooling, has been introduced for companies buying and selling shares, but private investors must continue to keep separate records.

(2) In the UK Stock Exchange's TALISMAN settlement system, all stock which has been sold by investors via their broker to a jobber, is pooled in the jobber's pool (called his trading account) and any bought stock is allocated from that pool. *See* TALISMAN.

portafoglio titoli (It). *See* PORTFOLIO.

portatore (al) (It). A BEARER security.

portatore di obligazione (It). The holder of a BEARER BOND.

portefeuille (Fr). *See* PORTFOLIO.

portfolio. A collection of stocks, shares or other securities held by an investor.

portfolio investment. Investment in securities contrasted with so-called 'real' investment in land, plant and equipment, stocks of commodities and work-in-progress.

portfolio investor. One who undertakes PORTFOLIO INVESTMENT.

portfolio management. The management by a professional manager of the portfolios of a group of investors, either private or institutional. All aspects of the portfolio may be managed, not only the collection of interest and dividends but also decisions on whether or not to take up rights issues and indeed the decision to change the securities in the portfolio. *See also* MANAGED FUNDS; DISCRETIONARY FUNDS.

portfolio theory. A theory of investment which uses statistical techniques to help investors decide the correct spread of their investment risk over a number of securities in their portfolio. In a naive form, it shows that the risk of holding specific shares can be substantially reduced by holding a portfolio of 10-15 shares. These shares can be selected at random. At a more sophisticated level, modern portfolio theory, now best represented by the CAPITAL ASSET PRICING MODEL (CAPM), enables the investor to diversify his risk even more efficiently by quantitative analysis of the expected rates of return on individual shares in combination with his own preference for the degree of risk he wishes to accept.

BIBLIOGRAPHY Janette Rutterford, *An Introduction to Stock Exchange Investment* (Macmillan, London, 1983), Chapter 7 and bibliography.

position. (1) The amount of stock a trader or market maker has outstanding on his book at any time (a BULL position) or the extent to which he has agreed to supply stock he does not have (a BEAR POSITION or SHORT POSITION).

(2) To buy or sell a security with the object of establishing a net bull or bear position.

(3) The amount of an investor's interest in a FINANCIAL FUTURES market as measured by the extent of his open CONTRACTS, either long or short.

position trading. A method of trading on a FINANCIAL FUTURES market whereby contracts are held for an extended period of time, as opposed to DAY TRADING or scalping.

posizione aperta (It). *See* OPEN POSITION.

Post Execution Reporting (US). A system used on the American Stock Exchange which is similar to DESIGNATED ORDER TURNAROUND on the New York Stock Exchange.

Post Office Register (UK). *See* NATIONAL SAVINGS REGISTER.

pound cost averaging. A method of investment whereby the investor buys shares in a company over a period of time so as to establish an average price between the peaks and the troughs of the share price. The word is often applied to an investment plan where a fixed amount of money is subscribed per month or per quarter and the number of shares or units which the money will buy varies inversely with the price.

pre-emptive bid. An offer for the shares of one company by another for the purpose of deterring another bidder. *See also* TAKEOVER BID; WHITE KNIGHT.

pre-emptive rights. The right of a shareholder to keep his stake in a company intact. Thus, when a company seeks new equity capital it should offer it first to its existing shareholders on a pro-rata basis. The existing shareholders may take up their rights, so maintaining their proportional stake. They may choose not to do so; but the important point is that they have been given the chance, as shareholders, to subscribe. In the United Kingdom, the Stock Exchange insists that existing holders are given such rights. In the United States such a right is not regarded as sacrosanct. *See also* RIGHTS ISSUE.

preference shares (UK). Shares which carry the right to a (normally fixed) dividend which ranks before the payment of a dividend to ordinary shareholders but behind the claims for interest by debenture and loan stock holders. Preference shares may also have a right to a further dividend if the company is successful. *See also* PARTICIPATING PREFERENCE SHARES; CUMULATIVE PREFERENCE SHARES.

preferred stock (US). The American equivalent of PREFERENCE SHARES.

pref. trick (UK). A method of avoiding the payment of United Kingdom TRANSFER STAMP DUTY in a TAKE-OVER BID. The payment of stamp duty on the acquisition of shares was often a significant expense of a take-over. To reduce it, the effective value of the shares to be taken over was drastically reduced and the amount of stamp duty payable was equally cut. The Inland Revenue in July 1984 announced its intention to exempt from stamp duty take-overs which involve share exchanges, thus removing the need for an artificial reduction of the shares' nominal value. Take-overs for cash will, however, be subject to stamp duty. The changes are scheduled for the 1985 Finance Act, but any take-overs following the Inland Revenue's announcement are subject to the new arrangements.

Preis (Ger). The method of quotation for occasionally traded shares on a stock exchange. Such dealings take place on the regulated unofficial market. *See also* KURS.

Preisnotierung (Ger). *See* QUOTE.

Preisverdienst-Relation (Ger). *See* PRICE-EARNINGS RATIO.

premie marketer (Neth). An options specialist on the floor of the EUROPEAN OPTIONS EXCHANGE in Amsterdam.

premier ou dernier cours (Fr). Opening or closing price. *Premier ou dernier cours* is one of the ways in which an investor can specify how he wishes to deal, the others being *au mieux* (AT BEST) or a *cours limité (*LIMIT ORDER). If a *premier ou dernier cours* order is received, such orders can be carried out whether at the opening or the closing price, depending upon their nature. If an opening price order is received during the session, it can only be carried out if it is still possible to do so, in other words, if the opening price still holds; closing price orders can only be given on the forward market (MARCHÉ À TERME) not the cash market (MARCHÉ AU COMPTANT).

premio a vendre (It). *See* PUT OPTION. More commonly called *un premio put.*

premio d'acquisto (It). *See* CALL OPTION. More usually referred to as *un premio dont.*

premium. (1) The difference between the par value of a security and a higher issue price.

(2) The difference between the issue price of a security and its higher current market price.

(3) The price paid for an option to buy or sell a security at a pre-determined price.

(4) The excess of one futures contract price over that of another or over the cash market price. *See also* DISCOUNT; INVERTED MARKET.

premium bond (US). A bond whose market price stands at a premium on its PAR value.

Premium Bonds (UK). Issued by the Government to private investors, Premium Bonds, introduced in 1956, pay no interest but all bonds go into weekly and monthly prize draws, where prizes range from £25 to £250,000. Bonds are of £1 each and are available in £5 units. New bonds do not enter the draw until three months after purchase.

prendere una barca (It). *See* BARCA.

prerefunding (US). Refunding is the issue of a new security to repay a maturing one. Prerefunding is the issue of such a new stock not at the time it is needed, but ahead of that time to take advantage of interest rates in the market.

presentazione fogli (It). The day on which the presentation of the appropriate documents must be made to the clearing house of the Bank of Italy for the settlement of the monthly stockmarket account.

present value tables. Statistical tables which show the present value of an amount to be received at a known future date, discounted by a particular rate. Used in conjunction with ANNUITY TABLES, present value tables can be used to calculate REDEMPTION YIELDS.

prête participatif (Fr). A participating loan. A borrowing instrument created to allow the widest possible participation of investors under the French LOI MONORY.

Prevention of Fraud (Investments) Act 1958 (UK). An Act governing the sale of securities to the general public and the ways in which they may and may not be persuaded to buy them. It is concerned primarily with the licensing and regulation of the conduct of intermediaries in securities dealing and the ways in which circulars soliciting the purchase of securities may be issued. Under the Act, anyone wishing to deal in securities must obtain a licence issued by the Department of Trade and Industry before he can deal. Members of the Stock Exchange are exempt from the provisions of the Act since they are effectively regulated by the Stock Exchange Council, while since 1983 members of the NATIONAL ASSOCIATION OF SECURITY DEALERS AND INVESTMENT MANAGERS have been similarly exempted from needing individual licences. The Secretary of State for Trade and Industry who grants the licences can also revoke them, although this power has seldom been invoked.

In recent years, the Prevention of Fraud (Investments) Act has been found wanting in a number of respects and the GOWER REPORT has recommended that it be replaced by a more comprehensive Investor Protection Act.

prezzo (di) carico (It). The price at which the security was bought.

prezzo (di) chisura (It). *See* CLOSING PRICE.

prezzo(i) (di) compenso (It). The average end-of-account price of a security. It serves to calculate the cost of carryover transactions, (CONTANGOS), the tax to pay on inherited securities, the value of client portfolios in order to calculate custodian charges etc.

prezzo (di) emissione (It). *See* ISSUE PRICE.

prezzo fatto (It). The price at which a listed security is effectively traded.

prezzo limitato (It). A limit order price.

prezzo lordo (It). The stockmarket price excluding any commission.

prezzo medio di storno dei diritti di opzione (It). The average price of rights to a capital increase. It is calculated by the COMITATO DIRETTIVO DEGLI AGENTI DI CAMBIO and based on the price fixed on the first five days of trading of the right. It serves to rectify the base of already stipulated option contracts.

prezzo medio di storno del dividendo (It). The calculation of the value in lire of a stock dividend. It serves to rectify the base price of already stipulated option contracts on the same security.

prezzo netto (It). NET PRICE, indicating that the broker's commission is already included in the price of the security.

prezzo nominale (It). *See* NOMINALE.

prezzo quotato (It). Quoted price. *See* QUOTE.

prezzo (di) riporto (It). The interest rate charged on a CONTANGO contract.

prezzo (di) riscatto (It). The price at which a management company agrees to re-purchase units of an investment fund. *See* BID.

prezzo di storno (It). The average current prices of securities calculated by the COMITATO DIRETTIVO DEGLI AGENTI DI CAMBIO on the occasion of the settlement of an insolvency.

price continuity (US). One of the measures of market quality used by the New York Stock Exchange. Price continuity is the size of a price variation, if any, from one trade to the next in the same stock. In recent years, over 85 percent of all deals have occurred either with no change in price or the minimum movement of one-eighth of a point. *See also* QUOTATION SPREAD; DEPTH (OF A MARKET).

price earnings ratio (PE or PER). The relationship between the price of a share and the company's net earnings attributable to that share, the result being expressed as the current share price divided by the latest available figure of EARNINGS PER SHARE.

The price earnings ratio is a useful guide for investors as to how a particular share is rated in the market; a share for which investors are willing to pay 30 times current earnings as evidenced by the market price, is obviously more highly rated than one for which investors are prepared to pay only five times current earnings. Such figures must only be used as a guide; the current earnings figure may be out of date on one share or the other in that the difference may represent the anticipation of investors that the next year's earnings will be much better (or worse) than the latest published figures. In addition, companies' accounting practices in reporting earnings may also differ.

There are two possible ways of calculating price earnings ratios, depending upon the treatment of the company's tax position: these two are the nil distribution and the net distribution bases. The differences spring from the United Kingdom's imputation system of ADVANCE CORPORATION TAX (ACT) on dividend distributions. Under the nil method of calculating earnings per share, it is assumed that the company distributes no dividends; earnings and hence the price earnings ratio are calculated on the basis of the company's profits after tax. The net method is the net cost of the dividend plus retained profits. Because Advance Corporation Tax on dividends may be offset against a company's mainstream Corporation Tax on its profits earned in the United Kingdom, these two methods will generally, in the case of companies whose profits have been made wholly within the United Kingdom, produce the same figure. However, for companies which earn profits overseas, Advance Corporation Tax is not offsettable against the company's mainstream Corporation Tax and so the nil method of calculating earnings will result in a higher earnings per share figure (and thus a lower price earnings ratio) than the net method. The *Financial Times,* in calculating the price earnings ratio of companies, which it publishes daily alongside the latest share price, uses the net distribution method, but where the nil distribution method would lead to a figure which is ten percent different from the net basis, the figure is shown in brackets.

price limits. The minimum and maximum prices specified by a FINANCIAL FUTURES exchange between which FLOOR TRANSACTIONS may take place during a trading session. *See also* MAXIMUM PRICE FLUCTUATION.

price sensitive information. Information about a company's trading or other affairs which, when known, might be expected to exert an influence on the share price. In particular such information would include, but certainly not be confined to, profit and dividend announcements and possible take-over bids. It is a cardinal rule of disclosure of information that all such price sensitive news must be made available to the market as soon as practicable and that no INSIDER should seek to profit from the use of that information before it has become generally available.

price spread agreement (UK). *See* OPENING PRICE CONVENTION.

primary dealer (US). Sometimes called reporting dealers, they are dealers in United States government bonds who stand ready to make continuous TWO-WAY PRICES in Treasury issues direct with the United States Government's agent, the Federal Reserve Bank of New York (FRBNY). There are 36 of these dealers, about one-third of whom are banks. They deal as principals for their own account. Before recognising and doing business with a primary dealer, the FRBNY requires evidence of capital of $10 million. *See also* INTER-DEALER BROKERS.

primary distribution (US). The initial selling of a company's shares or government bonds on a stock market. Also called the primary offering or public offering. *See also* SECONDARY DISTRIBUTION.

prime (Fr). *See* MARCHÉ À PRIMES.

primary market (1) The NEW ISSUE market in contrast to the trading or SECONDARY MARKET provided by a stock exchange.

(2) In financial futures terminology, the primary market is the principal underlying market for a financial instrument or physical commodity.

primary offering (US). *See* PRIMARY DISTRIBUTION.

prime rate (US). The lowest rate of interest charged by commercial banks in the United States to their most creditworthy corporate customers. Other rates, to less good credit risks, personal borrowers etc are often linked to the prime rate. The term is equivalent to the United Kingdom's BASE RATE.

principal. (1) A partner in a firm, one who is responsible for the debts of the firm and who is a full profit-sharing partner.

(2) One who initiates a deal or who bears the risk of a stock exchange deal by taking a position in the shares and not acting as an intermediary or AGENT. The term is therefore applied to investors and to the MARKET MAKERS as opposed to the brokers.

prior charges (UK). Debts on which interest has to be paid before any dividends can be paid on preference or ordinary shares.

prior charges market (UK). The market in company fixed interest stock.

Prioritätsaktie (Ger). *See* PREFERENCE SHARE.

prise de contrôle (Fr). A take-over.

private company (UK). One which does not have a stock exchange listing and may restrict the transfer of its shares.

private placement or **private placing.** *See* PLACING.

private sector liquidity (PSL) (UK). Two of the wider definitions of the money supply in use in the United Kingdom. *For definitions, see* MONEY SUPPLY.

privatization (UK). The term given to the action of the British Government from 1979 onwards of transferring back to private ownership companies which had previously been nationalized. Such companies as British Aerospace, Cable & Wireless, Amersham International, Britoil, Associated British Ports, Jaguar, British Telecom and British Airways either have been or are intended to be sold to the investing public, while additional tranches of Government shares in British Petroleum were also sold. National Freight Corporation, meanwhile, was bought by its workers. *See also* PUBLIC CORPORATION.

Privatplatzierung (Ger). *See* PLACING.

prix d'émission (Fr). *See* STRIKING PRICE.

prix d'offre (Fr). In a new issue of securities on a French BOURSE, the *prix d'offre* is the minimum price acceptable to the company and announced several weeks in advance of the issue. Bids are then called for and the actual offer price (COURS D'INTRODUCTION) is fixed according to the amount of supply and demand.

probate price (UK). The price accepted for the valuation of securities on the death of a holder. The closing SPREAD as shown in the Stock Exchange Daily Official List is taken, and the probate price is the lower of the two prices, plus 25 percent of the difference.

proceeds. The amount raised by a company or its directors at the time of a new issue. Gross proceeds, less such items as broking and merchant bank fees etc produce a figure of net proceeds.

profit. The excess of sales proceeds over acquisition cost. *See also* REALIZED PROFIT and PAPER PROFIT.

profit and loss account. One of the statutory pieces of information which has to be produced by a trading company. The profit and loss account details the company's turnover, consolidated with that of its subsidiaries if appropriate, less the cost of sales. From the resulting figure of gross profits net operating expenses are subtracted to arrive at the trading profit. Subtracted from this figure are taxation and any profits attributable to minority shareholders to arrive at a figure of profit attributable to shareholders. This amount is then available, either for distribution to shareholders or putting to reserves as retained profits. The profit and loss account will show how the directors intend to divide the net attributable profit between the two.

profit sharing. The participation of employees in the profits earned by the company for which they work.

In the United States, such schemes have been in operation for many years but the most popular one is now the EMPLOYEE STOCK OWNERSHIP PLAN which gives tax relief to employers and encourages employees to use such schemes to save for their retirement.

In the United Kingdom there are two major schemes allowing all employees to join: these are the SAVE-AS-YOU-EARN profit sharing scheme and the profit sharing schemes set up under the Finance Act of 1978 and substantially extended by later Finance Acts. Under this latter scheme, an employer may set up a profit-sharing scheme approved by the Inland Revenue. To gain approval, the scheme must be open to all full-time employees with over five years service with the company and not confined to a restricted group. Funds paid into the scheme by the company are offset against the company's Corporation Tax liability, provided they are used to pay for shares which are alloted to the employees pro rata to their earnings or in some other mutually-agreed way. No employee, however, may receive more than a specified value of shares in any one year.

The shares are placed in a trust and cannot be sold for at least two years. After that time the shares are vested with the employee who may choose to sell them. If he sells them before the end of seven years from the date on which they were first alloted and five years from the date on which the VESTING occurs, he is liable to pay income tax at his marginal rate on a portion of the benefit. If, however, he keeps the shares for seven years, the benefit is completely free of income tax. When he comes to sell the shares, the employee may be liable to pay CAPITAL GAINS Tax if his capital gain is large enough.

profit taking. The selling of shares to turn a PAPER PROFIT into a REALIZED PROFIT. Such action is the trigger for calculating any liability to Capital Gains Tax which is levied only on realized gains.

profitti per azione (It). *See* EARNINGS PER SHARE.

progressif (Fr). Rising; on a rising trend.

project finance. Money made available by a group of specialist lenders to finance a specific project. Often the lenders acting in a consortium will also have set up the planning and appraisal of the project in question, as well as financing it.

promoter. An agent who helps to launch a business, dealing with the establishment formalities.

PRONED (UK). An association for encouraging the appointment of non-executive directors to the boards of British companies. Set up in 1982, with the support and encouragement of the Bank of England and a group of City and management institutions. The main tasks of PRONED are to promote the wider use of non-executive directors and to bring together those company boards wanting to appoint such directors and those willing to serve.

BIBLIOGRAPHY *Role of the Non-Executive Director* (PRONED, February 1982).

property. Property, especially in the United Kingdom, is often thought of as land and housing but it can also be applied to anything which yields its owner an income, including stocks, shares and other securities.

proprietary company. A company owning the rights over a piece of land suitable for mining etc and which it lets out on a profit-sharing basis to other companies.

proprietors' stake. The paid up capital and accumulated reserves of a company. Also called SHAREHOLDERS' FUNDS.

prospectus. The document which must be issued by a company wishing to make an issue of shares to the public. The contents of a company prospectus are determined by the provisions of the various Companies Acts in the United Kingdom, supplemented by the Stock Exchange requirements, laid down in its ADMISSION OF SECURITIES TO LISTING. *See also* OFFER FOR SALE.

In the United States, the prospectus must be filed with the SECURITIES AND EXCHANGE COMMISSION. It has to give all relevant information to prospective shareholders and must contain the highlights of the REGISTRATION statement, which also has to be filed with the Commission. As with a UK prospectus, its American counterpart must contain details of the issuer's capital and business and a statement on the use of the proceeds, as well as details of the issuer's prospects and likely competition for his product or service. Details of the management team must also be given. A preliminary version of the prospectus is called a 'red herring' because of a notice which is printed in red on the front page. This notice warns that the preliminary prospectus is 'for information only' and that the registration statement which has been filed with the Securities and Exchange Commission has not yet become effective and does not constitute an offer to sell shares to the investing public. The 'health warning' also says that the information in the preliminary document is subject to 'completion and amendment' and the preliminary prospectus leaves spaces for the price of the offer, the underwriting discount and the proceeds for the company to be filled in later, along with the list of sub-underwriters to the offer.

prospectus issue (UK). An unusual method of selling a new issue to investors. In such a case, a company would offer securities direct, rather than through an ISSUING HOUSE. *See also* OFFER FOR SALE.

Prospekt (Ger). *See* PROSPECTUS.

Prospekthaftung (Ger). The responsibility for the accuracy of a prospectus which is borne by those issuing it and party to it.

prospetto (It). *See* PROSPECTUS.

provisional allotment letter. A communication in the form of a letter sent to shareholders by a company informing them of a provisional allotment of shares due to them under a RIGHTS ISSUE announced by the company. In form virtually identical to an ALLOTMENT LETTER in the case of a new issue for which the prospective shareholder has applied, the rights issue allotment letter is provisional in that the shareholder will not receive his allotment unless he sends his cheque to the company to pay for it. If he does not wish to take up his rights, the shareholder may sell the shares in the market and renounce his rights. Alternatively, he need do nothing, in which case the company will sell his shares in the market and send the shareholder the proceeds, providing they are above a small minimum amount. Proceeds below this level are retained by the company. *See also* NIL PAID.

provvigione (It). *See* COMMISSION.

proxy. One who votes for or on behalf of a shareholder at a company meeting. Shareholders who cannot attend meetings will fill in proxy cards stating which way they wish to vote at the meeting and these votes, normally one for each share held, will be cast in the designated way. In the United Kingdom, the procedure is relatively straightforward in that all shares are registered in the name either of the beneficial owner or a nominee company which knows who the beneficial owner of the shares is. In the United States, where bearer shares are more common, the gathering of votes for and against resolutions at a company meeting is a more complex matter as shareholders must be encouraged to notify their interest to vote. *See* PROXY STATEMENT.

proxy statement (US). A statement giving information which must be supplied to shareholders by proxy solicitors, those firms which are employed by companies to seek out shareholders of bearer shares and seek their votes for or against a resolution at a company meeting. *See also* PROXY.

prudential ratios. Ratios applying to banks which they must keep to ensure that they are capable of meeting their obligations as they fall due. In the United Kingdom, the Bank of England does not lay down hard and fast rules, but satisfies itself that the banks concerned are following prudent policies and adequate management systems to ensure that the laid-down policy is being followed.

BIBLIOGRAPHY 'The liquidity of banks', *Bank of England Quarterly Bulletin,* March 1981, pp 40-1. 'The measurement of capital', *Bank of England Quarterly Bulletin,* September 1980, pp 324-8.

prudent man rule (US). An investment standard for the guidance of trustees. In some states of the United States, the law requires that anyone acting in a fiduciary capacity, such as a trustee, may invest money only in a list of securities designated by the state, the so-called LEGAL LIST. In states where there is no legal list, trustees may invest in a range of securities of their own choice if they are those which would be bought by a prudent man of discretion and intelligence seeking a reasonable income and the preservation of his capital assets.

public company. *See* PUBLIC LIMITED COMPANY.

public corporation (UK). A commercial enterprise in the United Kingdom run by the state and not by private enterprise. The usual method of running such bodies is not for the Government itself to be responsible, but for a separate business unit, the public corporation, to be set up to run it. Such public corporations include the National Coal Board, the Central Electricity Generating Board, the Electricity Council, British Gas, British Rail, among others. As part of its political philosophy, the Government from 1979 onwards has followed a policy of selling back some of the public corporations to private investors. *See* PRIVATIZATION.

public enterprise. Services or goods the supplier of which is in the public sector. In the United Kingdom, these would mainly be public corporations or other organizations such as water authorities and local government bodies.

public funds. (1) The stocks of public sector bodies which are listed on the Stock Exchange.

(2) Money supplied by the government or other public sector body.

public issue. The issue of securities in a company to the general investing public. *See also* PROSPECTUS ISSUE; OFFER FOR SALE.

public limited company (plc) (UK). The standard form for a public company in the United Kingdom, introduced by the Companies Act 1980 and replacing the old form of 'Limited' or 'Ltd'.

A public limited company is defined as one limited by shares or by guarantee, whose memorandum states that it is a public company and which has registered as such. The words 'public limited company' or 'plc' must follow the company's name.

public offering (US). The American counterpart of a public issue. *See also* PRIMARY DISTRIBUTION.

Public Trustee (UK). A body appointed under the Public Trustee Act of 1906 to provide executor and trustee services on a permanent basis for members of the public. When first set up, the concept was a novel one, trustees having previously been private individuals, but was quickly taken up by financial companies in the private sector who also established such trustee companies. The Public Trustee has to deal with many small estates which are not commercially profitable to handle.

public utilities. (1) Public sector bodies set up to supply basic services such as water, gas, electricity, postal services etc. *See also* PUBLIC CORPORATIONS and PUBLIC ENTERPRISE.

(2) (UK). The securities of such suppliers listed on the Stock Exchange. These are now relatively few in number because since the 1950s the usual method of supplying such utilities with long term funds has been for the Government itself to borrow, by issuing more stock, using the proceeds in part to supply the capital needs of public sector organizations.

pulito (It). *See* MERCATO PULITO.

Punkt (Ger). *See* POINT.

punto (It). A unit (of stock).

purchase and sale statement. A statement made by a commission broker to his client showing that his FUTURES position has changed: the number of contracts involved, the prices at which they were transacted, details of commissions and fees, and a statement of the net profit or loss on the transaction.

purchaser. One who buys, in a securities market context, a security, option or FINANCIAL FUTURES contract.

put and call. In an options market the buying of a right either to buy or to sell a security at a given price before a specified future date. *See also* PUT OPTION; CALL OPTION.

put option. The rights to sell a given security at a pre-determined price by a specified future date. *See also* CALL OPTION; CONVENTIONAL OPTION; TRADED OPTIONS.

put through (UK). The United Kingdom's equivalent of a CROSS. A deal on the Stock Exchange in which the broker or agent finds both seller and purchaser of the security. Under the rules of the Stock Exchange, the broker must deal with the jobber as market maker and so he sells the security to the jobber and instantaneously buys back from him at an agreed rate. In other words he puts the deal through the jobber. The jobber has the right to take some of the stock on to his firm's account or to supply stock from it if he wishes to balance his book. *See also* JOBBER'S BOOK.

pyramiding. In a FINANCIAL FUTURES market where excess margins are paid out in cash, the use of positive VARIATION MARGIN on an existing futures POSITION to increase the size of the position, normally in successively smaller increments.

Q

qualified accounts. A set of published accounts of a company which have not been given a wholly satisfactory report by the company's auditors. In the United Kingdom, the normal unqualified wording from the auditors to the shareholders is that the auditors have examined the accounts of the company under the relevant accounting conventions and that they give a 'true and fair view of the state of affairs of the company' in accordance with the Companies Acts' provisions.

quality of markets (US). The efficiency with which prices are made and deals take place in a stock market. The New York Stock Exchange places such emphasis on maintaining the quality of its markets that it has a special committee making regular reports to ensure a high level of quality. Market quality is measured by PRICE CONTINUITY, QUOTATION SPREAD and market DEPTH.

quantitativo minimo di negoziazione (It). Minimum trading lot on the stock exchange. It is established for each share by the COMMISSIONE NAZIONALE PER LA SOCIETÀ E LA BORSA (CONSOB).

quasi money. *See* NEAR MONEY.

quick assets. Sometimes called liquid assets: those which can be quickly turned back into cash without loss.

quick assets ratio. *See* LIQUID ASSETS RATIO.

quotare (It). To QUOTE prices for shares.

quotation. (1) The listing of a security on a stock exchange. Before such a security can be admitted to listing, the documentation accompanying it must have been closely examined by the relevant authorities, both at the stock exchange on which the listing is sought and, if applicable, by the relevant government department or other statutory regulatory agency. In the United Kingdom, quotation (always referred to as 'listing') is granted by the Council of the Stock Exchange following examination of the application by the Quotations Department and the Quotations Committee. The requirements for a company seeking a listing are laid down in a document called ADMISSION OF SECURITIES TO LISTING, usually known as the Yellow Book from the (somewhat bright) colour of its binder.

In the United States, details of the issue have to be filed with the SECURITIES AND EXCHANGE COMMISSION as well as the authorities of the stock exchange on which the listing is being sought.

In France, the COMMISSION DES OPÉRATIONS DE BOURSE (COB) has, among its other duties, the responsibility for making sure that all listed companies issue all the required legal information at the appropriate times.

The listing of securities on any of the German Stock Exchanges is the responsibility of the listing committee (ZULASSUNGSTELLE) of the relevant exchange.

(2) The prices made by a MARKET MAKER. *See* QUOTE.

quotation di borsa (It). The LISTING of a company's securities on a stock exchange.

Quotations Committee (UK). The Stock Exchange Committee responsible for granting listing to securities under powers delegated by the Council of the Stock Exchange.

quotation spread (US). The difference between the BID PRICE and the OFFER PRICE of a stock. Quotation spread is one of the measures used by the NEW YORK STOCK EXCHANGE (NYSE) to measure the quality of its market. Clearly the narrower the spread the better the quality of the market; around two-thirds of the bids and offers monitored on the NYSE are within one quarter of a point of one another.

quotazione (It). The price(s) of a security established on the stock exchange.

quotazione ex (It). Indicates that the price of the share does not include any right to dividends or other benefits.

quote. The BID and OFFER prices currently being made by the market makers or dealers on a securities exchange.

quoted company. *See* LISTED COMPANY, which is now the preferred terminology for a company whose shares are dealt in on a stock exchange.

quote driven. The phrase used to describe a stock market pricing mechanism which is stimulated by market makers adjusting their prices in order to find the level at which business can be done. A quote driven system is contrasted with an ORDER DRIVEN method. The NASDAQ system in the United States and the competing market maker system in the United Kingdom are examples of a quote driven system.

Quotenaktie (Ger). A share of NO PAR VALUE.

quotient cours bénéfice. (Fr). *See* PRICE EARNINGS RATIO.

R

raccattore (It). To build up a holding of shares bit by bit in order not to influence prices.

rachet (Fr). *See* REDEMPTION.

raider (US). A person who aggressively sets out to buy stock in a company in order to acquire control.

rally. An upturn or recovery in security prices following a sharp downward trend.

random walk. The concept that share price movements cannot be predicted from past behaviour, but move in a random way. Thus, because a share price has risen, there is no statistical reason for it to continue to move in that direction; at the next trading session it is just as likely to move in the opposite way. The random walk theory was developed in the 1950s and 1960s and was later developed into the EFFICIENT MARKET HYPOTHESIS (EMH). *See also* HIGGLEDY PIGGLEDY GROWTH.

range. The high and low prices recorded for individual stocks in a securities market, or the high and low for contracts in a financial futures market at a specific time or over a specified period. Thus one may speak of a range of prices at the close of business of a trading session, the range during the day or, indeed, the range over a month or a year. *See also* YEAR'S HIGH; YEAR'S LOW.

rapport (Fr). *See* ANNUAL REPORT.

rapporte (di) conversione (It). The conversion ratio of a convertible issue into shares.

rapporto prezzo-utile (It). *See* PRICE EARNINGS RATIO.

rapporto (di) twist (It). The inter-relation between short and medium term interest rates.

rate of interest. The price of money in a lending and borrowing transaction. In practice there may be almost as many rates of interest as there are borrowing transactions and economic theory abounds with discussions on the determination of rates, both absolutely and in relation to one another, and their effects on an economy. Explanations of the absolute levels of interest rates include the relative supply of and demand for loanable funds, influenced in the long term by the degree of wealth and development of an economy, the extent to which people are prepared to sacrifice current consumption for the benefits brought about by current savings and investment on future production, the level of inflation in any economy and its expected future rate.

Among factors influencing relative interest rates in an economy are the length of the loan, with short term rates generally being below long term ones as the lenders are sacrificing liquidity for a shorter time and the lower degree of risk that the loan will not be repaid. Among other factors influencing the general level of interest rates are the levels of interest rates overseas in money markets which are competing for funds and the future expectations of exchange rate movements.

rate of return. (1) In measuring the benefit of a real, as opposed to a portfolio investment, the annual benefit derived from the investment as a percentage of its capital value.

(2) In recent years much academic work has been done to measure rates of return in order to assess the performance of investment managers in running the portfolios in their charge. These studies are based on the degree of risk inherent in a portfolio, as well as on the

of risk inherent in a portfolio, as well as on the timing of inflows of funds into given investment schemes. To allow for this latter problem, namely that some funds may experience cash flows at more advantageous times than others, the time-weighted rate of return technique has been developed. This enables a comparison to be made on the rates of return achieved over a period by allowing for changes in relative cash flows.

BIBLIOGRAPHY Janette Rutterford *Introduction to Stock Exchange Investment* (Macmillan, London, 1983).

rating (US). A grade given to a company's bonds or preferred stocks by a credit rating agency, such as Standard and Poor's. *See also* 'AAA' RATING, STANDARD AND POOR'S RATINGS.

rationalization. The act of amalgamation of parts of an organization in order to achieve greater profitability for the whole. Alternatively, to concentrate on a particular activity or group of activities, selling off those peripheral businesses which do not fit in with the main specialization.

ratios. The relationship of one variable to another. These may be business ratios such as profits to turnover, stock to sales etc, that act as benchmarks against which to measure performance. Alternatively they might be balance sheet ratios, measuring short term assets against short term liabilities. *See also* PRICE EARNINGS RATIO.

reaction. The opposite of a rally: namely a fall in market prices of securities following a sustained rise. Sometimes, however, used as a synonym for a rally.

real estate investment trust (REIT) (US). An organization similar to an INVESTMENT COMPANY but concentrating its holdings in property, or real estate, investments. Real estate investment trusts are required to distribute as much as 90 percent of their income so the yield is generally very attractive.

real investment. Investment in assets such as land, buildings, equipment, stocks and work-in-progress, as contrasted with PORTFOLIO INVESTMENT.

realize (gain or loss). To crystallize a PAPER PROFIT OR LOSS. *See also* REALIZED PROFIT.

realized profit. The PROFIT taken on an investment by selling it, thus realizing the PAPER PROFIT.

real rate of interest. The rate of interest on an investment after allowing for the effects of inflation. Thus an asset yielding a nominal interest rate of 10 percent will have a real interest rate of 4 percent if the rate of inflation is 6 percent but a negative real rate of 2 percent if inflation is running at 12 percent.

real time. Minute by minute. A piece of jargon emanating from the world of computers to highlight the difference between those computers which do their work in batches and produce output at the end, compared with those machines which constantly up-date and can be interrogated at will.

In securities markets, some indices of stock market prices are said to be calculated in real time, meaning that price information is constantly being fed into the computer and a new index of prices is being calculated continuously. Such indices include the STANDARD & POOR'S 500 and the DOW JONES AVERAGE in New York and the FINANCIAL TIMES-STOCK EXCHANGE (FTSE) INDEX in London. Other indices are calculated less frequently than these minute-by-minute indices: these include the FINANCIAL TIMES INDEX of 30 industrial shares (calculated hourly throughout the trading day) and the FINANCIAL TIMES-ACTUARIES ALL SHARE INDEX and its sub-divisions which are calculated just once a day.

receiver. An official, often an accountant or lawyer, appointed to wind up the affairs of a company.

receiver for debenture holders. An official appointed by the debenture holders of a company, in accordance with the terms of the debenture deed, to sell assets covered by the debenture for the benefit of the holders. A receiver may be appointed when the company is in default either of the interest or capital payments on the debenture.

receiving banker. A banker appointed to a NEW ISSUE to receive applications from potential investors and to send out letters of allotment to the successful applicants and letters of regret to those who have been unsuccessful in their applications.

receiving order (UK). One of the stages in the bankruptcy of an individual or partnership. A receiving order may be granted by the Court if a petition is made to it which substantiates that the person or firm has committed an act of bankruptcy. From that moment the affairs of the debtor are placed in the hands of a RECEIVER.

rechnen (Ger). To establish an estimated price for securities before any official price has been fixed.

reciprocal business. Business given by one organization to another in return for business passed in the opposite direction. Such business may be transacted between two similar organizations with different specializations or between two organizations in different fields of activity.

recognized marking names (UK). *See* MARKING NAMES.

reconstruction. The re-arrangement of a company and its capital base in order to put it on a better financial footing; to re-organize its structure in a way deemed more appropriate by its board of directors or to give effect to a merger. *See also* MINORITY SHAREHOLDER.

record date (US). The date on which a shareholder must be registered in order to receive a declared dividend or other benefit or indeed to vote on a company's affairs. *See also* PROXY.

recovery. *See* RALLY.

recycling. The redistribution of funds. The word came into common use following the oil price rises of 1973-74 and 1979. At those times, substantially more cash was being paid to the oil exporting countries for the oil, money which they were literally unable to spend on imports and capital investment. The funds, therefore, remained in the form of liquid balances which were invested in the world's money markets (or, in some cases, with international organizations such as the International Monetary Fund). These organizations then on-lent these funds to those countries suffering balance of payments problems as a result of the initial oil price increase. The wheel thus came full circle, hence the coining of the word recycling. The amounts of money involved in this recycling process totalled many billions of dollars and because of the amounts available, lenders often lent it on very fine margins to borrowers who could ill afford to repay. The matter came to a head when many of these loans fell due for partial or total repayment and in many cases the loans had again to be recycled, except this time it was called rescheduling, by the banker making money available to the borrowers so that they could maintain the appearance of paying back the original loan.

reddito degli investimenti (It). *See* INVESTMENT INCOME.

redeemable bond. A security which will be repaid on a given future date or at any time between two specified dates.

redeemable debenture. The same as a redeemable bond, except that the debenture is normally secured on a company's assets in the case of a default before the final date of repayment.

redeemable preference share. A PREFERENCE SHARE which, although being a part of capital rather than a debt obligation, does have a specified date or dates of repayment of the principal sum.

redeemable stock. *See* REDEEMABLE BOND.

redelivery (UK). A technical term used in TALISMAN, the Stock Exchange's system of equity settlement. Redelivery is the use by a buyer of stock to satisfy a later sold bargain using stock which has not yet been registered out of SEPON, the Stock Exchange nominee company. *See* TALISMAN.

redemption date(s). The date on which a redeemable bond or preference share will be repaid. Alternatively, such a bond or share may carry two redemption dates, the prospectus stating that the security will be repaid not earlier than the first of these and not later than the second.

redemption price. The price at which a bond will be redeemed. Usually this is at PAR but it may not be so. In some cases the stock may be repaid above par as a bonus to holders.

redemption yield. The return on a fixed interest redeemable security based on its present price and taking into account both the interest to be paid and any capital gain (or loss) over the period to redemption of the security. This yield is most particularly applied to government stocks where any risk of default on the repayment can be ignored and the redemption yield can thus be calculated with certainty.

If the current price is below the price at which the stock will be redeemed, then the redemption yield will be higher than the FLAT YIELD; if, on the other hand, the current price is standing above the redemption price, the redemption yield will be the lower of the two yields.

Although the principle of the redemption yield is clear enough, the calculation is somewhat complex and involves the use of ANNUITY TABLES and PRESENT VALUE TABLES, or a small computer or calculator.

BIBLIOGRAPHY Janette Rutterford, *Introduction to Stock Exchange Investment* (Macmillan, London, 1983), Chapter 3.

red herring. *See* PROSPECTUS.

redimere (It). To REDEEM a bond.

reduction of share capital (UK). The writing down of a company's share capital to a level commensurate with the present worth of the business.

A company may apply to the Court to have its share capital reduced if it is clear that the capital has been lost and providing creditors have agreed to the reduction.

refinancing (US). The issue of new securities to repay an existing issue. The object may be to reduce the cost of the existing issue or to lengthen the life of the issuer's debt. Also referred to as refunding.

refunding (US). *See* REFINANCING.

register, share. *See* SHARE REGISTER.

registered bond (US). A bond which is registered in the books of the issuing company in the name of the owner. It may be transferred only when endorsed by the registered owner. *See also* BEARER BOND.

registered capital. The maximum amount of owners' share capital which a company may have outstanding. *See* AUTHORIZED CAPITAL.

registered competitive market maker (US). A member of the New York Stock Exchange who trades on the floor of the market for his own or his firm's account and who has an obligation, when called upon by a New York Stock Exchange official, to narrow a QUOTE or improve the depth of an existing quote by his own bid or offer.

registered equity market maker (US). The American Stock Exchange equivalent of a REGISTERED COMPETITIVE MARKET MAKER.

registered market maker (US). A BROKER-DEALER member of the NATIONAL ASSOCIATION OF SECURITIES DEALERS who is registered with NASD as a MARKET MAKER in particular securities.

registered office (UK). The official address at which the official books of a company, such as its registers of directors and secretaries, members and debenture holders must be kept.

registered representative (US). The person in a broker's office who deals with clients. Under the rules of the New York Stock Exchange, the registered representative must meet the requirements of the Exchange as to his background and knowledge of the securities business. The registered representative is also known variously as an account executive or customers' broker.

Registered Representative Rapid Response System (R4) (US). An experimental system on the NEW YORK STOCK EXCHANGE, launched on a pilot basis in 1982, to enable NYSE member firms to offer near instantaneous EXECUTION of small orders to their clients.

registered share. A share the ownership of which is recorded in the books of the company and transfer of which is also recorded into the name of the new holder. Shares in the United Kingdom are normally in this form and communication between the company and its shareholders is made much easier for the payment of DIVIDENDS, the making of a RIGHTS ISSUE of shares, notification of benefits such as a SCRIP ISSUE, and other company communications such as voting by PROXY and soliciting acceptances or rejections in a take-over situation. *See also* BEARER SHARE.

registered stock. *See* REGISTERED BOND.

registered trader (US). *See* COMPETITIVE TRADER.

Register of Agents. *See* AGENTS, REGISTER OF.

Register of Companies (UK). The list maintained by the Registrar of Companies containing the names of all those companies who, having complied with the formalities, are duly registered companies.

Register of Debenture Holders (UK). A record of all those who have lent money to a company on the security of a debenture. The register has to be kept at the company's offices and to be available for inspection, both by those holding the debentures and any other interested party.

Register of Defunct and Other Companies (UK). A publication which used to be issued by the Stock Exchange in the United Kingdom, giving details of those formerly listed companies which no longer had a listing. The last issue of the Register as a separate publication was in 1979-80, since when details have been incorporated in the STOCK EXCHANGE OFFICIAL YEAR BOOK.

Register of Directors and Secretaries (UK). A record of a company's directors and company secretary, which has to be maintained by the company and available for inspection.

register of members. *See* SHARE REGISTER.

registrar. The official or corporate entity appointed by the company to maintain its share register and to communicate with its shareholders. *See also* REGISTERED SHARE.

Registrar of Companies (UK). The public official appointed to maintain the REGISTER OF COMPANIES and ensure that all companies comply with the necessary formalities leading to registration and the continuing obligations on them to provide regular public information such as their annual accounts, changes in directors and so on.

registration (US). The act of registering an issue of securities with the SECURITIES AND EXCHANGE COMMISSION (SEC). In the United States, such registration must take place before any public offering may be made of any securities by a company under the Securities Act of 1933. A registration statement is filed with the SEC by the intending issuer; this statement must disclose all relevant information relating to the company's operations, securities, management and purpose of the public offering.

In addition, before a security may be admitted to dealings on a national securities exchange in the United States, it must be registered under the Securities Exchange Act of 1934. The application for registration must be filed by the issuer with the exchange on which the listing is being sought and with the SEC. This application, too, must disclose all relevant information relating to the company's operations, management and securities.

registration application form (UK). A document attached to an ALLOTMENT LETTER and a PROVISIONAL ALLOTMENT LETTER which has to be completed if the shareholder in whose name the shares are to be registered (at the end of the period of dealing in the allotment letters in bearer form) is not that of the original allottee.

registration fees. The charges made by the CLEARING HOUSE of a FINANCIAL FUTURES market in consideration for registering members' contracts. Fees are calculated on a per contract basis and payable on registration.

Registration of Business Names Act (UK). An Act which was introduced in the United Kingdom in 1916 and continued in force until 1982. Under the Act, any sole trader or partnership operating a business in names other than those of the sole trader, or partnership, had to register that name under the Registration of Business Names Act. The Act no longer applies.

registration statement (US). *See* REGISTRATION.

registre des actions (Fr). *See* SHARE REGISTER.

registro delle azione (It). *See* SHARE REGISTER.

Règlement Général de la Compagnie des Agents de Change (Fr). The general regulations of the association of stockbrokers in France governing the conduct of trading on the markets. The regulations deal with the organization of the association and rules for the admission of securities to listing on the official market as well as on the SECOND MARCHÉ and the MARCHÉ HORS CÔTE. Other sections of the regulations are concerned with dealing practices and the determination of prices, the publication of those prices and the scales of stockbrokers' remuneration. Specific rules also lay down procedures which must be followed in regard to options contracts, take-over situations and portfolio management by brokers.

BIBLIOGRAPHY *Règlement Général de la Compagnie des Agents de Change* (Paris).

regular way delivery (US). Unless otherwise specified, securities sold on the New York Stock Exchange must be delivered to the buying broker by the selling broker and payment made to the selling broker by the buying broker on the fifth business day after the transaction. This is known as regular way delivery. Such delivery for bonds is the business day following the transaction.

Regulation Q (US). A regulation of the Federal Reserve System which fixed a maximum rate of interest which could be paid on bank balances. Its existence helped the EUROCURRENCY market to develop.

Regulation T (US). A regulation of the Federal Reserve, the US central banking system, governing the amount of credit which may be advanced by brokers and dealers to customers for the purchase of securities. *See also* MARGIN; REGULATION U.

Regulation U (US). A Federal Reserve System regulation governing the amount of credit which may be advanced by a bank to its customers for the purchase of listed securities. *See also* MARGIN; REGULATION T.

reisen für (Ger). To trade for someone's account, to act as agent.

relazione annuale (It). *See* ANNUAL REPORT AND ACCOUNTS.

relazione sul mercato (It). *See* MARKET REPORT.

remisier (Fr). A sub-agent or intermediary who brings business to an AGENT DE CHANGE on a French BOURSE in return for a share of the commission. New laws governing the activities of *remisiers* were brought into effect in 1972, following the publication of a report by the COMMISSION BAUMGARTNER.

rendement (Fr). *See* FLAT YIELD.

rendita di rimborso (It). *See* REDEMPTION YIELD.

rendite (Fr). The return on an investment expressed as a percentage; the yield.

renounceable certificates. Share certificates which allow the holder to renounce his holding and transfer it to another.

rente (Fr). (1) An undated French government stock.

(2) any interest-bearing stock.

(3) the annual income from such stocks, hence *rentier,* one whose income derives from investments.

Renten (Ger). *See* BONDS.

Rentenanleihe (Ger). An undated fixed interest bond issued by the government.

rentier (Fr). *See* RENTE.

renunciation. The foregoing of one's rights. In a United Kingdom securities context, an investor may renounce his rights to an allotment of shares by signing the letter of renunciation on the reverse of an ALLOTMENT LETTER.

re-open an issue (US). To issue an additional tranche of an existing Treasury bond rather than make an issue of a completely new security.

Repartierung (Ger). Literally, a spreading or rationing. The word is used to describe the allotment of shares as the result of an imbalance of buying and selling orders.

report (Fr). *See* MARCHÉ DES REPORTS.

reprise (Fr). A RALLY on a *bourse* following a fall in prices.

rescriptions (Fr). Short term bills issued by the government. Roughly equivalent to TREASURY BILLS.

reserve liability. That part of a company's authorized share capital, which may be called only in the event of a winding up of the company's affairs.

reserves. Shareholders' funds which consist primarily of profits retained in the business and accumulated over the years, rather than paid out by way of dividends to shareholders.

residence. Generally the place of domicile of an individual. More particularly, in the United Kingdom the basis on which the Inland Revenue decides whether an individual or company is liable to UK tax.

resistance level. A level of prices at which buying support or selling pressure will halt a falling trend in the former case, or a rising trend in the latter.

restare (in) collo (It). *See* COLLO, RESTARE IN.

Restrictive Trade Practices Court (UK). The Court to which the OFFICE OF FAIR TRADING may refer agreements which are *prima facie* in restraint of trade, for adjudication. It was this Court, presided over by a judge and sitting with lay assessors, before which the Stock Exchange's case would have been heard had it not been settled out of court beforehand. *See also* COMMISSION; LINK, THE; DUAL CAPACITY; SINGLE CAPACITY.

retail broker (US). A broker who acts for a wide range of small clients. Often these brokers have large operations spread over a wide area for the purposes of dealing for small retail clients as well as, perhaps, a large institutional dealing presence. Also sometimes called a wire house.

retail price index (RPI) (UK). The most commonly used and widely available consumer price index in the United Kingdom. In securities dealing this index is used as the reference point for the INDEXATION OF CAPITAL GAINS TAX, which has operated since 1982.

reversal. (1) A turnround in the price trend of a stock, rising after a sharp fall or vice versa.

(2) A fall in the price of a security following bad news.

reverse take-over. The acquisition of a larger company by a smaller one, or the buying of a company whose shares are listed on the Stock Exchange, by one whose shares are not listed. The object of this latter exercise is frequently to gain a listing for the non-listed shares by the back door, rather than by an OFFER FOR SALE.

reverse yield gap (UK). The difference between the YIELD on a risk free government stock and the average yield on industrial equities, when the government stock yields more than the equity. When the equity yield is higher, the difference is referred to simply as the yield gap.

Traditionally, equities were considered more risky than fixed interest government stocks, on which income was guaranteed and not subject to rises (and falls) along with the profitability of the company. The yield gap measured that difference.

In the late 1950s the yield gap began to narrow as investors began to appreciate that the return from equities included not only the dividend payments but also the prospect of capital growth, not available on a fixed interest stock. In 1959 the yield gap became the reverse yield gap for the first time as equity yields fell below those on gilt edged stock. Apart from a few minor occasions, the reverse yield gap has been the norm ever since.

revoca (a) (It). (1) In the case of a cash order, the order is valid until the end of the calendar month.

(2) A stockmarket order in the forward market which is valid until the date established on the Stock Exchange calendar for the Options Declaration Day.

revocable (Fr). The status of a deal on the forward market in France, which can be revoked at any time before the end of the month by the investor, on payment of an agreed premium. *See also* MARCHÉ À PRIMES.

revocation (Fr). The equivalent of a GOOD TIL' CANCELLED order. Orders given without a time limit are regarded as standing until fulfilled. In contrast, *see* JOUR SEULEMENT.

revue du marché (Fr). *See* MARKET REPORT.

Rialto (UK). A colloquial name sometimes used to refer to the trading floor of the Stock Exchange. The allusion is to the Ponte di Rivo Alto, the marble bridge across the Grand Canal in the centre of the commercial quarter of medieval Venice and referred to in Shakespeare's *Merchant of Venice.*

rialzista (It). *See* BULL.

rialzo (It). An upward movement of stock market prices.

riaprire (It). To reopen the call of a security. This occurs when one or more brokers realize that they failed to execute some orders which could have been concluded at the fixed price.

ribassista (It). *See* BEAR.

ricopertura or ***ricoprirsi*** (It). The purchase of securities previously sold short.

rifiuto (di un) ordine (It). To refuse a stockmarket order.

riflessivo (It). A market characterized by slightly falling prices.

right. (1) Any benefit attaching to the holding of a security, be it dividend, the preferential opportunity to buy additional shares etc.

(2) More specifically, the privilege given to shareholders to subscribe additional new capital to the company at a favourable price. *See also* RIGHTS ISSUE.

rights issue. When a company wishes to raise more funds by the issue of additional shares, it normally gives its existing shareholders the right to subscribe additional capital, on favourable terms, in proportion to the number of shares already held. Such a rights issue made by a company to its existing shareholders is the way of raising new capital often recommended by stock exchanges to issuing companies, since it allows shareholders to preserve their existing percentage stake in the business. Such an action is thus an important element of investor protection, in that a shareholder cannot suddenly find his percentage interest in the company reduced without his consent. This principle is often referred to as the PRE-EMPTIVE RIGHT of the shareholders to have the first chance to subscribe new money.

The rights issue is made by way of a PROVISIONAL ALLOTMENT LETTER to the shareholders, notifying them of the terms of issue and the number of shares to which they are entitled under those terms. Shareholders then have a period of time (for example, 21 days in the United Kingdom) in which to make up their minds whether or not to take up their entitlements.

They may do one of three things: first, they can elect to take up their rights by returning the provisional allotment letter to the company, together with a cheque for the due amount.

Second, they may sell their provisional allotment letter, which is a BEARER instrument, in the market place, where they will be traded in NIL PAID form. The buyer pays a premium for the allotment letter and himself has to find the cash to take up the rights (or resell the allotment letter on at a profit later). Such a market in allotment letters is possible because of the favourable price at which the new shares are being offered, thus attracting buyers, combined with the fact that, for various reasons, an investor may not wish to take up his rights, either because he does not have the money immediately available or because he does not wish to add to his holdings of that particular share because it might upset the balance in his PORTFOLIO.

Finally, the shareholder may simply allow his rights to lapse. If he does so, the shares to which he is entitled will be sold in the market by the company through its broker and the proceeds will then be distributed to those shareholders who allowed the offer to lapse. The benefit to shareholders is that they avoid the individual cost of disposing of the rights. The major drawback is that shareholders cannot choose the time of disposal and must accept the price obtained. For really small holdings, where the distribution to an individual shareholder would be, for example, less than £2, the amounts would not be distributed because of the costs involved, but would be retained for the company's benefit.

rights letter of allotment. *See* PROVISIONAL ALLOTMENT LETTER; RIGHTS ISSUE.

rigido (It). *See* LIMIT ORDER.

rimesse (Fr). A consignment or parcel of shares in a portfolio, a term usually applied to BEARER instruments.

rimettere (It). To suffer a loss on a stock exchange transaction.

ring. (1) A group of investors, acting in concert, who try to corner the market in a particular share or commodity, in order to drive the price up or down to their own advantage.

(2) (Fr). The bar on the Paris BOURSE around which the dealers congregate.

(3) The physical market of the London Metal Exchange where the dealers congregate in a circle to deal.

rinvio (dell')accertamento del prezzo (It). Should the price of a share fluctuate by 20 percent or more, the COMITATO DIRETTIVO DEGLI AGENTI DI CAMBIO will postpone the call of the security until the end of the session. In the case of a bond, this occurs if the variation is equivalent to 5 percent.

ripartizione (It). An ALLOTMENT of shares.

riportare (It). To postpone the settlement of a stockmarket contract by a carryover transaction or CONTANGO.

riporto (It). A carryover or CONTANGO transaction.

riporto (di) borsa (It). A CONTANGO for a precise period of time.

ripresa (di) borsa (It). A recovery of stock exchange prices.

riscatto (It). *See* PREZZO DI RISCATTO.

Risikoverteilung (Ger). *See* RISK CAPITAL.

risk capital. The capital subscribed to a business by its owners which risks being lost in the event of the company being unsuccessful in its trading activities. On the other hand, if the company is very successful, the original capital subscribed by its owners may multiply many times over in value, as well as benefitting from high and rising dividend payments. Such risk capital may consist of ORDINARY SHARES and DEFERRED SHARES and is also known as EQUITY or SHARE CAPITAL.

risposta anticipata (It). To exercise an option transaction before its expiry.

ristretto (It). *See* MERCATO RISTRETTO.

ritenuta (di) acconto (It). The withholding tax on dividend or interest payments.

riunione (di) borsa (It). A stock exchange trading session.

roll-over. The term used to describe the practice of extending a period of credit by a technical repayment followed by a further loan of the same amount for a further period. The terms of the loan may not be precisely the same, however. The lender might well take the opportunity to increase the rate of interest on the loan.

roll-up funds (UK). Schemes popular in the United Kingdom until 1983, when they were effectively stopped by the tax authorities. Roll-up funds were based offshore, that is outside the jurisdiction of the UK tax authorities, and invested their inflows of funds in high interest, but safe, investments. The income from these investments was not, however, paid out as income to the beneficiaries; it was ploughed back into the fund, where it accumulated as capital gain. When the term of the investment ended, the recipients received their share but it was taxed at the relatively low rate of CAPITAL GAINS TAX, rather than at the higher marginal tax rates on income. Such schemes were thus very popular with higher-rate tax payers. The roll-up funds were brought to an end by legislation, which effectively identified the gain as income and taxed it as such.

rottura (It). A sudden and considerable drop in stockmaket prices.

round lot (US). A unit of trading on the New York and other US Stock Exchanges. On the

New York Stock Exchange, the unit of trading is generally 100 shares and either $1000 or $5000 in the case of bonds. In some inactive stocks the round lot may, however, be as low as just 10 shares. The prices quoted by dealers for round lots are slightly more advantageous than those quoted for ODD LOTS.

round turn. The total FUTURES transaction, both in and out, which is completed when the initial LONG or SHORT position is OFFSET by an opposite transaction or by accepting or making DELIVERY of the actual FINANCIAL INSTRUMENT or physical commodity. A single commission may be charged at the time that the total transaction is completed. *See also* COMMISSION.

rovesciare (la) posizione (It). To conclude a speculative transaction in the opposite WAY and for a larger quantity of shares.

rubinetto (It). *See* CANNELLA.

Rücknahmepreis (Ger). *See* REDEMPTION PRICE.

Rule 394 (US). A New York Stock Exchange rule which required all business to be brought to the specialists on the stock exchange floor. No longer operative.

Rule 415 (US). A rule of the Securities and Exchange Commission dealing with the registration of securities. *See* SHELF REGISTRATION.

Rules of Fair Practice (US). A code of conduct drawn up by the National Association of Securities Dealers and incorporated into its Manual. The rules cover a wide variety of matters including the business conduct of members, recommendations of securities to investors, fair prices and commissions, the use of information received in a fiduciary capacity, the disclosure of interest in a security, and many others.

BIBLIOGRAPHY *Manual of the National Association of Securities Dealers Inc.* (Washington D.C., 1983).

running yield. *See* FLAT YIELD.

S

sacrificare (It). To sell a security just before a sudden and unexpected price rise and therefore obtaining a lower price than could have been achieved with a bit of patience.

saitori (Jap). A particular type of member of the Tokyo, Osaka and Nagoya Stock Exchanges. The *saitori* man the trading posts on the floors of the exchanges and receive buying and selling orders. When a buying and selling deal is struck, the *saitori* member sends details to the buying and selling brokers, notifies it to the settlement system and publishes details of the trade. The *saitori* members are intermediaries between the members who deal for the general public; they see all the business and help keep the market liquid. They do not deal direct with the public, nor can they trade on their own accounts.

salaried partner. A partner in a stockbroking firm who is remunerated in part by the payment of a salary, rather than sharing in the partnership profits. Nonetheless, he has the status of a partner and like the other partners is responsible for the debts of the firm. The precise nature of a salaried partner's position depends upon individual circumstances as set out in the partnership deed.

saldo del dividendo (It). *See* FINAL DIVIDEND.

sale docket (UK). A document issued by the Stock Exchange settlement system to selling brokers. The broker attaches the stock to the sale docket when he delivers the stock for settlement and the settlement centre can thus identify the bargain to which the stock relates.

Sallie Mae (US). *See* STUDENT LOAN MARKETING ASSOCIATION.

Sanierung (Ger). *See* RECONSTRUCTION.

Save-As-You-Earn (SAYE) (UK). Savings schemes in the United Kingdom for individuals who wish to save regular amounts on a monthly basis.

There are a number of different means of saving which all come under the general heading of SAYE. First are the regular monthly savings schemes under which an individual may place up to £100 a month with the Department of National Savings or with a building society. These savings must be made on a regular basis for five years, with interest added at regular intervals. After five years, the savings can be left in the scheme to accumulate further interest and, after another two years, a bonus of two months' contributions is added.

The second scheme is an index-linked SAYE scheme. Under this scheme, savers again agree to save on a regular monthly basis for a period of five years. Instead of interest being added, each of the monthly contributions is increased in line with the growth of the RETAIL PRICE INDEX (RPI) between the date of the contribution and the date when the SAYE contract matures at the end of the five year period. In addition, a supplement over and above the RPI has been paid in some years. If the amount invested is left in the scheme for a further two years, the savings are increased by a further two years' indexation and a bonus, amounting to two months' contributions, is again added.

A further variation of the scheme was introduced in 1980. This is the savings related share option scheme. Under this scheme, an employee can again save regular amounts, up to £100 a month from 1984 onwards (£50 maximum previously). In return for these regular savings, the employee's company grants him an option to buy shares in the company at a given option price when the scheme matures in five years' time. The price at which the option is granted is usually close to and a little below, the current price of the shares in the market, so that if the company is successful, the option price will be a very favourable one in five years' time and the market value of the shares the employee then acquires will be much higher than his actual savings over the period. If, on the other hand, the company is unsuccessful and at the end of the period the employee will not benefit by taking up the shares, he may fall back on the provisions of the ordinary SAYE scheme and receive interest and bonus benefits as described above. *See also* PROFIT SHARING.

sbracare (It). A sharply falling market.

scadenza (It). *See* MATURITY.

scalata (It). The systematic purchase of the securities of a company with the object of obtaining a controlling interest.

scale order (US). An order to buy or sell securities which specifies the total amount to be bought or sold and the amounts to be bought or sold at specified price variations. Thus an order might be to buy 1000 shares if the price is 500, but only 900 shares if it has risen to 510, 800 if it is 520 etc.

scalp. (1) To trade for small gains on a FIANANCIAL FUTURES exchange, trading actively by CLOSING positions quickly, often within minutes, always within the day.

(2) (US). To deal in an improper way, the trader putting his own commercial interests ahead of those of his client.

scappato (It). Literally meaning 'escaped'; in a stock market context, it indicates that a chance was missed in a sudden and notable change in the price of a security, so that it is no longer of any speculative interest.

scaricare (It). A general prevalence of sales. That is a bearish market.

scarto (di) garanzia (It). The percentage guarantee required on a CONTANGO or carryover contract, which may vary according to current stockmarket prices.

schedario generale titoli azionari (It). The general register of shareholders kept by the authorities, introduced in 1962. It is updated on the distribution of dividends to shareholders.

schedato (It). A person whose name has been included on the shareholders' register on receiving a dividend payable on the securities held.

Scheduled Territories (UK). An expression in UK exchange control regulations specifying the area within which investment could be made freely without the need for exchange control clearance. The popular name for the Scheduled Territories was the Sterling Area, and for many years it consisted of most of the countries of the Commonwealth, with the exception of Canada, plus a number of other countries which chose to link their currencies to sterling. With the decline in the importance of sterling as a world trading currency, many countries chose to link their currencies with the dollar instead and so passed out of the Scheduled Territories. When sterling was floated in 1972, the Scheduled Territories were reduced by the decree of the British Government to the United Kingdom itself (including the Channel Islands and the Isle of Man) and the Republic of Ireland, with Gibraltar later re-joining. The Republic of Ireland left when its currency joined the European Monetary System, and the Scheduled Territories ceased to have any practical significance with the effective ending of exchange control in October 1979.

scheme of arrangement (UK). *See* ARRANGEMENT.

Schiedsgericht (Ger). The arbitration tribunal of the two largest Stock Exchanges in West Germany, namely Frankfurt and Düsseldorf.

Schlussdividende (Ger). *See* FINAL DIVIDEND.

Schlusskurs, Schlussnotiung (Ger). *See* CLOSING PRICE.

Schuld (Ger). *See* DEBT.

Schuldscheindarlehen (Ger). Certificates of indebtedness issued by public authorities and listed on the German Stock Exchanges.

Schuldverscheibung (Ger). *See* BOND, DEBENTURE.

Schwach (Ger). A falling of stock exchange prices; price weakness.

scoperta (It). A SHORT sale.

scopertista (It). *See* BEAR.

scorched earth. A colloquial description of selling off property assets by a TARGET COMPANY in a TAKE-OVER BID to make itself less attractive to a bidder.

scrip. PAPER of a securities nature.

scrip issue. The issue of shares, free of charge, by a company to its shareholders in proportion to their existing holdings. Such an issue is also called a capitalization issue or a free issue. A scrip issue is made by a company transferring some of its reserves, which are shareholders' funds, to its share capital account, hence the term capitalization issue. The term free issue is only partially accurate, because although the number of shares held by each shareholder increases, the price of each individual share falls by an equivalent amount, the total value of the holding calculated by multiplying the total quantity by the price of each unit, remains the same.

The object of a scrip issue is to bring the share capital of a company more into line with its business needs and to reduce the price of each share while increasing the number available in order to make the shares more marketable.

scripophily. A term coined in the 1970s to describe the hobby of collecting antique bonds and share certificates.

scrutiny (UK). The term used to describe the various checks which are made by the Stock Exchange's central settlement system on stock deposited with it for settlement.

scuponato (It). A share in EX COUPON form.

seal. A die or cast used to imprint on wax to signify a formal agreement. A company purchasing shares of another, for example, must affix its seal to the document of application for it to be valid.

séance complémentaire (Fr). The official title for the late afternoon trading session on the Paris BOURSE which coincides with the first hour's trading on the NEW YORK STOCK EXCHANGE. Foreign securities are traded at this session, which makes ARBITRAGE easier for stocks also listed in New York. Unofficially, the session is sometimes called the *petite bourse*.

seat. Colloquially, membership of the New York Stock Exchange or other exchanges which restrict membership; New York, for example, has since 1953 had 1366 seats. Such seats may be bought and sold on terms which reflect the current state of supply and demand. The price of a seat on the New York Stock Exchange has varied in recent years from $515,000 in 1969 to just $55,000. The lowest ever recorded price for a seat in the NYSE was just $17,000 in 1942.

The LONDON INTERNATIONAL FINANCIAL FUTURES MARKET (LIFFE) sold its original 215 seats for £20,000 each in 1982; later sales were made at higher prices.

secchione (It). A security in which there is active two-way speculation and whose price is therefore fairly steady.

secco (It). *See* CORSO SECCO.

secondary distribution (US). Also known as secondary offering, a secondary distribution is the redistribution of a block of securities some time after it has been sold originally by the issuing company. The secondary distribution is handled off the floor of an exchange by a securities firm or a group of firms and the shares are usually offered at a fixed price related to the current market price of the stock. Usually the block of securities concerned is large, while the securities may be either listed or unlisted. *See also* PRIMARY DISTRIBUTION.

secondary market. The market in existing securities provided by a stock exchange. Also known as the trading market and distinguished from the NEW ISSUE OF PRIMARY MARKET.

The secondary market, by providing a method of buying and selling securities, overcomes the basic mis-match between the needs of the savers or investors who provide new money and the requirements of the capital raisers, be they companies, governments or other borrowers. Those raising money need large sums for long periods to develop their businesses or to carry out major public sector projects. The investors, on the other hand, can contribute only a proportion of the needs of the borrower and require liquidity, the ability to convert their holding of securities back into cash immediately and without loss. By providing a market where investors can buy and sell existing securities, stock exchanges or secondary markets encourage investors to put up money for new issues, enabling the borrowers to raise finance more easily and more cheaply than would otherwise be the case.

secondary offering. *See* SECONDARY DISTRIBUTION.

secondi prezzi (It). Prices fixed following the opening or closing call on the trading floor of the exchange.

Second Marché, le (Fr). The French equivalent of the UNLISTED SECURITIES MARKET, established in Paris in February 1983.

The requirements for companies to have their shares traded on the *second marché* are less onerous than for a full listing: a company has to make just ten percent of its shares available to outside holders, does not have to have its auditors approved by the COMMISSION DES OPERATIONS DE BOURSE (COB) and there is no rule about a minimum market capitalization before a company's shares can be traded.

Unlike the rules of the MARCHÉ HORS-CÔTE, a company may have its shares traded permanently on the *second marché,* but after three years its auditors must be approved by the COB, as for companies on the main market. In the interim, a company on the *second marché* must publish quarterly accounts.

In February 1983, on the launch of the *second marché,* 20 French and three overseas companies were traded. At the end of its first year of operation the total had risen to around 60 companies.

Second Section (Jap). One of the two sections of the Stock Exchanges in Tokyo, Osaka and Nagoya, the Second Section was established on the three exchanges in 1961 to provide greater organization for securities which had previously been traded on the over-the-counter markets. The listing requirements for the Second Section are less stringent than for listing on the FIRST SECTION but newly listed companies spend some time being traded on the Second Section of the market, even though they may be able to meet the more stringent criteria of the First Section.

secured debenture . A loan issued by a company which is secured on a specific asset or unspecified assets. *See also* DEBENTURE; FIXED DEBENTURE; REDEEMABLE DEBENTURE; SIMPLE DEBENTURE.

securities. A generic term for any financial instrument traded on a stock exchange. Such instruments may be FIXED INTEREST DEBT investments, with known interest payments made at regular intervals; they may be VARIABLE RATE STOCK, on which interest is paid, not at a fixed rate but at a variable rate, which depends upon the level of short term rates currently being paid in the money markets. Again, as a more recent trend, they may be INDEX-LINKED STOCK, with interest and capital repayment linked to changes in the retail price index or some other measure of price changes.

Most of the above types of securities are loans made by lenders to borrowers; the lenders are creditors of the company or other issuer and the loans normally carry a date of repayment. Interest on these loans is a CHARGE on the company which must be paid ahead of any dividends paid to shareholders.

The other main type of security traded on a stock exchange is SHARE CAPITAL. This is permanent money supplied by investors who are part owners of the business. Their reward is not fixed in money terms, but comes by way of DIVIDEND, a variable amount which fluctuates with the success or failure of the business.

Securities Act 1933 (US). The first major Act in the field of securities regulation introduced in the United States following the WALL STREET CRASH of 1929. The objective of the 1933 Securities Act was to give some measure of protection to investors following the abuses which had helped first to fuel and then to burst the speculation of the late 1920s.

The Act requires in most instances that details of any offering of securities to US residents must be registered with the SECURITIES AND EXCHANGE COMMISSION. The information required includes details of the company's history and its business, its directors and the amounts of the company's securities they hold, up-to-date information on income and expenditure and balance sheet figures, together with information on the use of the proceeds of the issue and details of the securities to be issued. *See also* REGISTRATION.

Securities and Exchange Commission (SEC) (US). The body set up by the SECURITIES EXCHANGE ACT 1934 to help protect investors. The Commission, with headquarters in Washington D.C. is responsible to Congress for the implementation of enacted securities legislation including the SECURITIES ACT 1933, THE SECURITIES EXCHANGE ACT 1934, the Securities Acts Amendments 1975, the Investment Advisers Act and the Public Utility Holding Company Act. In carrying out its duties under the Securities and Exchange Act, the SEC carries out investigations into dealings in a particular share and may institute proceedings against anyone believed to be acting to profit from INSIDER knowledge. The SEC normally leaves the regulation of dealers to the various stock exchanges and the NATIONAL ASSOCIATION OF SECURITIES DEALERS, but any dealers who are not members of such organizations are regulated by the Securities and Exchange Commission.

Securities and Exchange Law (Jap). The law enacted in 1948, and substantially based on US legislation, under which securities markets in Japan operate.

Securities Dealers Association (Jap). The Association set up in 1973 to help regulate securities trading on the Japanese Stock Exchanges. The Securities Dealers Association set up entry standards and examinations for all securities dealers and salesman and has an active role to play, along with the Stock Exchanges, in the self-regulatory aspects of securities regulation: both lay down rules, for example, on the degree to which members may actively stabilize prices of securities during the period of a further issue of securities, while the Securities Dealers Association helps control dealings in the over-the-counter market.

Securities Exchange Act 1934 (US). The second major piece of US securities regulation of the 1930s, the Act of 1934 was designed to improve the quality of information available to investors and potential investors in the United States, to prevent abuses in securities dealing, to control the practice of buying securities on

MARGIN and to curb INSIDER dealing in securities.

The Act laid down that all issuers of securities must provide specified information to the SECURITIES AND EXCHANGE COMMISSION under the REGISTRATION procedures. Secondly, all exchanges had to be registered and to agree to help enforce the provisions of the Act among their members. Finally, all broker-dealers have to be registered with the Securities and Exchange Commission before they are permitted to transact dealings in securities.

Anyone owning more than ten percent of a company's share capital must notify any dealings every month and profits realized as a result of sales within six months of purchase by such individuals may be recovered by the company or by other shareholders on the company's behalf.

Active trading to stimulate tape transactions and give a false impression of genuine interest in a security was also declared unlawful under the Act. *See* PAINTING THE TAPE.

Securities Industry Association (SIA) (US). A trade association for securities dealers in the United States to which many dealers, both on recognized stock exchanges and in the NATIONAL ASSOCIATION OF SECURITIES DEALERS belong.

Securities Industry Automation Corporation (SIAC) (US). An independent organization set up by the New York and American Stock Exchanges as a jointly owned subsidiary to provide automation, data processing, clearing and communications services. *See also* NATIONAL SECURITIES CLEARING CORPORATION.

Securities Investors Protection Act 1970 (SIPA) (US). Passed in the wake of difficulties in the securities markets in the late 1960s, the Act was designed to give additional protection to investors than that afforded by the SECURITIES AND EXCHANGE ACT 1934. Among its provisions was the establishment of the SECURITIES INVESTORS PROTECTION CORPORATION.

Securities Investors Protection Corporation (SIPC) (US). A non-profit making corporation set up in 1970 to provide funds where necessary to protect investors' cash and securities which may be on deposit with a securities firm which fails and is liquidated. Provided that such a firm is a member of the SIPC, its investors are protected against loss. All member firms of any of the national Stock Exchanges in the United States, plus members of the NATIONAL ASSOCIATION OF SECURITIES DEALERS, must participate in the scheme.

Originally the fund provided protection of up to $50,000, of which up to a maximum of $20,000 could be in cash. These figures have subsequently been increased substantially and now stand at $500,000 with a maximum cash content of $100,000.

securities market line. A graphical concept which relates market-related risk for a share to its expected return. The slope of the line represents the trade-off between the two. Risk is accurately measured as the BETA FACTOR.

BIBLIOGRAPHY Janette Rutterford, *An Introduction to Stock Exchange Investment* (Macmillan, London, 1983), Chapter 8.

seduta (di) borsa (It). The period of the stocl exchange daily trading session.

seduto (It). A calm period in the market aft a period of price rises and considerab volume.

segnare (un) prezzo (It). To indicate a pric fixed for a security which may be different from the current price on the stockmarket.

segregation. The separation of clients' account balances and securities from those of the broking firm.

seguire (un) titolo (It). To follow a share. To communicate to a client the price variations recorded for a security in a stockmarket trading session.

self-regulation. The term applied to regulation of securities markets, their members and listed companies by non-statutory bodies. In practice, all securities markets operate under a combination of legal statute and non-statutory (or self) regulation; the degree of one type of regulation compared with the other varies from country to country. In the United States, the securities market operates against a background of the legally established SECURITIES AND EXCHANGE COMMISSION and a plethora of legislation, but much detailed regulation remains with the New York Stock Exchange and the other stock markets throughout the country. Similarly, France, Italy and Japan all have securities commissions along the lines of the Securities and Exchange Commission.

In the United Kingdom, the Stock Exchange, while being ultimately responsible to the Government for the fair and efficient running of the market, has a generally free hand in the day-to-day business of regulation. The COUNCIL FOR THE SECURITIES INDUSTRY, the body with overall supervision of securities and related trading, is also a non-statutory body.

self-regulatory agency (SRA) (UK). The type of organization recommended in the GOWER REPORT to exercise control over a particular area of investment, to provide a regulatory body for members dealing in that area and to provide the necessary degree of protection for investors.

sellers' market. A market in which there is a predominance of buyers so that the terms which may be obtained on a transaction are highly favourable to any sellers.

seller's option (US). A special transaction on the New York Stock Exchange which gives the seller the right to deliver the stock or bond at any time within a specified period ranging from six business days to sixty business days ahead. *See also* DELIVERY; REGULAR WAY DELIVERY.

selling climax. An accelerated fall in the price of a security preceded by a steady fall in its price. Often regarded in TECHNICAL ANALYSIS as a pessimistic over-reaction which is likely to be reversed.

selling group. A group of banks collaborating in the new issue of securities to investors.

selling out (UK). The action of a seller of securities in the United Kingdom when the buyer fails to take up the stock. An official of the Stock Exchange sells the stock at the best obtainable price and any loss on the transaction, compared with the original price, is borne by the buyer.

selling short. *See* SHORT.

sell on close. In a FINANCIAL FUTURES market, to sell at the end of a trading session at a price within the CLOSING RANGE. *See also* BUY ON CLOSE.

sell on opening. To sell at the beginning of a trading session on a FINANCIAL FUTURES exchange at a price within the OPENING RANGE. *See also* BUY ON OPENING.

sell out. To COVER, offset or close out a long position in a FUTURES contract.

sepong. *See* STOCK EXCHANGE POOL NOMINEES.

serial bond (US). A bond issue which matures in part at periodic stated intervals.

series of options. All options of the same CLASS having the same EXERCISE PRICE and DELIVERY DATE.

service. To pay the regular interest payments on a debt.

settlement. The payment of cash for securities or, conversely, the delivery of the securities against payment: the concluding of a securities transaction by delivery.

settlement day. The day upon which bargains in securities must be settled. In the United States, for example, this is usually on the fifth business day after the bargain was struck. In the United Kingdom, settlement day for GILT EDGED transactions is the business day following the day on which the deal was made. For EQUITY transactions, settlement is made on an ACCOUNT basis, and the settlement day is six business days after the end of the account.

settlement price. The price calculated by the CLEARING HOUSE of a financial futures market on the basis of the CLOSING RANGE and other relevant price information and used for the purpose of calculating MARGIN.

shape (UK). The size of a Stock Exchange bargain as measured by the number of shares traded.

share. A security which represents a portion of the owner's capital in a business. In the United States referred to as COMMON STOCK. Shares represent the risk capital of a business, their holders are the owners of that business and share in its success and failure, measured by the amounts of DIVIDEND they receive and also by the price of the shares quoted on a stock market. Shares may be of different types conferring varying rights on their holders; such different types include DEFERRED SHARES, NON-VOTING SHARES, ORDINARY SHARES, PARTLY PAID SHARES, PREFERENCE SHARES and REDEEMABLE PREFERENCE SHARES.

share capital. The total of the owners' investment in the business. *See also* AUTHORIZED CAPITAL; ISSUED CAPITAL; PAID UP CAPITAL; UNCALLED CAPITAL.

share certificate. The piece of paper which gives evidence of title to the shareholder. The certificate is issued by the company registrar and states the number of shares owned by the shareholder. Over the next few years, the share certificate may become obsolete as securities markets move towards book entry transfer of securities, without the need for certificates as evidence of title.

shareholder. The owner of shares in a company. Shareholders may be individuals, charities or financial institutions such as pension funds, insurance companies, unit trusts and investment trusts, banks or industrial and commercial companies which may hold shares in other companies as trade investments. Shareholders, as contrasted with the holders of a company's debt, are the suppliers of the risk capital of a business. They share the increasing rewards by way of rising income and capital gain if the company is successful but stand to lose their whole stake in the business if it fails.

BIBLIOGRAPHY *The Stock Exchange Survey of Share Ownership* (The Stock Exchange, London). *Shareownership 1983* (New York Stock Exchange).

shareholders' funds. The liabilities of a business represented by its issued share capital and reserves. The issued share capital is the actual amount which has been subscribed by shareholders, either initially or subsequently. Reserves are largely built up from profits which have been retained in the business and not distributed to shareholders. These amounts, however, remain a part of shareholders' funds.

share index. *See* INDICES, STOCK EXCHANGE.

share option scheme (UK). A scheme which allows employees to buy shares in the company for which they work at a favourable price at a stated time or times in the future. *See also* PROFIT SHARING; SAVE-AS-YOUR-EARN (SAYE).

share pushing. The active selling to investors of shares which may be of doubtful worth.

share register. The list containing the names of the owners of registered securities in a particular company. On sale, details are passed to the REGISTRAR who deletes the selling shareholder's name and inserts the name of the buyer, issuing him with a new SHARE CERTIFICATE. Where a seller disposes of only part of his holding, the registrar will note the reduction and issue a new share certificate showing the balance of the shares now held.

shares of no par value. Shares which do not have a nominal or PAR VALUE. Although common in the United States, such issues are not permitted in the United Kingdom where all shares must possess a nominal value.

share split. *See* SPLIT.

share transfer form (UK). A form signed by the seller of securities relinquishing his rights in them. *See also* TALISMAN STOCK TRANSFER FORM.

shelf registration (US). The registration of details of securities with the SECURITIES AND EXCHANGE COMMISSION (SEC) under SEC Rule 415 which is filed and approved. There may be no intention to issue new securities immediately, but registration is made simply to speed up the whole procedure when the timing is considered appropriate. The details of the issue lie 'on the shelf' until needed and are available for inspection by investors. The Rule was introduced in October 1983 after an 18-month trial period, but is not normally available for smaller companies.

shell company. A company with few assets and available for take-over by a buyer at a low price. The buyer will then use the shell to develop his own business, often for a substantially different purpose from the original. Tea planatation companies registered in the United Kingdom were, for example, used to develop investment companies in the 1960s.

short. A POSITION on the stock market where a seller is committed to delivering shares which he does not have: the situation is often referred to as being short, going short or selling short.

On a FINANCIAL FUTURES market, the word has a similar meaning: one who has sold one or more futures contract(s) to establish a market position and who has not yet closed out that position through an offsetting purchase. *See also* LONG.

short covering. The offsetting purchase of securities to cover or close a short position. The investor will hope to do this at a profit (by buying the securities back at a lower price than that at which he originally sold short) but the price may have moved against him in the meantime and covering that position may cause an actual loss.

short dated (stock). Stock with less than five years to run to maturity.

short end of the market. Those securities which are repayable in the relatively near future. The precise definition depends upon the nature of the market: in money markets, the short end may be just a few days, in the government securities or bond markets, the short end is up to five years to maturity. *See also* SHORT DATED (STOCK).

short gilts (UK). Securities issued by the British Government which have less than five years to run to maturity, whatever their LIFE on the date of issue.

short hedge. The sale of FUTURES CONTRACTS for HEDGING purposes.

short position. *See* SHORT.

shorts. *See* SHORT GILTS, SHORT DATED (STOCK).

short sale. The sale by an investor of the securities he does not own in the hope of being able to buy them back later at a lower price, thus making a profit on the transaction. *See also* BEAR; SHORT; SHORT COVERING.

short selling. Establishing a market POSITION by an investor selling a security he does not possess, or selling FUTURES CONTRACTS or FINANCIAL INSTRUMENTS or commodities he does not own.

short tap (UK). The British Government sells its securities through the Stock Exchange by means of a TAP mechanism. The short tap is the particular security of less than five years to maturity which the GOVERNMENT BROKER has for sale at any given time.

short term. With only a short period left to maturity. *See also* SHORT END OF THE MARKET.

simpatia (It). *See* MOVIMENTO DI SIMPATIA.

simple debenture. A loan or debenture which is not secured on a company's assets: merely a debt of obligation which the company has executed under SEAL.

simple interest. A method of calculating interest by which the interest is calculated only on the principal and does not include any interest on previously-credited interest payments. The formula is:

$$A = P\left(1 + \frac{rt}{100}\right)$$

where *A* is the final amount
P is the original principal
r is the rate of interest
t is the number of period in which the interest is paid.

See also COMPOUND INTEREST.

single capacity. The concept that the roles of BROKER (agent) and JOBBER or other MARKET MAKER (principal), should be kept strictly separate and that a firm or company acting in one capacity shall have no involvement in the other. As the concept is currently enforced in the United Kingdom, the brokers agree to bring all their business to the market where the jobbers compete for it. The brokers must not deal as principals while the jobbers do not deal direct with the investing public.

The concept has been strictly enforced in the London Stock Exchange since 1912 and nationwide since the amalgamation of all the Stock Exchanges in the United Kingdom in 1973. In 1983, following the removal of the Stock Exchange case from the Restrictive Practices Court, and the commitment by the Stock Exchange to end minimum commissions by the end of 1986, the ability of pure single capacity to survive in conditions of negotiated commissions has been questioned.

The idea of a breakdown of single capacity springs from the concept of the LINK between single capacity and minimum commissions, which would have formed the basis of the Stock Exchange's case for retaining minimum commissions if it had been fought through the Restrictive Practices Court. Present proposals for changes to the dealing system following the abrogation of minimum commissions envisage the ending of strictly enforced single capacity among the Stock Exchange membership. Instead, a system of broker-dealers is envisaged. Such broker-dealers will be permitted to act in DUAL CAPACITY, although they will be free to elect to act only as broker or as market maker if they so wish.

sinking fund. Money set aside on a regular basis by a borrower in order to redeem outstanding loans. Normally such a sinking fund is set up in accordance with a debenture deed as added security for the lenders.

size. *See* MARKET SIZE.

società anonima (It). A public limited company.

società madre (It). *See* PARENT COMPANY.

società quotata in borsa (It). *See* LISTED COMPANY.

société (Fr). Company or association.

société anonyme (SA) (Fr). One of the basic types of company whose shares may be listed on the BOURSE and equivalent to public limited company in the United Kingdom.

société d'investissement à capital variable (SICAV) (Fr). Investment funds equivalent to UNIT TRUSTS in the United Kingdom or MUTUAL FUNDS in the United States. Such companies may be listed on the BOURSE and have shown rapid growth in recent years. They received a particular boost with the introduction of the LOI MONORY in 1978 when new investment via SICAV was eligible for the tax relief granted; much of the money invested under the provisions of this law was channelled through SICAV.

société en commandite par actions (Fr). Limited partnerships which are allowed to be listed on a French BOURSE. SEE ALSO SOCIÉTÉ ANONYME.

Société Interprofessionelle pour la Compensation des Valeurs Mobilières (SICOVAM) (Fr). The most important of the clearing systems in France for the deposit, withdrawal and transfer of securities. It was created in 1949, is operated jointly by the banking and stockbroking institutions and operates under rules laid down by the French Ministry of the Economy.

SICOVAM operates as a depository for French registered equities and bonds which are officially listed, oil certificates and equities dealt on the marché hors-côte, SICAV equities and bonds which may be traded on the money market.

BIBLIOGRAPHY Paul Stonham, *Major Stock Markets of Europe* (Gower Publishing, London, 1982).

Society for Worldwide Interbank Financial Telecommunication (SWIFT). An organization formed in 1973 and operated by over 200 banks worldwide. Its object is to enable the member banks to transmit funds and information between themselves more quickly than previously. The company itself is incorporated under the laws of Belgium and is based in Brussels.

soft dollars (US). Payment for services rendered by stockbrokers which is not made in hard cash. The services are provided out of payments made by way of commission and are not separately charged for. *Contrast with* HARD DOLLARS.

sold contract note (UK). A notification by a broker to his client that a sale has been carried out on the client's behalf, the price at which the deal was made and details of commission and other charges. Since the inception of the TALISMAN settlement system for equities in 1979, this information, in respect of deals settled through the system, is contained in a TALISMAN SOLD TRANSFER form.

sold stock account (UK). An internal account with the Stock Exchange's TALISMAN system to which all sold bargains are posted, pending settlement.

solvency ratio. The ratio of equity capital to total assets in a company's balance sheet.

sopra la pari (It). Above PAR.

sostenuto (It). A market characterized by generally rising prices.

sotto la pari (It). At a discount. To indicate a security priced below its nominal value.

sottoscrizione (It). A SUBSCRIPTION for shares or bonds.

soulte (de conversion) (Fr). The cash balance paid in the case of a conversion into shares which does not exactly match.

sous participation (Fr). The sub-underwriting of a share or bond issue.

souscription (Fr). *See* SUBSCRIPTION.

souscription préférentielle (Fr). The right of shareholders to an allotment of shares in proportion to their holdings.

South Sea Bubble (UK). The name commonly applied to stock market speculation in the year 1720 which eventually led to a collapse in the share prices of companies and, indeed, to the demise of many of the companies themselves. The speculation centred around the stock of the

South Sea Company, a company formed under Royal Charter in 1710 with a monopoly of trade in the Pacific Ocean and its islands and territories.

To boost the company's status, the directors hit upon the idea of taking over the United Kingdom's NATIONAL DEBT and, despite opposition in Parliament, secured the necessary legislation. Impressed, investors rushed to buy the shares of the company, which rose dramatically in price to over £1000 per £100 of stock. On the back of this speculation, many company promoters enticed investors to put their savings into companies which they had floated and which, in many instances, were no more than frauds on the investing public. The euphoria came to an end in August 1720 when the South Sea Company's stock collapsed, thus pricking the bubble and bringing ruin to thousands of investors, famous and unknown, large and small. As a result, it was almost three-quarters of a century before any form of share dealing became even moderately respectable again. On the credit side, the fortune made out of the stock by Thomas Guy, a stationer and former Member of Parliament, enabled him to found and endow Guy's Hospital in London.

BIBLIOGRAPHY John Carswell, *The South Sea Bubble* (Cresset Press, London, 1960).

special *ex* div. (UK). Standing for special *ex* dividend, the term is used to describe particular arrangements for dealing in interest bearing securities. Whereas normally a security is dealt *cum* dividend up to a particular date and *ex* dividend thereafter, in most government stocks it is possible to deal in them both *cum* and *ex* the dividend for a period of 21 days before the security is officially quoted *ex* dividend. The situation gives the advantage to the investor that he can choose whether to buy or sell with or without entitlement to the dividend and his choice will depend upon his tax status: a high rate taxpayer would buy *ex* dividend, a non-tax paying pension fund would buy with the dividend.

specialist (US). One of about 400 members of the NEW YORK STOCK EXCHANGE. The specialist has two main functions: first, to maintain an orderly market, insofar as is reasonably practical, in the stocks in which he is registered as a specialist. In order to maintain an orderly market, the New York Stock Exchange expects the specialist to buy or sell for his own account, to a reasonable degree, when there is a temporary disparity between supply and demand. Second, the specialist acts as a brokers' broker. When a COMMISSION BROKER on the Exchange floor receives a CLIENT ORDER, say to buy at $50 a stock which is currently being sold at $60, he cannot wait at the specialist's trading post to see if the price reaches the level at which his client has placed his buying order. So the commission broker leaves the order with the specialist who will try to execute it in the market if and when the price of the stock falls to the specified price. At all times, the specialist must put his customers' interest above his own. *See also* BOOK.

speculation. Investment on a short term basis hoping for quick profits. Safety of the investment in the longer term is a secondary consideration. Speculation may also carry the connotation of investing beyond the speculator's means. This may be done by investing on MARGIN or dealing within the ACCOUNT. In both of these cases, the speculator does not have to put up the full value of his purchase with his own money. Equally, speculation may also be undertaken on a fall in the value of the securities by the speculator's SHORT SELLING of the shares, hoping to buy them back and close the position at a profit. *See also* SHORT COVERING.

speculator. One who indulges in SPECULATION.

speculatore (It). *See* SPECULATOR.

speculazione (It). *See* SPECULATION.

spéculer à la baisse (Fr). To speculate on a fall in prices of securities. *See also* BEAR; SHORT COVERING; SHORT SELLING.

Spekulation (Ger). *See* SPECULATION.

Spekulationskapital (Ger). *See* RISK CAPITAL.

spin off. The separation of one member of a group of companies from the rest and its establishment, perhaps with its own stock exchange listing, as a separate legal entity. In return for the loss of such an asset, the parent company's shareholders may receive a share allotment in the new company.

Spitze (Ger). The fraction of a share which might arise as the result of an ALLOTMENT of shares by a RIGHTS ISSUE or a SCRIP ISSUE and which will be amalgamated with others to be sold in the market.

split. The breaking of the shares of a company into a larger number by means of issuing an additional one, two, three etc for every share already held.

split-level trust (UK). An investment trust whose capital is divided into two, each portion of which may be bought separately by investors. One section of the capital receives all the income accruing to the trust, which then pays it out to the holders of that portion of the capital. The second section of the trust is credited with all the capital growth achieved. Investors can therefore choose high income or capital growth, a choice which will depend upon their tax position and their relative desire for income or capital.

splitting. *See* SPLIT.

sponsor. The issuing house, stockbroker or investment bank which brings a company to the market.

spostamente di prezzo (It). A fluctuation in prices.

spot month. The next possible DELIVERY month available for each type of financial futures CONTRACT.

spread. (1) The difference between the BID and OFFER prices for a share quoted by a JOBBER or other MARKET MAKER.

(2) ON A FINANCIAL FUTURES market, the simultaneous purchase and sale of two different futures CONTRACTS in the expectation of a favourable change in their relative prices. Examples include purchase and sale of different DELIVERY MONTHS in the same CONTRACT (*see* STRADDLE), the purchase and sale of the same delivery month of the same contract on different financial futures exchanges or the simultaneous purchase and sale of different contract types.

spunta (giorno della) (It). The day on the stockmarket calendar when all operations executed during the account are checked for settlement purposes. It is the day immediately following the end of the account.

spuntare un certo prezzo. (It). To manage to sell or buy at a price previously fixed or regarded as favourable by the operators.

squeeze. A situation in which the shortage of supply of a security forces the prices up to the disadvantage of the BEAR who has gone SHORT. Sometimes the situation might arise as a result of changed expectations in the market about the prospects for the security in question; at other times, the situation may be engineered by other (and often official) participants in the market if they believe that the short selling has had a destabilizing effect on the market. This latter is more often seen in the foreign exchange markets, but can also be seen at work in government bond and stock markets from time to time.

Squirts' Guide (UK). *See* JOBBERS' INDEX.

Staatsanleihe (Ger). A government loan.

Staatsbesitz (Ger). *See* PUBLIC ENTERPRISE.

Staatsobligation (Ger). *See* GOVERNMENT BOND.

Staatsschuld (Ger). *See* NATIONAL DEBT.

stacco dividendo (o della cedola) (It). The detachment of the relative coupon in order to claim the dividend.

stag (UK). An applicant for a NEW ISSUE of shares who hopes to be able to sell them quickly at a substantial profit once trading starts on the stock market. The word has also acquired the additional connotation of one who applies for far more shares than he wants (or indeed, can afford to pay for if all his cheques were to be cashed) in the hope that one or more will receive an ALLOTMENT in a ballot.

The stag may profit from the FIXED PRICE OFFER FOR SALE, whereby all investors who wish to buy submit an application at the price fixed by the ISSUING HOUSE. He is less well placed in a TENDER issue, when potential buyers have to nominate the price they are willing to pay and the PREMIUM when trading begins is likely to be smaller than under a fixed price offer.

stake. The holding of an individual or institution in a company's share capital.

Stammaktie (Ger). *See* ORDINARY SHARE.

Stammeinlage (Ger). The shareholding of an investor in a company.

Stammkapital (Ger). The ordinary share capital of a company.

stamp duty (UK). *See* TRANSFER STAMP DUTY.

stampigliare (It). The stamping of a coupon in order to indicate that the relative right has been exercised.

Standard & Poor's (S & P) '500' Index (US). One of the major stock exchange indices in the United States. The '500' index covers securities which account for over 80 percent of the total value of securities listed on the New York Stock Exchange. Of the 500 securities in the Index, 400 are industrials and the remaining 100 consist of 20 transportation, 40 financial issues and the remaining 40 are public utilities. The Standard & Poor's '500' is a weighted index based on the number of shares in issue in each stock included. Thus a movement in the price of one of the companies with a large amount of issued capital will be given more weight in the index that one with a smaller amount of issued share capital.

Standard and Poor's ratings (US). Standard and Poor's Corporation's ratings are the best-known internationally of the credit ratings given to issuers of preferred and common stock in the United States.

The Standard and Poor's preferred stock ratings are based on the likelihood that the issuer will meet his obligations on the stock, the nature and provisions of the issue including sinking fund provisions, and the position of the issue in the event of bankruptcy or reorganization.

The Standard and Poor's preferred stock ratings are as follows :

AAA	:	highest quality
AA	:	high quality
A	:	good
BBB	:	adequate
BB, B, CCC	:	speculative, with greater degree of risk for CCC than B, and for B compared with BB
CC	:	payment of preferred stock dividends in arrears but is currently paying
C	:	a non-paying issue
D	:	in default
NR	:	no rating

The common stock ratings are based on the growth and stability of a company's earnings and dividends. Information on the last ten years' results is taken into account when making the rankings. Size of company also plays a part in the ranking, but a company with an exceptional earnings and dividend record might be included in a higher rating irrespective of its size.

The common stock rankings are as follows:

A+	:	highest
A	:	high
A−	:	above average
B+	:	average
B	:	below average
B−	:	lower
C	:	lowest
D	:	company in reorganization

BIBLIOGRAPHY *Stock Guide* (Standard and Poor's).

Standardwerte (Ger). Shares with the highest stock exchange turnover and capitalization and of the highest international standing.

star del credere (It). The payment of an extra commission when a commission dealer also guarantees payment of the stockmarket transaction. *See also* DEL CREDERE AGENT.

statement in lieu of prospectus (UK). A statement which must be delivered by a company to the REGISTRAR OF COMPANIES if it has no need to issue a full prospectus.

Statistiques Mensuelle de la Bourse de Paris (Fr). A monthly publication of the Paris BOURSE which gives statistical information on market activity and prices of listed securities.

statutory books (UK). The books which a company must keep by law. They are a minute book together with a register of directors, members and the names of the company secretary.

statutory company (UK). A company which is established, not under the Companies Acts, but by Act of Parliament. Such companies include nationalized industry bodies including British Gas, the Electricity Council etc.

statutory meeting (UK). A meeting of members which a company must hold by law at a date between one and three months from the date of its incorporation.

statutory report (UK). A report which must be issued to all members of a company at least seven days prior to the date of the STATUTORY MEETING in which the details of share allotments and other matters dealing with the establishment of the company, must be given.

stellage (Fr). A term used to describe transactions on a French BOURSE which are essentially PUT OPTIONS. The taker of the option pays a premium for the right to deliver shares at a specified price on or before a particular date. *See also* MARCHÉ À OPTIONS; MARCHÉ À PRIMES.

Stempelgebühr or ***Stempelsteuer*** (Ger). Stamp duty.

Sterling Area (UK). *See* SCHEDULED TERRITORIES.

sterling bonds (UK). A bond denominated in sterling and issued on the London capital market by an overseas-based company or other issuer. Such bonds became very popular in the early 1980s as sterling began to be seen as an oil-supported currency.

sterling securities (UK). Any share or loan issues which are denominated in British pounds and which pay interest in sterling terms.

stillhalten (Ger). To delay a decision on whether to exercise an option until the last possible EXERCISE DATE.

Stillhalter (Ger). The seller of an option.

stimmberechtigte Aktie (Ger). *See* VOTING SHARE.

stimmrechtslose Aktie (Ger). *See* NON-VOTING SHARE.

stock account (UK). A control account within the TALISMAN settlement system on the Stock Exchange in the United Kingdom, which specifies how much of each stock every participant in the system holds.

stock ahead (US). A phrase used in US markets to indicate to an investor why his deal has not yet been executed when other deals at the same price have already appeared on the TICKER. The reason is that there were orders ahead of his in the queue of the SPECIALIST and all deals must be executed in the order in which the specialist received them.

Stock and Exchange Board (US). A 19th-century American name for a stock exchange. The New York Stock Exchange was called the New York Stock and Exchange Board between 1817 and 1863.

stockbroker. An agent who buys and sells shares on behalf of his customers or clients. The broker will provide other services such as the collection of dividends or any other right attaching to the shares on purchase. He will also provide advice on share dealings backed by detailed analysis and research reports. Other services which major stockbrokers will supply include the management of clients' investment funds, personal financial planning, tax advice, other research and analysis and advice on related investments such as options and financial futures.

The broker acts as an agent and is rewarded for his services by commission. In almost all stock markets such commissions used to be regulated by the stock exchange authorities, but now this system is breaking down in many countries. *See also* ASSOCIATED MEMBER; BROKER-DEALER; COMMISSION BROKER; DEALER; FLOOR BROKER; HALF-COMMISSION MAN; INDEPENDENT BROKER; MEMBER FIRM; REGISTERED REPRESENTATIVE.

stock certificate. *See* SHARE CERTIFICATE.

stock dividend. A DIVIDEND payment made in the form of additional shares rather than cash. Normally such a stock dividend payment is made in the shares of the company paying the dividend, although in the United States it may be in the shares of another company (usually a subsidiary of the one paying the dividend).

Stock dividends enjoyed a brief popularity in the United Kingdom in the mid-1970s when there were tax advantages for the investor in taking additional stock or shares in lieu of dividend and benefits for the company's cash flow. However, the tax treatment was changed in 1975 so that it was no longer so attractive for investors and after that date companies, by and large, returned to cash dividend payments.

stock exchange. An organized marketplace for the buying and selling of stocks and shares. Sometimes referred to as the SECONDARY MARKET or trading market, a stock exchange is primarily concerned in its day-to-day turnover with existing securities. By providing this service, it overcomes the essential mis-match between the needs of borrowers who require large amounts of funds for long periods, and the needs of the providers of the funds, who each contribute relatively small amounts to a range of borrowers and who desire LIQUIDITY for their investments. A stock exchange provides the means of giving investors liquidity and allowing them to spread their risks while allowing the borrowers, such as companies and governments, to retain the funds for investment in their businesses or projects.

Over the years, in providing this marketplace, stock exchanges throughout the world have become regulatory authorities, controlling the activities of their members, the directors of companies whose shares are listed on the exchange and the investors. Most stock exchanges set their own rules of conduct but some are supplemented by a public sector body with strong regulatory powers. This latter case exists for example, in the United States through the SECURITIES AND EXCHANGE COMMISSION (SEC) in France via the COMMISSION DES OPÉRATIONS DE BOURSE (COB) and in Italy through the COMMISSIONE NAZIONALE PER LA SOCIETÀ E LA BORSA (CONSOB). In the United Kingdom, the COUNCIL OF THE STOCK EXCHANGE still largely administers the methods of trading on the stock market by means of non-statutory powers. In addition, there is a further non-statutory body, the COUNCIL FOR THE

SECURITIES INDUSTRY, which has a wide-ranging role in securities market regulation. Ultimately, both bodies must satisfy the DEPARTMENT OF TRADE AND INDUSTRY that they are carrying out their duties effectively. The Department itself has a role as the direct supervisor of those investment companies who are outside one of the recognized regulatory bodies, such as the Stock Exchange or the NATIONAL ASSOCIATION OF SECURITY DEALERS AND INVESTMENT MANAGERS (NASDIM).

Stock Exchange, The (UK). The united Stock Exchange of the United Kingdom and the Republic of Ireland was created in March 1973 as the culmination of many years of work to bring together the independent stock exchanges situated in many towns and cities throughout the United Kingdom and the Republic of Ireland.

Shortly after the second world war, there were over twenty stock exchanges. In 1965, as a forerunner of eventual amalgamation, many of these exchanges joined together into regional exchanges. Thus Manchester, Liverpool, Newcastle, Leeds, Sheffield, Huddersfield and Oldham formed the Northern Stock Exchange; Birmingham, Bristol, Cardiff and Nottingham joined to form the Midlands and Western Stock Exchange. Glasgow, Edinburgh and the other exchanges north of the border formed the Scottish Stock Exchange, while Dublin and Cork formed the Irish Stock Exchange. In addition, there were a few hundred brokers scattered throughout the United Kingdom, without access to a trading floor, who formed the Provincial Brokers' Stock Exchange. These regional exchanges entered into a federation with the LONDON STOCK EXCHANGE which lasted from 1965 to March 1973, when the planned amalgamation took effect.

Stock Exchange Automated Quotation (SEAQ) system (UK). The electronic price display system which is being planned by the Stock Exchange for the new trading system when it comes into being. All COMPETING MARKET MAKERS will input into the system their BID and OFFER prices along with the number of shares in which they are prepared to deal at that price. These competitive quotes will be displayed on screens in brokers' offices. Dealing will take place by telephone and will be subject to negotiation between the broker and the market maker.

Stock Exchange Compensation Fund (UK). A discretionary fund established by the Stock Exchange in 1950 to compensate any investor who, through no fault of his own, has lost money as a result of default by a member of the Stock Exchange. The fund is maintained in the Stock Exchange's balance sheet at around £2 million, but in fact is supported to an unlimited extent by members of the Exchange. If, therefore, as a result of a large default or a number of such failures, large claims were made on the fund, it would be topped up by a levy on members and/or member firms, in order to meet legitimate claims on it.

BIBLIOGRAPHY *The Stock Exchange Compensation Fund, a guide for claimants* (The Stock Exchange, London).

Stock Exchange (Completion of Bargains) Act 1976 (UK). The Act of Parliament which enabled the UK Stock Exchange to implement its TALISMAN settlement system for equities by allowing information contained on computer tapes to be acceptable as evidence of the purchase and sale of securities.

Stock Exchange Daily Official List (SEDOL) (UK). The daily publication of the United Kingdom Stock Exchange which gives information on securities traded on the Exchange. The List gives information on each security listed, when it was last quoted *ex* dividend, its closing quotation and the prices at which deals were done during the day.

Stock Exchange Fact Service (UK). The statistical information service of the Stock Exchange in the United Kingdom. It consists, basically, of a quarterly journal and a monthly

Fact Sheet. In addition, *Stock Exchange Companies* is a biannual publication which gives details of all companies listed on the Exchange, their market capitalization, points from their latest annual reports etc. Subscribers to the service also receive a number of other surveys published by the Stock Exchange.

stock exchange indices. *See* INDICES, STOCK EXCHANGE.

Stock Exchange Inspector (UK). An official of the COUNCIL OF THE STOCK EXCHANGE who carries out regular surveillance of Stock Exchange member firms or who may be called upon to carry out specific inspections on particular member firms if any aspect of their activities and finances give cause for concern to the Stock Exchange authorities.

Stock Exchange Official Year Book (SEOYB) (UK). The annual publication giving details of all securities and companies listed on the Stock Exchange. In addition, information on the history of the Exchange, taxes on securities, defunct companies and much other information is given.

Stock Exchange of Singapore Index (SESI) (Sing). The most comprehensive of the indices showing the pattern of movement of share prices on the Stock Exchange of Singapore. The Index consists of six weighted indices covering different areas of the market: industrial and commercial, finance, hotels, property, mining and finally, plantations.

There are several other indices covering stocks listed on the Singapore and Kuala Lumpur Stock Exchanges, including the STRAITS TIMES INDEX, Kuala Lumpur Stock Exchange Index, Business Times Index, Fraser's Singapore Industrial Index, Kay Hian Geometric Indexes, Overseas Chinese Banking Corporation Index.

BIBLIOGRAPHY Paul H. and Laurie J. Aron, 'The Asian Equities Markets', in Abraham M. George and Ian H. Giddy (eds.) *International Finance Handbook,* (John Wiley & Sons, New York, 1983).

Stock Exchange Pool Nominees (SEPON) (UK). The Stock Exchange nominee company into which all sold stock is transferred in the TALISMAN settlement process for equities and from which all buying orders are fulfilled.

BIBLIOGRAPHY *The TALISMAN settlement system,* (The Stock Exchange, London).

stockholder of record (US). A share holder whose name is registered on the books of the issuing company. *See also* REGISTER.

stock index futures. Contracts based on stock market indices which are traded on a FINANCIAL FUTURES exchange. They began in Chicago and were based on the Standard and Poor's 500 share index, spread to New York and have now reached the United Kingdom, where the LONDON INTERNATIONAL FINANCIAL FUTURES EXCHANGE (LIFFE) has since May 1984 traded a stock index future based on the FINANCIAL TIMES-STOCK EXCHANGE (FT-SE) 100 INDEX.

stock index option. Similar to stock index futures, a stock index option is also a contract based on movements in a particular stock exchange index. Such a contract has been dealt in on the traded options market of the Stock Exchange in London since May 1984.

stockjobber (UK). *See* JOBBER.

stock market. An organized mechanism through which stocks and shares may be transferred from one holder to another. Normally this takes place on the trading floor of a stock exchange, but a stock market can also be a telephone or electronic market.

stock note (UK). A document issued by the Stock Exchange settlement system as proof that stock has been allocated to a particular bargain. The stockbroker receiving this stock note can then present it to his CASH-AGAINST-DOCUMENTS (CAD) CLIENT for payment.

stock queue (UK). In the TALISMAN equity settlement system, transactions which result in the allocation of stock from jobbers' trading accounts are placed in a stock queue and are dealt with in relation to their position in the queue.

stock ticker symbols (US). Every company whose shares are traded on the New York or American Stock Exchanges or on the NATIONAL ASSOCIATION OF SECURITIES DEALERS QUOTATION SYSTEM (NASDAQ) is given an abbreviated identification symbol of up to four letters to help facilitate trading and ticker reporting: some are obvious, such as F (Ford), GM (General Motors) and IBM (International Business Machines), others are reasonably easy to understand, for example T (American Telephone & Telegraph), XON (Exxon) and XRX (Xerox Corporation). Others are less obvious; for example, X, does not immediately suggest US Steel to one who is not in the know, but that is what it stands for.

stock transfer form (STF) (UK). An old (pre TALISMAN) form which evidenced the sale of securities. Now replaced by a TALISMAN SOLD TRANSFER.

stop limit order (US). A STOP ORDER which becomes a LIMIT ORDER after the specified stop price has been reached.

stop loss order. *See* STOP ORDER.

stop order (US). An order to buy at a price above or to sell at a price below that prevailing when the order is given. Stop buy orders are generally used to limit loss or protect unrealized profits on a short sale. Stop sell orders are generally used to protect unrealized profits or limit loss on a holding. A stop order becomes a MARKET ORDER when the stock sells at or beyond the price specified. For example shares are sold short at 50. Stop buy orders may be given at prices of 40 and 55. If the stock reaches 40 the stop buy order will operate and the shares will be bought at that price thus realizing the paper profit on the transaction. If, however, the price rises to 55 the shares will again be bought, thus limiting the investor's loss.

A similar expression is used for dealings on the financial futures markets.

stornare (It). A transaction effected in the opposite WAY in order to close an operation. Often used in reference to intermarket arbitrage.

straddle. The simultaneous purchase and sale of FINANCIAL FUTURES or OPTIONS contracts for the same type of security option, interest rate or currency futures. The object of the operation is to make a profit when the price of the UNDERLYING SECURITY or FINANCIAL INSTRUMENT moves substantially in either direction, but to make such a profit the movement must be a large one.

straight debt. *See* STRAIGHT (FIXED INTEREST) STOCKS.

straight fixed interest stocks. Fixed interest company loans with no equity or CONVERSION element. In the United Kingdom such stocks are free from Capital Gains Tax liability if held by the investor for more than one year from the date of acquisition.

Straits Times Index (STI) (Sing). One of several indices of stock market prices on the Stock Exchange of Singapore. Beginning in 1948, the Straits Times Index now covers the six major Singapore groups: industrial and commercial, finance, hotels, property, mining and plantations. The Straits Times Industrial Index (STII) is identical in construction to the Financial Times Index in the United Kingdom consisting of an unweighted geometric calculation based on the prices of 30 leading industrial stocks.

For details of other indices covering stocks listed on the Stock Exchanges of Singapore and Kuala Lumpur, and for a short bibliography, *see* STOCK EXCHANGE OF SINGAPORE INDEX (SESI).

Straits Times Industrial Index (STII). *See* STRAITS TIMES INDEX.

stralciare (It). The request by one operator to another to accept a temporary document on settlement day as he is unable to deliver the effective document.

strappare (It). A sudden and unexpected rise in the price of a security.

Street, The (US). Abbreviation for WALL STREET.

street, the. *See* STREET MARKET.

street market. (1) Unofficial dealings in securities which take place outside a recognised stock exchange. *See also* KERB MARKET.

(2) At one time, dealings which took place after hours. *See also* KERB TRADING.

street name (US). Securities held in the name of a broker rather than the client are said to be carried in a street name. This often occurs when the securities have been bought on MARGIN or when for other reasons, the client wishes them to be held in the broker's name. *See also* NOMINEE.

striking price. In an OFFER FOR SALE by TENDER the price at which the shares are allotted, based on the demand for them in relation to the supply available and the wish to achieve widespread shareholding. All tenders at or above the striking price will receive an allotment of shares at the striking price, although the number of shares alloted may be pared down from the original number bid for. Those bids below the striking price will be unsuccessful.

Strohman (Ger). *See* NOMINEE.

Student Loan Marketing Association (SLMA) (US). An organisation often, along with its securities, called Sallie Mae, which makes a market in loans to students by banks and other financial institutions. SLMA raises funds by the issue of bonds on the securities markets.

Stützungskäufe (Ger). Purchases undertaken to SUPPORT a price.

subscribed capital. The amount of PROCEEDS contributed by shareholders to the ISSUED CAPITAL of a company. There may be a difference between the amount of AUTHORIZED CAPITAL and the lower amount of issued capital; more shares may later be issued to bring the issued capital up to the limit of the authorized and only at that time would this balance of unissued capital become subscribed.

subscription. The amount paid to a company for an allotment of shares in a new issue.

subsidiary company. A legal corporate entity which has at least 51 percent of its shares owned by another company and whose accounts may be consolidated with those of the PARENT COMPANY.

Substitut (Ger). A substitute for a KURSMAKLER.

sub-underwriter. A participant in the underwriting of a new issue of securities, other than the main UNDERWRITER. The sub-underwriters are usually investment institutions, such as pension funds and insurance companies. It is usual in many new issue markets to underwrite a new issue in order to make sure the borrower gets the proceeds he is expecting from the issue, even if the market suddenly deteriorates and the prospective firm investors do not take up the issue. The ISSUING HOUSE or INVESTMENT BANK does not carry the whole risk itself but spreads it among a number of sub-underwriters who, for an agreed fee, undertake to subscribe for all of the issue which is not applied for by other investors.

sul limite (It). When the stockmarket price fixed is within the price limits.

sunshine laws (US). A name applied to laws enacted in the United States which ensure the greatest possible disclosure to the general public of information on the operations of government regulatory bodies, including those responsible for the regulation of securities trading.

superannuation fund. *See* PENSION FUND.

support. Active buying of securities, usually government securities, by the 'official' buyer in order to increase the level of demand and thus moderate or reverse a fall in prices. Usually such support is provided by the Treasury or central bank of a country in order to prevent a sharp rise in rates of interest (the counterpart of a fall in fixed interest security prices). Such support measures are used to try to deter speculative activity by making it unprofitable. Support measures were employed in the United Kingdom, and elsewhere, to keep government stock prices reasonably stable, as this was believed to be the best way of ensuring a regular demand for them from investors. The difficulty with such support is that it puts money into the hands of domestic investors and this swells the MONEY SUPPLY, as measured by the amount of cash and bank deposits in the public's hands. With increased attention being paid to measuring the growth of money supply, support operations in the government stock market became less popular and, indeed, counter-productive for investor confidence.

support level. The level of prices at which SUPPORT buying takes place.

swapping (US). Selling one security and buying back a similar one at the same time, usually to establish a tax loss. Equivalent to the practice called BED-AND-BREAKFAST in the United Kingdom.

switching. (1) Selling one security and buying another simultaneously in order to establish a more favourable tax position or to take advantage of a price or yield anomaly which has arisen. In the United Kingdom, such switching between gilts qualifies for concessionary rates of commission so long as the minimum scales remain in being.

(2) Liquidating an existing FINANCIAL FUTURES position and simultaneously establishing a similar LONG or SHORT position in another futures contract of the same type.

Syndic (Fr). The chairman of the CHAMBRE SYNDICALE DES AGENTS DE CHANGE in France.

syndic délégué (Fr). The representative of the SYNDIC on the French provincial exchanges.

syndicat (Fr). *see* SYNDICATE.

syndicat d'émission (Fr). A collection of investment banks grouped together to arrange the new issue of securities for a company.

syndicate. An association of financiers or others who group together for a particular business purpose, such as the distribution of a new issue of securities.

Syndikat (Ger). *See* SYNDICATE.

T

Tafelgeschäft (Ger). Transactions made at the counter of a bank rather than on a stock market. *See* OVER-THE-COUNTER MARKET.

taglio (It). In reference to securities it indicates the nominal value or number of securities of each security certificate.

tail (US). In quoting a securities price, the tail is the 'small number' after the decimal point. If a security is quoted at $98.625, the tail is '.625'. The figure of 98 will be referred to as the BIG NUMBER.

take-over bid. The offer by or on behalf of one company for the share of another. Such a bid may be made in cash or by the issue of shares in the offerer company. The practices of some companies and their financial advisers in take-over situations, where the attentions of the bidder were unwelcome to the offeree and the bid was thus contested, have led to strict controls and rules of conduct in many market places, for which *see* CITY CODE ON TAKE-OVERS AND MERGERS; PANEL ON TAKE-OVERS AND MERGERS; OFFRE PUBLIQUE D'ACHAT.

Take over Code (UK). *See* CITY CODE ON TAKE-OVERS AND MERGERS.

taker. In a CONTANGO transaction one who agrees to grant the buyer a delay in payment.

TALISMAN (UK). The Stock Exchange's centralized computer settlement system for equities. TALISMAN is an acronym for Transfer Accounting, Lodgement for Investors, Stock Management for jobbers.

The system was set up in 1979 for UK equities and now also includes South African equities. It is currently expected to be enhanced to include Australian and North American stocks in due course.

The concept of TALISMAN is that all settlement of equities is carried out centrally by the Stock Exchange. All stock of the same company sold to a jobber goes into a pool (*see* SEPON) from which all bought bargains are satisfied. The system deals direct with registrars to facilitate transfer of the stock from one holder to another and the issue of new certificates.

BIBLIOGRAPHY *The TALISMAN Settlement System,* pamphlet (The Stock Exchange)

TALISMAN bought transfer (TBT) (UK). A legal instrument transferring a specified quantity of stock out of the name of the Stock Exchange nominee company, SEPON and into the name of the buyer of the stock.

TALISMAN sold transfer (TST) (UK). A legal instrument used to transfer a specified quantity of stock into the name of the Stock Exchange nominee company SEPON from the seller of the stock.

talon. A slip attached to a sheet of COUPONS of a BEARER BOND or a BEARER SHARE which is sent to the issuer when a fresh supply of coupons is required.

tap (UK). A method of issuing government stock to investors by trickling them out, on tap, via the stock market mechanism. *See also* TAP STOCKS; GOVERNMENT BROKER.

tap (Treasury) bills (UK). Treasury bills are short dated paper of 91 days' maturity issued by the British Government as a means of raising short term finance. They are either TENDER BILLS or tap bills. Tap bills are issued to government departments with spare short term funds to invest and are thus internal government funding. Some are also issued to overseas government agencies who wish to hold them They are, however, of little market importance.

tape (US). *See* TICKER.

tap stocks (UK). When the British Government undertakes a new issue of its own stock, it advertises a substantial amount for sale and seeks subscriptions. Rarely does the total amount of stock applied for reach the amount on offer and the balance is placed with the Bank of England. This amount is then sold via the GOVERNMENT BROKER to the jobbers in the Stock Exchange's gilt edged market as demand requires: it is available, in other words, on tap, hence the phrase. The Government Broker will usually have tap stocks available at any one time so that he can satisfy the demand from investors in gilt edged securities, whether that demand be for short or long dated issues.

target company. In a TAKE-OVER BID, the company whose shares are being bid for.

tariffa ufficiale dei diritti di mediazione per gli affari di borsa (It). The official rates of commission established by law.

tassa di bollo or ***tasse (sui) contratti di borsa.*** (It). Stamp duty applicable on shares and bonds.

tasso d'interesse (It). *See* RATE OF INTEREST.

tax credit. The amount of tax deemed to have been paid by a taxpayer on his dividend. Under the IMPUTATION SYSTEM of Corporation Tax operating in the United Kingdom, dividends on shares (but not interest on stocks) are declared and paid on a net basis at *x*p per share. By a process of GROSSING UP, the net dividend is increased notionally to calculate the gross dividend which, after allowing for tax at the basic rate, would have yielded the net dividend paid. The difference between the grossed-up figure and the net amount is the calculated tax paid and is shown on the shareholder's DIVIDEND WARRANT as a tax credit against his income tax liability.

The calculation of the tax credit is based on the current basic rate of income tax. If this is 30 percent, the tax credit is 30/70ths of the net dividend payable; if the basic rate were 40 percent, the tax credit would be 40/60ths, and so on.

Those shareholders who are due to pay tax at the basic rate have no further liability to tax; those who pay income tax at above the basic rate must later account to the Inland Revenue for the difference; those shareholders who pay no tax may reclaim the amount of tax credit from the Revenue.

The company pays over the full amount of the tax credits on the dividends to the Inland Revenue as ADVANCE CORPORATION TAX. This amount may later be offset against the company's liability to MAINSTREAM CORPORATION TAX.

taxe d'émission (Fr). A government tax on the issue of new securities.

tax haven. An overseas banking and financial centre with a less harsh tax regime than that of the investor's own country. Such tax havens are centres for OFFSHORE FUNDS.

tax shelter (US). A means by which an investor's liability to tax may be reduced or eliminated. They range from straightforward tax-exempt securities, often issued by government and local municipalities, to more complex arrangements designed to take advantage of tax concessions.

technical analysis or **technical research.** The method of research into share price valuation which relies on studies of the past trends in share prices in the belief that such movements form patterns which can be identified and used to predict future share price movements. A follower of technical analysis is often known as a CHARTIST. Technical analysis is contrasted with FUNDAMENTAL ANALYSIS, the study of the underlying position of a company rather than its share price movements.

Teilrecht (Ger). *See* RIGHTS ISSUE.

Telefonverkehr (Ger). The over-the-counter or telephone market in securities in West

Germany. Securities which are fully listed on a German exchange may also be traded on the *Telefonverkehr* in addition to non-listed stocks. The dealers on this market are the FREIE MAKLER and the investors are the banks and other financial institutions. Through the *Telefonverkehr* dealings may be done on an arbitrage basis with overseas securities markets at times when the German exchanges are closed.

tel quel (It). *Ex* dividend.

tendance (Fr). The trend of prices in securities markets.

Tendenz (Ger). *See* TENDANCE.

tendenza (It). *See* TENDANCE.

tender. To bid for an allotment of securities at a price specified by the intending buyer. The word is used in a number of contexts in banking and securities markets, but all have substantially the same meaning within the context of their own particular environment.

(1) An OFFER FOR SALE may be either a FIXED PRICE OFFER FOR SALE or may be by tender. In the case of a tender, prospective investors are asked to bid for the stock stating the price they are prepared to pay above the minimum stipulated. Successful investors are alloted stock at the STRIKING PRICE. Small investors may make bids at the striking price, without specifying an amount. UK Government stocks are also often issued in the same way.

(2) In a financial futures market, the word means to offer for DELIVERY against futures. *See also* TENDER BILLS.

tender bills (UK). TREASURY BILLS, other than TAP BILLS, are issued weekly via a tender organized by the Bank of England. The bidders are the discount houses which each make a bid for an allotment of the 91-day bills. The bills are issued in denominations of £5000 to £1 million with a minimum tender of £50,000. The banks do not usually bid for bills in their own name but buy them from a DISCOUNT HOUSE when they are closer to maturity. The discount houses no longer tender for the bills as a syndicate, as they did prior to 1971, but they are under a collective obligation always to cover the tender so that all bills will be taken up.

tender offer. (1) (US) A public offer to buy shares from existing shareholders of one public company by another, under specified terms holding good for a given period. Shareholders are asked to sell (or tender) their holdings for a stated value, normally at a premium on the current market price, subject to the tendering of a certain minimum and maximum number of shares specified by the bidder.

(2) (UK) An offer for sale by TENDER is sometimes referred to as a tender offer.

tenere (It). In reference to the stockmarket in general or of a specific security, it means that prices are steady.

termine (fermo) (It). A forward deal.

terzo mercato (It). The third market for unlisted securities and which is without any regulation or control.

third market (US). The trading of stock exchange listed securities on the OVER-THE-COUNTER MARKET by non stock exchange brokers.

Throgmorton Street (UK). A name sometimes applied to the UK stock market because of the situation of the Stock Exchange on Throgmorton Street in the City of London. It is equivalent to the name Wall Street for the New York financial markets and BEURSPLEIN 5 for the Stock Exchange in Amsterdam.

Thundering Herd, the US. A colloquial name applied to the American brokerage house, Merrill, Lynch, reflecting the size of its operations and the number of staff it employs.

tick. *See* MINIMUM PRICE MOVEMENT.

ticker (US). The telegraphic (or electronic) system, first introduced in the United States in

1867, which prints or displays the last prices at which deals were transacted on US stock exchanges and the volume of shares involved. The information is available on a moving tape, usually within a minute of each trade. If the ticker falls behind trading, as sometimes it does if volume is high, the information on volume of securities per trade is dropped to give the ticker a chance to catch up.

ticker tape. *See* TICKER.

ticket (UK). A claim for settlement of Stock Exchange bargains which is issued on the second business day of the settlement period.

ticket day (UK). *See* NAME DAY.

'tiger bonds' (US). A colloquial name for Treasury Investment Growth Receipts (TIGR) issued in the United States in 1984. The funds from the issue of these bonds is invested in Treasury bonds, but they themselves do not pay regular interest: the return to the investor comes in one payment on the maturity of the TIGR. In this respect they are similar to ZERO COUPON BONDS.

Tilgung (Ger). *See* REDEMPTION.

Tilgungsanleihe (Ger). Bonds redeemable by DRAWING by lot.

time bargain (UK). A deal on the Stock Exchange which is made on the basis that settlement will be delayed to the following settlement day. *See also* NEW TIME.

time deposit. (1) In banking, a deposit which may be withdrawn by a depositor only after due notice has been given.

(2) In a FINANCIAL FUTURES market, an interest-bearing deposit for a fixed period of time; on the London International Financial Futures Exchange contracts in sterling and dollars, the fixed period is three months.

times covered. *See* COVER.

time value. In an options contract, that part of the option premium arising by virtue of the length of time left to maturity. The longer the period, the higher the time value. It is contrasted with INTRINSIC VALUE, the value of the option arising from the valuation of the underlying security in relation to the exercise price of the option.

tip. Supposedly good or inside information on a company, which might give the user inherent advantage in his share dealings.

tirage au sort (Fr). The drawing of bonds for repayment by lot.

titoli (It). *See* SECURITIES.

titoli di assoluta fiducia (It). First class securities: GILT EDGED or BLUE CHIPS.

titoli di prestito (It). *See* LOAN STOCK.

titoli di Stato (It). *See* GOVERNMENT SECURITIES.

titoli quotata in borsa (It). *See* LISTED SECURITIES.

titoli stanziabili (It). Stocks which the Bank of Italy is prepared to discount.

titolo (a) breve scadenza (It). *See* SHORT DATED (STOCK).

titolo (a) interesse fisso (It). *See* FIXED INTEREST DEBT.

titolo patrimoniale (It). The security of a company which has invested all or most of its assets in land and/or property.

titolo (a) portatore (It). *See* BEARER BOND and BEARER SHARE.

titre (Fr). A share certificate or other evidence of title to securities and, by extension, the securities themselves.

titre a court terme (Fr). A short term security.

titre participatif (Fr). A security in wholly owned nationalized industries, issued to

French investors under a programme introduced in 1982. The security allows investors to receive dividends and is quoted on the stock markets, but does not carry voting rights.

titres de placement (Fr). *See* BLUE CHIP.

toccare (il) fondo (It). To touch the bottom. On the stockmarket the term is used to indicate the expected end of a sustained fall in prices.

Tochtergesellschaft (Ger). *See* SUBSIDIARY COMPANY.

Tokyo Stock Exchange (TSE) Index (Jap). Introduced in 1969 and based on 4 January 1968 as 100. It includes all FIRST SECTION stocks; the index is weighted and the base is constantly adjusted to take account of capital changes resulting from new issues, rights etc. Separate indices are also published covering large, medium and small companies and for 28 industrial sectors.

tombstone. An advertisement placed in the press as a matter of record showing the names of the banks and other financial institutions which participated in the issue of securities for a company or other borrower. It is specifically not an invitation to purchase any of the stocks or shares to which it relates.

TOPIC (UK). The Stock Exchange's viewdata system which disseminates prices, company news and other information to its subscribers. TOPIC is an acronym for Teletext Output of Price Information by Computer.

touch, the (UK) *See* JOBBERS' TOUCH.

trade. A deal or bargain most usually, but not always, used in a US context.

trace. The identification of a particular piece of stock through a number of intermediaries to establish the beneficial owner.

traded option. An OPTION is the right to buy or sell a given amount of a particular security at a stated price on or before a particular future date. The distinction between a CONVENTIONAL OPTION and a traded option is that the latter has a standardized contract of trading, is made at standardized exercise prices and with standardized delivery dates. Because of this standardization of the basic terms of the contract a market in the options themselves can be made. Whereas a conventional option is a non-transferable contract which lapses unless exercised, the traded option always has its own value and the option position can itself be closed, rather than being exercised by taking up or selling the UNDERLYING SECURITY.

Traded options began in Chicago in 1973 and have spread rapidly: there are traded options exchanges in Amsterdam, London, New York, Singapore and other centres. Originally, only the shares of some individual companies were subject to traded options contracts but more recently, traded options have been introduced on general stock market indices such as the STANDARD & POOR'S 500 AND 100 and on the specially constructed FINANCIAL TIMES-STOCK EXCHANGE INDEX.

trader (US). (1) An individual who buys and sells securities for his own account on a short term basis.

(2) An employee of a broker/dealer or financial institution who specializes in handling purchases and sales of securities for the firm and its clients.

(3) In a FINANCIAL FUTURES context, a trader is one who buys or sells CONTRACTS in the expectation of profit without, unlike a HEDGER, having an opposite position in the CASH MARKET.

trading. (1) Generally dealing in securities.

(2) Assuming a price risk in the expectation of profit through dealing in FINANCIAL FUTURES.

trading account (UK). An account held by the Stock Exchange settlement system TALISMAN for each jobber in a particular security. Sold stock is added to these accounts when delivered from brokers' accounts and bought stock is allocated from the trading account when settlement is due.

trading company (UK). A commercial company formed for the purpose of carrying on a commercial enterprise with a view to profit.

trading crowd (US). The dealers interested in a particular security or group of securities who congregate around the same pitch, or pit in the case of traded options and financial futures dealing.

trading floor. The physical market place or trading area on which dealers gather to buy and sell securities.

trading halt. A temporary suspension of dealing in a securities or options market.

trading hours. The hours during which dealings on a stock market officially take place. Some markets, such as the London market, permit after-hours dealing; others, because of the nature of their systems, cannot. New York's specialist system comes into this category.

The trading hours on various stock exchanges around the world are as follows :

North America	
New York	10:00 - 16:00
American	10:00 - 16:00
Pacific Coast	10:00 - 15:00
Toronto	10:00 - 16:00
Europe	
United Kingdom	09:30 - 15:30
(after dealing hours permitted)	
Frankfurt	11:30 - 13:30
(after hours dealing permitted)	
Paris	(bonds) 11:30 - 12:30
	shares 12:30 - 14:30
Milan	10:00 - 13:45
Brussels	12:30 - 13:30
Copenhagen	10:30 - 13:00
(close variable, depending upon level of business)	
Vienna	11:30 - 13:00
South Africa	
Johannesburg	09:30 - 16:00
Australia and the Far East	
Sydney/Melbourne	10:00 - 12:00
	and 14:00 - 15:00
Tokyo: Daily	09:00 - 11:00
	and 13:00 - 15:00
Saturday	09:00 - 11:00
(except 2nd Saturday in the month)	
Hong Kong	10:00 - 12:30
and (except Wednesdays)	14:30 - 15:30
Singapore	09:30 - 11:00,
	11:15 - 12:30
	and 14:30 - 15:30

trading market. The market in which existing stocks and shares are traded; a secondary market in securities.

trading partnership. *See* PARTNERSHIP.

trading post (US). A place on the floor of the New York Stock Exchange at which securities are traded. About 100 securities are traded at each trading post. Although the market system of dealing differs between New York and London, the nearest London equivalent of the trading post is the JOBBERS PITCH.

trading range. The difference between the highest and lowest prices at which transactions in a security took place during a specified period, such as a trading session on a stock exchange.

trading session. *See* TRADING HOURS.

traditional option. *See* CONVENTIONAL OPTION.

tranche. A slice. Applied to an issue of stock made at a different time and, perhaps, at a different price from another block or slice of an otherwise identical issue. Thus, a further issue of an existing stock may be referred to as another *tranche* of that existing stock.

tranchette (UK). A word derived from TRANCHE and used to describe the small additional issues of existing government stocks made by the GOVERNMENT BROKER to the UK gilt edged market. The practice of issuing additional units of existing stock in this way was introduced in the early 1980s.

transaction charges (UK). On the LONDON INTERNATIONAL FINANCIAL FUTURES EXCHANGE, the charges levied by the Exchange on its members in respect of each transaction they undertake.

transaction costs. The costs of buying and selling securities. Such costs include brokers' commission and any taxes and other imposts.

transfer. (1) The delivery of a stock or share certificate from the seller to the buyer through their broking agents and the legal change of ownership.

(2) To record such change of ownership in the books of the REGISTRAR.

transfer agent. (1) The broker or bank which acts as the investor's agent in carrying out a change of share ownership.

(2) In US terminology, the rough equivalent of a REGISTRAR in the United Kingdom.

transfer receipt (UK). A paper issued by a registrar acknowledging the receipt of securities documents for transfer.

transfer register (UK). *See* REGISTER OF TRANSFERS.

Transfer Stamp Duty (UK). A levy made on transfers of property in the United Kingdom, levied both on real property, land, etc. and on the transfer of securities. The earliest stamp duties were introduced in the reign of William and Mary (1689-94) and have a continuous subsequent history.

For stock exchange securities the present rates of duty are as follows:

Consideration		Duty Chargeable
exceeds	does not exceed	
£ 0	£ 50	£0.50
50	100	1.00
100	150	1.50
150	200	2.00
200	250	2.50
250	300	3.00
300	350	3.50
350	400	4.00
400	450	4.50
450	500	5.00
500	1.00 per £100 or part £100	

The Inland Revenue issued, in September 1982, a discussion document on the future of stamp duties. The responses to this document and subsequent decisions may lead to a radical reform of such duties in the near future.

Treasury bill (UK). A financial instrument issued by the Bank of England on behalf of the Government as a means of raising short term finance for the Government, pending receipts of taxation.

Treasury bills are of two types, tap and tender. The tap bills are issued to government departments, which are temporarily holding large sums of cash, as well as to overseas banks who wish to hold them.

The Treasury bills with which the money market is mainly concerned are the TENDER BILLS, so called because of the method of issue, namely, the weekly tender. Bills issued through the tender have, generally, a life of 91 days. They are available in denominations of £5000, £10,000, £25,000, £50,000, £100,000, £250,000 and £1 million, with a minimum tender of £50,000.

The bills do not carry a rate of interest. They are bid for at a DISCOUNT on the PAR VALUE and are repaid at par on the due date, the difference between the two prices constituting the investor's return.

Each week, the Bank of England announces how many bills in total will be issued at the following week's tender and calls for bids. The bidders will notify the Bank of the amount of bills for which they wish to bid and the price per £100 they are prepared to pay. The Bank then ranks the bids and allots the bills to the successful bidders. By traditional agreement, the DISCOUNT HOUSES cover the whole amount of the issue to save the Government the embarassment of not selling all its bills each week.

The Treasury bill was introduced in 1877 as the invention of the economist and writer Walter Bagehot, who suggested the idea of short term government money being raised by means of a financial instrument already familiar to the London financiers, namely the commercial bill. In fact, the Treasury bill is identical in concept to its commercial progenitor, with the exception that it is not 'accepted' by an ACCEPTING HOUSE. Such a procedure is unnecessary, since the credit of the British Government does not need the 'support' of an acceptor for the bill to be negotiable in the money market at the finest rates.

BIBLIOGRAPHY 'The Treasury bill - The Story of an Economist's Invention', *Midland Bank Review*, February 1961, reprinted in J.E. Wadsworth (ed.), *The Banks and the Monetary System in the UK, 1959-1971* (Methuen, London, 1973).

Treasury stock. (1) (UK). Securities generally, but not always, carrying a fixed rate of interest, issued by the British Government. *See also* GOVERNMENT SECURITIES.

(2) (US). Stock issued by a company but later re-acquired. It may be held in the company's treasury indefinitely, re-issued to the public or 'retired' (cancelled). Treasury stock receives no dividends and has no vote while held by the company.

trend. A general movement of security prices in one direction or the other.

triangle. An expression used in TECHNICAL ANALYSIS to describe a particular pattern of share prices characterized by a widening or narrowing of the gap between the high and the low over a period of time.

Trittbrettfahrer (Ger). A short-term speculator. Literally a 'traveller on the running board': one who buys shares on the back of a general rise in prices, hoping thereby to profit from them by a later sale. Also sometimes called a *Mitläufer.*

troppo pieno (It). Excessive buying by operators. It normally coincides with a prolonged price upturn.

true rate of interest. The rate of interest paid on a loan which reflects the rate to the borrower based on the principle that his repayments include regular amounts of capital as well as interest. The true rate of interest may differ markedly from the nominal rate quoted by the lender. Thus, on a loan of £1000 repayable in equal monthly instalments over two years, the lender may calculate a total amount of interest to be paid of £200 and describe that rate as 10 percent a year: i.e.

$$\left(\tfrac{200}{1000} \div 2\right) \times 100$$

In practice, the monthly instalments of £50 (£1,200 ÷ 24) will consist approximately of £42 capital and (again approximately) £8 interest and thus the average amount of the outstanding loan over the period is a little under £500, on which £200 of interest is being paid.

The true annual rate of interest, as defined by the Consumer Credit Act 1974, in the United Kingdom is calculated as follows :

$$100\left(\left(1 + \frac{\text{total charge for credit}}{\text{amount of credit}}\right)^{\frac{1}{t}} - 1\right)\%$$

where t is defined as the length of time over which the loan is to be repaid.

trust. (1) Trust can have a number of general meanings, but in a securities market context, it is taken to be a business enterprise which is run by a group of trustees. A few commercial companies are run along these lines, but in general the word is applied to investment management companies such as INVESTMENT TRUSTS and UNIT TRUSTS.

(2) (US). A cartel or group of companies which is considered to exercise restraint of trade in its operations and therefore to act against the public interest. Such companies have been subject to much regulatory legislation stretching back to the Sherman Act of 1890.

trust corporation (UK). A corporate body which may act as a trustee. *See also* PUBLIC TRUSTEE.

trust de valeurs, trust d'investissement (Fr). *See* INVESTMENT TRUST.

trustee. One who holds assets for the benefit of others in financial or business arrangements.

Trustee Investments Act 1961 (UK). This Act modified an earlier Act and lays down certain requirements which a security must meet before it can be bought by trustees. The object of the Act was to allow trustees to invest in equity shares, giving their beneficiaries the prospect of capital growth, while on the other hand protecting beneficiaries from reckless actions by the trustees.

The Act lays down that a half of the investments must be in fixed interest securities while the other half may be in equity shares, building societies and unit trusts.

BIBLIOGRAPHY *The Trustee Investments Act 1961* (HMSO, London, 1961). *The Stock Exchange Official Year-Book* (London, annually) reprints the legislation.

trustee securities (UK). Securities which are authorised for investment by trustees. *See also* TRUSTEE INVESTMENTS ACT, 1961.

turn. The amount of profit taken, as measured by the difference between the price at which something is bought and that at which it is sold on again by a trader or market maker in a securities market. *See also* JOBBERS' TURN.

turnover. Generally, the total value of business undertaken by a company in the course of a particular period. In stock market terminology, the value of dealings carried out in securities between members of a stock exchange. The word in this context might also mean the actual number of dealings or the total number of shares traded, rather than the value, so the context in which the word is used is important in order to determine its precise meaning. Equally, in making comparisons of turnover between one stock exchange and another, it is important to know precisely how turnover information is measured. As an illustration, the New York Stock Exchange measures turnover by totalling the amount or the value of stock which passes in deals; London, on the other hand, calculates its turnover figures from the information supplied by brokers who have bought and sold stock on behalf of their clients. To illustrate the difference, a parcel of 2000 shares being dealt on New York will show as turnover of 2000 shares, but in the United Kingdom, the selling broker will report he has sold 2000 shares to the jobber, the buying broker that he has bought 2000 shares from the jobber. In this case, turnover will be calculated as 4000 shares.

turnover rate. The volume of shares traded on stock exchanges in the course of a year, expressed as a percentage of the total number of shares in issue.

two-dollar broker (US). *See* INDEPENDENT BROKER.

two way market. The phrase used to describe a market in securities (or in a particular security) in which there is a lot of buying and selling business without a few large orders dominating it. In such a market a lot of dealing can take place without moving the price of the stock too much in one direction or the other.

two way prices. The BID and OFFER prices for a security at which the market maker is prepared to deal not just to quote a nominal dealing price.

U

Übernahmeangebot (Ger). *See* TAKE-OVER BID. Sometimes also means the price offered by the bidder.

Übernahmekonsortium (Ger). A syndicate of banks which buys new securities from the issuer and sells them on to investors. The syndicate acts as an underwriter and any shares unsold are its responsibility; this type of issue consortium is now more common than the agency-only BEGEBUNGSKONSORTIUM.

Übernahmevertrag (Ger). The agreement between a syndicate of banks formed to market a new issue of securities. When a new issue is made, the normal method for selling the shares is via such a syndicate, which ensures a rapid distribution of the shares. The syndicate agreement fixes, among other things, the size of the quota which each participant will receive and be responsible for selling. The profit comes from the difference between the price at which the shares are underwritten and the selling price obtained from investors. The syndicate, however, is responsible for the full risks involved in selling the shares if the sale price to the final investors falls below expectations. *See also* BEGEBUNGSKONSORTIUM and ÜBERNAHMEKONSORTIUM.

über Pari (Ger). Above par. *See* PAR.

umsteigen (Ger). To switch. To sell one stock and buy another with the proceeds. *See* SWITCHING.

unauthorized clerk (UK). *See* BLUE BUTTON.

uncalled capital. The amount of capital on PARTLY-PAID SHARES which shareholders are under an obligation to subscribe if called upon to do so by the directors of a company, but which remains uncalled for the time being.

uncovered. A trading position in a securities or similar market is said to be uncovered if the trader or investor is exposed to a risk which he has chosen not to OFFSET. *See also* COVER.

undated stock (UK). An interest bearing security, usually issued by the British Government, which has no final date of repayment of the principal sum. There are eight such stocks at present traded on the UK Stock Exchange: these include 2.5 percent Consols, the repayment date of which is technically given as '1923 or after'. The significant phrase being '...or after'. Most stocks have two REDEMPTION DATES, not this open-ended option on the government's part. The market values the securities on the basis that the principal amount will not repaid and they are referred to as undated stocks. *See also* CONSOLS; DATED STOCK; GOVERNMENT SECURITIES; WAR LOAN.

underlying security. The security which forms the basis upon which an options contract is made. A participant in an options market, be it a TRADED OPTIONS or a CONVENTIONAL OPTIONS market, will contract to buy options contracts giving him the right to buy (CALL) or to sell (PUT) a specified amount of a particular stock or share at or before a given date. That stock or share is the underlying security of the options contract.

underwriter. An investor or investing institution agreeing, for a fee, to purchase the balance of an issue of securities, should investor demand not be sufficient to take up the whole issue.

In the United Kingdom, GOVERNMENT SECURITIES are not underwritten, although the short term (91 day) issues of TREASURY BILLS are taken up by the DISCOUNT MARKET if outside or firm bids are insufficient. When a company issue is made on the stock market, it is usual for such an issue to be underwritten in order to ensure that the issuer receives the full value of the issue. The underwriters are normally large investing institutions such as insurance companies, pension funds and the like. Underwriting is normally undertaken both for issues of shares in companies which are totally new to the market and also to RIGHTS ISSUES of new shares by existing companies.

The underwriters who are called upon to take up a new issue when public demand proves insufficient, may either take the shares into their own portfolios and hope to sell them later when the price improves in the market, or they may sell immediately at a loss and thus weaken the market price further.

On the other hand, when an issue is successful, the underwriters will retain the UNDERWRITING COMMISSION as their reward for having taken the risk that the issue might not be fully subscribed.

underwriting commission. The amount obtained by the UNDERWRITERS for taking on the risk involved in a new issue of shares by a company to the investing public. The fee or underwriting commission in the London market is normally around 1.5 percent. These commissions are paid whether or not the underwriters are called upon to take up shares which other investors have declined to buy. So when an issue is successful, the underwriters obtain a useful additional income but, in return, they accept the risks involved in an unsuccessful issue. Generally speaking, underwriters are prepared to accept a degree of risk for all issues coming to the market and do not seek to charge a higher underwriting commission for an issue which may or may not be successfully floated. Such a system, while appearing at times in a bull market to give underwriters easy, risk-free profit, does help smaller and more risky new issues in that they may be underwritten at a lower commission than would otherwise be the case.

unearned income. Income accruing to an individual from assets rather than arising from work. Thus interest on stocks and dividends on shares are referred to as unearned income, as are rents from property etc. Income from salaries, wages and pensions is classed as earned income. At one time, so-called unearned income was charged at a higher rate of tax than earned income in the United Kingdom; although a more equitable tax treatment between the two was instituted in 1973, an INVESTMENT INCOME SURCHARGE was levied on investment income over a certain amount until the Budget of 1984.

unfranked income (UK). Income from securities which does not carry an accompanying certificate stating that tax has already been paid and, therefore, subject to tax at the taxpayer's own rate. The distinction between franked income and unfranked income created a number of distortions in investment decisions by investing institutions. Prior to 1980, when the law was changed, dividends were franked income, interest from fixed-interest stock was not. Thus institutions receiving unfranked income had to bear tax on it before passing it on to the ultimate beneficiaries. In effect, such income was being taxed twice over, as it was again subject to tax in the individual beneficiary's hands. Such distortions were recognized in 1980 in order to encourage institutions to invest in fixed interest securities.

unfunded debt. Obligations owing to holders which are not covered by a SINKING FUND. Colloquially, short term government debt.

ungesichert (Ger). Unsecured. *See* LOAN STOCK.

unico azionista (It). The concentration of all the shares of a company in the hands of a single shareholder. To prevent such a shareholder, in the event of the company's failure, obtaining the benefits of limited liability, the Italian Civil Code says that whenever such a situation occurs the shareholder's liability shall remain unlimited.

unissued capital. That part of a company's AUTHORIZED CAPITAL which remains unissued.

unità (di) contrazzione (It). The minimum trading lot on the Stock Exchange for each security.

unit-linked policy (UK). An insurance savings scheme linked to investment in a unit trust. The premiums are invested in units and the income and capital gain from them goes to enhance the value of the policy. The emphasis between one type of unit-linked policy and another may vary with individual schemes: in some, the emphasis is on the life assurance aspect, with the bulk of the premiums being used to provide the life assurance cover in the normal way, with a little invested in a unit trust to give extra capital growth. In others, the emphasis is placed on the unit trust investment aspect with the majority of the premiums going into such investment and just a little going to provide the basic insurance cover.

The advantage of investment in unit trusts via unit linked policies has, until recently, been the tax relief investors received on insurance premiums which was not available for investment directly in unit trusts. Such benefit has been abolished under the Finance Act of 1984 for new policies taken out after 14 March 1984.

unit of trading or **unit of contract.** In a TRADED OPTIONS market, the number of shares of the UNDERLYING SECURITY covered by a single traded options CONTRACT.

unit trust (UK). A fund which collects together the savings of small investors and puts these collective savings into a range of stocks and shares. Unit trusts are designed to allow savers to invest in equity shares, to obtain capital growth for their savings, while at the same time allowing them to spread their risk over a large number of securities in a way which would be impossible, or at least wholly uneconomic, if the savers were themselves investing directly in individual shares.

Unit trusts began in the United Kingdom in 1929 when the investment company M. & G. set up the first. A unit trust is an open-end fund, which means that its capital is not fixed but may rise, or fall, depending upon the willingness of new investors to put more money into the fund or, conversely, existing investors' desire to sell units. Buying and selling of units generally takes place via the managers of the trust who, on the basis of the value of the shares in the fund, quote two prices: a bid price at which they will buy back existing units from current holders and an offer price at which they will sell new units to buyers.

The activities of unit trusts are closely regulated by the Department of Trade and Industry, which fixes a formula on which the value of the units must be calculated, as well as the types of security a trust may or may not hold and the charges which managers may levy on investors.

There are now over 400 unit trusts authorized by the Department to carry on business. Some of these are general trusts, attempting to give their unit holders the benefits both of income and capital growth; others may concentrate on the one or the other. Still others may specialize in different market sectors such as oil, commodities, financial companies etc, while some undertake investment primarily in overseas markets such as North America, the Far East or Australasia. *See also* INVESTMENT TRUSTS; UNIT TRUST ASSOCIATION.

Unit Trust Association (UTA) (UK). The trade association of the UNIT TRUSTS in the United Kingdom. The Association represents the views of the unit trust movement to government and acts as the trusts' voice on a number of representative bodies including the COUNCIL FOR THE SECURITIES INDUSTRY.

unlimited company (UK). A form of corporate entity whose shareholders do not enjoy the privilege and protection of LIMITED LIABILITY and who may thus be called upon to contribute, to the extent of their personal assets, to meet the debts of the company in the event of its failure. This form of corporate entity is highly unusual, although all partners in a PARTNERSHIP will normally be liable for the debts of the partnership to an unlimited extent.

unlimited corporate member (UCM) (UK). A type of organization for a member firm of the UK Stock Exchange. Although the most common type of firm is a partnership, the Stock Exchange rules allow corporate entities to trade as member firms. In order to protect investors, however, the rules insist that all principals in the firm must remain liable for the full extent of the debts of the organization. *See also* LIMITED CORPORATE MEMBER.

Unlisted Securities Market (USM) (UK). A market set up on the trading floor of the Stock Exchange in London in 1980, in which shares of certain non-listed companies can be traded.

Companies may apply to have their shares traded in this market, and to do so they must abide by three initial criteria: first, they must make available at least ten percent of their shares to the market and to OUTSIDE SHAREHOLDERS; second, they must have been in business for at least three years, or they must have a product which has been fully developed but which needs extra financial resources to market successfully; third, they must make specified information available to potential shareholders at the time of the issue and must make all PRICE-SENSITIVE INFORMATION available to investors via the Stock Exchange as soon as possible on a continuing basis.

These requirements differ from those for a LISTING in that the latter requires 25 percent of shares to be available for trading, a minimum track record of five years and the amount of information which has to be made available and advertised at the outset is often greater and more expensive to disseminate.

For the investor, the USM offers the opportunity to invest in newer and, he hopes, growing companies, but often, because of their shorter track records, they are more risky investments.

The Unlisted Securities Market has been very successful in attracting to the Stock Exchange companies which had previously not taken advantage of its facilities and in the first four years of operation attracted well over 250 companies to its ranks. It has also been the model for similar markets in other countries, notably the SECOND MARCHÉ in Paris.

unlisted shares. Shares of companies which have not obtained a listing on a stock exchange. Shares traded on the UNLISTED SECURITIES MARKET (USM) are regarded as unlisted for the purposes of CAPITAL TRANSFER TAX relief in the United Kingdom, but not as unlisted for the purposes of the BUSINESS EXPANSION SCHEME legislation. Unlisted shares outside the USM may be dealt in by brokers on the Stock Exchange, but only on an occasional basis and after the specific permission of the Stock Exchange to the deal and its price has been obtained.

Unlisted shares may also be traded on an OVER-THE-COUNTER MARKET but without the protection to the investor afforded by trading on a the Stock Exchange through a member whose dealings and conduct are regulated by its authorities.

unlisted stock (US). The American equivalent of unlisted shares. Such stock may be traded on an OVER-THE-COUNTER market in the United States.

unrealized profit(loss). *See* PAPER PROFIT(LOSS).

unsecured loan stock. *See* LOAN STOCK.

upstairs. The word used to describe a securities deal which takes place not on a trading floor or in competition with other dealers and market makers, but in the broker's office, the broker finding both sides of the transaction.

up tick (US). A term used to designate a transaction made at a price higher than the preceding transaction. Also referred to as a plus tick. A plus sign is displayed throughout the day next to the last price of each relevant stock at the TRADING POST on the floor of the New York Stock Exchange to indicate a price higher than a previous trade. *See also* DOWN TICK; ZERO PLUS TICK.

urgenza immediata (It). An order valid only for 15 minutes.

urgenzando (ordine) (It). An order which is valid only for one hour.

usi di borsa (It). The set of rules regulating the daily function of the Stock Exchange.

utile (It). A profit.

utile sulla carta (It). *See* PAPER PROFIT.

V

valeur (Fr). The literal meaning is 'value'; the prices or values of securities listed on a stock exchange and, by extention, the securities themselves.

valeur admise à la Bourse (Fr). A security which has been admitted to LISTING on a stock exchange.

valeur à revenu fixe (Fr). *See* FIXED INTEREST SECURITY. A stock or bond.

valeur à revenu variable (Fr). A variable rate security; a share.

valeur au porteau (Fr). *See* BEARER SECURITY.

valeur de tout repos (Fr). *See* GILT-EDGED SECURITY.

valeur marchand (Fr). The MARKET VALUE of a security.

valeur nominale (Fr). The NOMINAL VALUE of a security as distinct from its MARKET PRICE.

valeurs non cotées (Fr). *See* UNLISTED SHARES.

valore (It). A SHARE.

valore nominale (It). *See* PAR VALUE.

valore (al) portatore (It). *See* BEARER SHARE.

valora di mercato (It). *See* MARKET VALUE.

valuation. The estimate of the worth of something; in a stock exchange context, the worth of a share, a portfolio, the entire market or a sector of it. *See also* MARKET CAPITALISATION.

value, market. *See* MARKET VALUE.

value, nominal. *See* NOMINAL VALUE.

Value Added Tax (VAT) (UK). A tax on consumption of goods and services, introduced in the United Kingdom in 1973 to replace Purchase Tax and Selective Employment Tax. It is a tax designed to be levied on consumers and imports: any business which is an intermediary and which itself pays VAT on its purchases may claim it back as a credit against the VAT it must send to the tax authorities in respect of its sales.

In a stock market context, VAT is levied on the commission charged by stockbrokers to their clients in the United Kingdom. The French equivalent is also charged on brokers' commission in France, but the other European countries do not impose their own expenditure taxes on brokers' commission.

variable annuity (US). A life insurance policy where the annuity premium is invested in a portfolio of securities. When the annuity falls due to be paid, its value at that time will depend upon the performance of the securities in which it has been invested. The variable annuity has some similarities to a UNIT-LINKED policy.

variable rate stock (UK). A government security introduced in 1977, the interest on which is not fixed at the outset but varies with short term interest rates, according to a predetermined formula.

The stock was introduced as a means of providing an additional type of security for investors in government stocks and to help the authorities to sell government debt in difficult market conditions. Demand for a fixed interest security is very variable; strong when interest rates are expected to fall and the price to rise, but very slack in the opposite circumstances, since investors are unwilling to put their money into fixed interest stocks if they think that by waiting they will get a higher rate of interest and not suffer capital loss. This alternating glut and drought, so far as demand for gilt edged stock was concerned, led the government to introduce the variable rate stock which did not suffer the same drawbacks and gave investors an attractive alternative gilt edged investment at periods when interest rates were generally expected to rise.

variabler Kurs (Ger). The continuous quotation market on the German Stock Exchanges. On each of the eight West German exchanges, the BÖRSENVORSTAND, or governing body, can approve requests from companies for their shares to be traded, not only by the single quotation (EINHEITSKURS) method, but also on a continuous basis during the trading session which runs from 11:30 to 13:30. Only companies with a large number of shares available for trading may be dealt in on this basis. The MAKLER collects the bids and offers and fixes his prices on the same lines as he does in the single quotation market.

variation margin. The gains or losses on OPEN CONTRACTS in FINANCIAL FUTURES which are calculated by reference to the market price at the end of each trading day and credited, or debited, by the CLEARING HOUSE to the CLEARING MEMBERS' accounts and by the members to their customers accounts. If the amount of MARGIN maintained in those accounts is insufficient, the holders will have to deposit additional margin; if there is surplus margin, this can either be left to the credit of the holder or paid back to him.

vendita (in) danno (It). The sale by auction on the trading floor of securities not paid for by the brokers' client. The rough equivalent of SELLING OUT.

vendor. A seller.

vendor consideration. Shares issued by a listed company to the sellers of a business in consideration for the sale of that business to the listed company. *See also* VENDOR PLACING.

vendor placing. The PLACING by a stockbroker of shares issued to the sellers of a business as VENDOR CONSIDERATION. The successful bidder will, in this case, have paid for the acquisition by issuing its own shares to the sellers of the acquired company. These shareholders may not wish to keep the bidder's PAPER but prefer instead to turn the holding into cash. The sale on the open market of large blocks of shares at the same time would drive the price down sharply. To avoid this, a stockbroker would place the shares in the firm hands of clients.

vente à découvert (Fr). An UNCOVERED sale. The sale of shares a trader does not have, in the hope that he may reverse the transaction, to his profit, when the shares have fallen in price. *See also* BEAR.

venture capital. *See* NURSERY FINANCE.

Vereeniging voor de Effectenhandel (NL). The Association for Trading in Securities, set up in the Netherlands in 1876; a private corporation which is effectively the management committee of the Amsterdam Stock Exchange; the Association owns and operates the stock exchange building and regulates securities trading in it.

Verfall (Ger). *See* MATURITY.

verkaufen (Ger). To sell.

Verkaufsofferte (Ger). *See* OFFER FOR SALE.

Verkehrswert (Ger). The market value of securities.

Verlust (Ger). A loss on a transaction.

Vermögensanlagengesetz (Ger). The law relating to capital investment in West

Germany which deals with general conditions relating to the issue of securities to the investing public.

Verteilungsbrief (Ger). *See* ALLOTMENT LETTER.

vertical integration. The linking of economic activity in such a way as to bring the whole process of production, from raw material to final product, within one organization. The cost benefits of such integration are often used as an argument to justify the amalgamation of two or more companies at different stages of the production process in one corporate group. *See also* HORIZONTAL INTEGRATION.

Verwaltungsrat (Ger). The board of directors of a limited company.

vesting. The placing in the hands of a beneficial owner shares or other property which had previously been held in trust by a nominee.

V formation. A term used in technical analysis to describe a sharp fall in prices followed by an equally sharp rise. An inverted V formation is a sharp rise followed by a fall.

vigilanze (sulle) borse (It). The regulatory control of stock exchanges, exercised by a series of bodies such as the government, the chambers of commerce, and various stock exchange bodies.

vinkulierte Aktie (Ger). A particular type of share sometimes traded on the German Stock Exchanges. Such a share enjoys only limited transferability and is found most frequently, though not exclusively, in the insurance company market. It is a registered share which may be transferred only with the consent of the company.

volando (ordine) (It). A stockmarket order which is valid for only 15 minutes.

volume. The amount of TURNOVER on a stock exchange, either in a particular security or in the market as a whole. Generally, volume is applied to turnover as measured by the number of deals or the number of shares traded, but occasionally it is loosely applied to the value of the transactions.

As with TURNOVER, care must always be taken when measuring volume to make sure precisely how the figure is being obtained. The LONDON INTERNATIONAL FINANCIAL FUTURES EXCHANGE lists three possible definitions of volume in its own glossary of terms: these are volume by number of contracts traded; by transactions, irrespective of the number of contracts in each transaction; and finally, by number of deals, where both the buying and the selling sides of the same transaction are counted.

voluntary liquidation. The winding up of a company on the petition of the company itself, either because it cannot pay its debts or, more frequently, because its business has been taken over or merged into another larger entity.

von ihnen (Ger). *See* AN SIE.

vorbörselicher handel (Ger). Business done on a German Stock Exchange prior to the official start of business.

vorgeben or ***vornehmen*** (Ger). To purchase for one's own account in anticipation of a rise in prices.

vorläufige Dividende (Ger). *See* INTERIM DIVIDEND.

Vorrangsbelastung (Ger). PRIOR CHARGES on the earnings or profits of a company to be met before any payment of dividend is made to shareholders.

Vorstand (Ger). A board of directors of a limited company or other type of organisation. *See for example* BÖRSENVORSTAND.

Vorstandsmitglied (Ger). A member of a company board; a director.

Vorugsaktie (Ger). *See* PREFERENCE SHARE.

voting right. The entitlement of a shareholder to exercise a voice in the running of the company by way of a vote. Most company shares give shareholders the right to vote on a one-share-one-vote principle. But occasionally share voting rights are restricted in some way: for example, to a maximum number of votes irrespective of the number of shares held. Such restrictions are not popular with shareholders and the growth of powerful institutional shareholdings has led to companies being put under pressure to amend their voting structures. *See also* NON-VOTING SHARE.

voting share. A share which enjoys a VOTING RIGHT.

vuoto (It). Lack of business on the stock market.

W

Wachstumswerte (Ger). *See* GROWTH SHARE.

waiter (UK). The name popularly applied to the attendants on the floor of the Stock Exchange in the United Kingdom. The term arises from the origins of the Stock Exchange in the London coffee houses of the 17th and 18th centuries, when those who served the needs of the dealers in stock really were the coffee house waiters. A similar term exists in the Lloyds insurance market for the same reason.

Wall Street (US). The name colloquially applied to the New York financial and securities markets, the New York and American Stock Exchanges. The equivalent of THROGMORTON STREET in the United Kingdom and BEURSPLEIN 5 in Amsterdam.

Wall Street crash (US). The name given to the dramatic fall in share prices on the New York Stock Exchange in October 1929 which heralded the economic depression. Following an intense bull market, often fuelled by trading on MARGIN, stock market prices peaked in August 1929, when the index had risen from around 100 to 450 in just five years. The market began to drift downwards through September and early October, but the break came on Saturday 19 October when stocks fell sharply in some of the heaviest Saturday trading ever recorded. A further sharp fall on Monday 21 October was followed by a rally on the Tuesday. On Wednesday and Thursday the market plunged again until organized support caused it to rally briefly. The real fall began on the following Monday 28 October and continued unabated on the following day. Despite occasional rallies, the market continued to plunge in early November and fell back to around half of what it had been just over two months previously. The 'crash' itself was over, but the market continued generally to drift lower for another three years and reached a low in 1932.

BIBLIOGRAPHY J.K. Galbraith, *The Great Crash 1929.* (Hamish Hamilton, London, 1954; Penguin, London, 1961).

Wandelobligation (Ger). *See* CONVERTIBLE LOAN STOCK.

Wandelparität (Ger). The conversion price of bonds or stocks into shares. *See also* CONVERSION RIGHTS.

Wandelpreis (Ger). *See* WANDELPARITÄT.

warehousing. The practice of a number of investors acting in concert to acquire the shares of a particular company. Each builds up a stake to a figure just below the level at which a holding in another company has to be declared (currently five percent). Thus the target company is unaware of concerted purchases of its shares or, if it is aware, would find it difficult to discover who the owners are and if they are acting together. Such practices are frowned upon by the securities authorities, and in the United Kingdom legislation has been introduced to outlaw the practice.

War Loan (UK). Government stock first issued in 1917 as a means of raising money to finance the war effort. Subscriptions to the stock were regarded almost as a patriotic duty. The stock, however, was an undated stock repayable in 1952 or after. During the periods of high inflation and high interest rates of the post-1950 period, the value of War Loan has fallen to as low as £14 per £100 nominal value of stock even in current money values. In real terms, after allowing for inflation of more than twentyfold since 1914, War Loan is practically worthless.

warrant. A document attached to a debt security giving the holder the right to buy shares in the company at a pre-determined price, at a date or on one or more of a number of future dates.

warrant, dividend. *See* DIVIDEND WARRANT.

watered stock (US). A shareholding in a company which, while remaining constant in absolute terms, has become a smaller percentage of the total issued share capital as the result of further issues. *See also* DILUTION OF EQUITY; PRE-EMPTIVE RIGHTS.

way. The direction, buying or selling, in which a client or his broker wishes to act. The normal practice on the UK stock market is for the broker on the floor to ask the dealer for the bid and offer prices of the stock without disclosing to the dealer whether he wishes to buy or sell. The dealer will respond, but if he particularly wishes either to buy or to sell he may ask the broker which 'way' he wishes to deal and, if it is acceptable to the dealer, he may quote a finer price than his original quote in order to attract the business.

weighting. The level of importance given to the prices of the constituent shares in a share index. In order to give a view of the market corresponding to the level of importance of particular shares in a market, each share in an index may be weighted according to its relative market valuation compared to the whole. Thus the movement in price of a share whose total value is ten percent of the market value of the whole index is deemed to be ten times more important than a price movement of the same absolute amount in a share whose share of market value is only one percent of the total. The first share is, therefore, given a weighting ten times greater than the latter, in to order reflect more accurately its impact on the market as a whole.

Wertpapier, Wertschrift (Ger). Documents of title or securities.

Wertpapierstatistik (Ger). Stock market statistics; a general term covering market capitalization, new issues, turnover, prices etc.

Wertschriftentrust (Ger). *See* INVESTMENT TRUST; UNIT TRUST.

Wertzuwachsteuer (Ger). Capital gains tax.

W formation. *See* DOUBLE TOP and DOUBLE BOTTOM.

when issued (US). A shortened form of the phrase 'when, as and if issued'. The term indicates a conditional transaction in a security authorized for issue but not, as yet, actually issued. All 'when issued' transactions are on an 'if' basis, to be settled if and when the actual security is issued. This contrasts with the situation in the United Kingdom, where permission to deal is granted only after admission to LISTING.

white knight. A term originating in the United States, but now spreading to the United Kingdom. It is the phrase applied to a company making a counter-bid for another company which is the target of an unwanted take-over. Often the second bid is an agreed and acceptable one for the target company, in contrast to the initial offer. Hence the analogy of the white knight rescuing the damsel in distress. *See also* PRE-EMPTIVE BID.

widerstreitende Interessen (Ger). *See* CONFLICT OF INTEREST.

winding-up. The compulsory or voluntary liquidation of a company either because it is unable to pay its debts or for some other reason. *See* COMPULSORY LIQUIDATION; VOLUNTARY LIQUIDATION.

wire house (US). *See* RETAIL BROKER.

withholding tax. A tax imposed by the tax authorities in one country on the payment from that country of interest and dividends to overseas residents. Many countries have reciprocal agreements which give double taxation relief to the recipients of interest or dividends which have already borne tax in the country of origin. Under such double tax conventions, the recipient can offset any overseas tax payment from a country with which a convention has been signed, against his domestic tax liability. If there is no such bilateral tax treaty, he must pay tax again on his receipts of interest and dividends.

working capital. The amount of capital available for the day- to-day operations of a company after allowance has been made for the provision of fixed assets and such intangibles as goodwill etc. Working capital may be used in the purchase of raw materials, payment of wages and salaries etc, and is topped up by the cash flow emanating from sales and any other current income.

working control (US). The 51 percent ownership of the voting shares of a company which gives the holder control of that company. In practice, because of the spread of shareownership among a diverse range of investors, it is usually possible to exercise effective control with a holding of less than 51 percent.

World Bank. *See* INTERNATIONAL BANK FOR RECONSTRUCTION AND DEVELOPMENT.

X

XA (UK). Abbreviation for 'ex all', meaning that a share deal has been made in which the buyer has bought the share without the right to any of the benefits currently announced, such as a DIVIDEND, RIGHTS ISSUE or SCRIP ISSUE.

XC (UK). Abbreviation for 'ex capitalization', meaning that a share has been sold without entitlement to participate in a recently announced capitalization or SCRIP ISSUE.

XD (UK). Abbreviation for 'ex dividend', meaning that a share has been sold without the right to participate in the next DIVIDEND distribution.

XR (UK). Abbreviation for 'ex rights', meaning that a share has been sold without qualifying for a forthcoming RIGHTS ISSUE.

Y

Yankee bond (US). A dollar denominated issue made by an overseas issuer to attract American investors.

yearling bond (UK). A short term security issued by a local authority or public board in the United Kingdom. The bonds most commonly have a life of just one year, hence the name, but bonds issued for periods of up to five years to maturity, are still colloquially known as yearling bonds. They are issued through banks and stockbrokers each week and a group of local authorities and public boards will participate in an issue with identical terms. When the bonds fall due for repayment they are often covered by a ROLL-OVER issue on terms which are current in the market at that time.

year's high. The highest level a share price has reached during the course of a calendar year. This figure is usually shown alongside other details of the company's shares such as the yield, current rate of dividend etc. In the early months of a new calendar year, the year's high figure covers the last calendar year plus the early months of the new year, to give a better idea of the RANGE of prices at which the stock has traded over a reasonably long period.

year's low. The lowest level a share price has reached during the course of a calendar year. *See also* YEAR'S HIGH.

Yellow Book (UK). The colloquial name for the UK Stock Exchange's publication ADMISSION OF SECURITIES TO LISTING. Called the Yellow Book because of the somewhat bright colour of its binding.

yield. The dividends or interest paid by a company on its securities expressed as a percentage of the current market price.

yield curve. The pattern of yields in a fixed interest market at a particular time. Normally yields on short dated stocks are below those on long dated ones, reflecting the relatively lower liquidity of long dated stocks, but the liquidity on, say, a 10-year stock is not vastly different from that on a 30-year stock, given the ability to sell in the market. The difference between a one-year stock and a ten-year stock is much larger because of the different nature of the market and, normally, the extra demand for the very short dated stock. A yield curve plots the yield on the *y*-axis and the time to maturity on the *x*-axis. The normal pattern is of a sharply rising curve from around three months to two years, rising thereafter at a much slower rate, thus making the yield curve much flatter.

This describes the normal pattern. Occasionally, if short term rates are exceptionally high and are expected to fall, the yield on short dated stocks will actually be higher than that on longer dated issues. The yield curve will thus show a falling pattern at the short end before flattening out later.

yield gap. The positive difference between the yield on variable rate shares and that on risk-free fixed interest securities. Economic analysis suggests that the yield on the riskier investment should be higher than that on the risk-free fixed interest stock and for many years, this was reflected in yields in the financial markets. However, in recent years the prospects of capital growth in equities have outweighed the risk in investors' minds and the normal yield gap has been reversed, with equities yielding less than fixed interest stocks, which have no prospect of real capital growth. *See also* REVERSE YIELD GAP.

yield to maturity. The yield of a security to maturity takes into account the price discount at which the stock currently stands below its redemption price or, indeed, of the premium it currently commands over the redemption price. These factors are added to the current interest yield to produce the yield to maturity OR REDEMPTION YIELD.

Z

Z account (UK). A type of account opened by the Bank of England to allow large dealers in the gilt-edged market, such as JOBBERS, insurance companies and a few others, to register transfers of stock quickly. The account is a privilege granted to major dealers in the market in order to assist dealing and liquidity.

zaibatsu (Jap). The large, conglomerate, privately owned holding companies which controlled much of Japan's trade and industry in the period up to the second world war. A decree of 1948 forbade members of the old *zaibatsu* families from official positions in these companies in the future. Nonetheless, the conglomerate holding company as such remains a potent force in Japanese business.

Zeichnung (Ger). The subscription for a new issue of stock.

Zeichnungspreis (Ger). The price at which a new stock is issued.

Zeitgeschäfte (Ger). Dealings on a forward market.

zero coupon bonds. First issued in the United States in 1981 by companies. As the name suggests, they pay no interest, but are issued at a substantial discount on the eventual redemption price. The advantage to the company is that it has no continuing annual interest payment to meet. For the investor, his return comes wholly from capital gain rather than interest receipts, which may well benefit him, since capital gains tend to be more lightly taxed than income.

In the United Kingdom, zero coupon bonds have not been issued because of tax problems.

zero plus tick (US). A term used for a transaction in securities dealt at the same price as the immediately preceding trade which itself was higher than the preceding different price. *See also* MINIMUM PRICE MOVEMENT; UP TICK.

Zertifikat (Ger). *See* CERTIFICATE.

Zins, Zinsfuss, Zinsrate, Zinssatz (Ger). Interest paid for the use of capital. *See* RATE OF INTEREST.

Zinsschein (Ger). *See* COUPON.

Zirka Auftrag (Ger). *See* LIMIT ORDER.

zukünftige Lieferung (Ger). Future delivery of goods or securities.

Zulassungsstelle (Ger). The Listings or Admissions Committees of the German Stock Exchanges. The Listings Committee is partly independent and its role is to licence securities prior to their being admitted to official listing. It examines the issue documents and ensures that all the requirements laid down for listing have been met and all relevant information made publicly available.

Zusammenlegung von Aktien (Ger). A reduction in the share capital of a company.

Zusammenschluss (Ger). *See* AMALGAMATION; MERGER; TAKE-OVER BID.

Zuteilungsschein (Ger). *See* ALLOTMENT LETTER.

Zwangskonversion (Ger). Compulsory conversion. The offer of one stock into another in which the offeree has no cash alternative and must take the new stock offered.

Zwangsliquidation (Ger). *See* COMPULSORY LIQUIDATION.

zwei Weibchen (Ger). To have two investors both of whom wish to deal either as buyers or as sellers and the dealer is therefore unable to carry out a transaction.

Zwischenbilanz (Ger). *See* INTERIM STATEMENT.

Zwischenhändler (Ger). An intermediary, agent or broker.